D0881253

THE HOUSE ON *Diamond Hill*

The House on Diamond Hill

THE UNIVERSITY OF NORTH CAROLINA PRESS Chapel Hill

A CHEROKEE PLANTATION STORY

Tiya Miles

This book was published with the assistance of the Z. Smith Reynolds Fund of the University of North Carolina Press.

The paper in this book meets the guidelines for permanence and durability of the Committee on Production Guidelines for Book Longevity of the Council on Library Resources. The University of North Carolina Press has been a member of the Green Press Initiative since 2003.

Library of Congress Cataloging-in-Publication Data
Miles, Tiya, 1970–
The house on Diamond Hill : a Cherokee plantation story / Tiya Miles.
p. cm.
Includes bibliographical references and index.
ISBN 978-0-8078-3418-3 (cloth : alk. paper)
1. Chief Vann House (Spring Place, Ga.) 2. Cherokee Indians — Georgia — History.
3. Plantations — Georgia — Spring Place — History. 4. Plantation life — Georgia — Spring Place. 5. Vann, James, 1765 or 6–1809. I. Title.
E99.C5M5325 2010
975.8'31 — dc22

2009052891

Title page illustration: *The Vann House: Monument to a Chief* by Ken Morrison. Used by permission of the artist.

cloth   14 13 12 11 10   5 4 3 2 1

To my parents, with gratitude and love:
mother and father, Patricia Miles King and Benny Miles
stepmother and stepfather, C. Montroue Miles and W. James King

For Pleasant, Patience, and Grace,
who called me

Contents

Illustrations and Maps

The Vann House with luminaries and holiday wreaths.
Courtesy of the Chief Vann House.

Housewarming

A PROLOGUE

"Something about this house inspires lunacy in people."
—Julia Autry, interpretive ranger, Chief Vann House State Historic Site,
December 2006

I had trod this Georgia road many times before, but never at night, never in winter. The air was frigid, the sky gloweringly black. But out of the darkness, off in the distance, the grand house glowed. Candles shone in every window. Beribboned wreaths of evergreen hung from the double doors. The promised warmth of interior spaces, hidden from view, beckoned through the gloom. It was lovely, this old plantation house, perched, as it was, atop a hillside. Striking in its grandeur. Alluring in its light. I could almost believe, staring up at the glowing, Palladian window panes, that the year was 1806, that Cherokees still possessed the lands of northern Georgia, that the wealthy Cherokee family who once dwelled in this home would appear at a doorway in waistcoats and bustles.

But this was not 1806. It was 2006. The family who had built this house had long passed into memory, and the home was owned and cared for by Georgia's Department of Natural Resources. I had come here to attend the Chief Vann House State Historic Site's Christmas by Candlelight celebration. And I found that, as William Chase Parker, an eighteen-year-old employee of the Vann House had put it, the "Christmas Spirit of the community" was very much in evidence.[1] A team of local volunteers from the nonprofit group Friends of the Vann House had readied the home for show. In the place of modern lighting, candles had been lit throughout the house and luminaries positioned along exterior pathways. Natural embellishments of dried okra pods, oiled magnolia leaves, and fanned cedar boughs festooned the interior rooms. The hand-carved mantels were topped by crimson-bowed wreaths, and inside every working hearth, a warming fire had been lit. The ornate dining table was set for a sumptuous holiday meal fit for a king or an Indian chief.

In addition to staging this event, the Friends group volunteers also hosted it, standing in the stead of the long-gone Vann family. The women Friends who

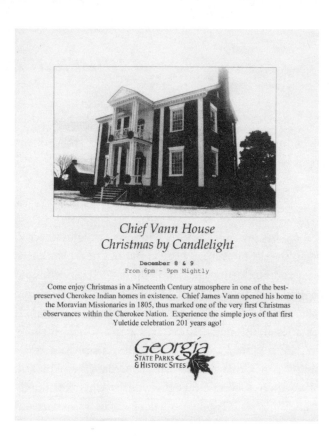

guided visitors on the house tour were dressed to match the stately rooms, in festive red wraps and shawls and gold-toned jewelry that shone in the candlelight. In the parlor, Tim Howard, past president of the Whitfield-Murray Counties Historical Society, played a tune on the piano. A female tourist joined him, singing an impromptu Christmas carol to spirited applause. Children of the Friends of the Vann House members, wearing period dress of breeches and homespun cotton, also guided visitors through the home. On the third floor, in what would have been the Vann family's children's rooms, young tour guides described the games that Cherokee boys and girls would have played.

In a cozy cabin adjacent to the main house, chief interpretive ranger Julia Autry, one of the two full-time employees at the Vann House, welcomed visitors with cookies and cocoa by warming firelight. She answered questions about the home and described colorful individuals in the Vann family. Christmas by Candlelight was the most popular annual event that the Vann

The dining room in the Vann House decorated for the Christmas by Candlelight program, with Joseph Vann's portrait on the wall. Courtesy of the Chief Vann House.

House museum sponsored, and Ranger Chase Parker captured in words the recurring magic of the scene:

> The Christmas Candlelight Tour is the most authentic celebration held at the site today. . . . I believe that when walking through the home during those candle lit nights, one gets the closest glimpse possible of how the home looked during Joseph [Vann's] time. The night hides so much of the modernization inside and surrounding the home. Also, the way that candle-light affects people today is probably the same way that it affected people two hundred years ago. So the feeling people get when they see the candle's flame flicker and the fires' reflections sway on the walls is a feeling much like the visitors of the Vanns' did in the early eighteen hundreds.

The rare feeling that Ranger Parker described of being transported into the past was one that the public hungered for, as evidenced by the one hundred to two hundred people who were expected to tour this tucked-away historic house over the course of the two-day event. This particular 2006 holiday season, Ranger Autry explained, their numbers had reached that projected highpoint on the very first evening. And as I write these words in the spring of 2009, the Vann House has just announced that the 2008 Christmas event broke past records, drawing over eight hundred visitors to the "delightful" fires "inside the old mansion."[2]

Throughout the year, visitors travel to the Vann House from nearby towns, the city of Atlanta, the states of Tennessee and Oklahoma, across the United States, and even around the world. This night, almost all of the tourists were white and southern: young adults with babes in arms, elderly couples, adolescents. Latino teens made up the second largest group, reflective of the changing population dynamics of many southern cities. As the only African American person I could visually identify, I may have stood out among the crowd. Nor did I note, on the single night that I was there, the presence of Cherokees or other Native American people. Some visitors were seeing the Vann House for the first time, but many others had been there on several occasions before. The latter spoke animatedly and knowledgeably about members of the historical Vann family, debating theories about the Vanns' personalities and the motivation for acts undertaken long ago. The second set of guests returned to this place again and again, as if it were their own ancestral home.

The volunteers, too, had walked these grounds many a time, following in the footsteps of generations of family members from Murray County, Georgia, and surrounds, a predominantly white area. The children who guided tours on the upper floor of the home spoke of their grandparents' work as volunteers at the Vann House. A young man who led guests through a Cherokee cabin on the grounds explained that he was following in his elder brother's footsteps as a Vann House worker. The inherited aspect of Vann House volunteerism was so pronounced that site employees recognized it in their seasonal newsletter, writing: "[T]he Vann House somehow seems to produce this special type of generational selflessness."[3] The devotion of local volunteers amazed Ranger Autry, who compared their unflagging love for this house to a rather less enthusiastic embrace of Cherokee political historic sites in Georgia. A woman of wry but good-natured humor, Autry called some volunteers' passion for the Vann House a form of "lunacy."[4]

And perhaps this manor home in the foothills of the Blue Ridge Mountains did hold just a bit of the moon's magic. People fell for this place—the home, the hills, the mountains on the horizon. The Vann House has a way of casting spells, creating an aura of eras past. Its massive porticoed entry doors, framed in brightest white, double as a portal to another time. For many visitors and volunteers alike, the effect has been a sense of connection, a feeling of comfort, serenity, pleasure, and release from the cares of our day-to-day world. And I was really no exception. This Christmas marked my fifth visit to the site, and if I had been immune to the house's beauty, it is doubtful I would have chosen to write this book. But, I am compelled to ask, what is it we are connecting with when we walk the oak halls of this exquisite plantation home—one hundred and seventy years after Cherokees were forcibly removed from the South, one hundred and forty years after African Americans slaves were emancipated from slavery? What *really* took place on these well-worn grounds? What does this house *stand for*?

That wintry evening, during the Christmas tour, I visited the cellar of the Chief Vann House. Unlike the above-ground rooms that hummed with the movement of scores of guests, this space that formed the home's foundation was quiet, empty. A lone volunteer, a young man of about thirteen dressed in period clothing, stood ready to describe the cold, desolate rooms. "This is where the slaves would have worked," he told me. "Shackles were found in the corner," he said.

Instead of climbing the basement stairs to reenter the warm, bright body of the house, I made my way outside through the cellar's slim side door. From this angle, facing away from the burnished brick home, all was dark, all was chill.

THE HOUSE ON *Diamond Hill*

The oldest known photograph of the Vann House, 1898.
Courtesy of the Chief Vann House.

This Old House

AN INTRODUCTION

Can we read the history of a place in its buildings? The skyscrapers of
Manhattan; the wooden, wide-porched farmhouses of Iowa; the broad streets
of Chicago; the narrow-streeted neighborhoods of Boston; the brick colonials
of Philadelphia; the white-columned manors of Georgia . . . all stand witness to
the past, conveying the personality and ethos of a place.
—Phoebe S. Kropp, *California Vieja: Culture and Memory in a Modern American
Place*, 2006

The Chief Vann House in its faded dignity and its romantic decay, appealed
to many minds and attracted not only historians but also those persons whose
imagination loves to live in the past.
—Clemens de Baillou, "The Chief Vann House," 1957

On Diamond Hill

Generations of enthusiasts of southern historic sites have sought to "read the
history" of northwest Georgia in the former Cherokee building known as the
Chief Vann House. This lovely brick plantation home, embellished by forty-
eight of the iconic white columns for which southern architecture is recognized, has long been a source of pride in the state.[1] After falling into disrepair
in the decades after Cherokee Removal, the Vann House was restored in the
early 1950s by local community organizers in partnership with the state-run
Georgia Historical Commission. The home was and remains beloved by community members as well as by local journalists, who over the years have described it as "palatial," "lofty," "a monument to its owner," "a shrine to the
Cherokees," having "all the elegance of a fine Virginia mansion," and "more
grand than the palace of Versailles."[2] As the executive secretary of the Georgia
Historical Commission (GHC) wrote to the Keeper of the National Register
of Historic Sites in 1968: "The Vann House [was] one of the most important
structures in the state of Georgia."[3] Primary among the home's many extolled
virtues was that it had been built by the Cherokee Indians and was, according
to an early GHC brochure, "the finest home in the Cherokee Nation," which
"dominat[ed] the countryside for miles."[4]

CHIEF VANN HOUSE

STATE HISTORIC SITE

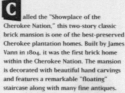

A Vann House brochure. Courtesy of the Chief Vann House.

ANNUAL EVENTS

- Artifact Identification (May)

- Vann House Day (July)

- Candlelight Christmas Evenings (December)

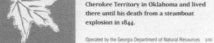

Called the "Showplace of the Cherokee Nation," this two-story classic brick mansion is one of the best-preserved Cherokee plantation homes. Built by James Vann in 1804, it was the first brick home within the Cherokee Nation. The mansion is decorated with beautiful hand carvings and features a remarkable "floating" staircase along with many fine antiques.

"Feared by many and loved by few," Vann was both a hero and a rogue, and he was responsible for bringing the Moravian missionaries into the Cherokee Nation to build schools. Toward the end of his life, Vann became a heavy and often violent drinker. He killed his brother-in-law in a duel, fired a pistol at dinner guests through the floor of an upstairs bedroom, and once even shot at his own mother. Vann himself was shot and killed at a local tavern in 1809.

His son, Joseph Vann, inherited the home and went on to become a Cherokee statesman. He expanded the family wealth in property, slaves and a line of steamboats. The Georgia Militia evicted "Rich Joe" Vann in 1835 for having unknowingly violated a new law making it illegal for Indians to hire Whites. Joseph then settled in the Cherokee Territory in Oklahoma and lived there until his death from a steamboat explosion in 1844.

Operated by the Georgia Department of Natural Resources 3/00

From the 1950s to today, citizen-restorers and local historians have pledged their hearts to this old plantation home, reading into it their own identities as white southerners living on former Cherokee lands. Those who played a role in the restoration, and even descendants of restorers, speak of the home with tenderness, reverence, loyalty, and love.[5] They describe the Vann House as a keepsake of and tribute to their region's past. I, too, want to read a history of place through this southern building, but with a radically different perspective than that expressed by many of its devoted followers. Rather than viewing the Vann House as a symbol of Georgia's proud history, or, as the Georgia Historical Commission deemed it, "the show place of the Cherokee Nation," I see it as a sieve for contemporary place-based identity formation and as a site of historical struggle for human dignity and survival.[6] And rather than excising the history of slavery from the memory of this plantation home, as so many public representations of southern manors do, I aim, in this book, to expand the story of the Chief Vann House beyond the celebrated domicile and onto the plantation grounds that surrounded and supported it. The famous brick house, which was actually built in the final chapter of the Cherokee plantation's history, has been central to visitors' memory of and attachment to the place. The image of the home appears on postcards, T-shirts, tote bags, engraved Christmas ornaments, tourist websites, Cherokee history books, and original art, like the watercolor that graces the frontispiece of this work. The home retains central importance in the history I will tell as a symbolic, referential, and evocative structure, even as I attempt to stretch the story back in time to the decades before the house was built, out in space to the far corners of the plantation, and forward, briefly, into our own contemporary moment.

The brick manor house, intended to be the crown jewel of the Vann family's Diamond Hill plantation, was spectacular in the Cherokee Nation and Georgia frontier of the early 1820s. But the plantation proper, developed at the turn of the nineteenth century, existed long before the house that would hold it in memory for present-day Georgians and tourists. This book tells a story of the historic place of Diamond Hill, the people who dwelled there, and their memory in modern times, tracing the plantation from its prehistory, to its heyday and downfall in the 1820s and 1830s, to its restoration and commemoration as the Chief Vann House State Historic Site from the 1950s onward. On Diamond Hill, one of the first and most prosperous Cherokee plantations, American Indians, enslaved people of African descent, and Euro-American missionaries, craftsmen, and laborers lived incredible, intersecting lives. Their experiences, set against the backdrop of American colonization of the Cherokee Nation, the spread of black chattel slavery across the South, and a premarket revolution set in motion by the American War of Independence, reveals the gradations of everyday life across multiple color lines, the brutal injustices of race-based systems of slavery and land seizure, and the creative ability of human beings to adapt and survive against the odds.

In the early 1800s, a Cherokee man named James Vann built a fortune in the north Georgia hills on land possessed by the Cherokee Nation. As the son of a Cherokee woman and a Scottish trader who had emigrated from South Carolina, James Vann inherited both Cherokee citizenship from his mother's family line and valuable property from his father. Bold, savvy, and inventive, Vann soon amassed control of at least four hundred to nearly eight hundred acres of rich agricultural land bordered by the Conasauga River and watered by a series of natural stone springs. By 1801, he had named his estate Diamond Hill, inspired, perhaps, by the striking quartz crystals that were strewn about the property below the soil's surface.[7] Vann then invited missionaries from the Moravian Church, a culturally German, Protestant denomination based in Salem, North Carolina, to found a Christian mission and school on his grounds. In 1803, Vann successfully lobbied the U.S. government for a proposed federal road to pass by his estate. Once the road was in place, he developed a string of hospitality businesses far to the east of Diamond Hill in what is now Forsythe County, Georgia, alongside the thoroughfare's Chattahoochee River route. These included a tavern with sleeping quarters for travelers, a campground for low-budget visitors, a trading post, and a ferry service.[8]

Meanwhile, Vann expanded his plantation base at Diamond Hill, building a large two-story home most likely constructed of logs in 1804–1805, developing agricultural fields and cattle herds, commissioning the first mill in the area, constructing a whiskey still, and opening a store — all accomplished with the indispensable aid of black slave labor.[9] Property in enslaved blacks was one of the most valuable commodities Vann had inherited from his father, and at the time that he consolidated his business ventures, Vann owned nearly seventy women, men, and children of African descent. This was the principal workforce that grew and harvested field and orchard crops on Vann's estate, transported supplies, constructed buildings, prepared meals, cleaned living quarters, wove textiles, tended cattle, and delivered goods. As Vann extended his business transactions into Charleston and Augusta, trading the corn, wheat, fruit, and cotton his plantation enterprise produced for dry goods, household supplies, alcohol, tools, and clothing, he also bought and sold black slaves. By 1805, Vann had taken to calling his string of businesses on the northern Cherokee-Georgia frontier Vannsville.

Together, Vannsville and the adjacent plantation community of Diamond

Hill made for a bustling place, a cosmopolitan center of activity tucked in the Cherokee wilderness. Travelers from points north, south, and even Europe passed this way as they crisscrossed the southern region of the young United States. The Moravian mission station, named Springplace after the area where it was located, was a destination for fellow Christians as well as prominent U.S. citizens, weary travelers, and poor American Indians in need. James Vann's prominence as a Cherokee political leader meant that Diamond Hill was the site of meetings for the Cherokee Council and the distribution center for federal treaty annuities to Cherokee people in the vicinity. Cherokee subsistence farmers and residents from regional Upper Towns settlements gathered on and near Vann's landmark estate to do business; to engage in community social activities; to seek food, translation assistance, and other forms of aid; and to enroll their children in the Springplace Mission school. White laborers from Georgia and other states relocated to Vannsville to work in Vann's employ as clerks, overseers, construction workers, and craftsmen. The population of enslaved blacks on Diamond Hill was one of the largest in the Cherokee Nation. On any given Diamond Hill day in the early 1800s, a blend of cooking smells would have mingled in the air: Cherokee hominy and bean soups, African-inspired sweet potato or boiled peanut dishes, and fresh slaw prepared from the bounty of the Moravians' garden. A symphony of sounds, too, rode the gentling breeze, as residents conversed in Cherokee, African, English, and German languages. On Christmas holidays and Saturdays, the steady beat of African drums emanated from the slave quarters, resounding through the night.

Amid the constant, variegated flow of people and goods that characterized the area, James Vann's intimate companions on Diamond Hill were his mother, Wali, who had her own home and field there, a number of Cherokee wives, most of whom deserted Vann in quick succession, several sons and daughters, and Vann's political allies on the Cherokee Council who often visited. The only wife of James Vann to stay with him permanently was Peggy Scott, also the daughter of a Cherokee woman and European man. She, along with Vann's favored son, Joseph, inherited a portion of the Diamond Hill estate. When Joseph became the master of Diamond Hill in the eighteen-teens, he commissioned the now famous brick manor house.

In 1809, James Vann was murdered by an unknown assailant. Peggy Scott lost her life to consumption in 1820. And Joseph Vann died in a steamboat accident on the Ohio River in 1844. Across the decades, Diamond Hill changed from hand to hand: first owned by Georgia land-lottery winners in the period of Cherokee Removal and then by a series of Georgia planters and families, and finally falling into a condition of abandonment and disrepair. Today, the restored remainder of Vann's estate is owned by the state of Georgia and known as the Chief Vann House State Historic Site.

This shift from Cherokee ownership to Georgia state stewardship was precipitated first by Cherokee Removal, and then by the concerted effort of local white residents. Encouraged by the house museum movement that had gathered steam in the 1890s in southern cities like Charleston, as well as by the successful development of Cherokee, North Carolina, as an Indian-themed tourist attraction, community members in north Georgia labored in the 1950s to save the Vann family's house.[10] Dicksie Bradley Bandy, high-society maven and head of the Whitfield-Murray Historical Society, penned dozens of letters on the home's behalf and involved herself intimately in minute details of construction, decoration, landscaping, and event planning. As a result of her efforts, Bandy became known as a "lady detective, historian, and champion of the Indian cause."[11] Bandy was joined by Ivan Allen, a businessman fascinated by local history, whose family hailed from the historic Spring Place township. Allen was among a core group of Vann House devotees who convened in 1951 to save the structure. The *Atlanta Constitution* reported that in October of that year, "a number of Georgians, not necessarily of Indian blood but interested in the Indian history of Georgia," gathered at the Henry Grady Hotel in Atlanta to form the Joseph Vann Historical Association. The meeting had been called by Decatur resident Gertrude Ruskin and had as its primary goal the formation of a group "to raise money somehow to buy the old Joseph Vann house at Spring Place, Georgia, and convert it into a museum to the fabled Cherokee." Attendees at the meeting were "prominent Georgians from Cartersville, Chatsworth, and the surrounding regions, whose interest in the Cherokee is profound." Allen, a founding member of the association, contributed the first $500 to the cause. To spur interest in the campaign, the Vann Association sponsored an essay contest in the *Atlanta Constitution*. The winner, Onie Starr of Atlanta, the widow of a former Georgia state senator, had written about spending her honeymoon in the Vann home sixty years prior. By 1952, the community group had raised the $5,000 needed to purchase the house along with six acres of the original plantation grounds.[12]

Contemporaneously with the association's efforts, the Georgia state legislature authorized the GHC to mark and protect historic places. The commission commenced its work by interpreting sites from the Civil War era and then began purchasing sites related to Georgia's American Indian history. Due to the enthusiastic advocacy of residents in and near Murray County, the first purchase of property made by the Georgia Commission was the Chief Vann

House.[13] Funds raised by the Joseph Vann Association were used to buy the home, and on July 5, 1952, the GHC took legal acquisition of the property. An inspection by architect Francis Smith of Atlanta revealed that the house was in "deplorable condition." Nevertheless, the "remarkable hanging stairway" was still intact, and "the detail of mouldings and the curious wood inlays," which the architect found "most interesting," "could be restored in large part." The house might be returned nearly to its original condition, Smith concluded, if the GHC dedicated at least $15,000 and secured a "competent builder."[14]

Lobbied by the GHC, the state made an initial appropriation of $10,000 for the Vann House revitalization project. The GHC then hired noted Maryland architect Henry Chandlee Forman to undertake a painstaking six-year restoration. A 1957 guidebook to southern homes included the Vann House among its listings and noted that the site, "stunningly restored by Henry C. Forman," was "open during restoration."[15] After Forman completed his work, Dalton, Georgia, designer Marjorie Rhodes scraped peeling paint and wallpaper to reveal the home's original paint colors and planned the interior decor. Volunteers furnished the home with donated antiques and Vann family items identified in Oklahoma.[16] In July of 1958, the Vann House was dedicated in a grand opening ceremony organized by Dicksie Bandy.[17] Between 5,000 and 8,000 people attended the event that society columnist Mary Well of Chatsworth described as "[a] big day in our county . . . quite the largest crowd we've ever had in our county, on any occasion."[18] Soon, a glossy brochure produced by the GHC heralded the "Chief Vann House, the finest home in the Cherokee Nation . . . completed in 1804 by James Clement Vann."[19]

The Chieftains Trail

The restored Vann House is a featured stop on what the contemporary Georgia legislature has termed the Chieftains Trail, a route of exploration through Native American history in northwest Georgia, which also includes the restored Cherokee capital of New Echota, the museum home of Cherokee leader Major Ridge, and the Etowah Mounds from the "prehistoric" Mississippian Chiefdom period.[20] The over one-hundred-acre Vann site encompasses a brick house museum; an Interpretive Center complete with film, exhibit hall, and gift shop items; various log outbuildings; a stone springhouse; and a streamside nature trail. Though extensive in acreage, the site is run by only two full-time staff members with the aid of young-adult part-time employees. Local volunteers organized as the Friends of the Vann House contribute much-needed labor, funds, energy, and imagination to the site by orga-

Local historian Dicksie Bradley Bandy with Joseph Vann's portrait, 1950s. Courtesy of the Chief Vann House.

nizing and carrying out special programs. The Vann House sits on Highway 225, also called the Trail of Tears Highway and the Joseph Vann Highway, which traces the stretch of the federal road for which James Vann lobbied back in 1803. The Vann House is situated in the historic town site of Spring Place, just three miles outside of the tiny town of Chatsworth, in Murray County. A mile down the road on Highway 52, formal markers and a commemorative headstone identify the Moravian Springplace Mission and God's Acre cemetery that once adjoined Vann's estate. Farther south, heading the ninety-two miles toward Atlanta, the Joseph Vann Highway intersects with Interstate 75. Forty miles north and west of the Vann House, Georgia borders Tennessee near the city of Chattanooga.

The lush boundary region between northern Georgia and southern Tennessee, where forested mountains meet tumbling hills and winding rivers range through the countryside, was Cherokee territory in the time of the Vanns. In an 1826 "Address to the Whites," delivered at the First Presbyterian Church of Philadelphia, Cherokee newspaper editor Elias Boudinot described his home

Designer Marjorie Rhodes with drapery in front of a Vann House fireplace, 1950s. Courtesy of the Chief Vann House.

region as "one of the Garden spots of America." "Indeed," he added, "I would not be guilty of exaggeration were I to say, that the advantages which this country possesses to render it salubrious, are many and superior." The "lofty" mountains, he wrote, "placed there only to exhibit omnipotence, contribute to the healthiness and beauty of the surrounding plains and give us to that free air and pure water which distinguish our country."[21] Today this alluring area attracts rural and urban tourists of both historical and environmental persuasions. The historic sites on the Chieftains Trail are nestled between the Chattahoochee National Forest to the west and Fort Mountain State Park (land donated to the state by Ivan Allen) to the east.[22] The Cohutta Mountains—end caps of the Blue Ridge range and home to Fort Mountain State Park—host retreat sites and vacation homes with stunning views. The Vann House is nestled in the valley of this range and features a Cohutta vista to the east.

Visitors to the Vann House reach into the thousands annually. In the year 2000, over 7,000 tourists visited the site; in 2005, that number had grown to over 10,000; and in 2007, the number of visitors was nearly 13,000.[23] William Chase Parker, a young and talented ranger who has worked at the Vann House for over three years, described the site's many tourists as a diverse lot: "Our visitors to the Vann House vary as much as the colors of a rainbow. We have visitors who are rich and poor. We have members of [the] upper, middle, and lower class . . . as well as the famous and the not famous. . . . We have visitors of every race and ethnicity. . . . We have visitors from out of this country. . . . I have often said that it surprises me how so many people from all over the world can find the Chief Vann House, which is in a little town in the mountains of North Georgia."[24]

The diversity of backgrounds that Ranger Parker notes among tourists must certainly result in a range of experiences at the historic site. Even so, visitors of many stripes leave the Vann House with an overwhelming sense of positive connection to the place and its history.[25] Visitors report being awestruck by the architecture of the home, lulled by the natural setting, touched by the barely sensed presence of spirits of the dead, and transported into scenes of times gone by. To mark their impressive experience, tourists purchase items imprinted with the Vann House image, revisit the site time after time, or become active members of the Vann House community advocacy group.

Playing Southern, Playing Indian

The feelings of connection, sublimity, and escape inspired by the Vann House in its visitors are also generated by southern plantation home tours more generally, offered at historic sites, at annual home and garden events, and in virtual form in architectural books and shelter magazines. Homes of the "early" South, notably those dated before the onset of the Civil War, capture the American imagination like few other architectural styles in the country. Images of snow-white columns, wide porches framed by azaleas, glossy-leaved magnolia trees, and moss-dripped oaks hold a unique and enduring place in our mind's-eye map of the nation. As one midcentury guidebook put it: "It is hardly necessary to introduce the South as a place where stately and romantic early homes abound. Too many people have now heard of the glamorous charms of Natchez, New Orleans, and Charleston; of Williamsburg's patrician splendors, the matchless country mansions of Virginia, and Maryland's aristocratic tidewater manors."[26] For the South, in its mythical image of sun-doused splendor, luxury, and leisure, retains the memory of a genteel America elegant with agrarian grace. Southern living has epitomized, in the words of an early-twentieth-century North Carolina journalist, "the most glamorous of all folk legends of America — the legend of the plantation civilization of the Old South."[27]

For many tourists, old plantation homes and their gardens mark, contain, and represent a persevering spirit of the grand southern past. These lovely houses set the stage for imagined, romantic scenes—bedecked and dazzling ladies gathered at garden parties, crisp and lacy crinolines hung from scented wardrobes, refreshing mint juleps served on the verandah—a time when life was easy, sweet, and slow. As southern historian W. Fitzhugh Brundage has put it: "The tourist South became a stage on which southerners presented the South both as they wanted to see it and as they imagined tourists wanted to experience it. . . . Americans gravitated to these historical settings, which offered a vivid intensification of experience and a magical suspension of time."[28] Historian Phoebe Kropp has likewise observed that a "national fascination with the Old South" developed because tourists "found great psychic relief in a vision of gracious hegemony." "From Uncle Remus to Scarlett O'Hara," Kropp continues, "the Old South came to evoke for many white Americans a happier time and a less hurried pace of life."[29]

These historians' descriptions of southern tourism in the early 1900s continues to resonate today, since the southern "dream world" of "private gardens and homes" still entrances many Americans, who treasure aged plantation houses as icons of better days gone by.[30] These classic homes cum heirloom antiques and romantic memorabilia erase, if only for a moment, the hectic surge of twenty-first-century life, the present-day reality of financial strain, and, most pointedly, the social complexities of modern race relations. The Old South still functions, writes literary scholar Jessica Adams, "as a site of whites' leisured longing."[31]

Southern, northern, and western tourists alike, especially those of Euro-American heritage, can enter and enjoy these plantation "scenes of nostalgia."[32] White southerners whose identity coheres around the Lost Cause of the U.S. Civil War, for instance, cherish such architectural icons of a prewar era, remnants of the South's fleeting cotton kingdom golden age. Other white southerners, who have witnessed or heard tell of grand plantation homes being passed down in families for generations, experience these houses as "strongholds of identity," "dispensaries of memory," and "connective tissue to their ancestors."[33] Nonsoutherners whose regional identity is rooted elsewhere but whose popular imaginations have been fed by *Gone with the Wind's* fabled Tara can also access antebellum southern mythology as part of a larger American heritage. Indeed, for nonsoutherners the South is an ideal vacation spot—temperate, storied, long defined as exotically and culturally distinct from other regions of the United States, yet easily accessible by highway and railway.[34] The elephant in the plantation parlor, however, is black chattel slavery, which mars the purity of mint julep moments, undoes the pleasure of white-only leisure, and justifies the wreckage of a bloody Civil War. Plantation home tours and photographic representations of plantations steadfastly avoid the elephant, whose presence, if recognized, would trample the fantasy of better times recalled. To avoid the elephant, these tours and images must accomplish a stunning sleight of hand: separate "slavery from the meaning of the plantation" and reduce the working plantation to the comfortable status of "home."[35]

In prominent ways, the Chief Vann House is a plantation show-home akin to many others. The elegant brick Georgian facade signals a stately air. White columns, porches, and porticoes echo the lines of classic estates. Its "floating" staircase and elaborate woodwork suggest an extravagance of architectural style. Its rooms showcase a bevy of antiques, including a priceless highboy dresser, a canopy bed of mahogany, a porcelain chamber pot, and a singular nineteenth-century quilt. Rolling grounds and award-winning gardens signal an Eden of repose. And the home's placement atop a scenic rise sets it apart from the town below, beset by streetlights busily flashing, gas stations hawking Doritos, sports bars, pharmacies, and the greasy spoons of modern-day life. At the same time, though, the Vann House holds a major distinction from other plantation homes: it was built for and owned by American Indians. This unexpected aspect of the home's origins is one that fascinates many visitors, many of whom associate Native Americans with plains-style teepees and simplistic, static lifestyles. As cultural historian Philip Deloria has argued, nonindigenous Americans have long imagined native people as existing outside of the categories of modern life, and representations of Indians that challenge such expectations have therefore been discomfiting. The anomalous Indian history of the Vann House, though, seems to have an oddly reassuring effect on local stewards of the site as well as on many visitors from the outside. For local community members have claimed the Vann family as fellow southerners and experience the Vanns' architectural achievement as their own. Visitors, too, are able to fold the unexpected aspect of Native American history into their enjoyment of the site. For both these groups, the movement from discomfort with Indians found in the "unexpected" setting of the southern plantation to pleasure in an "exotic" Indian presence in this same setting hinges on the specific Indians in question—Cherokee Indians—who have often been categorized as uniquely "civilized" in American historical and popular representations.[36]

Georgian writers have long defined Cherokee Indians in this civilizational light. Cherokee history was a point of pride for local communities precisely because Cherokees were viewed as a uniquely cultured and illustrious tribe.

A local newspaper editorial praising the Vann House restoration intimated as much when it hailed the "splendor" of the house, stated that the Cherokees "were highly civilized and educated," and noted that "savage" Indians of the far west were nothing like the Indians in Georgia. A compendium of Georgia history similarly boasted that, unlike other tribes, the Cherokee Nation had reached what was "for Indians . . . a highly advanced stage of civilization . . . had become a settled society of farmers and Negro slave owners—rather than nomadic groups of hunters—and had its national capital two miles east of what is now Calhoun, GA." Georgia State University historian Henry Malone published an essay titled "The Cherokees Become a Civilized Tribe" in *Early Georgia* magazine's 1957 Cherokee issue, in which he stated: "With the help of Christian missionaries, friendly government agents, and wise counsel from within the tribe, these Indians became more nearly civilized—in the white man's sense—than any other red men of their day." And Governor Marvin Griffin commented in his speech at the Vann House dedication that the "landmark" site was symbolic of the "great dignity" of both the "Indian" and the "settler" cultures that had melded there. As historian Andrew Denson has succinctly put it: "Cherokee history, in particular, the 'civilized tribe' image, had become part of the state's heritage, a unique feature of the [Georgian] past."[37] Rather than being a point of discomfort for Georgians, the Cherokee origins of the elegant Vann House makes local sense. And stewards of the Vann House have sought to share this local understanding of Indians with visitors to the site.

Because Cherokees have long been understood as different from (and better than) other Indians, especially in this specific southern locale, they are intelligible in what would otherwise be viewed as a non-Indian plantation space. A Cherokee historical presence at the Vann House not only makes sense in this regard but also renders the plantation scene all the more alluring. For similar, in a way, to southern ladies in hoopskirts and lace, Native Americans have long represented a romantic past in mainstream American culture. Once Indians were expelled from their homes, or exterminated, or "pacified" in various moments of the sixteenth, seventeenth, eighteenth, and nineteenth centuries, they became objects of fascination for the perpetrators of such violence and for their descendants. White Americans, and some African and Mexican Americans, too, embraced memories of a past peopled with Indians through dress-up, dramatic reenactment, and commemoration of historic sites, participating in what some scholars would call "imperialist nostalgia" or "playing Indian."[38] Native Americans, reviled in person by those who sought their fertile lands, were cherished at a distance of time and space. This is because it was *their* presence, *their* "wild nobility," *their* indigenous "essence" that had distinguished America from Europe and made this country unique. In short, as Deloria has put it, Indians "spoke for the 'spirit of the continent.'"[39]

Americans longed to possess not only Indian land but also what they perceived as the Indians' special connection to it; they wanted to belong to this place that was America as truly and as mystically as had the original inhabitants; they longed, in other words, to capture the Indian "spirit." Colonial historian Nancy Shoemaker has described this embrace of distant Indians as a process of "national mythmaking," writing: "[A]s time passed and the newly independent United States cultivated a distinct national identity rooted in the North American landscape, narratives of American history looked for Indians to place among the nation's founding fathers. Towns and cities — especially those located in the East, where Indians had already been vanquished — celebrated the Indian heritage of their communities."[40] As a remarkable structure from an unusual chapter in Native American history, the Chief Vann House makes a vivid impression. It allows visitors to enter into the once private space of a famous Indian's home, to participate most intimately in a national mythmaking process in which absent Indians are celebrated as central to the spirit of America. And therein lies the rub. In order for this feeling of patriotic celebration to function, Indians must be exorcised and non–Native Americans must be enabled to forget their own culpability for native exile, extermination, and detribalization. For if Cherokees and other American Indians still occupied their historic places on the American landscape, there would be no state-operated Chief Vann House museum to wistfully recall a vanished Indian heritage.

The Vann House is therefore a typical *and* atypical plantation home, combining elements of antebellum southern nostalgia and American Indian historical enchantment that capture deep and differing aspects of the American popular imagination. Tourists at the Vann House can participate in the imagined, combined reenactment of southern antebellum and Native American life. And the connotative pleasures of the site are even greater for local residents, who have a particular regional investment in its meanings. The Vann House is a statewide icon, representative of Georgia's glorified past in terms of both antebellum southern culture and American Indian history. Just as images of antebellum grandeur permeate the state's sense of itself, so too do notions of an extraordinary Indian past, which lend a sense of ancient mystery, foreign exotica, and aristocratic ambience to the locale. It seems no coincidence that the Georgia Historical Commission turned first to preserving Civil War sites, remembrances of the Lost Cause, and then to purchasing Native American structures like the Vann House and the Etowah Mounds. For the notion of an Old South took on new and richer meaning when Native American history was folded into the story. The region could now be heralded as an ancient South dating back to indigenous times and continuing through the apex of southern civilization.[41]

And beyond the acquisition of an ancient South inheritance, the notion of Indians as slaveholders offers an additional positive link between the southern plantation mythology and the historical Vann family. When the Vanns lost their plantation despite the existence of a Cherokee state that had fought for Cherokee rights, their experience mapped even more closely onto that of white southerners who had failed to sustain a Confederate state and lost all in the Civil War. Cherokees and southerners had a common enemy: the federal government that had passed the Indian Removal Act and crushed the South in battle. As Civil War historian David Blight has observed: "Unlike most parts of the United States, with Native Americans the obvious exception, the South was conquered." In this and other ways, the Cherokee Vanns can be viewed as having undergone a quintessential southern experience. Cherokees and southerners alike had fought for a noble, lost cause.[42]

It would seem, then, that when local Vann House enthusiasts embrace this home and its history, they are also embracing a notion of themselves as southerners. The Vann House is a distinctive place for the projection of southern visions of a landed aristocracy that nobly defended states' rights. While black slavery conjures feelings of guilt, defensiveness, and even denial among many white southerners, especially in the civil rights era when the Vann House was first restored, Indian Removal can be viewed as a point of connection between martyred southern whites and ousted southern Indians.

The Bosom of the House

In addition to this potent blend of southern mythology and Native American mystique, the Vann House, because it is a house (rather than, say, an aged municipal building), becomes for visitors an especially intense source of comfort and pleasure. This process, argues French philosopher Gaston Bachelard, is fundamental to the human concept of the house itself. In Bachelard's view, the house, whether hovel or castle, is an elemental sign of safety that draws and succors human beings and allows for the spinning of intimate dreams. Delving into psychology and phenomenology, Bachelard asserts that because "life begins . . . enclosed, protected, all warm in the bosom of the house," the house takes on magical qualities in the human mind. Protected within the sturdy walls of a house, residents ponder, think, and dream, experiencing their most intimate moments and forming their most secret desires. People bond most especially with the homes in which they were born but also with all of the places in which they have lived, tucking away precious memories and bits of themselves into corners and attics. "[I]f I were asked to name the chief benefit of the house," Bachelard writes, "I should say: the house shelters day-dreaming, the house protects the dreamer, the house allows one to love in peace." The magical role of protector-muse that the house plays in human emotional life leads people to "experience the house in its reality and in its virtuality." The house therefore becomes more than real in the human imagination, as "one of the greatest powers of integration for the thoughts, memories, and dreams of mankind."[43]

Bachelard's notion of the house as both "cradle" of new life and incubator of dreams may indicate why a place like the Vann House exhibits a special power to arrest imaginations. A structure that symbolizes shelter and promotes fantasy, the Vann House, in its very house-ness, exudes a mystical magnetism. And because the original inhabitants of this house were displaced nearly two centuries ago, visitors are free to roam its rooms, unleash their imaginations, and claim its protective powers for their own. Perhaps this is what Vann House chief interpretive ranger Julia Autry meant when she said that, unlike the restored government buildings of the old Cherokee capital of New Echota, "something about this house inspires lunacy in people."[44] The Vann House's combination of southern allure, Indian aura, and essential house-ness is a siren's call to those "whose imagination loves to live in the past."[45]

But few visitors whose imaginations are so moved, with the clear exception of Cherokee tourists, recognize the irony of their adulation for an Indian home no longer possessed by Indians. If they did, perhaps they would share the ire of eighty-eight-year-old Virginia Vann Perry, great-great-great-granddaughter of James Vann, who said, when asked about the Vann House: "I'll tell you exactly what I think: I think the white people around were jealous of the culture and prosperity of the Indians and one of the homes [they envied] was the Vann House and that's why they wanted them out of Georgia, Tennessee, and other places." Or perhaps, if encouraged to tour the home with guarded and discerning minds, visitors would understand the ambivalence of Cherokee political activist and historian David Cornsilk, who has led two Oklahoma-based Cherokee groups on tours through the Southeast and commented that the Vann House "is representative of the tremendous losses suffered by Cherokees, both rich and poor, because of the theft of our homeland." Although Cornsilk would like to see "all historic sites in Georgia, Alabama, and Tennessee and the rest of our ancient homeland turned over and jointly controlled by the three federally recognized bands of Cherokees," he has consigned himself to an unsettling compromise. "If [the Vann House] must be in the hands of the state responsible for our ouster, so be it. Its preservation is the most critical issue." For Cornsilk and other Cherokees who cherish the Vann House despite its shadowed history, the home is "symbolic of our tribal claim to our original homeland . . . a beacon or focal point to which all Cherokees can pay homage."[46]

Book Objectives and Organization

Over the years, the Chief Vann House has attracted a devoted following among white Georgia residents. The Vann House advocacy group, Friends of the Vann House, is the oldest organization of its kind in the state, and no other Native American site along the Chieftains Trail is as well loved and well tended by members of the local community. Ties of dedication to and passion for the Vann plantation extend back in time for generations, from the original purchase and preservation of the home and acreage in the 1950s to the careful stewardship of the site by community groups today. But absent in the Vann House enthusiast tradition has been an exploration of the reasons why this particular old house has inspired such a groundswell of grassroots activity. Why is a Cherokee Indian plantation so powerful a place in the hearts and minds of modern-day Georgians? What stories are allowed and disallowed, voiced and suppressed, at this beloved historic site? Posing questions such as these can point us toward new understandings of the meaning and value of historical sites to our sense of regional as well as racial identity. And exploring possible answers to these questions allows us to peer beyond a glamorous architectural facade to an era of unbridled violence set in motion by U.S. expansion and colonialism, a time of desperate accommodation to Euro-American cultural dictates, an epoch of expanding race slavery in Indian nations and the southern states, and a period of layered and entangled culpability for both black and Indian suffering.

The story told in this book describes these overlapping contexts and circumstances, portraying the people, both famous and forgotten, who lived in this place in trying times. In writing it, I was first inspired by enslaved people of the past whose voices rose from the written records of the Vann estate. Later, I was encouraged the more by interpretive ranger Julia Autry, who pointed out that there had never been a book written about the Vann plantation. Although many scholarly articles, newspaper stories, local history booklets, and fanciful genealogical narratives have been penned about James Vann and his estate, it is indeed the case that no full-length study, scholarly or popular, has yet been produced. As early as 1957 archaeologist Clemens de Baillou commented on the wealth of material yet scarcity of accurate information on the Vanns' home, observing: "While hobos and animals were seeking shelter in it, mystery stories of hidden treasure and legends about its origin were growing. . . . Although much has been told and written about the Vann House, very little was actually known."[47] It is my wish that this book contributes to public knowledge and debate about the Vann plantation, Diamond Hill, in all its facets—the factual and the fabled, the past and the present. I can only hope that through this telling, Cherokees out West and down South, descendants of slaves once owned by Indians, Euro-American southerners, African American southerners, and lovers of old, history-laden homes will discover some small thing of value for the tending of identities and the shaping of communal civic lives.

This book is written in tripartite sections that offer different ways of thinking about Diamond Hill history. The prologue, introduction, and conclusion deal principally with the Vann House as a museum and its contemporary memory and interpretation as a public historic site. Three appendices (along with detailed footnotes) include information for fellow researchers about the research process and the kinds of sources used. This appended material also makes new and rediscovered sources (the Diamond Hill black population chart from the Vann House slavery exhibit and the faith biography of Peggy Scott Vann Crutchfield) available to readers.

Six chapters at the core of the book reconstruct late-eighteenth- and early-nineteenth-century life on Diamond Hill. Chapter 1 is a contextualized biographical treatment of James Vann, the infamous founder of Diamond Hill. This chapter summarizes and assesses previous writings about James Vann's character and ponders whether his unpredictable personality and tragic demise were as much due to the extremities of his times as to fatal flaws in his character. Chapter 2 describes James Vann's development of a thriving plantation with a focus on the years 1800 through 1805, his marriage to Peggy Scott, his early business and political ventures, his adoption of racial slavery, and his invitation of settlement to Moravian missionaries—all within the context of Cherokee cultural change.

Chapter 3—about the family and community lives of over one hundred enslaved and free blacks on the premises—is the heart of this book. The subject matter of this chapter is where my research on the Vann plantation first began, and the centrality of this material to the larger work is signified by the relative length of the chapter. This section picks up where Chapter 2 leaves off, at the moment of Diamond Hill's consolidation, and draws a vivid portrait of communal black life on a native-owned plantation, a picture I believe has been missing in the historical literature thus far. Chapter 3 focuses on the years 1805–09, the peak of Diamond Hill's productivity under James Vann's management. But because many members of the slave population outlived James Vann and because I aim to follow the arcs of particular life stories, I bring in documentary material from the period after Vann's death in 1809 through the 1820s. This chapter also departs from strict temporal content when I gather and describe relevant examples, again from 1810 to the 1820s, to illustrate various points about black community and culture that hold true for the period of James Vann's administration.

Chapter 4 moves from the subject matter of enslaved blacks' experience to an analysis of the equally unknown and chronologically overlapping experience of Cherokee women in the contained environment that was the "plantation household."[48] While offering a thesis about the early-nineteenth-century increase of domestic violence in Cherokee society, this chapter also links a set of dramatic events on Diamond Hill between the years 1805 and 1809 — a robbery and an escape perpetrated by slaves, a family duel, and James Vann's involvement in the Lighthorse police force — to a larger point about the escalation of violence in the Cherokee Nation. Chapter 5 covers a period of monumental transformation on Diamond Hill between 1809 and 1812, beginning with the murder of James Vann and chronicling the watershed Christian conversion of Peggy Scott Vann (the first recorded Cherokee convert) and the Cherokee traditionalist spiritual revival of 1811–12. Chapter 6, focused on the years 1812–29, describes the redistribution of James Vann's estate, the remarriage of Peggy Scott, the inheritance and expulsion of Joseph Vann, and the opportunities and vulnerabilities faced by Vann-owned slaves in this volatile period of flux. This chapter covers the natural deaths of several principal figures on the plantation in the 1820s and 1830s, including Peggy Scott's, and concludes with Joseph Vann's loss of Diamond Hill in the Georgia land lottery. An epilogue describes the fate of Joseph Vann, Diamond Hill's sole surviving heir, in the 1830s and 1840s, including the removal of the Cherokees from the Southeast, and the death of Joseph Vann in a steamboat explosion as recalled by his slaves.

Historical and Cultural Arguments

The Vann House is the best-preserved plantation home in the Cherokee Southeast, and it is also the best documented. Life on Diamond Hill in the nineteenth century is richly recorded in a range of primary source materials. By investigating the historical record and imagining Vann's place of the past, we gain a unique view of the lives of Cherokees, blacks, and whites in the early 1800s, a pivotal moment in Cherokee, African American, and American history, when Cherokees struggled to rebalance after the onslaught of American statehood, African Americans in the South faced an expanding slave system and an intensified internal slave trade, and white Americans worked toward the consolidation of political, cultural, and economic systems. Along with a rich sense of the complex social world of a Cherokee-owned plantation, studying Diamond Hill yields valuable observations for Native American history and African American history in Indian nations. Three unseen elements in the public representation of the Chief Vann House — the subtleties of American colonization and Cherokee resistance to it; the experience of Cherokee women of the slaveholding upper class; and the texture of life in the slave quarters — become visible in this portrayal of one plantation's story.

From the vantage point of Diamond Hill, we can closely observe the pace and shape of cultural change in the slaveholding microculture of early-nineteenth-century Cherokee society. The American state placed inordinate pressure on Cherokees to reorder their lives. How did various Cherokee subgroups respond to this pressure? Nineteenth-century observers and reformers, as well as some historians of the Cherokee Nation publishing in the 1950s–70s, have positioned Cherokees as an eagerly acculturating tribe, the most civilized of southern Indians, who readily embraced white ways. In one example, Grace Steele Woodward writes on the first page of her 1963 monograph that the Cherokees, having moved "from dark savagery into the sunlight of civilization . . . reached a higher peak of civilization than any other North American Indian tribe."[49] In some cases, Cherokees of the nineteenth century provided support for this sort of view, a primary example being Cherokee statesman John Ridge's letter to ethnologist Albert Gallatin in 1826, in which Ridge lauded Cherokee progress toward "civilization."[50]

This commentary contributed to a widely held public perception in the nineteenth century that Cherokees were more advanced, and hence less authentically Indian, than other native people. As historian Alexandra Harmon has explained: "Many Americans questioned whether enterprising tribal citizens were Indians at all."[51] In our time, the inheritance of this perception lives on in the criticism, sometimes leveled by other American Indians, that Cherokees gave in early to Euro-American colonialism by frequently intermarrying with whites, building wealth, and accepting Christianity. This is a perspective that contemporary Cherokee and non-Cherokee scholars are working to dislodge.

To note just a few examples, Cherokee literary scholar Daniel Heath Justice challenges the way in which Cherokee people are imagined by non-Cherokees as being "civilized savages or washed out wannabes." Religious studies scholar Justine Smith likewise seeks to "question both popular and scholarly notions regarding Cherokee religious identity—namely that Cherokees, because of their widespread acceptance of Christianity, desire rapid assimilation into White America." Historian Tom Hatley muses that "what exactly went on in the houses of the Cherokee elite . . . was in all likelihood consistent with what had gone on before." And historian Theda Perdue argues that rather than being solely white identified, mixed-race Euro-Cherokees (and other southern Indians) retained aspects of "red" identity. "We are blinded by the spectacle of Indians living in mansions, owning plantations and African American slaves," she writes. "In our analysis of mixed-blood Indians, we have privileged white-ness, and as a result, we have underestimated the power and persistence of the culture into which they were born and chose to live."[52]

The history of Diamond Hill complements the argument advanced by these and other scholars that even amid change, Cherokees remained in many ways and for a long while "Cherokee-centered."[53] For here, the pace of Cherokee accommodation to Euro-American views and practices was slower than many have believed, indicating that even mixed-race, wealthy Cherokees struggled long and hard to maintain cultural, as well as political, integrity. In fact, the very structure that has often been said to symbolize early Cherokee progress toward "civilization"—the Vanns' iconic brick manor house—turns out to have been built nearly twenty years later than the official celebrated date.

Generational shifts in one Cherokee family's acceptance of white American ideologies and practices are visible on this plantation, most evidently when projected against a backdrop of black chattel slavery, a form of human sub-jugation that did not exist in Cherokee society until after contact with Euro-peans.[54] The first generation of Vanns on the premises, represented by James's mother, Wali, who was born in the 1740s, owned black slaves acquired mainly through inheritance from white forebears. However, Wali did not pursue the heady profits of plantation expansion, and Wali stands out among the Vann family members for her frequent social intercourse with enslaved blacks in her own home, a stance of social flexibility that is not apparent among those of her equivalent status among the white slaveholding elite. The second gen-eration, as represented by Wali's son James, born in the 1760s, found greater interest in plantation expansion and profitability and less comfort in black society. Although James was certainly known for having slaves in his home during social occasions, his engagement with blacks differed slightly from his mother's. James socialized with slaves only when inebriated (a frequent occurrence), and he often had them provide musical entertainment (fiddling) for his other guests.[55] In the third generation, Joseph Vann, born at the turn of the nineteenth century, extended the plantation's borders even farther and tightened the managerial regime, supervising slave labor and leisure time to a degree unimagined by his elder family members. Joseph Vann is never described as inviting blacks into his home to participate in social events as had his father and grandmother before him. Instead, his relations with black slaves echoed the social distance practiced by white elites since the early eighteenth century.[56] For Joseph, a third-generation Cherokee slaveholder, the line between black and red had become bold and fixed.

[margin handwriting: Generations and slave-holding]

It took two generations of slaveholding before the Vanns exhibited any sign of what historian Peter Parish has described as the "prime motive" of nineteenth-century southern slaveholders: the obsessive accumulation of land and slaves.[57] It took three generations for the Vanns to distance themselves socially from blacks in a way that mirrored the racial prejudices of the white southern elite. In part, this time lapse is owing to what historian Philip Morgan has called "the sheer fact of precedence": Cherokees began holding blacks as slaves much later than Euro-Americans did.[58] But the Vann family's delayed application of some aspects of southern styles of mastery also fits into a larger practice of cultural persistence and selection employed by Cherokees in different walks of life. While most Cherokees "remained quite different" from the wealthy Vanns and their ilk, these class-differentiated social groups were "not completely apart."[59] Albeit to varying degrees and levels of intensity, the Vanns, like other Cherokee families, were squeezed by colonial imposition and adopted particular Euro-American practices while rejecting others. In the 1820s when Joseph Vann attempted the kind of systematic, tightly run operation that was idealized in mainstream plantation advice manuals, the Vanns would finally be in step with predominant slaveholding views in the South.[60] Even so, in this third generation represented by Joseph, the Vanns were not embraced by whites of their economically equivalent planter class, who viewed the Vanns' home as gaudy and commented on the dark skin of Joseph's Cherokee wife.

By 1800, most of the white slaveholding South had already discovered staple crops like tobacco, rice, indigo, and cotton that had propelled black slavery into an increasingly mammoth, rigid, and brutal race-based system and deepened the social chasm between blacks and whites. Meanwhile, the Vanns, though certainly guilty of cruel exploitation, were socializing with black slaves in the private spaces of their Cherokee homes. The story of Diamond Hill illustrates that even elite Cherokees like James Vann who were most acculturated to Euro-American habits early on, held back from full acceptance of foreign beliefs and total enactment of foreign systems. And it indicates, further, that cultural change for Vann's Cherokee family was generational, occurring slowly over time.[61]

In addition to the *pace* of cultural change within the Vann family, the *shape* of that change, or, the forms it took most prominently, is also discernible on Diamond Hill. James Vann first began to set himself apart from the majority of his people by adopting individualistic entrepreneurialism and engaging in unbounded acts of violence, both of which played out in his embrace of plantation slavery as well as his mistreatment of female family members. But at the same time that Vann habituated himself to these behaviors, he steadfastly refused to entertain the belief system of Christianity. His primary wife, Peggy Scott, also rejected the Christian faith for the first nine years of the Moravian missionaries' tenure. We can infer, then, that communal, noncommercial economics and cultural containment of violent acts were among the first aspects of Cherokee life to bow under the weight of Euro-American colonialism in the Vann family's experience, while their Cherokee spirituality remained resilient for the longer term. Although James Vann did develop a thriving, independent, commercial enterprise and practiced racial, gender, and ritual violence in ways familiar to white southern culture, he did not assimilate into Euro-American life immediately or fully. He did not become a substitute southern white man, in his own mind or in the minds of whites he interacted with. James Vann was a *Cherokee* person of mixed racial ancestry who generated great wealth. His life lived out on Diamond Hill reflected the growing gradations of Cherokee experience amid a changing cultural world.[62]

And James Vann's is not the only style of life to come into focus through this microhistory. Reading the social landscape of Diamond Hill yields the first sustained historical portrait of Cherokee women of the slaveholding class.[63] Peggy Scott Vann, along with her in-laws, Wali and Nancy Vann, faced, just like the men in their families, the tumult of pressured cultural transformation. Shifting Cherokee attitudes toward women's role in politics and domestic spaces, often propelled by U.S. agents and white missionaries, profoundly affected these women's lives. Peggy Scott was among a first generation of Cherokee women to endure serial domestic violence at the hands of her husband, a cultural shift brought about by access to alcohol, and exacerbated, it can be argued, by the volatile context of a gendered and racialized plantation order. Even as Peggy Vann skillfully wove river cane baskets in the ways of her Cherokee foremothers and spoke the Cherokee language, she took on

[handwritten marginal note: How he remained Cherokee]

the mantle of plantation mistress, learning how to discipline and commodify black slaves even as her husband disciplined her. We see in Peggy Scott's world of Diamond Hill the ways that race and class, together with gender, shaped individual experience, interactions between groups, and new social patterns.[64]

Through a study of the Vann plantation, we also gain a refreshed view of African acculturation to Cherokee lifeways. If James Vann viewed the world through the eyes of a native man who stood at the center of an emergent social formation — a Cherokee plantation elite — how did blacks possessed by him interpret and react to their surroundings? Recent scholarship on blacks among Cherokees and other southern Indian nations has highlighted the adoption of native cultural ways by black slaves, the desire for black slaves and freedpeople to be recognized as culturally Indian, and the integration of blacks and Afro-Indians into native communities.[65] These kinds of processes certainly did take place for many blacks who lived among Native Americans. But the Diamond Hill case multiplies, diversifies, and differentiates our conception of black experience as slaves of Indians.

Blacks on Diamond Hill had no doubt of their enslaved, subjugated status. They recognized James Vann as an unexceptional master in the main, just as cruel and pecuniary as any rich planter in the white South. Regardless of his Cherokee-centered behavior in political and religious arenas and despite his willingness to drink with slaves, in the realm of plantation oversight, Vann was a tyrant. And yet the specific surround of a Cherokee-owned plantation in a Cherokee settlement in a Cherokee society, a framework that stretched beyond the personal orientation of James or Joseph Vann, created space for the maintenance of African-derived practices that could sustain and succor the black community.

Unlike most farms in preremoval Cherokee territory, Diamond Hill was a massive place, sizeable enough to support a community of over one hundred slaves. Blacks here were not isolated one from another as was the case on small Cherokee farms. As a result, the men, women, and children owned by the Vann family created a social circle and smaller enclaves within it. They lived in cabins near one another and worked side by side. They shaped nuclear families and extended relational networks. What is more, the Vann slaves' large numbers and concentrated living quarters created the possibility for reinforcing African-based cultural ways. This was especially true for a subset of slaves who were sent to care for Vann's cattle or to work at his mill on the far borders of the plantation; many of these men and women were recently transported from Africa, spoke African languages, and held African spiritual beliefs. Blacks on the Vann estate engaged extensively with Cherokees of the wealthy and poorer classes through assigned work tasks and on a variety of social occasions, but they always had the slave quarters to return to. The aspects of Cherokee culture that these slaves adopted would have therefore been balanced by or blended with African-inspired cultural habits. Unlike the generalized picture we may have of blacks in Cherokee society becoming primarily Indianized, or longing for Indian identity, blacks on the Vann plantation are better described as "creolized." They, like blacks in other locales who were developing racialized and culturally distinctive African American identities, "drew upon richly diverse African traditions and adapted them creatively and dynamically to a new physical and social environment."[66] Blacks on Vann's plantation did not stand outside of the economic, social, and cultural forces that compelled the creation of an African America; instead, they were one of "many African American societies" with "distinctive social and cultural configurations" located in one of "many Souths."[67]

While bondsmen and -women owned by the Vanns adopted some Cherokee ways of life, they retained memories of Africa and black life of the quarter as a cultural home base. This dynamic retention was especially possible here because the broader Cherokee cultural milieu contained features in common with the slaves' African home-cultures. Blacks found protective cover for some indigenous African-derived practices in an indigenous American nation with similar cultural elements. But enslaved blacks on Diamond Hill also found space for cultural reinforcement because Cherokee ways of being were reformulating under duress just as rapidly as African slaves'. Cherokees under American colonialism, like black slaves of the Atlantic world, lived in an environment in which they were compelled to re-envision cultural life. The increasingly diversified culture of Cherokee society, characterized by indigenous features and Euro-American adaptations, created an experimental openness that allowed black slaves to carve out a space for African rememory. Their daily lives therefore reflected a heterogeneous pattern, a rich cultural intermixture of African, Cherokee, and Euro-American elements.

The fertile documentation of life on Diamond Hill, together with the remarkable artifact that is the house itself, allows us to be transported. We can imagine standing on the fine home's porch, peering in through its windowpanes, and catching a close, prolonged glimpse of a Cherokee, African, and Euro-American world. We must bear in mind though, as we take in the view from here, that even with the rich documentation that exists, we are consigned to gazing through a glass darkly. Our vision is blurred by the passage of time, the distance of place, the biases of the historical record, and the blinders of our own culture-bound perspectives. In this case, African American author Alice Walker's personal reflections after visiting a former Georgia plantation home can also be instructive for us: "Whenever I visit antebellum homes in the South, with their spacious rooms, their grand staircases, their shaded back windows that, without the thickly planted trees, would look out onto the now vanished slave quarters in the back, this is invariably my thought. I stand in the backyard gazing up at the windows, then stand at the windows inside looking down into the backyard, and between the me that is on the ground and the me that is at the windows, History is caught."[68] We, too, must be mindful, as we peer at the past through the Vann House windows, of Walker's "me," or the experience of the watchers watching. For we can discern, in this pose of contemplative observation, not only the somber "catch" that is history at this public site but also the faintest reflection of our modern-day senses of self.

CHAPTER 1

This Soul-House Built of Mud

Let me live out my years in heat of blood!
Let me die drunken with the dreamer's wine!
Let me not see this soul-house built of mud
Go toppling to the dusk—a vacant shrine.

Let me go quickly, like a candle light
Snuffed out just at the heyday of its glow.
Give me high noon—and let it then be night!
Thus would I go.
—John G. Neihardt, "Let Me Live Out My Years,"
in *A Bundle of Myrrh* (1907)

Introducing James Vann

What manner of man was James Vann? What was the content of his character? These questions troubled Vann's Cherokee countrymen from the Upper Towns on the Little Tennessee River, who described Vann as "a turbulent and dangerous man" in a meeting with President Thomas Jefferson in 1808.[1] Another Cherokee, the young leader John Lowrey, charged that Vann "intended to turn boney part" in the way of the famed French ruler Napoléon Bonaparte, who had recently wrested power through military prowess and political stealth.[2] More nettled still were white contemporaries who viewed James Vann with anxious consternation. Federal officials labeled him a "villain," "assassin," and "desperado," and Christian missionaries claimed he was caught in the "hands of the evil enemy who has him completely under his power!"[3]

Modern-day historians and visitors to the Chief Vann House are also beset by the problem of Vann's personality. Attend a Vann House gathering, read a local history bulletin, and the question of Vann's boorish behavior is always at the fore. In 2008, the Athens-based Georgia Gazette radio show posted a less than becoming riddle for listeners to solve on its blog:

Here stands the home of a would-be assassin,
A man so drunk he could not kill
A leader so vengeful no one would test him
Especially his wives, whom he beat for cheap thrills

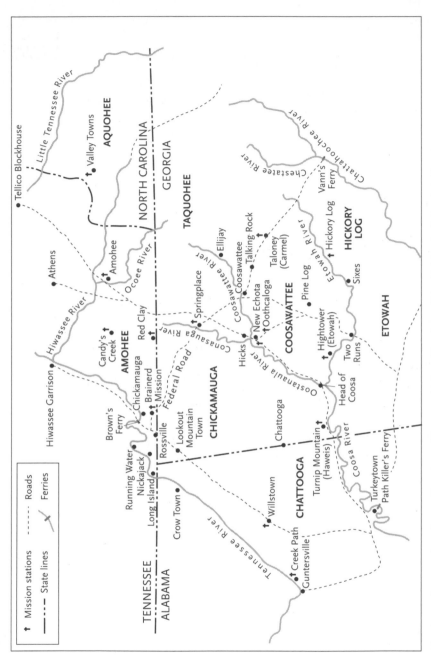

Cherokee settlements, circa 1817–23. From Henry Thompson Malone, Cherokees of the Old South: A People in Transition (University of Georgia Press, 1956). Used by permission of the University of Georgia Press.

Around 1800, this man found religion
And he brought the lord's workers to teach his tribe
But he kept drinking whiskey like it was a source of nutrition
Clutching a bottle and glass even as he died.[4]

The answer to the riddle was the Chief Vann House, the man profiled so harshly, James Vann. By many accounts both then and now, Vann was a selfish, impulsive person who drank heavily, angered quickly, and often resorted to violence. But several letters penned by Vann and posted to the federal Indian agent document behind-the-scenes political activities that show Vann to be a principled protector of fellow Cherokees. Rather than the boorish, caricatured figure of the radio riddle, my research, in conjunction with the more sensitive historical accounts, reveals James Vann as a person whose life was marked by contrast, as would befit his time and position in a Cherokee Nation pressed by aggressive U.S. settler colonialism. Vann fought valiantly for Cherokees harassed by white frontiersmen, while abusing members of his own Cherokee family. He looked and dressed like a white gentleman but battered whites who visited his home. He welcomed missionaries of the Christian faith yet rudely rejected their God. He danced and drank with black slaves but burned them alive in punishment. According to John Howard Payne, a journalist and playwright who interviewed Cherokees for a work of history in the 1830s, James Vann was "aristocratic, impetuous, and full of chivalric daring" and acted in ways both cruel and patriotic. In a 1950s classic work on Cherokee history, Henry Thompson Malone embellished Payne's portrait, describing Vann as "a peculiar combination of benevolent leader and rip-snorting hoodlum."[5]

Throughout his life, James Vann collected a series of enemies, from indignant American officials who criticized his lack of "respectability," to Cherokee leaders who envied his growing political influence, to righteous black slaves seeking self-liberation and justice.[6] It should not be surprising that a man like this lost his life to an act of violence. One missionary who lived near Vann's estate even predicted such an outcome for him, writing in a letter in 1806: "We don't believe that he will die a natural death for his life style and his behavior is such that one can presume he will some day be done in before he expects it."[7] That fateful day came on the 19th of February in 1809. On this blustery evening, James Vann was downing whiskey in a tavern owned by Thomas Buffington. Vann held a bottle in one hand, a glass in the other, and was accompanied by an unnamed slave who was armed, like his master, with "a double pair of pistols, a rifle & a dirk."[8] Vann's favored son, Joseph, a boy of eleven, was sleeping soundly in a chamber on the upper floor. All was well until midnight, when, according to John Howard Payne's account, "the door [of the tavern], which swung loosely, was silently pressed open by the point of a rifle. In an instant, James Vann was dead, and no one has ever known his slayer. He was forty four." John Norton, a Cherokee raised in England and later adopted by Mohawks, wrote just after Vann's death: "It is said, that the deceased, altho' of considerable natural talents and capable of serving his country; on account of his violent disposition was not generally beloved: this perhaps may be the reason why no greater exertions have been made to bring the culprit to justice."[9]

After Vann was gunned down in the dead of night, his missionary neighbors opined that he had been a "well-known man, loved by few, hated by many, feared by almost the whole Cherokee Nation."[10] William McLoughlin, a preeminent historian of Cherokee life, wrote in 1984: "Vann had never been a popular leader and had many enemies. . . . He seems to have been reckless, a man grown rich and cynical and tired of living."[11] The list of possible suspects for the crime was so long, and the murderous act, in many onlookers' view, so justified, that no one was charged with the shooting. Payne reported, as Norton intimated, that a criminal investigation was never pursued.[12]

And it is no wonder. The James Vann of nineteenth-century primary accounts was shrewd, selfish, and unpredictable; his oddly paired passions for violence and justice seemed to know nearly no bounds. And the motivating force behind Vann's conduct remained cloaked in mystery upon his death, further disquieting those who sought a plausible cause. Hence, for the two centuries since James Vann lived and died, observers have speculated about the nature of his character. Many contemporary writers have sought to pinpoint the catalyst for Vann's erratic aggression, which was unparalleled among his Cherokee compatriots. Their interpretations — perhaps influenced by our modern-day cultural surround of pop psychology and addiction awareness — range from the political to the psychological and even to the metaphysical, indicating what William McLoughlin has described as the "many dimensions" of James Vann, "this intemperate patriot."[13]

In written speculations on what motivated Vann's extreme behavior, alcohol addiction is the most common conclusion. Historian Thurman Wilkins describes Vann as "homicidal," "a thoroughly godless man," who "kept gargantuan supplies of brandy and whiskey and dealt drinks like a lord to his followers." Wilkins suggests that alcoholism enabled Vann's brutal conduct, writing: "He was himself frequently in his cups and when drunk was liable to turn vicious and become as deadly as a water moccasin."[14] Georgia historian Don Shadburn, an expert in the local documents, argues that Vann's uncontrolled drinking shaped Vann's later adulthood, which Shadburn terms "the outlaw years." "He had taken to the bottle so often," Shadburn writes, "that his once charitable, diplomatic nature suddenly turned to acts of violence and personal vengeance."[15] These interpretations of alcohol addiction are grounded in the primary documents from Vann's era, but they take on added connotations in public discourse today in which the stereotypical drunken Indian permeates popular culture. The Georgia radio contest described above stigmatizes Vann in a way that taps into that racialized stereotype, as do, it must be noted, historical accounts that describe Vann in animalistic terms such as "water moccasin."

Contemporary memoirist and Vann descendant Barbara Vann Pommer attempts to defend Vann against the charge, and perhaps the stereotype, of drunkenness. She asserts in an undated, self-published book that Vann had schizophrenia, a condition that she argues has been overlooked due to a focus on his drinking. Vann House chief interpretive ranger Julia Autry also speculates about the possibility of mental illness. She wonders if James Vann contracted syphilis at a young age and slowly deteriorated as a result, since syphilis was a commonly undiagnosed illness in the nineteenth century that could lead to brain damage and mental and emotional instability.[16] Autry also points to an odd exchange between Vann and his missionary neighbors in the summer of 1805. Vann called for the missionaries to come see him, at which point one of the brethren found Vann "almost out of his mind with pain because a live creature had gotten into his ear," and reported that "[h]e [Vann] himself believed he would pass away on this occasion."[17] Autry speculates that since the summer of 1805 marked the height of Vann's violent activity, this "creature" may have been a behaviorally debilitating parasite.

Building on Autry's observation of the importance of this passage and drawing from the anthropological notion of ethnomedicine that ascribes experiences of illness and healing to particular cultural understandings, another interpretation of this incident is that Vann *believed* there was a creature in his ear as the result of a spiritual assault.[18] Like many peoples then and now, Cherokees believed in witchcraft and sorcery. They saw the witch's chief talents as the ability to think bad things into being and attributed to witches the malevolent insertion and withdrawal of objects into and from the body. The latter characteristic was so fundamental to the witch's being that one Cherokee term for sorcerer (dida:hnese:-sgi) was translated by Cherokee anthropologists Jack and Anna Kilpatrick as meaning: "putter-in and drawer-out of them, he."[19] As a Cherokee who steadfastly rejected Christianity, Vann would have known that "psychological discomfort or pathological illness" could be caused by a witch's "magical introjection of objects or minute animate beings into the victim."[20] He also knew himself to be a man with many enemies. Vann's exchange with the missionary might have reflected Vann's belief that he had been bewitched by the implantation of a live foreign creature. This spiritual attack, or the belief in it, could have led Vann to paranoia, increased substance abuse, and the deterioration of his mental faculties. Vann's missionary neighbors would have agreed with Pommer's assessment that Vann, because of causes natural or supernatural, was at least temporarily mentally ill and concurred with Autry's dating of the onset of that illness to the summer of 1805, since they wrote in their diary in July of that year: "Recently he [Vann] conducts himself generally so that one might think he has lost his mind."[21]

Continuing in a vein more psychoanalytical then psychomedical, in a biographical booklet, Vann descendant James Bell attributes Vann's "inexplicability" and "turbulence" to his "half-blood nature" and the "conflicts inherent in these two ethnic worlds."[22] In what would now be viewed by many readers as overly simplistic phrasing that discounts the cultural sophistication of Indian individuals, Bell explains that Vann, the child of a native mother and European father, struggled to "adapt to the ways of the white man" yet was "compelled to follow the way of his ancient tribal heritage" and was therefore "a man torn between two worlds." Added to this internal burden, Bell rightly argues, were the extreme pressures of leadership in a native nation beset by turmoil.[23] William McLoughlin shares this view of acculturation strain, writing: "[Vann] desperately wanted to be admired and respected, but only on his own terms. Caught between the irreconcilable worlds of red and white, he was consumed by a profound impulse toward self-destruction."[24]

Although some of these interpretations are tinged by limited views of Native American subjectivity, each contains a measure of insight. It is persuasive that a combination of causes — alcoholism, mental instability caused by physical illness or the belief in supernatural attack, the pressures of identity strain and leadership responsibility, and the character flaw of impetuous arrogance — could have produced a man like James Vann. But borrowing from the recent work of Native American studies scholars like Ned Blackhawk, Philip Deloria, and Andrea Smith, we might add to these an additional, critical factor: the context and culture of U.S. colonialism and concomitant violence. James Vann was surely idiosyncratic in his quest for personal dominance, and he may have had an Achilles heel–like addiction to alcohol, but overshadowing these personal failings and even shaping them, was the reality of European and American conquest of indigenous nations. In short, the content of James Vann's character was shaped by both his unique personality traits and the socio-historical circumstance he shared with other Cherokees. The story of James Vann and his plantation enterprise emerges from a larger framework that Ned Blackhawk has called the "[h]arrowing, violent histories of Native peoples caught in the maelstrom of colonialism."[25]

From the time of James Vann's boyhood in the 1760s to the time of his young manhood in the 1790s, the Cherokee Nation was under a devastating economic and military attack that had begun with British incursions in the late 1600s and would continue long after Vann's death.[26] Vann learned early, and above all else, of the vulnerability of the Cherokee people and the role of violence in their subjection and defense. Like youngsters born into battle-scarred countries in our own time, James Vann was a child of war. Perhaps this is why, in the absence of sufficient documented material about James Vann's early life, two legendary stories about the young Vann survive. Both stories feature a boy in mortal danger amid the chaos of cultural disorientation and the onslaught of violence. In the first story, Vann himself is the boy in trouble; in the second, he attempts to rescue another boy from harm. Both tales highlight a context of limited options in which unthinkable bloodshed is the inevitable outcome.

The single surviving story of James Vann's childhood can be traced back to one of the most extensive English-language sources on Cherokee history — John Howard Payne's fourteen volumes of notes compiled in the early nineteenth century. Claiming Vann's relative, Major Waters, as his source, Payne describes a moment in Vann's youth that initiates and frames Vann's violent tendencies later in life. The scene, set at a "drinking party" in the 1780s, is one of implied cultural destabilization. The mostly young men gathered together were inebriated when an older man among them, Chief Sour Mush, began to insult a man of another clan. The man then "fell upon the aged chief and beat him," and when Sour Mush's clan members stood by and did nothing, he "mourned the degeneracy of the times. He said when he was a youth, neither he nor any other youth of the Blind Savannah blood, would have seen an old clansman used this vilely, without vengeance."[27] Later, the shamed clan members of Sour Mush beat the offending man, causing his death. According to the unwritten Cherokee cultural code of clan revenge, which authorized and compelled members of the same clan (or extended kinship group), to avenge the death of another in that group, the dead man's Paint Clan members would now either seek the life of the perpetrator or another one of Sour Mush's relatives. Knowing this, "[t]he kinsmen consulted" and the killer of the man is said to have influenced the victim's relatives to "leave him untouched & to select for their victim James Vann. James Vann was a boy ungovernable and unpromising. He had never yet done anything for the good of his country and could be spared without regret."

Learning of this decision, friends informed the teenaged Vann of the place and time of a planned ambush. Nevertheless, Vann did not change routes. Payne recounts:

> He [Vann] passed on the way he had intended and at the very hour. Crossing a creek, five voices hailed him from different points. He made no stop. He dashed on the faster to the opposite shore. His horse was fleet. Behind him his blanket [was] in a roll, like a knapsack. Obtaining no notice, the lurking Indians fired: two balls struck the blanket, one broke the right wrist of the hand in which he bore his rifle: one missed its aim; and he presumes another missed fire. . . . He flung his rifle from the wounded arm to the other [,] put his horse to its full speed, and escaped.

In a memorable feat of derring-do, the young James Vann made good his escape, but because the man's death had not been successfully avenged, Vann was still in danger.

Later, at a social gathering, Vann spied his attackers and knew they would try to take his life or the life of another Blind Savannah Clan member. To shield himself, Vann "deliberately walked up to his uncle and shot him dead." This, Payne quotes Vann's relative, "quieted the claim." In later versions of the story, Vann's uncle is said to have set him up to take the fall for the clan, an added detail that helps to justify Vann's unconscionable action. Still, Vann's willingness to kill a family member to avoid death himself violated Cherokee expectations and marked him as truly "ungovernable," a man of extremes. Payne ends this story with the summary statement: "James Vann now grew into fame & importance, as he grew into maturity. But his impetuosity and decision[s] sometimes degenerated into cruelty."[28]

Various elements of this story tell us something about the unstable context of James Vann's upbringing. We know that he is young at a moment when Cherokee cultural ways are already under strain from the territorial and cultural encroachment of whites. The Cherokee men are drunk from rum supplied by white traders; a seemingly helpless boy is singled out for sacrifice in a way that violates the norms of clan justice; and that boy defends himself by committing the unfathomable act of murdering his own uncle. The balancing effect inherent in the traditional system of clan revenge is shown to be askew, and James Vann's response, shocking to his peers, is the result of both the changing cultural context and his tempestuous personality. The story also serves as a cautionary tale that sets the young James Vann on a path toward national defense. He was singled out as a target because he "had never yet done anything good for his country" and thus "could be spared." We see through the telling of this event that political apathy was not only noticed by Vann's fellows but also dangerous for those who engaged in it. This fundamental story of Vann's boyhood is at once a tale of culture out of balance, violence out of bounds, and nationalistic exhortation, the combination of which sets the stage for Vann's imperfect character development.

The second surviving story from Vann's younger years places him as a young man in the 1790s. Unlike the first tale, this one is difficult to trace definitively to eighteenth- or nineteenth-century primary sources, indicating the likelihood that it is more legendary than factual. This second story does date back to an early-twentieth-century secondary source titled *Old Frontiers* by John Brown. In 1988, fiction writer John Ehle renarrated the story in his popular history *Trail of Tears*, and later authors and website writers reproduced the Ehle version. The outlines of the tale — the main event, date, and place — also appear in an eighteenth-century letter and travel narrative and in secondary sources from the early and mid-1900s, but the role played by James Vann in the Brown and Ehle renditions is attributed to a different person altogether in the earlier documents.[29]

In this second story, we re-encounter Vann as a young man in his twenties. The famed Chief Tsiyu Gansini (Dragging Canoe) of the Chickamauga towns is leading a revolt against American colonists who have been victorious in their rebellion from Great Britain. Since the Cherokees had sided with England during the revolution, believing that the distant king was more likely to protect their land rights than American settlers, Cherokees were the targets of Patriot slash-and-burn campaigns. Refusing to accept the authority of the young United States with the famous rallying cry, "we are not yet conquered," Dragging Canoe inspired and led a seventeen-year guerrilla resistance.[30] He and his fellow rebels struck the backcountry of Cherokee territory where white settlers claimed jurisdiction for their newly forming states. In 1793, as the story goes, James Vann had joined this revolt, and was riding with noted rebel chiefs Doublehead and John Watts in an attack on Knoxville, Tennessee. Along the way, the 1,000-strong Cherokee force, which had been joined by Creeks and Shawnees, attacked white settlements, killing residents and destroying property. According to a witness who described the attack to the secretary of war: "They made an invasion into this district . . . in force, as is generally believed not less than a thousand; in many places they marched in files of twenty-eight abreast, each of which 'tis supposed was composed of forty men; besides, they appeared to have about a hundred horse [*sic*]."[31] The warriors stopped at a small settlement known as Cavet's Station, where family members of Alexander Cavet had barricaded themselves. In Ehle's version of this story, "Doublehead insisted that the army pause to loot all the settlers' cabins, to steal blankets, clothes, hams, corn, to kill and scare whites, and to burn the barns." Brown gives the reader more on Doublehead's motivation, writing: "Doublehead, fierce and sullen by nature, was angered by the death of his brother, Pumpkin Boy." In Brown's view, Doublehead was intent on punishing the residents of Cavet's Station, sending them to their deaths just as the Tennessee militia had killed his own brother, "a handsome warrior, well equipped with trinkets."[32] But seeking to block Doublehead's unchecked rage, "James Vann rode his horse into the mob and pulled a white child up behind his saddle. Doublehead saw him and with a leap broke the child's head open with his ax. Baby killer, Vann shouted at him. Doublehead swung the ax at Vann."[33]

In this legend, James Vann has matured since the initial story set during his adolescent years. He is doing "good" for his country by fighting in the rebellion, and he has developed a moral sense of just and unjust violence. In the chaos of frontier conflict, Vann attempts to save a boy's life from the misdirected vengeance of Doublehead, just as Vann had saved himself years before from the misdirected use of clan revenge. But the lesson here is ambiguous, for the context of Euro-American colonialism is even more pointed than in the first story. Cherokees are fighting for their lives, liberty, and land base, and mercy may have no role to play. Despite Vann's selfless attempt at a rescue, Doublehead brutally kills the boy. Vann shames Doublehead for violence against a helpless child by labeling him with the derogatory term "baby killer." But whether this story is apocryphal or accurate, one thing is certain — Vann later adopts the same behavior that Doublehead displayed of unleashing his rage on the innocent and the powerless.

In the absence of traditional historical documentation, these biomyths (or biographical mythologies) illuminate the texture, if not the verifiable facts, of James Vann's early life.[34] As a boy he was surrounded by interlinked forms of violence — the external violence of white aggression and of Cherokee resistance to it, and the internalized violence of Cherokee cultural disaffection and despair. Vann emerged from this crushing context brash, brave, and itching for a fight. He also emerged cold, callous, and lacking in empathetic spirit. The love he felt for Cherokees as a people, the dedication to his nation, failed him in the most intimate contacts of his daily life.

Writers attempting to understand Vann's complex character have debated the overall theme of James Vann's legacy, struggling to determine how this volatile man should be remembered. Descendant James Bell worries about the "unkind" writings of "[e]arly white historians" who "portrayed [Vann] as a cruel, power hungry, blood thirsty savage, bordering on almost a demonistic personality." In Bell's view, Vann deserves better: "[H]e did a great deal of good for his people and the Cherokee Nation. He was a true Cherokee patriot and champion of Cherokee rights."[35] William McLoughlin also fears that James Vann has been denied his due regard. McLoughlin writes of his intention to "stake out a claim for James Vann as an early, if ambiguous, hero among the Cherokees."[36]

Although this book will be a chronicle of James Vann's life and times that shines the brightest of possible lights on the experience of black slaves and Cherokee women who suffered by his hand, fundamentally, I assent to Bell's concern and sympathize with McLoughlin's heartfelt stake of claim. Previous authors *have* misrepresented Vann in a manner that feeds and authorizes public fascination with the Indian savage and drunken Indian stereotypes — cultural expectations that further the functional invisibility of real native people in contemporary American society.[37] And a sensitive portrait of Vann's character *would* by necessity reveal a streak of bold and caring activism. The documentary record bears out that James Vann was a fierce protector of Cherokee people. He believed in Cherokees' collective right to political sovereignty and individual right to human dignity.

But despite righteous convictions, Vann traded in brutality. Violence became his method for pursuing Cherokee freedom, as well as his measure of his standing in social relationships. Within an eighteenth- and nineteenth-century Cherokee worldview that cherished harmonious relationships above all else, James Vann's behavior pushed him beyond the pale. Anthropologist Robert Thomas's summation of Cherokee ideals — "to maintain harmonious interpersonal relationships with his fellow Cherokee by avoiding giving offense" — perfectly un-describes James Vann. And yet the second part of Thomas's description — "giving himself to his fellow Cherokee in regards to his time and material goods" — partly captures what was best about Vann.[38] Although Vann was self-interested when it came to material goods, even hording meat at the expense of others, he devoted his time and influence to protecting Cherokees' safety and security.[39] Raymond Fogelson, a foremost anthropologist of Cherokee culture, ventures a definition of what he calls Cherokee ethnopersonality, or, a culturally derived understanding of the meaning and enactment of being human. Fogelson explains that for Cherokees of the past there were two kinds of people: those who were "just," "right," "straight," "honest," "true," and "upright," and those who were "unmitigatingly evil." An evil person, incapable of "soul," "heart," and "feeling," was not a person at all but akin to the supernatural entity of the witch.[40] Vann's contradictory biography presents a challenge to these categories. He sought justice for Cherokee people; he pursued what he viewed to be true and right, but the damage done by a history of violence in the context of colonialism might have robbed him of interpersonal sensitivity. He was therefore a Cherokee person on the margins of acceptability, saved from the appellation of evil only by his devotion to the nation.

A dark haired, pale-skinned boy of not even ten, Vann had seen the Cherokees weakened and demoralized, their towns and fields destroyed by foreign wars. Later, he watched Cherokee rebels fending off Americans in a protracted backwoods guerrilla war. And according to legend, he had joined in that struggle, as had his maternal uncle before him. It is not difficult to imagine the rage James Vann would have felt growing up a Cherokee in the eighteenth century, or to see how violence could become the primary language of his life. Rather than seeking to label Vann a hero or antihero, perhaps we are called upon to recount and recognize the context of colonization that contributed to his character.

A History of Violence

The European backwoods settlers of the South Carolina colony saw their world as a series of zones. Farthest east, across the Atlantic Ocean, lay Great Britain, the home from whence they had come and the seat of their colony's political authority. Next came the coastal city of Charleston, where wealth and civility were concentrated. Next were the middle towns, founded just in the 1730s but developed by now with churches, mills, and gentry plantation establishments. Finally came the more remote backwoods or "backcountry" territory, home to white hunters, families seeking land, and men engaged in trade with the Indians. Beyond the backwoods was the "frontier," an interstitial space betwixt the European settlements and Indian country. And farther still were Indian towns occupied by communities of Cherokees, Catawbas, Creeks, Choctaws, or Chickasaws. The presence of indigenous people just beyond backcountry homes was a source of constant anxiety for frontiersmen and women, many of whom viewed Indians as "bloodthirsty, cruel and untrustworthy . . . more beast than human."[41] And as white settlers drove deep into the woods, clearing and building on native land, they ran the risk of attack from the Indians on whose territory they infringed. Hence the South Carolinian backwoods plan of defense, consisting of sturdy forts and fourteen militia captains at the ready, was oriented north and west toward the native towns.[42] Far greater than the fear of Spanish attack from Florida or assault by the Mississippi Valley–based French, was fear of an Indian ambush.

It is in this frontier zone and beyond, the place of white settlers' projected fears, that John Vann, a self-described "Indian Trader," plied his trade.[43] A Scotsman by birth who numbered among the English, German, and Ulster Scotts peopling South Carolina in its mid-eighteenth-century period of expansion, Vann was enterprising and unscrupulous. Like other Europeans with licenses from the provincial government, he transported manufactured goods like kettles, tools, cloth, and guns to the Indian towns in exchange for cleaned and dressed deerskins.[44] Although Indian traders were contractually limited to only one town before 1752, many bought and sold where they could. Men like Vann, who traveled with few companions and crossed the boundary between the white and Indian worlds, were viewed as bold and rough-edged by others in South Carolina society. But the image of the Indian trader as brave and solitary, "[a]s he counted off the weary miles, or rested himself by clear waters, or hunted game and searched for stray horses in the forest ... [and] came to know the country as few others could," was matched by a record of unethical dealings, in which traders systematically overcharged their Indian counterparts or sought to sway native hunters with the liberal provision of alcohol.[45]

John Vann may have been of the latter sort. Despite serving as an interpreter for the South Carolina governor's "interview with the Indians" in 1746, Vann was a shady businessman.[46] In that same year, he petitioned the South Carolina legislature to acquire "liquor for the Indians."[47] In 1747, he partnered with Charles McNaire and several other men in the establishment of a new firm that would trade primarily with the Choctaws. Entrusted by his associates to deliver "fifteen hundred pounds of powder and twice that weight of bullets" to the Choctaws, Creeks, and Chickasaws, Vann took eight months to complete a three-month journey, "excusing himself on the ground of floods and lack of forage."[48] In addition to completing the task dramatically behind schedule, Vann was suspected of "losing" some of the goods along the way. Perhaps better suited to independent business, Vann had already extended his trading activities into Cherokee towns. By 1751, he owned a settlement "of unsavory character" at Ninety Six, a town at a confluence of creeks near the Saluda and Broad rivers. Vann resided with his Cherokee wife along with "three Negroes, a Mulatto and a half-breed Indian," a motley crew in the eyes of Vann's colonial contemporaries. The "half-breed Fellow" at Vann's was "known for his Roguery"; one of the black men had been branded on the cheek for past acts, and Vann himself was criticized for his "Bravados," which took the form of railing "against Authority."[49] While his homestead gained the less than favorable reputation as a "bandit communit[y]" on the "border between the tribe and the colony," Vann himself became known as a "white Indian."[50] When Cherokee hunters of the Lower Towns were robbed of 331 deerskins, Vann first harbored the escaping white thief, then turned on the man, "sen[ding] one of his negroes, ostensibly to seize [the accused thief] in his hunting camp, but really to kill him and thus prevent his telling tales."[51]

By the best accounts of genealogists and descendants, John Vann was James Vann's grandfather. Beyond this clear assertion, however, the precise ancestry of the Vann family leading up to James's birth is uncertain (see notes 52 and 56 for varying interpretations). In the reckoning of Cherokee genealogist James Hicks, John was James's maternal grandfather; according to descendant James Bell, John was James's paternal grandfather. In the more detailed lineage offered by Hicks, John (the "trader") Vann II (Scottish, born circa 1715) was the husband of a woman named Sister of Raven (Cherokee, Wild Potato/Blind Savannah Clan, born circa 1726). John and Sister of Raven had three children: John (the "Cherokee") Vann, Wali (or Polly) Vann, and Betty Que-di Vann. According to Hicks, James Vann's mother was Wali, the eldest daughter of Sister of Raven and John (the trader) Vann. James Vann's father was Joseph Vann, a white man and the son of John (the trader) Vann's brother (which would have made Joseph Wali's first cousin on her father's side). Clement Vann, who is sometimes described in historical treatments as James Vann's birth father, was actually his uncle and stepfather — being Joseph Vann's half brother and Wali's second husband.[52]

Wali and her first husband, Joseph, had married and started a family in tumultuous times for the Cherokee Nation. After losing nearly half their population to smallpox in 1738–39, followed by an additional outbreak in 1759, the Cherokees were caught in the military conflict known as the Cherokee War. The governor of the South Carolina colony declared war against the Cherokees in 1759 in reaction to a series of skirmishes with Cherokee warriors and against the backdrop of the French and Indian War in which Cherokees supported the French.[53] Cherokees launched a defense, but the toll on their communities was great. According to James Mooney, an early ethnologist and historian of the Cherokees, by the end of the war in 1761,

> [t]he Cherokee were now reduced to the greatest extremity. With some of their best towns in ashes, their fields and orchards wasted for two successive years, their ammunition nearly exhausted, many of their bravest warriors dead, their people fugitives in the mountains, hiding in caves and living like

beasts upon roots or killing their horses for food, with the terrible scourge of smallpox adding to the miseries of starvation, and withal torn by factional differences . . . it was impossible for even brave men to resist longer.[54]

In 1763, as the bested French signed a peace with the British, the Cherokees also conceded their loss and paid a price for resistance. "[T]he period between the end of the Cherokee war and the opening of the Revolution," Mooney wrote, "is principally notable for a number of treaty cessions by the Indians, each in a fruitless endeavor to fix a permanent barrier between themselves and the advancing wave of white settlement."[55] In the wake of this crushing defeat for the Cherokees, Joseph Vann applied to the Georgia colonial legislature for 150 acres of land on the Savannah River. Around the year 1768, Wali and Joseph Vann had their baby boy, James (Tigalohi), or "Jemmy" to his mother.[56]

Wali and Joseph Vann's mixed-race Cherokee family predated the desired arrangement of early-nineteenth-century federal Indian agent Return Jonathan Meigs, who believed that Indian-white intermarriage would facilitate Indian advancement toward civilization and ensure peaceable cross-cultural relations. In 1804 Meigs would write: "It seems as if the Graver of time had fixed the savage character so deeply in the native Indians . . . that it cannot be effaced: but where the blood is mixed with the whites, in every grade of it, there is an apparent disposition toward civilization, and this disposition is in proportion to its distance from the original stock."[57] And over a decade later Meigs would claim this position more boldly, writing to Secretary of War William Crawford: "[S]ome will say that I have always encouraged such intermarriages since I have been in the Cherokee Agency. I presume that nearly one half of the Cherokees are the offspring of intermarriage and to this may be attributed the considerable advances the Cherokees have made in civilization and in some instances we may say refinement. In time by such a measure the shades of complexion will be obliterated."[58] In the view of Agent Meigs, marriages between Indians and whites bestowed a high assimilative potential on Indian communities. By these lights, the Vanns were a model Indian family.

When James Vann was born in the 1760s, followed by sisters Jennie and Nancy, his family was among the first in a new assemblage of the Cherokee population — mixed-race Euro-Cherokees. Although Agent Meigs had overestimated the size of this group in 1816 (the figure was closer to 15 percent or less of the Cherokee whole), this cluster of Cherokee society was taking root in the mid- and late 1700s, as Cherokee women like James's mother married white traders and Indian agents.[59] Cherokee women most likely did so to advantage their families and clans by integrating newcomers with special skills and access to resources. Missionaries observing this practice misunderstood the aims of Cherokee women, assuming them to be motivated by personal greed: "[T]he intermixings of Cherokees with white people are unbelievably many and are becoming more daily, as the Cherokee females are exceedingly mercenary," wrote John Gambold, the chief Moravian missionary to the Cherokees, in 1816.[60] But prominent historian of southern Indians, Theda Perdue, better conveys Cherokee women's reasons for marrying white men: "Native people recognized that intermarriage brought material advantages to the families to whom traders, soldiers, agents, and other officials connected themselves."[61]

Children of these unions were certainly influenced by the cultures of both parents, but they did not, as many modern-day observers have sometimes believed, transfigure into "whites." Perdue has demonstrated that "mixed-blood" Indians identified as Indian, claiming political affiliation with their nations and expressing native cultural identities. Their fellow group members, in turn, claimed them. She writes: "When Native women bore children by white men . . . they considered the children to be Indian, not white or 'mixed blood.'"[62] Missionary John Gambold expressed a similar observation in 1810, writing: "All the children of white men raised with Indian mothers belong without question to the family and lineage of the mother."[63] And Louise Philippe, the future French king who traveled through the Cherokee country in the 1790s wrote, accordingly, "The children of white men and Indian women are Indians like the others. The Americans call them half breeds. They live precisely as the others do, neither read nor write, and ordinarily speak only the tribal tongue."[64]

James Vann and his sisters, by the reckoning and recognition of everyone around them, were Cherokee children. But Cherokee though they were, their lives were different from most other Cherokees in identifiable ways. Even in a matrilineal kinship system, the white fathers of mixed-race Euro-Cherokee children shaped their upbringing in a manner that Cherokee uncles or fathers would not have. These children heard the English language spoken, if not between their parents, then in their father's work transactions, and they were able to gain a facility in that tongue. They observed and learned skills in business, animal husbandry, and agriculture before other members of their nation. They were exposed to the values of their fathers' moral, religious, and economic belief systems. And they had access to their fathers' financial resources. For unlike most Cherokees who farmed for subsistence, European men among the Cherokees labored to make a profit in trade or benefited from government salaries. As a result, their Cherokee families lived in environments of relative domestic comfort and economic surplus. These children's descent from white fathers did not exclude them from Cherokee identity but instead created an increasing racial and economic diversity in Cherokee society.

Within this small but growing population of Euro-Cherokees, the Vann family was successful and prominent.[65] In addition to profits from their trading business, their wealth derived from ownership of black slaves. Since black slaves were few in the South Carolina backcountry, numbering 250 in the 1740s and 1750s, and since they were even fewer in Cherokee country, numbering only 100 by 1794, the families who owned slaves had a scarce and valuable resource. John Vann, James Vann's grandfather, was among these privileged few.[66] John's daughter Wali and son-in-law/nephew Joseph inherited slaves and their "increase" and with the aid of this capital grew the family business.

At a time when the Cherokee Nation was fast becoming a consumer society, Joseph Vann developed a trading post to supply individuals with manufactured goods. Cherokees had been introduced to European things at least as early as the 1690s and had come to prefer kettles to baskets, cotton skirts to deerskin dresses. The cost of these luxuries was dear, however. A skilled hunter might acquire fifty skins in one season, but he would pay thirty-five skins for a gun, fourteen for a petticoat, five for a shirt, and one for a knife.[67] By 1745, Cherokees were so accustomed to the use of Western goods that Chief Skiagunsta wrote to the governor of South Carolina: "My people cannot live independent of the English. . . . The clothes we wear we cannot make ourselves. They are made for us. We use their ammunition with which to kill deer. We cannot make our own guns. Every necessary of life we must have from the white people."[68]

This situation advantaged white traders like Joseph Vann and, later, mixed-race traders like his son, James, who operated in a seller's market. And even as traders did business in Cherokee communities, reaping rewards from an out-of-scale system of exchange, white settlers continued to penetrate the frontier zone, squatting on Cherokee lands and shrinking the population of wild game. Historian Robert Meriwether noted in 1940 that it was this access to cheap land that defined America as a place of opportunity: "The impartial distribution of the soil, matched in varying degrees in the back country of the other southern colonies, was the chief basis for an equality of wealth and opportunity that was the most significant characteristic of the American frontier."[69] But this same process was happening to Cherokees in reverse. They were losing land, and it would be their undoing.

In 1763, just after the Cherokee War, King George III of England issued a proclamation on Indian affairs. It prohibited colonists from settling in the Indians' territory west of the Appalachian Mountains and forbade the purchase of Indian land without the crown's consent. Nevertheless, hundreds of settlers love-struck by land, including the iconic Daniel Boone, wantonly broke this law, searching out passages and Indian trails to force their way through the mountains. In 1775, when James Vann was just about seven or eight, a set of unscrupulous colonists violated the law in a most spectacular way. Richard Henderson and a clutch of North Carolinians convinced a handful of headmen to sell a vast tract of Cherokee land west of the Appalachians. The land in question — the present-day state of Kentucky and the Cumberland Valley of Tennessee (27,000 square miles or 20 million acres) — was the priceless upper hunting ground that Cherokees shared with the Shawnees and the Iroquois.[70] This plentiful region, according to one observer, had been "full of deer, elk, bears, and buffaloes," with "rich uplands, as well as the alluvial bottoms of the rivers" that were "covered with cane-breaks."[71] Historians suspect that the chiefs who made the deal believed they were merely selling use rights to this land, which might explain why the price they accepted was shockingly low, just "a few wagon loads of goods, worth about 10,000 pounds."[72]

The Henderson sale was negotiated at Sycamore Shoals in March of 1775, a month before shots rang out at Lexington and Concord. James Vann's father, Joseph Vann, moonlighted as an interpreter for colonial officials and others by independent contract. At the Sycamore Shoals event, Joseph Vann was the principal "linguister," and James may have accompanied him to the gathering.[73] If the young James had been there, he would have heard the passionate protest made by Dragging Canoe, who predicted a "dark and bloody" outcome of the sale before storming out of the meeting.[74] British officials were likewise outraged at the affair and criticized the actions of "our bad People."[75] But although colonial representatives warned Henderson's group to retract the agreement, the land speculators stood their ground.[76] By this massive land transfer, Mooney wrote, "the Cherokee were shorn of practically all their ancient territorial claims north of the present Tennessee line and east of the Blue Ridge and the Savannah, including much of their best hunting range."[77] And things would only grow worse for them in the coming months when the American colonies launched a revolution.

In 1776 the Americans declared their independence and Washington crossed the Delaware in a miraculous midnight march. The early events of the American Revolution hold mythical meaning for many of us. But what did the Cherokees think as they watched these developments from points south? In the aftermath of the Henderson sale and so many land grabs before it, experience told Cherokees that the Americans were no friends of theirs. Cherokees feared if the settlers won, the king's proclamation of 1763, which had hardly held back the tide of expansion before the colonists' war preparations, would be null and void. Their concerns were prescient, as colonial historian Alan Taylor has argued that Americans sought independence in part to corral more Indian land. "Colonial settlers and land speculators, who wanted free sway in western expansion, . . . fed the American Revolution," Taylor writes, "which created an independent republic dedicated to facilitating white settlement and Indian dispossession."[78] The Cherokees despaired at the prospect of just such an outcome. They knew that if the Americans won, they would lose.

The outspoken leader Dragging Canoe boosted this anger and fear, warning that older chiefs suffered from cowardice and urging young warriors to strike before the southern militias gathered strength.[79] John Stuart, British Indian agent to the southern nations who remained loyal to the crown, dissuaded Cherokees from immediate action, preferring instead to hold them in check until the British army called upon them. But Dragging Canoe and his supporters had no interest in playing a passive role. Spurred on by a delegation of Shawnees, Delawares, and Mohawks who also wished to defend against a new American state, the Cherokee rebels laid their plans in May and June of 1776. In June and July they struck, attacking white settlements in the South Carolina backcountry, Georgia, North Carolina, and into Virginia, and causing widespread panic across the South.[80]

This preemptive strike, as bold as it seemed, would backfire on the Cherokees. For unlike Dragging Canoe's warriors, who conceptualized the battles as a series of raids, the southern militias pursued systematic and comprehensive warfare. General Charles Lee, commander of the continental army in the South, urged a "powerful punitive expedition" against the Indians, and in late summer, the southern militias launched a devastating three-month campaign.[81] In August, South Carolina soldiers attacked the Cherokee Lower Towns with a force of over one thousand men; in September, North Carolina militia pummeled the Middle Towns; in October, the Virginia regiments approached the Overhill Towns, whose residents fled for the mountainsides. "From north, east, and south, their enemies had come to lay waste to their towns," and the effects were devastating.[82] The South Carolina expedition had burned each town site to the ground, leaving thousands of refugees to pour across the smoking fields. The North Carolina troops had done the same, destroying homes, council houses, property, and food stores.

Cherokee victims of these attacks remembered the terror vividly. A girl named Nancy from the Lower Towns was captured and sold into slavery after soldiers invaded her family's camp. Two elder chiefs, including Chief Sour Mush, who had been an important character in the early legend of James

Vann, recounted her story to the Cherokee agent in an attempt to secure her freedom: "In the early part of the Revolutionary War, the Cherokees were encamped on a mountain near Field Town on Seneca River. The white people approached their camp to attack it and the Cherokee fled, that a Cherokee woman named Olufletoy, having a little girl with her about eight years old — when the Cherokees fled, the woman and her child were left behind, that the white people killed the woman Olufletoy and took the little girl off with them."[83] The captive girl, Nancy, also recounted her suffering, testifying that "she was taken when a child from her mother, that the white people afterwards boasted that they held their guns over her mother's head to frighten her when they took her away: that sometime afterwards she was carried a great way on horseback to a place where there were a number of houses . . . that she had two masters before Mr. Fulton bought her, that she had brothers and sisters when she was taken away from her mother."[84]

In this single family caught up in the Cherokees' Revolutionary War battle, a mother was brutally murdered and a defenseless daughter was captured and sold into Virginia slavery. The added terror of sexual assault is never broached in the testimony, but as native women, Nancy and her mother would have been especially vulnerable. In her study of rape in early America, historian Sharon Block points to the lowering of prohibitions against sexual violence for men engaged in battle. Female war captives were subject to sexual assault as a display of conquering soldiers' prowess, and documented examples of this particular kind of violation exist for the American Revolutionary War.[85] Although white women were sometimes raped by soldiers during the conflict, native women were much more likely to be viewed as sexually violable. Block writes: "As 'Heathen,' Indian women were vulnerable to particularly sadistic assaults that were expressions of more than men's overt sexual gratification. Sexual interactions with nonwhite women were characterized by a degree of hostility and brutality that moved beyond simple sexual pleasure into torture as a purposeful expression of superiority."[86] Nancy could well have witnessed her mother being sexually assaulted during the attack, and although she was just a pre-adolescent, Nancy may have been a victim herself.[87]

James Vann, a boy of eight during the Cherokee battles of the Revolutionary War, may have witnessed such scenes. Cherokee communities lay in tatters around him. And he and his family, like thousands of others, were likely reduced to refugee status, seeking safer ground in the Georgia hills or North Carolina mountains. James's uncle, Richard Rowe, recalled the war this way in testimony to the Cherokee agent in 1829: "[H]e was a small boy about the close of the revolutionary war. [T]he war between the whites and Cherokees became very oppressive to the Cherokees, so much so that his father removed his family to the south side of the Etowah [River] or what is commonly called the Hightowah where he considered them safe from the whites."[88]

By November of 1776, the Cherokee military effort was spent, and most of the people were desperate for peace. In 1777 and 1783, Cherokees agreed to treaties with the southern states, ceding additional land.[89] In 1785, the Cherokees signed the Treaty of Hopewell, their first formal agreement with the United States, which gave the United States jurisdiction over trade and the right to punish crimes against whites that occurred in Cherokee territory, gave American traders the freedom to do business in any Cherokee town at will, pledged Cherokees to abandon the practice of clan revenge, and declared the Cherokees to be "under the protection of the United States."[90]

The Cherokee Nation was nearly undone by the series of losses in the 1760s and 1770s. Their ability to gain leverage by playing European powers off of one another had evaporated. Their land base had shrunk, and the core of their country had shifted west. Even the sacred "mother town" of Chota, a city of refuge and beacon of peace, was lost in the war and would not be rebuilt until 1823.[91] In his study of southern Indians and the Revolutionary War, historian James O'Donnell describes the enormity of this defeat for the Cherokees: "The results of the war were to break the power of a major Southern tribe. . . . Patriot leaders would find that the commitment of more than 4,500 men and the expenditure of several million dollars in the effort against the Cherokee were of lasting importance."[92]

Against the backdrop of famine and an uneasy peace, Dragging Canoe and his followers did not accept defeat. They deserted their ruined towns in southern Cherokee country and relocated to the Tennessee hills, where they founded a new town called Chickamauga. And for ten years following the Treaty of Hopewell, they attacked white settlements that infringed on Cherokee territory. James Vann's maternal uncle, John, was a member of this resistance. In 1788, a party of settlers led by Colonel James Brown was approaching the Cherokee towns of Running Water and Nickajack by boat when "suddenly four canoes, with white flags raised, and naked savages skulling in them as rowers, glided out into the river." Witnesses later reported that "John Vann, a well-known half-breed, who spoke good English, was the leader of the party." Vann convinced Brown to let him come aboard, and then proceeded, along with the warriors he commanded, to take the Brown party captive and commandeer their black slaves. The Brown party's presence, Vann declared, "was a violation of the Treaty of Hopewell" and the town chief would "punish the marauders."[93] As a young man in his twenties, the legend goes, James Vann followed in his uncle's footsteps, joining Dragging Canoe's forces in a group led by Chiefs Doublehead and Watts in an intended attack on Knoxville. But this resistance, too, would fail.[94]

Setting Up Shop

Like many other Cherokees, the Vann family probably migrated during the Revolutionary War years, resettling in the Georgia mountain zone. Describing the movement of these war refugees, historian William McLoughlin wrote: "The Chattahoochee and Connesauga rivers [area] was filled with Cherokees who had been forced out of towns further east when their land was ceded to the states of South Carolina and Georgia."[95] According to descendant James Bell, James Vann's father, Joseph, rebuilt his trading post in present-day northwest Georgia, and "once again had a flourishing trade business ... [and] gained a considerable amount of wealth."[96] But within a few years, American militiamen would destroy Joseph Vann's settlement. In 1782, during the Chickamauga resistance, Colonel John Sevier of Tennessee led reprisal attacks on Cherokee villages. When Sevier's troops "entered upon the territory of the hostile Indians ... they marched, immediately, against Vann's Towns, and reduced them to ashes."[97] A young teenager at the time of this assault, James Vann had lived amid war or its aftermath for his entire life. When an older James rebuilt a trading post near the ruins of his family's home, he did more than establish a business. He acted in defiance of a predominant settler-colonial mentality that sought to wipe Cherokees off the map.

James Vann was enterprising, clever, bold — but hostage to historical trauma and the personal flaws of arrogance and avarice. Sometime in his early adulthood, probably after the fall of the Chickamauga resistance and de facto peace between Cherokees and the U.S. government in 1794, Vann made a momentous decision.[98] If the Cherokee people could not fend off the Euro-American invasion, Vann would beat the Americans at their own game. By the 1790s, with his father now dead, James had the makings of a flourishing new settlement. While still in his twenties, he operated his own mercantile post, established a ferry, and cleared land with the labor of black slaves he had inherited. He was also intent upon increasing his property, and acquired, through less than estimable means, slaves belonging to his sisters. Missionary John Gambold, who safeguarded the papers of Vann's estate upon his death, reported that "Mr. Vann's father had given personally to each of his two daughters, Jenny and Nancy, according to the custom of this country, still during his lifetime, a Negress; James Vann had, however, arbitrarily kept these as well as the rest of his father's estate for his own possession."[99] James's larceny extended to his mother when he stole her family inheritance as well. Gambold recorded: "John Vann . . . had ordered before his death that his entire estate was to be divided between his two step-sisters, one of whom is the mother of James Vann. But James Vann had sold his mother's share, consisting of 19 horses and 15 or 16 heads of cattle and had invested the money in his business and kept it."[100]

As a result of these self-serving entrepreneurial moves, Vann saw remarkable economic success. But these acts, it need be said, did not remake him into a virtual white man. James Vann was by no means a typical Cherokee farmer in terms of persona or financial ambition, and yet Vann's accommodation to some, but not all, Euro-American practices was something he had in common with many other Cherokees. Individual Cherokee men and women determined in multiple manners and to varying degrees the ways and extent to which they would comply with colonial imposition. The Cherokees of Vann's Upper Town region, which included some of the oldest settlements in the nation as well as the new towns founded by refugees of war, had long been willing to cooperate with whites in the hope that this gesture would preserve their homeland.[101] Though some young men in these towns had left home to fight with the Chickamaugans, most Upper Towns people worked to maintain a fragile peace with whites. Cherokee residents of the Upper Towns gravitated toward negotiation and change as a means of self-protection.[102] And James Vann, an outspoken and controversial resident of this region, gravitated along with them.[103]

This choice of the Upper Towns people was one of two clear means of survival in a moment of widespread tumult at the end of the eighteenth and start of the nineteenth century. Cherokee literature scholar Daniel Heath Justice, richly describes these two means of survival as "complementary" Cherokee philosophies that emerged at a critical historical moment: a "'Chickamauga consciousness' of physical and/or rhetorical defiance" and a "'Beloved Path' of accommodation and cooperation."[104] James Vann had walked each of these roads with his fellow Cherokees, defying the American settlers *and* adopting some of their ways. But since both routes were imperfect, born, as they were, in response to colonial oppression, neither was satisfactory to him. Perhaps for this reason, along with others motivated by personal demons and flaws, Vann's was a life of disaffection and discomfiture. Moravian missionary Anna Rosina Gambold wrote about Vann: "[H]e is—one can notice it—restless; and he is trying to chase away his restlessness in other ways."[105] John Lowrey, a Cherokee compatriot and political opponent, once said disparagingly of Vann: "[H]is life is a misery to him."[106]

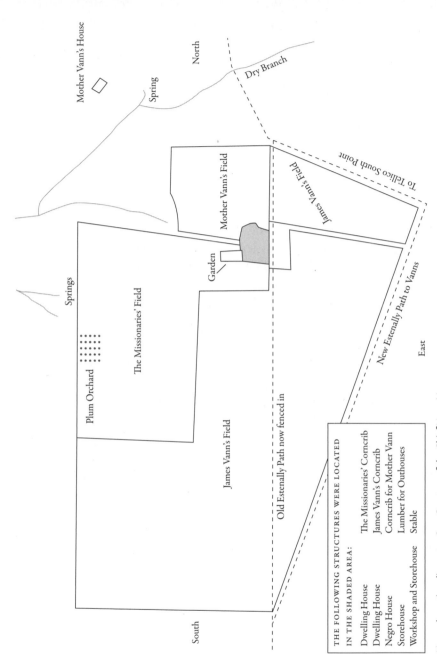

Mother Vann's House

North

Spring

Dry Branch

Mother Vann's Field

James Vann's Field

To Tellico South Point

Garden

Springs

The Missionaries' Field

New Estenally Path to Vanns

East

Plum Orchard

James Vann's Field

Old Estenally Path now fenced in

South

THE FOLLOWING STRUCTURES WERE LOCATED
IN THE SHADED AREA:

Dwelling House	The Missionaries' Corncrib
Dwelling House	James Vann's Corncrib
Negro House	Corncrib for Mother Vann
Storehouse	Lumber for Outhouses
Workshop and Storehouse	Stable

Vann plantation diagram, 1805. Courtesy of the Chief Vann House.

CHAPTER 2

House-Raising

And as the expert conchologist can determine by studying an empty shell
just what species of mollusk inhabited it, and how the internal anatomy of the
dweller was organized and where and under what conditions it led its life, so it
is generally easy by examining a human house to tell where it was built . . .
and what sort of man built it and under what conditions he lived.
—J. Frazer Smith, *Plantation Houses and Mansions of the Old South*, 1941

The Cherokees' New World

In August of 1783, the year the Peace of Paris concluded the American Revolutionary War, Peggy Scott, James Vann's future wife, was born to a Cherokee mother and English father. Peggy Scott's parents, Sarah Hicks of the Wolf Clan and trader Walter Scott, lived with their four daughters in a Cherokee town, where Walter Scott had once drawn a salary of "5/per day," as assistant commissioner in the Cherokee Nation under the direction of John Stuart, British superintendent of southern Indian affairs. The configuration of Peggy Scott's family reflected the imperfect intimacy that Cherokees had forged with European colonists over the decades since their settlement. For Peggy Scott's own mother was herself the child of a Cherokee woman and Englishman, and Peggy's grandmother was descended from Cherokees on her mother's side and Germans or Hollanders on her father's side.[1]

The influence of her mother's family on Peggy's upbringing was significant, especially in a matrilineal society in which a child inherited the clan membership and identity of the mother. Peggy Scott spoke Cherokee, believed in the value of Cherokee nationalism, knew how to harvest local foods in the ways of Cherokee women, and remained close to her Cherokee relatives throughout her life. But English cultural norms would also have shaped Peggy's development. As a mature woman, she recalled an example of her father's parental influence: "My father, Walter Scott, who was a white man and formerly an agent among the Cherokee Nation, protected me from heathen entertainment; once he kept me away from a dance on account of which I, out of love for him whom I lost to death all too early, still avoid to this day."[2] In the childhood moment Peggy recounts here, her father had dissuaded her from attending a traditional Cherokee dance and thereby inculcated the belief that such festivities were immoral. This teaching had a lasting effect on Peggy, who recalled it in explaining her conversion to Christianity later in life. The cultural preparation she received from her father enabled Peggy Scott to develop fluency in the ways of the English and Americans in addition to the indigenous practices of her mother. In this way she was similar to other mixed-race Indian women of her nation and generation: Cherokee in identity, Cherokee in belonging, and Cherokee in the cultural practices of daily life at a time when the very features of Cherokee culture were being influenced by European norms.

As Peggy Scott reached adolescence in the 1790s, the once great Cherokee Nation was still struggling to recover from the wreckage of the Revolutionary War and its aftermath, through which Cherokees had lost not only a third of their population but also massive swaths of land, including hunting grounds, villages, and sacred sites.[3] Vanquished militarily, Cherokees faced increasing pressure to adopt cultural change at the direction of the Americans. In the 1791 Treaty of Holston, the Cherokee Nation accepted the terms of the young United States: cultural adaptation in exchange for both material assistance like spinning wheels and plows and protection from America's land-hungry citizenry. Elements of Anglo-American culture were therefore everyday aspects of Cherokee life by the 1790s, especially in mixed-race, well-endowed families like Peggy Scott's.

The shape of this new multicultural Cherokee world is evident in exchanges between U.S. Indian agent Benjamin Hawkins and Cherokee women he encountered on his observational trip through Georgia in 1796. Hawkins had "a negro woman for [his] interpreter" on the journey, a fact that points to the relatively new practice of black slaveholding among southern Indians and confirms the primacy of indigenous languages. Hawkins would have been unable to converse fluently with these women in English because they spoke Cherokee. But, although their grasp of the English language was tenuous, the women Hawkins encountered reported an incorporation of Euro-American gender-specific tasks alongside of Native American gender-specific tasks. They were spinning cotton as the Treaty of Holston dictated, while continuing the Cherokee practice of river cane basket weaving, a practical art with sacred meaning at which they excelled. Hawkins reported: "They exhibited to me a sample of their ingenuity in the manufacture of baskets and sifters, out of cane the dies of the splits were good and workmanship not surpassed in the United States by white people." On his travels Hawkins also encountered the mixed-race Euro-Cherokee women Sally Waters and Sally Hughes (the former a half sister of James Vann's mother), who were fluent in Cherokee, spoke English adequately, and had plans to learn the new skills encouraged by the U.S. government. Hawkins recorded: "They said they would follow the advise [*sic*] of their great father, General Washington, they would plant cotton and be prepared for spinning."[4]

Benjamin Hawkins's interactions with these Indian women show the persistence of Cherokee cultural ways at the same time that they suggest the adoption of Euro-American practices in a context of U.S. colonialism and coercive surveillance. It was, after all, Hawkins's job as Indian agent to represent the U.S. government and assess Cherokee "progress" toward greater "civilization." Failure to visibly adopt the changes of the U.S. civilization program could have meant a decrease in material aid and loss of promised protection from white intruders, both of which Cherokees sorely needed. Peggy Scott was thirteen at the time of Hawkins's travels through Georgia, and she was among the first generation of Cherokee women to come of age in a country shadowed by absolute military defeat and perforated by European cultural influences. Emerging from a context in which Cherokees incorporated white family members and Euro-American ways of life, Peggy Scott was culturally primed to become the wife of James Vann, an early adopter of American-style business enterprise and southern-style plantation slavery.

The Mistress of Diamond Hill

A young teenager at the time of her marriage and fifteen years her husband's junior, Peggy Scott was surely relieved to find her sister already in residence. For before marrying Peggy around the year 1797, James Vann had married her eldest sister, Elizabeth (Betsy) Scott. Over the course of his lifetime, Vann would marry several women (sources vary on the exact number), including Nancy Brown, Jennie Doublehead Foster, and Peggy's second older sister, Mary Polly Scott. Vann's multiple spouses piqued and confounded white onlookers, one of whom, the Moravian missionary John Gambold, complained: "There is no one who can make sense of the genealogical register of the Cherokees. . . . 'The people live like valued cattle and wild sows.' Not only does a man often have more than one wife (I know some who have six of them), but there are also women who have several husbands at the same time."[5] Perhaps due to ethnocentric misunderstanding, Gambold exaggerated Cherokee marriage customs and maligned the nature of their genealogies, but the kind of familial arrangement found on the Vann plantation was not unusual for Cherokees. Polygamy was an accepted practice that could strengthen communities by forging ties across clans and towns. Through marriage to the Scott women in particular, James Vann drew a closer link not only to an influential former

Indian agent but also to Charles Hicks, the maternal uncle of Peggy, Elizabeth, and Polly and a respected Cherokee political leader.

Although James Vann had several wives over the years, and, it seems, more than a few consorts, most of these women would leave him in quick succession. For in Cherokee society of the eighteenth and early nineteenth century, a wife could divorce her husband with ease. Because women owned the homes, a wife could place her husband's things outside of the cabin door, thus signaling her desire for his departure. The children, the cabin, the household items — all would remain with the woman, and the husband would return to his mother's home or to the communal town house for shelter. The particular domestic situation of James Vann's wives, however, was a novelty for Cherokees, as they had joined him on the plantation that he owned in much the same way that an English or American wife would leave her parents to live with her husband. Nevertheless, Cherokee values around women's conjugal freedom persisted. Vann's wives likely had their own sleeping quarters on his grounds. And when Vann's wives were through with him, they picked up and left. No repercussions befell them, and no shame shadowed their lives. Some of Vann's former wives continued to live in the general vicinity, as did his children by them.

In 1801, when Moravian missionaries first visited Vann's place, they encountered two principal wives, one older and one younger, about whom they said in their diary: "Mr. Vann had here two (sisters) women, half Indian but mostly white, they were busy spinning and weaving cotton."[6] The younger wife in this description was Peggy Scott, who was fourteen when she married Vann and seventeen at the time of the Moravians' visit. By 1805, Peggy became the sole spouse of note and the only wife living on the Vann plantation grounds.

Peggy Scott was, by all accounts, a captivating woman. Lovely, with a calm disposition and sensitive aspect, she deeply impressed those who came into contact with her. John Norton, a Cherokee visitor, said of Scott: "[S]he is of a comely countenance, is tall and has a dignity of carriage softened by mildness."[7] Moravian missionaries described her as "very pretty," "industrious and skilled," with a "clear and bright" singing voice and a love of going "riding every day."[8] Peggy was also a woman of some means, having been promised an inheritance from her father upon his death in 1796. Privy to the records of the Vann estate, missionary John Gambold noted: "Walter Scott, had put together quite a considerable wealth and on his death-bed expressed the wish that his widow should enjoy that as long as she lived and then bequeath it to his children."[9] And even before her mother's death in 1816, Peggy had inherited one black slave woman, cattle valued at $700, and land on the Savannah River in South Carolina from her father's estate. Perhaps it was this combination of beauty, wealth, and charisma that led Peggy Scott to hold an opinion of herself as "superior to other of her countrywomen." Peggy would, however, lose a substantial portion of her personal wealth upon marrying James Vann. For Vann commandeered his young wife's property just as he had his mother's and sisters'. John Gambold wrote: "[H]er husband had added a large part of her property—for her husband and wife among these Indians have their own private interests—to his own from time to time before her very eyes."[10] To advance his business interests, Vann set aside Cherokee understandings of women's individual property rights in favor of Euro-American legal culture that sanctioned male authority over female family members. His rapid accumulation of capital, the foundation of his mounting success, depended on the subjugation of two groups: Cherokee women, whose wealth he pilfered, and African slaves, whose bodies and labor made up much of that wealth.

When Peggy Scott arrived at the plantation home that her husband had christened Diamond Hill, she found a majestic setting for her daily horseback rides. Vann's development lay deep within the Cherokee wilderness near the Conasauga River, where scattered log houses were separated by stands of old-growth forest and wandering tributaries. The area where Vann lived was known for its abundance of natural rock and sand springs. The closest towns were the Cherokee settlements of Coosawattee and Oostanaula, twenty miles to the south, and Chickamauga, thirty miles to the northwest. The U.S. agency to the Cherokees at Fort Southwest Point and the Tellico blockhouse, a U.S. military post and center for trade, were approximately eighty miles north, in Tennessee, a full day's journey away.[11]

This sparsely settled countryside was stunningly lush, with crisp springs, verdant fields, and blue-peaked slopes in the distance. English trader James Adair, when traveling through the mountainous region of Cherokee territory, concluded that "the Alps of Italy are much inferior to several of the Cheerake mountains," and continued, "There is not a more healthful region under the sun, than this country; for the air is commonly open and clear, and plenty of wholesome and pleasant weather. I know several bold rivers . . . which are almost as transparent as glass."[12] Journeying through the northwest Cherokee lands, Jeremiah Evarts, the corresponding secretary for the American Board of Commissioners for Foreign Missions (ABCFM), was also taken by the beauty of the natural terrain: "The forest, though generally the trees are not thick, afforded a grateful shelter from the rays of the sun. The herbage and flowers were in their most beautiful state, having all the freshness of spring, and beginning to show the luxuriance of summer. I am told, however, that flowers in variety and abundance are to be seen in the woods here, from the first of

March to the first of December."[13] And in his journal, John Norton depicted the land of this region as "both fertile and picturesque, being composed of a delightful mixture of hill and dale, moderately covered with timber of a fine growth; the water issues from the clearest fountains." Norton's described approach to the Vann plantation, in particular, reads like reverie: "[W]e crossed a ridge of hills, from the summit of which, we had an extensive view of the country, till bounded by a range of mountains, on the South East, whose blue tops were hidden among the clouds. In the afternoon, we passed a river called Kaneghsague, a branch of the Coosa; it is navigable for boats."[14]

In addition to this embarrassment of natural riches, Peggy Scott did not want for equine company on her husband's plantation. For James Vann owned more than one hundred horses, including a "Bay Paces natrel aboute fifteen hands high," which Vann described in his own hand in extant personal papers.[15] Nor did she want for economic resources. Although Peggy was skilled at sewing and applied that skill when she chose, she had the financial means to send sewing work out to a white woman in the area. Perhaps due to her economic standing, her demonstrated capabilities, or her outward beauty, a streak of pride colored Peggy Scott's character. This pride in her "good life," as she herself phrased it, is an attribute Peggy would struggle with when she later contemplated Christian conversion.[16]

The mountainous and riverine region where Peggy Scott lived was splendid country, and her husband was gaining proprietorship over hundreds of acres there. Because Cherokees did not permit private landownership, any unoccupied ground within the nation's boundaries was free for the taking to Cherokee citizens. In order to hold land in this system, James Vann had simply to claim it through evident use, like clearing forested plots into fields, raising fences, constructing buildings—or, more accurately, by having his slaves do these things. Moravian missionaries described this principle of Cherokee common landownership, noting: "Private property is safeguarded together with the improvements made on cultivated land. The land itself, however, is not private property. It is the property of the nation. No individual holds a piece of it in fee, but all are tenants in common. Each may occupy a piece of unoccupied land, clear it, and locate wherever he pleases."[17] French traveler Louis Philippe also took note of this practice, adding, as a point of comparison, the private possession of "movable goods" like African slaves: "Ownership of the land is common among all Indians, but they acknowledge the individual ownership of crafted and movable goods. . . . They even recognize the ownership of Negroes and their descendants."[18] For James Vann, the Cherokee value of communally owned land made available for private use, together with the increasing acceptance of black slavery in Cherokee society, proved immensely profitable.[19] Once he had inherited slaves from his father and swindled slaves from his sisters and wife, he possessed a ready-made plantation enterprise.

The Headman of Vannsville

Fertile, scenic, and far enough removed to allow for independent management, the Conasauga River valley was ideal for James Vann's ambitious vision. As Vann continued to develop acreage, his many business ventures flourished. By the early nineteenth century, just as slavery was expanding and intensifying in the U.S. South after the invention of the cotton gin, Vann's main plantation, Diamond Hill, was a multistructured, self-supporting, highly profitable establishment, producing crops of wheat, cotton, corn, and fruit that Vann sold to white frontier settlements for profit and exchange.[20] His complex was located in the northwest dells of four agricultural regions in what would later make up the state of Georgia: the small valley sector in the northwest, an adjacent mountainous area, a wide-swathed piedmont plateau to the south, and a sizeable Atlantic coastal plain across the bottom half of the state. While the coastal plain would become the state's rice and cotton slaveholding hub, and the plateau would hold a sizeable number of cotton plantations, Vann's valley region and the parallel mountainous zone would only support modest grain and livestock farms as late as 1860.[21] This meant that at the turn of the nineteenth century, when James Vann built Diamond Hill, his establishment dwarfed not only other Cherokee farms but also white farms in the bordering areas of northeastern and north central Georgia.

Vann's extraordinary gem of a plantation extended for miles across Cherokee territory. The center of the grounds held two wood dwelling houses, a slave cabin, a vegetable garden, a storehouse, a workshop, a corncrib, outhouses, a blacksmith shop, and a stable. Just beyond this central core were a series of cultivated fields, orchards, the home of Vann's mother, Wali Vann, and additional dirt-floored slave cabins. On the far boundary of his plantation, Vann built the first gristmill in the area on what is now Mill Creek, for which he ordered in a millstone by boat.[22] And beyond the villagelike perimeter, but still on land that Vann claimed, were additional slave dwellings and grazing space for cattle. Surrounding and meandering through Vann's cultivated land were miles of poplar forest, thick with brush and vines.

Vann's nearby Conasauga River trading post and ferry, known as Vannsville to travelers, were operational by 1800.[23] By 1804 Vann owned a second store, tavern, plantation, and ferry on the Chattahoochee River, ninety miles to the east.[24] Nineteenth-century novelist F. R. Goulding memorialized Vann's Chattahoochee complex in *The Woodruff Stories*, a trilogy of Indian-themed children's novellas. In "Sapelo; or, Child-Life on the Tide-Water," Goulding devotes two chapters to events on and around "Vann's Ferry," including this picturesque description:

> In the course of two or three days, we came to a river, which was crossed by means of a ferry-boat. . . . It was a broad, shallow, flat-bottomed thing, with double floor, built of very thick planks, having space enough for a large wagon and team. . . . A rope of twisted hide was stretched across the river and fastened to a tree on each side.
>
> The river was very beautiful, its waters clear as crystal, and overhung to their very edge by luxuriant trees and vines, growing in the rich banks. . . . A short distance above the ferry, the river was double; for there the waters of two rivers unite in their sparkling race to the Gulf of Mexico. The Chestatee above the junction and the Chattahoochee below it, formed the boundary, at that time, between the ill-starred Cherokees and white people of the State of Georgia.[25]

To best conduct his business, James Vann regularly traversed this boundary between the Cherokees and whites, traveling to Charleston and Athens for days at a time with wagonloads of deerskins and crops, then returning to the Cherokee Nation with piles of manufactured goods to stock in his stores. He also sold, in his own words, "a quantity of young fatt cattle which I would wish to dispose of on good terms."[26] And he owned, sold, and rented out scores of black slaves, whose combined value increased his capital just as their labor increased his profits. In contrast to the U.S. South, where the economic worth of slave property was second only to private land holdings, in the Cherokee Nation enslaved black people were the most valuable form of property imaginable.[27] Just one of Vann's adult black slaves, at a cost of approximately $300 each, was exponentially more valuable than a typical Cherokee family's log home, which could range in worth between $10 for a simple fourteen-foot-square cabin to $60 for a well-crafted, one and a half story sawed log dwelling house.[28] James Vann, who possessed over one hundred slaves by the end of the first decade of the nineteenth century, was wealthy beyond measure among his Cherokee peers.

Vann's interest in slave trading and the profit it could produce was most apparent in his business partnership with James Blair, a white associate from Georgia. By 1809, the two men had "formed a kind of company" for which they purchased hundreds of oxen, drove them to Pennsylvania for sale, then used the proceeds to purchase and resell black slaves.[29] In this venture Vann took part in the U.S. domestic trade in black bondspeople that grew after the Revolutionary War and exploded in the wake of the 1808 congressional ban on the importation of African slaves. Vann's actions, together with those of other professionalizing slave traders known at first as "Georgia-men," forced thousands of blacks into new areas of the South as slavery expanded westward, launching what historian Ira Berlin has called "the Second Middle Passage."[30] Residents of the Cherokee Nation were direct witnesses to this forced relocation of bondspeople, as white slaveholders began to use Cherokee territory as a passageway for travel to Natchez, Mississippi.[31]

About his participation in the commodification of other human beings James Vann showed no apparent hesitation or concern. Some scholars might argue that his comfort with slaveholding rested in Cherokees' familiarity with the presence of unfree people among them — Indian people taken in wars for territory and retribution. For Cherokees had long captured prisoners of war that they themselves described as "owned" individuals. But war captives among Cherokees had very different qualities from those of black slaves among Europeans. Cherokee war captives were drawn from any number of ethnic groups and did not have a unifying, indelible, and inheritable physical trait, such as "black" skin color, to demarcate and facilitate their subordination. War captives were held for a brief period of time before being adopted or ritually murdered by their captors; there was no interest, therefore, in exploiting them as a subjugated labor force. War captives did not occupy their degraded status long enough to constitute a stigmatized class, let alone to pass on that caste status to offspring. And although some southeastern nations, like the Westos and the Chickasaws, made a business of trading Indian war captives to whites for use as enslaved laborers, Cherokees were never especially active in the Indian slave trade.[32] While it is possible that Cherokees' customary practice of holding war captives had primed Vann for the act of keeping others in a state of bondage, it is more likely that the influence of his European father and relatives had normalized *racial slavery* — a new and particular form of exploitation born of European transnational capitalist expansion — as a means of economic advancement. As historian of comparative slavery David Brion Davis has noted, many forms and degrees of slavery existed around the world for centuries (and Cherokee captive-taking might arguably qualify as one such form), but racial slavery in the Americas "became the ultimate form of inhuman bondage."[33] For James Vann, acquiring and selling black slaves for profit was not a practice he shared, historically or contemporaneously, with most other members of his nation. Indeed, Vann's embrace of black slavery and his private accumulation of the incredible wealth it created was the principle feature that set him apart from other Cherokees.

From the very start, Vann was intentional about his business plan. In his English-language personal library, he kept a copy of George Fisher's *The American Instructor; or, Young Man's Best Companion*, a British guide to "spelling, reading, writing, and arithmetic," adapted "to the Use of the youth of the United States." The guide promised to "qualify any Person for Business, without the help of a Master" and included instructions on bookkeeping in the Italian manner, account making, waterway shipping practices, legal writing, and business writing. To oversee the daily activities of his many ventures, Vann had hired Valentine Geiger, a German American whose extended family had deep roots in the South Carolina Indian trade.[34] Geiger served as Vann's accountant, secretary, and manager of the Conasauga River store. In addition to Geiger, Vann hired a series of white overseers to supervise his slaves and contracted white workmen to man his blacksmith shop and build new structures. He developed a pattern of in-sourcing skilled labor, bringing in white men to carry out needed tasks. With an eye toward the future, Vann even adopted a "well-bred," orphaned white boy, Aquila Churchwell, whom, the Moravian missionaries supposed, Vann planned to train to manage the local store.[35]

In his business acumen and application, James Vann showed an uncommon talent. He was discontent to labor in a single field of endeavor. He wanted more than a single flagship trading post. He diversified into agricultural production and into providing much-needed services in an isolated area that he could develop and control. He even had plans early on to profit from the extension of U.S. federal services through his area. First, and most consequentially, Vann worked behind the scenes to convince reluctant Cherokee Council members to consent to the laying of a U.S. federal road through Cherokee territory. When Indian agents Benjamin Hawkins and Return Meigs presented their proposal for "a road from this part of Tennessee to the frontier of Georgia," Cherokee leaders balked, fearing the increased traffic of whites through their country and suspecting that a hidden land cession would be written into the deal.[36] But James Vann argued for the turnpike, thinking ahead to the personal profitability such a thoroughfare could bring. Agent Meigs saw Vann as the ideal Cherokee citizen to make the U.S. government's case. Not only was Vann influential enough to win the debate nearly single-handedly, but he was also geographically placed to benefit the most. "[Vann] is conveniently situated," Meigs wrote, "living nearly on the middle of the distance between Tennessee

& Georgia. — He has the means almost in his own hands to effect it. — He will establish a good house of entertainment on the Chattahoochee where the road will cross the river & will keep horses always ready for the mail carriers." And Vann did not disappoint the federal agent, who wrote in a private postscript: "Mr. Vann has done much in bringing the minds of the Indians to the measure of agreeing to the opening of the road, and yet they do not know it, and he wishes it to remain so."[37]

When Vann helped to deliver a hard-won diplomatic victory to the federal government, he was rewarded by the location of the road, which passed directly beside his plantation buildings at Diamond Hill, and by a contract to operate a ferry near the road's path at the Chattahoochee River. And since maintenance would be necessary, Meigs wrote to Secretary of War Henry Dearborn, "A turnpike company can easily be formed for keeping the new road in repair [and] Mr. Vann has authorized me to inform you that he will become a member of it, his engagemt [*sic*] will ensure that business being done to the Satisfaction of the public."[38] Vann profited from the road in numerous ways: a steady flow of customers passed his stores and taverns; he could take part in a road-maintenance company; the U.S. government now owed him a debt of gratitude; and he would benefit from the more efficient route to his own trading destinations. In his enthusiasm for the road, Meigs outlined the incredible savings it would bring to American merchants and their home states, exclaiming: "When the road thro the Cherokee nation is opened, the travel from Knoxville to Augusta and Petersburg in Georgia will not exseed 300 miles — by which the expence of the carriage of goods may be reduced at least 3/7 (tres) wherely There will be saved 17.440 Dollars on this number of [wagon] loads in one year."[39] James Vann was one of the merchants who traveled these routes and would save on the expense of transport, thus increasing his profits.

After ensuring that the new turnpike would lead paying travelers right to his doorstep, Vann then lobbied successfully to manage dispersal of the U.S. mail, which was sure to increase with American traffic. In 1803, William Lovely, assistant U.S. agent to the Cherokees, reported to Meigs, his supervisor: "I am requested by Mr. Vann to inform you . . . Mr. Vann wishes to be engaged in the mail business — so that no person may presume on any prior engagement thro you."[40] Vann's partnership ventures with the U.S. government yielded steady returns over time. Jeremiah Evarts, ABCFM secretary, described the federal turnpike in 1822: "The road from Augusta to Nashville has been a good deal traveled, since it was opened through the Cherokee Nation, eighteen years ago. . . . It has been quite an object, therefore, with several white men, who were settled here, and several natives of the country, to furnish food and shelter to travelers."[41]

In seeking myriad ways to diversify his ventures—through in-sourcing labor, winning government contracts, and dealing in cash as well as bartered goods, James Vann embraced the post–Revolutionary War economic shift that signaled America's first steps toward a commercial market economy. He was ahead of his time *and* place, making choices that were foreign to most Cherokees as well as to most white yeoman farmers in the South. His models may have been his successful trader father and grandfather, or the moneyed white men with whom he did business in coastal cities. He may even have been influenced by southern Indian agent Benjamin Hawkins, who had set up a model plantation on the Chattahoochee River in Creek country soon after his arrival in 1796. Hawkins's farm showcased "demonstration gardens," "scientific" methods, modern tools like the plough, and Hawkins's own transported black slaves. Vann was certainly in contact with Hawkins, as Hawkins wrote a letter advocating for Vann to receive a private trading permit in 1797. Whether Vann's models for expansive agricultural and mercantile ventures were white relatives, Indian agents, or business associates, they surely were not the majority of his fellow, farming Cherokees.[42] For Vann's decisions to use land to produce a surplus crop for profit, to siphon off property from female kin, to accumulate and stash cash inside his home, and even to own black slaves— ran counter to Cherokee common practice. The Cherokee cultural system was oriented around communal life and mutual responsibility, the sharing of material resources and the redistribution of goods. As historian Cynthia Cumfer has explained it, "spiritual and communal principles dictated the material relations of the Cherokees."[43] But Vann sought wealth, and he sought it for himself alone. Although he extended credit to Cherokees who shopped in his establishments and allowed countless visitors to stay in his home and drink his rum, James Vann was not a philanthropist. He adopted an entrepreneurial individualism that was new to Cherokees and indicated an early chink in the Cherokee armor against American cultural imposition. Vann had chosen to be a new kind of Cherokee—a fat cat of the planter elite microculture.

As Vann diversified his ventures and amassed amazing wealth, he also garnered influence with white government officials and Cherokee political leaders. Vann raised a Cherokee settlement from the ground up and then, as would happen, became the headman of the area. Indian agent William Lovely relocated to Vann's jurisdiction and regularly posted letters from Vann's Diamond Hill. In 1806, Vann gained prominence at the highest levels of Cherokee national government when he was elected "as a Chief in the Council," or, a formal member of the Cherokee Council governing body.[44] Soon he found himself hosting core Cherokee government functions, like council meetings and the distribution of annuity payments, on his estate. By 1808, James Vann could be described as one of "the two most powerful men in the nation," and his influence was noted by Cherokees and whites alike.[45] According to his Cherokee contemporaries, as quoted by Secretary of War Dearborn, Vann was a man "of whom care ought to be taken."[46]

James Vann was a maverick merchant-turned-statesman, destined to become the richest man in his region and one of the wealthiest men in his nation. His means set him far apart from most Cherokees, but he was among a small cohort of Cherokee men, many of them his regional neighbors, who were making a fortune from new market opportunities. Just after Vann's death, John Norton said of his establishment: "Mr. Vann, a half Cherokee, the son of a Trader; he had himself been very successful in trade, and had thereby acquired an immense property; he possessed at his death *a hundred negroes* employed on different plantations, besides a great sum in specie, and numerous herds of cattle; horses and hogs."[47] Vann's town drew, as if by magnet, masses of Cherokees and some Creeks, as well as residents, workers, and visitors from backgrounds far beyond the Cherokee borders. He created a cosmopolitan center along the Conasauga River that encompassed the diversity not only of the turn-of-the-century Cherokee Nation but also of the American state that steadily surrounded it.

The Arrival of the Missionaries

Members of the Moravian Church had a long memory of minority status. In fifteenth-century Europe, their Czech forebears had formed a radical sect that challenged the precepts of the Catholic Church long before the formally designated Protestant Reformation. After their first spiritual leader, John Hus, was burned at the stake as a heretic, his followers relocated to Bohemia, called themselves the Unity of Brethren, and embraced values of social equality under the banner of Christian love. Members of the church faced persecution and exile because of their radical vision that undermined the sanctioned belief in social and class hierarchy. They worshipped in underground communities across Eastern Europe until the early 1700s, when a group of German believers who had migrated to Moravia found refuge with Count Nikolaus Ludwig von Zinzendorf of Germany.[48]

Zinzendorf was a Protestant reformer who championed the notion that one knew God through experience and feeling rather then formal religious practice. He was, however, far more traditional in his views on social hierarchy than his new Moravian tenants. As the numbers of Unity of Brethren refugees on Zinzendorf's estate increased, they fused aspects of their radical views with Zinzendorf's interpretation of Protestantism, embracing beliefs in social hierarchy, passionate Christ-centered spirituality, simplicity, pacifism, and fervent international evangelism. Along with this new theology, Zinzendorf and a Council of Elders rethought the structure of community life, developing practices for believers that stressed spiritual communalism. Men and women were separated into age, sex, and marital-status cohort groupings called "choirs," and they lived and worshipped with same-sex choir members rather than with their nuclear families.

In the 1730s and 1740s, in response to both a call to evangelism and renewed persecution in Europe, the Unity of Brethren, or Moravians, formed settlements in North America. They purchased land in Pennsylvania and in North Carolina, creating the communities of Nazareth, Bethlehem, Wachovia, Salem, and so on. Here they replicated their former ethos of dedicated worship, same-sex housing, and purposeful evangelism. As their communities grew and stabilized, the Moravians set their sights on missionary endeavors to the indigenous nations of their new home country.[49]

With missions already established in Greenland, the West Indies, and Delaware, the Moravian Church of the Southern U.S. Province, headquartered in North Carolina, explored the possibility of beginning a mission to the nearby Cherokee Indians. In 1784 and 1790, Moravian representatives broached the notion with Cherokees, to no avail. But in 1796, after the Treaty of Holston had mandated Cherokee advancement toward civilization, the Cherokees expressed lukewarm interest in the possibility of allowing missionaries into the nation. In 1799, Moravian envoys Abraham Steiner and Frederic de Schweinitz met with U.S. Indian agents to gain support for their plans, and in 1800, they convened with the Cherokee chiefs in council to gauge their level of interest. At the council meeting, Steiner and Schweinitz explained their primary aim of introducing Cherokees to God's word and eventual Christian conversion, but the gathered chiefs, including prominent chiefs from the Lower Towns, such as Doublehead, Little Turkey, and Bloody Fellow, resisted.

James Vann was also present at the meeting, and he supported the missionaries' plan, provided that it included an educational component. Uninterested in the religious aspect himself, Vann gambled that having the Moravians build a church inclusive of a school would be better than losing the educational opportunity altogether. In the prime of his early thirties, wealthy, well dressed, and outspoken, Vann must have cut an impressive figure. Although his Upper Towns region near the Georgia-Tennessee border had far less national influence than the Lower Towns toward Alabama, his will held sway. He and his close allies from the Upper Towns, including his wife Peggy Scott's uncle, Charles Hicks, met with the missionaries privately. They hoped the missionaries would settle in their region, giving their children first access to formal education. Together, Vann, Hicks, and their allies not only convinced the other chiefs to grudgingly agree to a missionary establishment, but they also convinced the missionaries to settle near Vann. Already a regional power broker through his ownership of trading posts, now Vann would have a controlling influence over a new and vital Cherokee resource: Euro-American educators. According to nineteenth-century writer John Howard Payne, after the agreement was struck, "James Vann giving [the Moravians] his hand said 'Now I dare call you my country men.' . . . On the following day the Missionaries started with James Vann for Oostenally."[50]

Moravian missionaries were meticulous observers of the world around them, a habit they had developed with the founding of their first missions in the West Indies in order to update their fellow congregants back in Europe.[51] As Steiner and Schweinitz journeyed to James Vann's region in the autumn of 1800, they took in the changing scenes and memorable personalities around them. In a first impression of their host, they wrote: "Mr. Vann is a half Indian but in his dress [,] color and conduct is quite like a white man," and they took immediate notice of Vann's unruly behavior, noting, "he is namely very fond of drinking whiskey."[52] When they arrived at Vann's plantation, they observed that Vann's two wives were spinning thread and weaving cotton. They also noted,

> He had several Negroes and a white overseer who takes care of the plantation. There also was a German named Zeiger who bought hogs for him and Mr. Vann to drive them to Georgia. Mr. Vann had about 100 heads of horses, for as he is a trader he must have a good many pack horses, about 400 heads of cattle and plenty hogs of which the wolves get a good many. Mr. Vann trades mostly to Charleston and Augusta. He gets goods with wagons from the Jews west of Georgia about 70 miles from here and then they are brought here on pack horses.[53]

Vann showed the missionaries all about his property, taking them to his cow pens five miles out and then farther to a "plantation where Vann's mother and sister lived." The next morning, Vann was so busy with customers that he was unable to see the missionaries off as planned. They wrote: "We intended to set off in the morning and Mr. Vann intended to go a piece with us, but [so] many people came to trade with him that our horses were saddled from morning till after dinner. At last he told his customers they had to wait till he came back."[54]

By the end of the tour, Vann and Hicks had proposed two primary sites and two secondary sites to the Moravian envoys, who took the information back to church elders in Salem. The first site on the list was the Springplace plantation near Vann's own home that Vann had promised he would purchase and then sell to the missionaries for their use.[55] Led, they believed, by God's divine guidance, the elders selected Vann's grounds for their Cherokee mission complex. Hence, "[t]he Country about James Vann was finally fixed upon for the Mission settlement & the necessary information being given to & full permission obtained from the Government."[56] The U.S. government not only consented to this plan but also supported the mission with funds and supplies in the interest of Cherokee civilization. Agent Meigs championed the goal of the Moravians "to implant in the hearts of the Cherokees the Knowledge & principles of the Christian & Religion." And although he recognized the triple language barrier that existed between German-speaking missionaries, Cherokee-speaking Indians, and an English-language curriculum, Meigs believed that "[t]he [absence] of an Interpreter will at first be a hindrance to the progress of the mission: but there must be a beginning—If a few minds can be impressed it will be more easily communicated afterwards."[57]

In the spring of 1801, Abraham Steiner and Gottlieb Byhan set out from Salem to begin the first Christian mission in the Cherokee Nation, which they would name the Springplace Mission in keeping with the original plantation site and in honor of the plentiful natural springs in the area. That November, when Steiner returned to Salem for health reasons, accompanied by Byhan, Dorothea Schneider Byhan and Johann Jacob Wohlfahrt traveled to Cherokee country with Byhan to continue the endeavor. They arrived on December 16 and settled in a cabin beside Vann's home since the farm Vann had purchased for them was still occupied by the previous owners. They found that Vann was away on business. "Two days later," they reported "they went to Mr. Vann's place to deliver presents. The younger wife of Vann was not home. His older wife seemed happy over the presents. The small daughter of Vann upon receipt of a gift gave the Byhans a shawl."[58] The women and girls of Vann's family greeted the missionaries with generous hospitality, as was the Cherokee way. Vann's elder wife offered gifts of meat; his sister, Nancy, promised to deliver two milking cows. Meanwhile, Valentine Geiger, the plantation administrator, delivered a letter from Agent Meigs expressing his appreciation and offering assistance of any kind, and James Vann loaned out his enslaved men Tony, Ned, and Tom for the missionaries' use. The relational and material foundations for a successful mission station seemed to be in place.

But as the new year dawned, the Moravians faced disappointment. Their first church service, held on May 10, 1801, did not attract Cherokees, but instead drew an audience of Vann's black slaves.[59] As they strove to hold religious services in Vann's home and in the homes of other Cherokees to broaden their base, they often found Vann, his employees, his slaves, and various visitors drinking whiskey, listening to the fiddle, or completely incapacitated. Brother Steiner lamented in a letter: "It was too bad that I could not preach at Vann's last Sunday. There must have been a dozen white people there, who had been expecting me, as I heard later, and then there were about 30 Indians and several half-breeds. . . . But perhaps it is good I did not go there, for there was whiskey there and everything went topsy turvy."[60] The missionaries found that in addition to excessive drinking, the Cherokees around Vann's place believed in spiritual forces that ran counter to Christian theology. They met one man who "informed them that he was able to catch witches and that recently he had caught a grey haired one."[61]

Soon enough, they also realized that although the Vann family women extended hospitality, what they sought from the missionaries were practical skills, not religious teachings. Peggy Scott and her sister asked Mrs. Byhan "whether she would teach them to sew," but Peggy maintained an emotional distance from the missionaries and ignored their evangelical overtures. For his part, James Vann also "prove[d] by comments that he cares nothing about religion."[62] In June of 1801, as the Moravians finally settled onto the forty-acre farm that Vann had purchased on their behalf (thirty acres of which Vann would retain for his own use), they felt that they had come into a spiritually and morally bankrupt country. "It looks very dark in this land," Brother Byhan wrote, "all sins and scandals are going in full swing and one can see clearly that the prince of this world still keeps them bound with chains of darkness."[63] Even the wild house cats that plagued the missionaries' compound and would "jump on persons, bite them and then run" seemed a party to the evil environment.[64]

The Cherokees' Old World

Part of what the missionaries saw as "chains of darkness" was the negative consequence of European and Euro-American influence. Vann's constant procurement and abuse of alcohol was one such example. But other aspects of life on

Diamond Hill to which the missionaries objected because of their own parochial values were long-standing features of Cherokee cultural practice. The rejection of Christian faith that James Vann and Peggy Scott maintained suggested an unwillingness to forfeit their indigenous views about the nature of things in the spirit world. In addition, Cherokees and black slaves from the area constantly came by the mission to borrow garden seed, turnips, peaches, melons, and other foodstuff. The Cherokee culinary culture of sharing what one had miffed the missionaries, who viewed the Indians in their fields as little more than thieves. "Borrowing is an endless affair here," they wrote, "and we dare not refuse." Instead, to counter this problem, the missionaries set about building fences and asked James Vann to provide them with locks.[65] The Moravians also found that Cherokee ceremonial life was thriving even amid colonial disruption. They described the festival of green corn, which Cherokees commemorated in August to mark the first harvest and to engender a spirit of reconciliation and rebirth. The missionaries wrote of the celebration: "The 15 dances which they performed were quite simple and all were quite rhythmic. The dances were staged on a wide circular enclosure formed by boughs and shrubs. At the center of the carefully swept dancing area was a tall pole at which sat or stood one or two Indians to beat the time and chant words which no one seemed to be able to understand. To Steiner they sounded like hanaaji, hanaaji, hanaai, johnani." The series of dances featuring turtle shell rattles, rifles, bows, and "wild shout[s]" were the very kind of "heathen" activity the missionaries would strive to keep their congregants from attending in later years.[66] And in all of these circumstances, the missionaries depended on interpretation, translation, and pantomime, for everyone around them conversed in Cherokee.

In addition to their expectation of shared provisions, the Cherokees living near Vann's place wanted one thing from the missionaries: an English school where Cherokee children could learn needed skills. In 1803, when the missionaries still had not opened a school, the Cherokee chiefs registered their disapproval, expressing "a wish that the Missionaries might leave the country."[67] If the missionaries could not provide educational lessons, the chiefs complained, there was no reason for them to be in the Cherokee Nation. Even James Vann voiced his displeasure, posting a letter from Diamond Hill to Brother Steiner in Salem as follows: "Sir, I take this opportunity . . . to inform you that the Indians suppose themselves disappointed in their Expectations of having their Youth instructed. . . . I have always acted as a friend to the Business, provided it was carried on agreeably to what was understood by them & myself, that a school should be erected for their Instruction."[68] The desire of the chiefs prevailed. Although the church elders back in Salem regretted the promise of a school, they had no choice but to fulfill it. After they had accepted an enslaved woman purchased by Vann, and thus had the necessary domestic labor, the missionaries launched their educational program. "[W]e take steps, now that we have acquired a Negro woman, to receive 4 Indian children for schooling," they wrote.[69] In January of 1804, the missionaries had a dormitory built for the students, some of whom would board at the mission and others of whom would live in the home of James Vann or his mother.[70] The Moravians had come to Vann's place to impress their faith on the Cherokees, but they found instead a social world where Cherokee cultural ways persevered and Cherokee community agendas predominated.

Although Vann had made their mission possible and benefited financially from the commercial business they provided him (Vann outfitted the mission at a 25 percent markup because, he instructed his clerk to explain, "the transportation of the wares costs a lot"), he was willing to see the Moravians ousted for the greater good of the Cherokee people.[71] James Vann strove for personal gain in ways that exposed Cherokees to white intrusion and influence, but when Cherokees were misled or threatened directly by whites, he leapt to his people's defense. In the realm of economics, Vann acted out of self-interest; in the realm of negotiation with the U.S. government and white settlers, he consistently represented communal interests. He took on the role of ambassador, advocating for Cherokees when they needed a hearing and intervening with the U.S. agents when he saw situations that made Cherokees vulnerable. His letter to the Moravians in support of the chiefs' demand for a school is one such example. In 1801, in another example, Vann wrote to Meigs to lobby for a Cherokee man who had been jailed for stealing a horse. Vann explained that the man had been tricked into the action by white ne'er-do-wells and their Creek co-conspirator. Vann wrote that the captive man's family "wish you to make enquiry respecting the matter and rectifying the mistake." Agent Meigs replied by asking Vann to take depositions of Indian witnesses even though "the Law knows nothing of the Evidence of Indians." In 1802, as the case was ongoing and the Cherokee man was still imprisoned by whites, Vann wrote to Meigs on behalf of "the headmen of Oostenally, Rabbittrap & Cusawattee" to say that these town chiefs wanted the prisoner returned so that he might "have his punishment according to the Law of *this* Country."[72]

Later that year, Vann wrote to Meigs again in the aftermath of a terrible crime. A Cherokee man "happening to come into the [white] settlements [on the Georgia frontier] . . . in a drunken frolic, came to a Plantation, where he behaved shockingly." The man threw a baby into the fire, killed a young woman with a pickax, and molested the woman of the house. Her husband then killed the intruder. James Vann's interest in informing Meigs of this event was to protect other Cherokees from retribution, since whites made a habit of punishing any and all Cherokees for the actions of a few. Vann wrote: "I wish that this circumstance may not make such a sensation, as to breed further troubles. . . . I hope likewise that the government will not look upon it as the [crime] and deed of the Nation, as it certainly was done without the concurrance, nay even without the knowledge of the nation." In this case Meigs agreed with Vann and said that the man had received just punishment: "The white people have no right to consider this murder done by a drunken Indian as an Act of hostility of the Cherokee nation. . . . As a chief having great influence you will [place] the matter in its proper light to the Real People [meaning Cherokees] — I will do the same to the white people."[73]

And in another example, in 1803 Vann sought Meigs's intervention to help catch a white man and his cronies who "stole sixty deer skin from me" and who "whee[p]d an Indian woman and abus[ed] her very much, Likewise took her Earbobs from her." Vann suspected the white man who brutally attacked the Cherokee woman and stole her earrings and her horse of having twice robbed his Chattahoochee River store.[74] It was white men like this, violent and lawless, that Vann labored to keep outside of the Cherokee Nation's boundaries. He consistently fought against proposals to cede tracts of Cherokee land to Euro-American settlers. But the numbers of whites who illegally squatted in Cherokee territory was increasing in the early 1800s. According to Meigs, their tactic was to build homesteads, incite violence with Cherokees, and then pressure the U.S. government to buy the land on which they lived, thus "making a merit of their Crimes."[75]

In 1804, James Vann urged the Cherokee Council to resist selling significant acreage near the Georgia border that was overrun by white squatters headed by the Wafford family. Secretary of War Dearborn hoped Vann would support the sale of "Wafford's tract" and even instructed the U.S. negotiator "to use any means he may possess to induce Van to favor the views of the Government; if by two or three hundred dollars in Money or goods, Van can be induced to use his influence in favor of the cession." Agent Meigs, however, was skeptical of this ploy, noting that Vann was "so independent of mind and circumstances that the ordinary motives for some persons would not succeed with him." Vann, Meigs argued, was too rich and too strong-willed to be effectively bribed.[76]

Vann fought tooth and nail against the Wafford land cession and others to follow, but this was one fight he could not win. Pressed by the U.S. government, and crippled by leaders who did take money made available for bribes, the Cherokee Council agreed to sell Wafford's tract for five thousand dollars.[77] Though he was rapacious in his appetite for wealth, Vann had limits. He would not accept cash, or goods, or land to advance territorial dispossession. Vann bartered a good many things in his life, including, some have said, his soul— but he refused to sell out the Cherokee Nation. This sense of peoplehood and a passionate tie to the homeland were qualities that James Vann shared with many others of his nation. If entrepreneurial individualism and a fervent quest for wealth set Vann apart from his people, ardent patriotism held him within the national fold.

House Hunters

Vann's economic and political influence continued to grow in the first years of the new century. Soon he decided he needed a house to grow along with it. Traditional Cherokee housing had consisted of round-roofed mud plaster (wattle-and-daub) winter homes and blowsy, open-air summer shelters made of wood.[78] In the 1700s, Cherokees changed their primary construction material to timber and began to build year-round dwellings. By the turn of the nineteenth century, Vann and most of his fellow Cherokees lived in snug log cabins, but Vann wanted something more. Inspired, perhaps, by the leggy homes of big-city merchants or by the "respectable white clapboard houses" built by "white leading men of the colonial backcountry," Vann proposed to build a wood-frame house, two stories high, with porches.[79] This was no small undertaking in a remote valley of the Blue Ridge Mountains, where laborers skilled in western architectural design ran scarce.

The building of Vann's new home, begun in 1803, took months of planning and years of construction. His first hurdle, not surprisingly, was location. Vann had hundreds of acres at his disposal, but he also had a number of intimate neighbors, namely his mother and the Moravians, with a vested interest in where he built. Two years prior, the missionaries had moved onto an old farm adjoining Vann's estate, with "land quite level and fertile" bordered by "all-purpose woods."[80] But they now harbored hopes to secure greater independence by relocating at a distance from Vann. They wrote in their mission diary: "Vann's overseer, Crawford, acts as though he were master of our land. Vann is still quite pleasant but he continues to expand into our land more and more. What can we say against the strong hand he wields in this part of the country? We are hardly able to hold onto our houses and I begin to wonder if it is worth the effort to do anything toward building some distance from our place."[81] Even as the missionaries were feeling hemmed in by Vann's plantation expansion, Vann's mother, Wali, was feeling too isolated. She was having a new house of her own built closer to the center of Diamond Hill, where she would live with her husband, Clement, and her grown daughter, Nancy.[82]

The missionaries informed Vann of the place where they wanted to resettle, "on the other side of his field," to which he broached no objection. But several months later, they "heard that Vann was planning to build on a hill close to where we wanted to build."[83] It turns out that Vann did have his eye on a hilltop close to the sand spring, the very hilltop the missionaries had designated. Before the Moravians knew it, Vann's builder, Mr. Vogt, "had arrived to build a house for Vann in back of our field where we had planned to build."[84] The ensuing negotiations grew tense, as Vann told the missionaries to "build somewhere else," adding in a subtle rebuke that indicated he knew they were trying to escape him, that "we weren't too close for *him* and he could get along with us."[85] Since Vann had decided to build his new house on the opposite side of the coveted sand spring, the missionaries chose to remain where they were. They would relocate their mission buildings closer to the small spring near their current station and oversee the construction of additional new structures: two new houses (sixteen by twenty feet), a kitchen, a small house for a new missionary, and workshops for the Indian pupils. The disadvantages, in their view, were that "our fields border on those of Mr. Vann" and "the Negroes would remain quartered in their huts [nearby] until Mr. Vann will have completed his new house."[86]

But just as the missionaries settled on this plan, James Vann changed his mind again. He would not build by the sand spring after all. Instead, he would move into his mother's house and have her move into the missionaries' old building. "I must first get the consent of my mother before I can firmly settle anything," Vann is quoted to have said. Brother Byhan recorded, "[T]hat old Mother Vann refused! But Mr. Vann would not be turned away from his intention, but will build partly on his mother's place." Wali Vann "offered him permission to build at her house," and the matter was finally settled. The Moravians were now "going to build along our Sand spring on an elevation in our cornfield, on the spot where we had planned to build in the first place."[87]

James Vann now commenced to build a two-story house on the "northerly spring" near his mother's place.[88] His original builder, Vogt, seems to have made his exit during the long months of bickering between Vann and the missionaries, and now Vann hired a visitor to the mission, Brother Martin Schneider from North Carolina, along with Brother Byhan, to carry out the bulk of the construction work.[89] Vann contracted Brother Wohlfahrt, as well, to craft the doors, cabinets, and glass-paned windows that would add elements of style to the house.[90] Meanwhile, Vann made plans to build a distillery and commissioned a local millwright to survey locations for a gristmill. The millwright promised that if Vann's "Negroes would build the dam and the house under his supervision," he would build the mill for just $133.50.[91] The mill was operational by August of 1804, while the building of the main house made slow progress.

In April of 1805, when early spring crops were just beginning to sprout, James and Peggy moved into their new plantation home. They gave a gift of two cows to their missionary neighbors, who felt, nevertheless, that the Vanns were now too close for comfort.[92] For unlike white southern planters who signaled high status in the social order by blocking access to their homes through the use of architectural "threshold devices," the Vanns had an open-door policy.[93] Cherokee guests of lower class status were not held back at a gate, the porch, or front rooms of the house but were instead ushered into interior spaces on equal footing with the Vanns. Rich Indians, poor Indians, relatives, passers-through, blacks, whites, enslaved, free—all could be found frequenting the Vann family home. By August, Vann was already hosting tribal council sessions. By December, the home had become a gathering place for raucous social occasions, where visiting Indians sold "spirits" and "Vann's people, Negroes and Indians [,] were all drunk."[94] Vann's house was often so crowded with guests that the missionaries had to meet with him in his mother's home. Watching events unfold around them, the Moravians feared, "It is more and more apparent that no mission station can ever come out of this place where we are now, nor can it be one, because we are too close to Vann's."[95]

As master of this vast estate and owner of this ample home, James Vann stood apart from most of the people in his nation. He was far richer than many of them combined; he did business with the U.S. government; he hired white laborers and supported Christian missionaries. Other Cherokees in the area complained that they were "dissatisfied about the white people that now live around Vann's . . . [and] threatened Mr. Vann that they would take his life if he didn't get rid of the white people."[96] But if Cherokees could not see their lifestyle fully reflected in Vann's, neither could the Euro-Americans whose presence the Indians objected to. Vann stood up for Cherokees in trouble. He fought against the dispossession of Cherokee land. He refused to listen to Christian teachings. He had two wives. He drank with black slaves inside his own house, and he never attempted the kind of order expected of prosperous plantation owners. If the mark of a southern gentleman was his "proper house," surrounded by symmetrical gardens and neatly arranged fields,

Vann's place widely missed the mark.[97] The Moravians lamented that only one Cherokee slaveholder known to them had anything approximating an orderly house and plantation — fellow member of Vann's elite planter class and future principal chief, John Ross.[98] In the missionaries' eyes, even the dirt of Vann's plantation was an unusual combination of elements that hinted at (racial) disorder, made up as it was of a "mulatto top soil with red soil beneath."[99] Despite his great wealth, pale skin, and fine dishware, James Vann could not pass for a white planter of the southern elite. Nor, it would seem, did he wish to.

James Vann's new house was not the grand, brick structure of southern fantasy landscapes. It was, instead, a wood-frame house that symbolized his bicultural experience. Vann built a home to rival log cabins in the area, highlighting his economic standing in the way that a southern slaveholder might. But in direct opposition to the spatial intentions of southern manor homes, he threw his doors wide open to nearly anyone and everyone. In the coming years, Vann's new house would continue to show his acclimation to — and simultaneous rejection of — the Euro-American colonial presence. It stood as the backdrop to scenes of black enslavement and domestic gender violence, even as it served as a staging ground for political resistance to Cherokee oppression.

CHAPTER 3

The Big House/
The Slave Quarter

The ironies of plantation slavery were many and profound, for although
the plantation system was the very reason people of African descent were
enslaved, it also provided them with an arena in which they could begin to
piece back together their shattered lives. . . . Comforted by the fellowship
of the quarters, they were able to confront the injustice of their captivity.
—John Michael Vlach, *Back of the Big House: The Architecture of Plantation
Slavery*, 1993

The Slaves' Plantation Map

The upkeep of the Vann family's household, the operation of their various
business ventures, the growth of their fields and gardens and orchards, and
the care of their personal welfare depended on the toil and suffering of enslaved people of African descent. As in too many other places in the slaveholding South, the lives of those in the "big house," as the master's home was
termed by blacks, and the lives of those in the "quarters" reserved for enslaved
laborers, were inseparably and dreadfully linked on the Diamond Hill plantation. The Vanns depended on human chattel for economic livelihood and the
demanding services of daily life, while black slaves depended on the Vanns for
a hoped-for stability and basic standard of living. In the course of their long relationship, though, Vann family members and the slaves owned by them would
each violate these warped dependencies. The Vanns denied stability and material well-being to their slaves by selling members of the black community, applying corporal punishment, and doling out miserly food and clothing rations.
In turn, enslaved blacks disrupted the Vanns' livelihood and daily routines by
organizing work slowdowns, destroying tools, running away, and taking their
own lives.

When Cherokee travel diarist John Norton arrived at Diamond Hill in
1809, he saw people of African descent as little more than an abstracted labor
force. Norton's reportage on the black slave presence was limited and flat, reducing blacks to a head count and a description of the inanimate dwellings

A preserved slave cabin at Carter's Quarter Plantation, Georgia (formerly in the Cherokee Nation). Courtesy of Hargrett Rare Book and Manuscript Library/University of Georgia Libraries.

they occupied. From Norton's perspective as a traveler who had traversed the Cherokee Nation, Vann's slave quarters stood out: "The house is surrounded by a cluster of *negro* buildings," he wrote, "which give the place the appearance of a village." This villagelike scene that Norton described, created by the assemblage of the main house, slave cabins, and a series of outbuildings, was a hallmark feature of southern plantations in the nineteenth century.[1] Typical in its architectural configuration, the Vann grounds of the early 1800s probably looked something like Virginia plantations described by architect Frederick Law Olmsted on his travels through the South in 1852: "A good many old plantations are to be seen; generally standing in a grove of white oaks, upon some hill-top. Most of them are constructed of wood, of two stories, painted white, and have, perhaps, a dozen rude-looking little log-cabins scattered around them, for the slaves."[2]

Norton gives us the perspective of an outsider looking toward the slave quarters, similar to the view Vann would have had from the porch of his newly built wooden house. But what was the view from the inside of those clustered "negro buildings"? How did blacks enslaved by Vann map and interpret *their* plantation world?

Black men, women, and children working on the Vann estate rarely left testimony about their experience. It is possible, though, to imagine their spatial perspective or, as historian Stephanie Camp has termed it, their "rival geography" and thereby to draw informed inferences about the shape of their lives.[3] Diamond Hill encompassed improved landholdings, agricultural fields, and various industries spreading out at least three to four miles from Vann's big house. Around the main house that Norton described, enslaved individuals and family groupings lived in a set of bare-bones cabins. The residences occupied by Vann's slaves were spare, with dirt floors and poor protection from the elements. Their dwellings would have appeared like many others on southern plantations, "rickety, unpainted, cramped . . . with earth floors and windows without glass, swept by drafts in winter, stifling in the summer heat, choking with smoke, or swarming with insects." Nevertheless, these structures, this bit of plantation ground, was home to enslaved blacks, "the place where the slaves could shut the door on the master — though never with complete assurance of freedom from intrusion — and where their family and communal life could take root and take shape."[4]

This set of central structures housed slaves who operated Vann's stable, worked in the barn, transported goods, packages, and letters, carried messages, handled negotiations with whites, did housework and cooking, served as personal attendants to adults and children in the Vann family, engaged in agricultural work, and even, on occasion, worked as criminal investigators. A string of slave residences also stretched alongside Vann's acres of cultivated fields, apart from the main house complex. Blacks who lived here cleared forested land, worked Vann's fields and orchards, and were periodically dispatched to his Chattahoochee River plantation to do the same. Black men could be summarily assigned to haul building materials and raise new structures. Black women were often called on to care for Vann family members or their friends in times of illness. Boys were told to search the woods for stray pigs or other items, and girls were sent to the Moravian mission to assist with domestic work and childcare. Respected older black men and women were sometimes assigned supervisory roles, and very elderly slaves were loaned out until they

Mill Creek, a location of Diamond Hill slave cabins. Courtesy of the Chief Vann House.

were too frail to work any longer. On the northern border of Vann's estate near Mill Creek, another set of a dozen slave cabins housed workers who operated the mill. Many of these laborers were African-born, as was the elderly couple that tended Vann's cattle, also based at the plantation's edge. Beyond this plantation border was wild woodland forest, punctuated by widely spaced Cherokee farms.[5]

Slave quarters on the Vann estate were divided into sectors, with some cabins located close to the big house and others situated far across Vann's fields near his milling and cattle enterprises. Blacks stationed on the far corners of the plantation could not spy the big house from their vantage point, rarely saw their Cherokee master, and almost never saw whites. Enslaved supervisors operated the mill, and the cow pens were run solely by blacks, who sometimes played host to an occasional traditionalist Cherokee houseguest, such as a healer named Earbob. Blacks in the field cabins also lived lives apart from the big house, although they were subject to command by a hired white overseer during the workday. Even slaves posted close to the Vann home, those with the least privacy from their owners, far outnumbered the Cherokee family they served and the handful of whites working for Vann. Far off in the mill cabins, and closer in at the field cabins, black slaves hosted dances that were attended by fellow slaves as well as invited Cherokees. By all indications, slaves on James Vann's premises traversed the plantation at will, visiting various slave quarter enclaves in the evenings, on weekends, and on holidays. Enslaved blacks were therefore not only part of distinct neighborhoods zoned by location and the type of labor carried out there but also part of a larger circle of resident blacks whose lives were intertwined. While traveler John Norton could look upon the first set of slave quarters as dependencies to the main house "village," slaves posted there could look beyond the main house to a black, and increasingly African, sphere of life.

The precise size of the black population on Vann's estate at any given moment is impossible to pinpoint, since those numbers changed over time and complete business records of Vann's concerns did not survive into the present day. Documentation does show, however, that James Vann purchased many slaves at once, in groups of twelve and even twenty, and that upon his death he owned more than one hundred human beings. Of the thirty-seven slaves whose place of birth was recorded by Moravian missionaries, fourteen were said to be from Africa.[6] Vann's sizeable unpaid workforce placed him in the social and economic category of the southern planter, which historians have defined as a person in possession of twenty slaves or more. As a member of this group, Vann stood out as one of a privileged few in the South. As late as 1860, only 12 percent of white slaveholders fit this description of a planter, and most of those owned only twenty to thirty slaves. Vann's reported ownership of more than one hundred slaves in 1809 elevated him to the highest and most rare class of planters — those who owned estates that could be classified as manors.[7] Vann stood out, too, for his ability to hire overseers. For most southern slaveholders, hiring a plantation manager was a luxury that could scarcely be afforded.[8] Within the United States, the scale of Vann's enterprise was exceptional; within the Cherokee Nation, it was extraordinary. John Norton described Vann as one of the two largest slaveholders he encountered while on his travels, and historian William McLoughlin called Vann "a member of the new entrepreneurial class" who was "perhaps the wealthiest man in the Cherokee Nation."[9]

In the first years of the 1800s, when Vann was growing his estate, black slaves were available to him from a number of sources. Like other Cherokees who descended from white propertied fathers, Vann inherited enslaved men and women. He could also pay or trade for slaves in a small intranational exchange of blacks who were taken as booty by Cherokees during the Revolutionary War or other conflicts.[10] He could buy slaves from the Creeks or other southern tribes.[11] He could travel to major port cities like Charleston to purchase newly arrived Africans, and he could purchase slaves in any number of places across the South. He would, of course, also benefit from the natural increase of the slaves he already owned. The records do not suggest that professional slave traders visited Diamond Hill with merchandise for sale during

James Vann's lifetime. This is perhaps because Vann himself served as a provider of human chattel to others in the area, making black men, women, and children another lucrative commodity produced by his farms.

Vann regularly dispersed blacks on loan to members of his family and nearby residents, separating black families in the process and violating loving bonds. Along with sales of wheat, sugar, beef, and salt, Vann rented James, Mima, and Johnson to Major William Lovely, assistant U.S. agent to the Cherokees.[12] He also regularly dispersed black children. "James Vann namely had the habit," the missionaries wrote, "of giving Negro children to his relatives and acquaintances to raise and was happy and thankful when they received their upkeep and learned to work in *this* manner."[13] When Lovely's wife needed a slave girl, she got one from Vann. And when "Mrs. Lovely no longer needed the little girl, [Vann] gave her to [the missionaries]." Before this second trade-off took place, "Vann gave the child's mother to his sister."[14] On another occasion, when the Moravian missionaries were displeased with an enslaved woman Vann had bought on their behalf for "$350 dollars cash" and asked to return her, they revealed that Vann maintained purchase orders for slaves: "Vann showed irritation about [the request] until I referred him back to our order. He will sell her to someone else who had also ordered one by him."[15] Vann also caught and remanded runaway slaves when he came upon them hiding in his vicinity.[16] With his frequent travels to slave-market cities and purchase of blacks "in bulk" for sale, James Vann could include slave trading among his many business activities.

From the time that he took over his father's trading post in the late 1700s to the successful development of his plantation enterprise in the first decade of the nineteenth century, James Vann learned many tricks of the southern slaving trade. He absorbed acreage and acquired slaves, worked them hard, and sold them. He employed corporal punishment to exact his slaves' obedience and staged their public executions to instill group fear. And beyond his authorization of harsh disciplinary methods, Vann sometimes rampaged through the slave quarters, terrorizing his bondsmen and -women with the sheer unpredictability of his actions. One night, for no known reason, he burned down the cabins of two black families "and would have burned them all if Mr. Geiger and some more white people, who were there, had not prevented him from doing so."[17]

In many ways, James Vann's actions as a mean and avaricious expropriator of black slave labor seemed indistinguishable from those of white southern planters.[18] And when the passage of time is taken into account, there was, in fact little difference between the ways that Cherokee elites and white elites were prepared to commodify their human property. True, Cherokee slaveholding in the early 1800s still incorporated flexible features similar to American colonial slaveholding of the 1600s, such as recognition of slaves' linguistic and interpretive skills, wide allowances for slaves' property ownership and independent economic activities, and lesser containment of slaves' mobility (no evidence of bondspeople needing passes to travel or of regular slave patrols exists in the Diamond Hill record), but when Cherokees were introduced to black chattel slavery in the mid- and late 1700s, Euro-Americans had already had a century and a half's head start in the business. Over time, James Vann became a more capable and profit-producing planter, making him similar, in terms of slaveholding practices, to southern white elites. His penchant for drinking and merrymaking with slaves inside his home was one feature of social life that continued to set him apart from most white planters. But James Vann's son, Joseph, would take this transformation even further, eschewing social contact with blacks and exhibiting "an intense devotion to the capitalistic spirit of accumulation" that southern planters shared.[19]

By the time Joseph Vann and other wealthy Cherokees reestablished plantations in Indian territory in the mid-1800s, they had adopted a strict legal system of restriction and punishment for enslaved blacks. With time and experience, members of the Cherokee slaveholding elite, a microcultural minority in Cherokee society to be sure, adopted the practices, and even the race-based authoritarian identity, of white southern slaveholders. Enslaved blacks transported to Diamond Hill in the early 1800s thus faced a bleak, unambiguous bondage, even as their experience of relative physical mobility, economic opportunity, and a degree of social interaction with people outside of the slave class surpassed that of peers living on many white-owned plantations.

Four Women

The routes enslaved blacks took in their forced journeys to Diamond Hill were varied, circuitous, and arduous. Caty, a woman described as having a "very sweet attitude of heart" and an "honest disposition," was "born in Cherokee country." Caty's birth to black parents already living within the Cherokee Nation had meant her immediate and prolonged exposure to Cherokee lifeways. The missionaries said of Caty, "Like the Indians themselves, [she] was ignorant of God and godly things," suggesting inadvertently that she was knowledgeable, instead, of Cherokee things. Like other enslaved blacks who had lived their entire lives in a larger Cherokee context, Caty most certainly spoke Cherokee, perhaps to the detriment of her English-language ability.

Caty may have been the child of slaves owned by Peggy Scott Vann's family, for she worked as a personal servant to Peggy, and, according to the missionaries, "her mistress . . . loved and protected her to an unusual degree." Peggy's feelings of attachment to Caty were most evident when Caty became deathly ill and "Mrs. Vann nursed [her] with much faithfulness as though it were her own child." Upon Caty's death, Peggy Vann longed "to bury her in her garden in order [to] recall at her grave the last days and hours as well as happy departure from this life of this Negress whom she really loved dearly." But Peggy's depth of feeling for Caty was not boundless. When Caty, on her deathbed, needed to be moved out of her slave quarter cabin, Peggy did not have Caty transported to the big house but arranged instead for Caty to sleep in the plantation's weaving house, where she died in 1808.[20]

Unlike Caty, who was born on Cherokee land, Patience was born in "Guinea" (a reference, most likely, to Senegambia) on the African continent. She wore "an old felt hat, which was completely torn up," and she spoke her native African tongue interspersed with broken English. After surviving the unspeakable trauma of the Middle Passage, Patience "arrived in Charleston with some other Africans." James Vann purchased her there in the winter of 1805, and she was among "twelve quite new ones whom he bought from a ship and brought along, presumable to resell part of them." Patience would have arrived on a ship like the *Louisa*, which delivered ninety-nine Africans purchased in Goree and Senegambia to the Charleston port that year, or a ship like the *Hiram*, which transported 103 slaves to Charleston after losing 10 percent of the "cargo" en route. After the purchase, Vann forced the shoeless Patience to walk nearly 375 miles to Diamond Hill. Patience's feet froze on the long journey, and she forever lost the use of them. To carry out her assigned duties in the plantation's weaving house, where she pulled cotton for Peggy Vann, Patience had to "scoot on her knees." To secure enough food for her two young children, she was compelled to drag herself across the long distances of Vann's estate. After their first encounter with Patience when she came seeking food for her hungry little ones, the missionaries reported in their diary: "We had to cry when we saw her coming while crawling on her knees across the field with her two little friendly children at her side. She cried as well. Dire distress had driven her here and then she had lost her way in the woods."[21]

Becoming disabled due to the cruel indifference of her master was just one of Patience's many, many sorrows. Patience married an African man called Gander, who was also new to Diamond Hill. Gander's "barnyard animal" first name and lack of a surname reflected the absence of dignity reserved for him in a slaveholding society. In 1806, Gander, who was said to be "Mr. Vann's favorite," died in Mill Creek after he reportedly "jumped into the water to bathe."[22] In 1810, when Patience made a request to move in with her second husband, who worked at Vann's mill, she learned that he had been sold by the administrators of Vann's estate and would soon be transported out of the Cherokee Nation. Patience's unfathomable emotional suffering was exacerbated by physical abuse. In 1813, while in her third trimester of pregnancy, she was "horribly beaten" by Samuel Tally, overseer at Diamond Hill and husband to Nancy Vann. After this vicious assault, Patience was unable to move and "remained lying on the spot where he had abused her for several hours."[23] Whatever became of Patience and her little ones after this date is unknown. This terrible moment is the last notation on Patience's life to appear in the Moravians' Springplace Mission Diary.

Grace, a devout Christian, came to Diamond Hill in 1808, the same year in which Caty died. She did not hail from as close as Cherokee country or as far away as Africa. James Vann had purchased her family members along with several other women, men, and children from a slave owner gone bankrupt in Virginia. The bonds between Grace and her loved ones proved indelible. For Grace had been legally free in Virginia and "came into this land out of love for her husband and children," who were now the property of James Vann. Grace was sixty-seven at the time her arrival, and her husband, Jacob, was of similar age. Like the million and more slaves who were sold from the Upper South to the interior South and Southwest in what Ira Berlin has called the "migration generations" of the early 1800s, this elderly couple, abruptly uprooted, was forced to make new lives in what was to them a foreign country.[24]

In Virginia, Grace had been industrious and financially savvy, perhaps applying her skills in sewing to purchase her freedom and earn income for her family. She would experience a reversal of circumstances when her family was sold to Vann. After arriving at Diamond Hill, Grace lamented that "she had to leave behind on the loom a piece of cotton cloth from which she wanted to make some clothes for her children, as well as eighteen dollars that someone owed her. During her journey through Georgia, some blankets were also stolen from her, so she arrived poor as a church mouse." Worse, after relocating to Diamond Hill, Grace would be classed among the slaves there.

Grace's husband, Jacob, who had been highly valued by his former owner, was appointed to supervise the work at Vann's mill. Grace assisted in this managerial task and also became a revered mother figure to many female slaves on the estate. Grace gave counsel to Jenny and Pleasant, organized the burial of slave children, and during the long illness that eventually took Caty's life, Caty was under "Grace's care." The missionaries summarized Grace's potent influence, writing: "She is appreciated by her mistress as an intelligent faithful negress, and respected by the negroes as a mother."[25]

While Grace arrived at Diamond Hill a convert to Christianity, Pleasant firmly rejected the faith throughout her entire life. As a slave owned by the Wachovia Administration of the Moravian Church, Pleasant is said to have proclaimed to slaves on the Vann estate: "[T]hese people's religion is nothing but hypocrisy, this place is a very hell on earth."[26] Pleasant knew of what she spoke. The Moravians, who professed a passionate love for Christ, sanctioned the ownership of black slaves.[27] Before her sale to the church, Pleasant had been the slave of Caspar Stolz, a farmer who lived near the Moravian settlement of Bethabara in North Carolina. Stolz was eager to sell Pleasant, who was three months pregnant (it may be surmised, by Stolz's own transgression). And since the Moravian missionaries had in mind a "Negress long desired for Springplace," who could perform the domestic labor for the church and school, they accepted Stolz's overture and rock-bottom price point. The church records indicate that "[t]he Negress Pleasant, bought for the Cherokee mission, was paid for in 16½ acres of land and fifty dollars in cash, so cost only one hundred and thirty dollars."[28] The newly appointed chief missionary to the Cherokees, John Gambold, was given power of attorney over Pleasant, who was considered "among the assets" of the Moravian Church.[29]

Brother John Gambold had "often expressed his willingness for service of the Gospel among the heathen," and in September of 1805, he set out on a 400-mile journey from North Carolina to the Springplace Mission.[30] With him was Sister Anna Rosina Kliest Gambold, the new wife he had sought to join him in this calling. Anna Rosina, whose marriage to John had been sanctioned by the church, was highly regarded among Moravians in her own right. She was a poet, artist, botanist, and former beloved schoolteacher in the Bethlehem, Pennsylvania, Moravian settlement. Later she would be described by a famous New England poet as "[t]hou mild Moravian sister" of "tender and ardent zeal" who "discharged her duties" with "the most tender sentiments of piety."[31] Despite these apparent graces, Anna Rosina Gambold relied on the labor of black slaves, and "[took] with her [to Cherokee country] a black Servant, named Pleasant, the better to be able to get the necessary housework done, which is much increased by boarding and washing for said scholars."[32]

To John Gambold's expressed displeasure, Pleasant, being far advanced in her pregnancy, was unsuited for the difficult journey. John Gambold complained that Pleasant's condition had not only slowed their pace but also cost them additional funds:

[W]e used up $94.34 which is a terrible amount for such a trip. A lot of that is to be charged to the confinement of Pleasant, for in addition to the fact that I had to pay $4 to the midwife and nurses, we lost a lot of time for her sake; for two days we lay on one spot, then we traveled but like snails, 8, 9, 10 miles a day, and during that the consumption of provisions for man and beast went on continuously.... But we have to give thanks that in addition to Pleasant another little negro or mulatto has been acquired for the Mission.[33]

Church leaders agreed with Gambold's assessment that despite the cost and inconvenience, Pleasant's delivery of a child was fortuitous. A report to the conference of elders exclaimed: "The Black Pleasant has now been entered in the Administration books. On Sept. 29th, on the Way to Spring Place, she gave birth to a mulatto infant.... I hope the Brethren may be fortunate enough to raise him for useful service, such as plowing and the like."[34]

The white paternity of Pleasant's baby boy, a "mulatto infant," in the Moravians' words, became clear upon his birth. Because Pleasant was in her forties when the baby was born, this child was probably not her first. Perhaps she had been forced to leave a family behind when she was sold and then transported out of state. The Moravian records are silent on this dim probability.[35] Adding insult to heartless injury, once Pleasant's child was born en route, the Gambolds assumed the right to name him. They would call the baby Michael in remembrance of his arrival on the Christian holiday, St. Michael's Day. On Michael's first birthday, when he had become "a pretty, sturdy boy . . . a very nice looking child," John Gambold deemed Pleasant an unfit mother and declared his and his wife's intentions to further delimit her parental role. Gambold wrote about Michael: "[F]rom time to time some Negro naughtiness does show itself, and his mother does not have [the] gift to train him, therefore his god-mother Anna Rosel will have to assume chief responsibility for his bringing up when he is a little older. A short time ago we had to take a firm stand with her, Pleasant, so that I almost had to reach for the whip."[36]

No matter how many times she might have been threatened by Gambold's whip, Pleasant never settled in to her life in the Cherokee Nation, never accepted her role as the Mission slave. Pleasant thwarted her Christian owners at every turn, answering their demands with sarcasm, working at her own pace, and spreading negative information about them to slaves on the Vann plantation. The missionaries often complained of her sharp tongue and lack of diligence, even as they confessed their absolute dependence on her labor. In

1819, the Gambolds wrote about Pleasant: "The Negro woman Pleasant is not as useful to the mission as she probably should be; at times she is disagreeable, due to her sulky behavior, and offensive and injurious to others, due to her scolding and swearing. Nevertheless a servant is indispensable for milking, laundering, cooking, baking etc., and one cannot deny that this work, which is no small matter in our household establishment, has hitherto been done by her in great part."[37] This was just one of a series of criticisms, many of them much harsher and inclusive of the threat of violence, lodged against Pleasant by the missionary couple.

Pleasant longed to return to North Carolina, where perhaps she had older children, other relatives, a husband. In 1811, when a rumor circulated that all whites would soon be expelled from the Cherokee Nation, Pleasant was "beside herself with joy," thinking that the Moravians would be forced to go home.[38] But this did not occur, and Pleasant worked at the Springplace Mission until she reached her seventies, when she was "too old to be able to do much anymore."[39] In the end, Pleasant would spend nearly twenty-five years of her life in Cherokee country, a greater span of time than any of the missionaries sent by the Moravian Church spent there.

A Community of Slaves

Pleasant and Patience, Caty and Grace, were single individuals on the Vann estate whose lives were interwoven with those of many other people of African descent. Although they did not possess themselves by Cherokee law or custom, every slave on Diamond Hill possessed a name, a life, a story. Nearly one hundred of these souls are identified in the descriptions of daily events found in the Moravian Springplace Mission Diary (and listed in Appendix 2 of this book). As family members, companions, confidants, and competitors, all of the slaves on the Vann plantation, named and unnamed, comprised a sizeable black community like few others in the pre-Removal Cherokee Nation. And the place where they lived, the slave quarters of Diamond Hill, was the site of an active, diverse, dynamic, sometimes secret community existence.

Despite the harsh and unforgivable nature of chattel slavery, blacks developed viable family and community lives in North America. Those located on the same landholdings knew each other as intimates, depended on one another in the struggle to survive, and reinforced cultural knowledge and practices derived from their African homeland. Though not utopian by any means, black communities in slavery were real. As Stephanie Camp has described it, "Even as slave 'communities' were fractured by rifts of status, gender, and personal conflict, bondpeople living in the rural South also typically understood themselves as a common people, a contradictory, unequal 'we.'"[40] This was especially the case where enslaved blacks were in the majority and isolated from whites for long months out of the year, such as on the Georgia and South Carolina coastal plantations where African-based Gullah culture was nurtured for centuries. But the creation and continuation of interactive black communities also occurred on large inland plantations, where segregated slave quarters drew a veil of separation between the lives of slaves and the oversight of their owners, thereby allowing for some degree of autonomy and privacy for enslaved blacks. Behind this curtain, Africans and African Americans courted, married, bore children, raised families, tended the sick, grew gardens, ran an economy, shared spiritual observances, held social gatherings, celebrated joys, nursed sorrows, created art, and mourned and buried their dead. On James Vann's plantation, where the Cherokee master gave no indication of paternalist interest in his slaves and was frequently away on business, where the white population was a small minority, and where the farthest set of slave residences was located a full three miles away from the big house, blacks were able to attain degrees of autonomy. The Moravians, frustrated at this circumstance, commented that "[t]he negroes here have too much liberty, so that one does not get much from them," and complained that "[w]hen [Vann] is not at home then his negro people carry on terribly."[41]

Of the 583 black slaves in the Cherokee Nation in 1809, the Vann family possessed 115, nearly 20 percent of them. Well-off families (most of them mixed-race and headed by white men) owning ten slaves or more possessed another 124 of all black slaves in the nation at that time. The Vanns, together with the next eight richest families, owned between one-third and one-half of the 583 slaves in Cherokee country. This meant that although most Cherokee slave owners possessed only a few slaves, one out of three blacks in the Cherokee Nation in this period knew a large farm or plantation experience. Put another way, a significant proportion of blacks in Cherokee country lived on the ample plantations of a few Cherokee elites in the first years of the nineteenth century. By 1835, when the slave population had almost tripled, those numbers of elite ownership would hold steady, with forty-two of the wealthiest families owning over 525, or nearly a third, of the 1,592 slaves in the nation.[42]

These approximate figures are important for understanding the experience of black slaves among Cherokees. As scholars of Cherokee slaveholding have documented, prior to Removal, most Cherokee-owned slaves resided on smaller farms where daily contact with their owners was common and relative integration into Cherokee familial and social affairs was likely. However, a sizeable number of Cherokee-owned slaves — one out of three — had an experience that more closely approximated that of slaves in the white antebellum South, where "a majority belonged to holders of twenty or more."[43] Blacks enslaved by Vann met and exceeded this normative southern plantation experience. For Vann's plentiful plantation housed numbers of blacks that surpassed those congregated in all but the largest white-owned concerns. Here on Diamond Hill, bondsmen and -women were able to develop a sense of communalism, interdependency, and group identity in relationship with other blacks. As the flagship plantation in its region, Diamond Hill housed a vigorous black community, and the slave quarters there, a black social and cultural domain, became a meeting ground for other people of African descent in the area.

As the stories of Caty, Patience, Grace, and Pleasant illustrate, in the early 1800s the black community on Diamond Hill was composed of a diversity of people and family groupings, each with distinct experiences and backgrounds. The majority of slaves there were Afro-American English speakers, having been acquired from other parts of the United States. Pleasant was among this group, as was Grace, and the young woman Jenny, whom Grace took under her spiritual wing. In the white communities from which they came, each of these women was exposed to a different sect of Christianity: Pleasant to Moravian Protestantism, Grace to mainstream Protestantism, and Jenny to Catholicism.

A second population among the enslaved community was newly arrived Africans, who, according to John Norton, were favored by Cherokee owners. Although they "did not yet speak either English or Cherokee," African slaves were, in Norton's words, "simple and honest, for which reason, the Cherokees esteem them more than those who are brought up in the United States."[44] The Africans purchased by James Vann represented a potential range of West African ethnic and language groups. Many of them probably hailed from Senegambia, the region that South Carolina and Georgia planters preferred. One African man on Diamond Hill called Suniger Jacob was said to be from the Tjamba Nation, known by Europeans as the Kassenti tribe. Suniger Jacob's homeland would have been in the Dagomba territory of northern Ghana, but his unusual name indicated that he might also have spent time at a Dutch slave fort or in the Dutch West Indies.[45] One woman on Diamond Hill, Crawje, retained what seems to have been an African name, and there may have been others like her whose appellations do not appear in the missionary records. Patience was African-born, and so were Betty, her husband, July, and her relative, the aforementioned Crawje, none of whom could communicate well with English or Cherokee speakers without an interpreter. This interpretation duty was often carried out by Grace's husband, Jacob, who said he picked up bits and pieces of the Africans' language from living with them in the slave quarters at the mill.[46]

A third group in the black community was made up of slaves who had been born in the Cherokee Nation and spoke the Cherokee language. These individuals might best be described as Afro-Cherokee in cultural orientation. Caty was among this group, as was Isaac, an accomplished fiddler who sometimes played at James Vann's parties. Isaac was smart, resourceful, and brave, and he could often be found in the company of his wife, to whom he was greatly attached. Isaac's translation abilities were so regarded that the missionaries expressed relief when he was in the vicinity because he could translate for Cherokees visiting the mission.[47] Isaac even succeeded in bartering his Cherokee fluency for lessons in English literacy. In 1802, the missionaries recorded: "The Negro Isaac found out from Br. Byhan what he would have to give if he gave him instruction in reading. Br. Byhan replied that he wouldn't expect anything from him, except that in return he should give him instruction in the Cherokee language, which he promised to do."[48] Though Isaac stood out for his personal dynamism and linguistic skill, other slaves on the Vann plantation also spoke Cherokee. Toney "grew up among the Indians here in this country and understands and speaks their language as well as English."[49] The missionaries purchased earthenware bowls from two Indian women, thanks to the "Negro [who] was [their] interpreter for this." They were grateful, likewise, when blacks owned by Vann came to work for pay on Sundays, because the missionaries could "at least speak some with the Indians through them."[50]

This third group among the enslaved population also may have included the offspring of Cherokee and black couplings. For in the Cherokee Nation as a whole, children inherited the clan status of their mothers. Biracial Afro-Cherokee children likewise followed the condition of enslaved mothers unless their fathers intervened to secure their freedom. There are hints in the historical record of sexual relations between Cherokee owners and enslaved blacks in this pre-Removal period, suggesting that such interactions did occur, though not with great frequency. An example is the story of Coyeetoyhee and Sarah. Coyeetoyhee was among the group of Cherokees who, along with James Vann's uncle, John, attacked a company of white settlers led by Colonel James Brown after the Revolutionary War. Coyeetoyhee captured black slaves during the raid, including a fifteen-year-old girl named Sarah. Twenty-eight years after the episode, Brown's son and members of the Tennessee militia broke into Coyeetoyhee's home on the Flint River. The party forcibly seized the eight blacks living there, collectively valued at $1,200, to return them to slavery in the Brown household. Coyeetoyhee protested the seizure to Indian agent Return Meigs, arguing in a written complaint that he "became possessed of said Sarah according to the laws of war." By this time, Sarah had seven children, ranging in age from two to twenty-three years. With the exception of the two eldest, all of the children had Cherokee names. Richard Taylor, the interpreter and scribe for Coyeetoyhee, added as a supplementary note at the bottom of Coyeetoyhee's appeal: "All the children & grandchildren descendents of Sarah as before stated are of mixed Blood, their fathers are Cherokees."[51]

Another example pointing to sexual relations between Cherokee owners and black slaves comes from the second Moravian Mission, called Oothcaloga, in Cherokee territory. Missionary John Gambold wrote the following about Susanna Ridge, wife of Cherokee statesman Major Ridge and a frequent visitor to the mission:

> On Sunday the 13th of this month, Sister Ridge had to speak seriously with a young person, her half brother's son, about his lewdness towards her Negro woman. This, which she had already done repeatedly without fruit, made him angry and since no one else was in the house (Major Ridge and his son have been called to a "Council" of the Creeks) this person grabbed his aunt Mrs. Ridge and struck her so that she has been in bed since. Then he went to an Indian who [had told] Mrs. Ridge about his relationship with the Negro woman, and beat him so that he could hardly crawl home.[52]

This description of sexual misbehavior and domestic violence points to exploitative intimate relations and the possibility of mixed-race offspring in the enslaved population of the Cherokee Nation.

Finally, a vaguely worded case from the extended Vann family history indirectly suggests relations between a Cherokee woman and a black or Afro-Cherokee man. In 1819, Agent Meigs asked David McNair and Richard Taylor to go to "Samuel Tally's residence and demand & receive into your care a certain colored boy named James, son of Sarah Vann, whose affidavit with other papers explaining the business I have put into the hands of Captain Taylor." The accompanying papers were not preserved, but Meigs's cover letter outlines a situation in which Samuel Talley, Vann's notoriously cruel overseer, seized an Afro-Cherokee child and held him as a slave. The child's mother, Sarah Saunders Vann, appealed to Meigs, and Meigs threatened Talley with the force of the "magistrate of Georgia," promising "to prosecute as far as shall be necessary to secure the freedom of said James."[53]

Although the precise relationship of Sarah Saunders Vann to the Diamond Hill Vanns is uncertain, the involvement in her case of Talley, Vann's former overseer, and David McNair, Vann's son-in-law, indicates that she and her son moved through Diamond Hill's orbit. A review of genealogy and census records further suggests that Sarah may have been descended from the Cherokee Saunders (or Sanders) family who lived relatively near Diamond Hill in the Coosawattee and Etowah districts. The extended Saunders family included slaveholders, and Sarah may have had a child with a black man before later marrying a Vann. She may also, it may be conjectured, have married a Vann who was partly of African descent. James Vann did have children by unknown women, and not all of his children were named in his will. It is possible, though not verifiable, that James Vann had a son with a black woman and that this son took the Vann surname, married Sarah Saunders, and had a "colored" child with her. Even more intriguing is the fact that Sarah's kidnapped son was called James. Although it has proven impossible to reconstruct Sarah and the missing boy's link to the Diamond Hill Vanns, it is clear that the boy and his mother warranted the immediate action of the Cherokee agent. In his last lines to the would-be rescuers, Meigs wrote: "Your compliance with my request . . . may save a human being from slavery—who has a natural right to his freedom." And in an urgent postscript Meigs added: "I wish this letter to be kept safe. I have not time now to copy it."[54]

Little evidence documents sexual relations between Cherokee owners and black slaves, which would likely have taken place in private spaces beyond the purview of outside observers. But the scant information that does exist indicates that a minority of slaves in the Cherokee Nation had Cherokee and black forebears. This was probably also the case in the large black population on Diamond Hill. Like Caty, Isaac, and Toney, members of this group would best be described as Afro-Cherokee—in ancestry as well as cultural orientation.[55]

Because Diamond Hill was the site of the largest black community in the Cherokee Upper Towns, enslaved blacks from nearby plantations and free blacks from various walks of life often visited there. A midwife from a neighboring plantation came to Vann's place to tend "an African woman in her confinement." When the midwife visited the newborn two weeks later, she "found the baby very frail." The midwife carried the ailing child to Pleasant in the mission kitchen, and the baby died in Pleasant's arms. Sam Kerr, a free, self-described "Ethiopian" preacher from South Carolina with "white hair" and the ability to "read well," traveled to the area to visit old acquaintances and to urge the slaves at Vann's toward a Christian awakening. Indian pupils at the Springplace Mission became attached to Sam Kerr, broke into tears when he was injured by a billygoat, and influenced the missionaries' decision to tend Sam's wounds and offer him shelter.[56] The lives of these enslaved and free blacks and many more were knit together into the fabric of community. As

African-descended people whose stories unfolded on common ground, they shared the rhythms, losses, and pleasures of everyday life in the Cherokee Nation.

The community created by blacks on Diamond Hill in the early 1800s had core features in common with slave communities across the South. Blacks there forged and maintained family ties to the very best of their ability. They developed an economy in which they tended their own garden plots, worked on their days off to earn money, sold and traded with Indians, and possessed a variety of personal goods. A Cherokee law in 1819, the first to consider slaves' economic activities, reviewed the case of a "runaway negro man" who had sold a stolen horse to a Cherokee called Otter Lifter. The Cherokee National Committee heard the case and found that the runaway's former owner was not liable for the illegal sale, since masters held no responsibility for any "contract or bargain entered into with any slave or slaves." Not only did this decision document that slaves acquired property and entered into contracts, but it also assigned a degree of autonomy to slaves in their business dealings. Although Cherokee restriction on slaves' property rights would tighten over time with the passage of an 1824 act banning slaves' ownership of "horses, cattle, or hogs," in the early 1800s blacks owned by the Vanns had the license to earn money, acquire diverse goods, and engage in economic exchanges.[57]

The slaves' economy at Diamond Hill was well developed, and by every indication, blacks there knew the monetary value of their labor. The missionaries once complained that the "negroes and negresses are in fact willing to earn something extra on Sundays" but that they charged "⅛ per dollar and food" for a day of hoeing, a price the missionaries deemed too high. Blacks used their personal earnings to supplement Vann's meager clothing allowance. The missionaries recorded in 1806: "[S]ome of Vann's Negroes, men and women, who had asked to assist us on Sunday with the great amount of fieldwork which we now have, arrived for this purpose. We showed them plenty of work, which they undertook with pleasure. They only receive *one* piece of clothing from their master each year, so they are happy to find an opportunity to earn something for themselves on Sunday and to be able to dress themselves as needed."[58] Blacks also used their economic wherewithal to acquire special possessions of which they felt protective. When southern slaves faced property theft, they sought justice by publicly revealing the crime in song, forming investigative committees made up of other slaves, and turning to divination techniques to unveil the culprit.[59] On Diamond Hill, Isaac reacted just as indignantly when he found that his bridle had been stolen. Isaac boldly confronted the Cherokee man whom he suspected of the deed. Although the Cherokee at first denied the accusation, he soon gave in to Isaac's shrewd questioning. Eventually, the cornered thief relented and led Isaac "to the furthest end of the corn field, where he had hidden [the bridle] in the tall grass."[60]

In addition to building families and developing a strong internal economy, blacks on Diamond Hill, like slaves on countless other southern plantations, maintained a vibrant communal social life. Enslaved men used their leisure time during the Christmas holidays to go out shooting together, suggesting that they had the liberty to carry guns.[61] Enslaved women advised and chastised each other on relational matters and questions of propriety, such as how to interact with one's husband in public and how to bury a stillborn child.[62] Blacks on the Vann grounds also hosted lively parties, with drumming, fiddling, and dancing that echoed through the night. As on many plantations dotting the southern landscape, women here probably prepared pots of food on party days, secretly stealing time from Vann's work assignments. They may have wrapped their heads in colorful scarves, or straightened their hair with twine, or topped off a dress with a homemade straw hat. They may have taken special care to embellish dresses for themselves out of cotton they wove in the evenings and natural berry dyes.[63] Once at the party, women and men would have danced for pleasure and competition, partaking of prepared foods and imbibing bootleg liquor. On one occasion, the Moravian missionaries admitted their distress that their slave, Pleasant, gave in to "the great impulse to accept invitations from the Negroes in our neighborhood," thus rendering her incapable of attending morning church services as directed.[64] Pleasant, along with other members of the black community, set her own social agenda to the extent that she could.

Black community experience here, as elsewhere in the slaveholding South, also included resistance to the condition of bondage. Documentary, archaeological, and oral history evidence shows that enslaved people in every locale refused their reduction to the status of property. Historian Celia Naylor, whose research focuses on slaves and freedpeople in the Cherokee Nation after Removal, has demonstrated that Indian country was no exception, despite the popular belief in our own time in "a particular construction of Indian spaces as solely sites of African American refuge."[65] Through everyday acts of defiance and plots long in the planning, slaves in the United States and the colonized native nations within it thwarted the power of owners to fully control and restrict their lives. Historians have mapped slave resistance along a number of axes: from an internal, psychosocial resolve to preserve one's human dignity; to subtle external acts like negotiations with the master for greater autonomy; to slowdowns in work productivity and brief departures from the plantation; to outright attempts to poison the master, commit arson, or take full flight. This range of action on the part of blacks in refusal of their dehumanization and forced captivity also occurred on Diamond Hill.

Pleasant's unwillingness to work quickly, diligently, and humbly for her Moravian masters was an expression of her rejection of their complete authority over her. John Gambold complained of Pleasant's "foul mouth," which was "much more active than her hands." Anna Rosina Gambold bemoaned that when the missionaries try to correct Pleasant, "she always knows everything better and won't let us get to the point."[66] In a letter to a church member back in Salem, Anna Gambold criticized Pleasant's unpredictable work habits and the skill she manifested at manipulating her circumstances: "Of our poor Pleasant I can only say . . . Oh how often I have already sighed and cried to the Savior for her sake. . . . I have noticed that whenever I praise her, even if she is not aware of it, she always pulls a trick. . . . I have often thanked God and you for her, for it is sure that without such help we could not get by. . . . If she can only once learn to know herself thoroughly and turn to the Savior in her need, then I believe she can become a noble person."[67] In the same letter, Anna Gambold alluded to Pleasant's recent disagreeable actions, writing: "For a while back our Pleasant was in a very bad way which made us very much dissatisfied with her, but she is somewhat better now." The "bad way" to which Gambold referred could have been the time in May that Pleasant "cursed" Mrs. Byhan, another missionary, "in the most horrible way," or it could have been the unidentifiable ailment Pleasant complained of that summer that prevented her from completing her assigned tasks efficiently.[68]

Anna Gambold probably suspected that Pleasant was "pulling a trick" by lodging this medical complaint, but she had no choice but to respond to Pleasant's demands. Because Pleasant did most of the cooking and cleaning for the missionary couple in charge, their frequent guests from the home mission in Old Salem, visitors from the surrounding Cherokee towns, the Cherokee children enrolled at the school, as well as her own young son, any further decline in her productivity would have crippled the operation of the mission. For her part, Pleasant may have used her ailment as a form of work stoppage, and perhaps she even requested a house call by a local healer. For she, as much if not more so than her mistress, stood at the center of the mission's domestic life and tended the needs of various and sundry Cherokee visitors. After one year of bondage at the mission station, Pleasant must have been somewhat familiar with Cherokee people and practices. The potential ripple effect of having Pleasant out of commission compelled the Gambolds to seek a remedy unfamiliar and undesirable to Moravians. They turned to Earbob, an elderly Cherokee man who "began to distinguish himself as a conjurer among his nation" and lived as a guest in James Vann's home.[69] In July of 1806, Anna Rosina Gambold reported: "The Old Indian Earbob bled [Pleasant] yesterday around the ankles with a flint-stone because she complained of pain there."[70]

In addition to verbal and behavioral "trickery" that preserved their self-respect, enslaved blacks boldly defended their interests through acts of aggression. In 1806, "the new Negroes [recently arrived from Africa] threatened the overseer with an axe because he insisted they husk corn in the evening. . . . [T]hey went so far that he had to leave quickly as he could. . . . Such actions are not punished by the master, which the Negroes certainly know."[71] In 1807, Ben, after he was sold by James Vann, joined forces with a white man to steal $150 from Vann's store on the Chattahoochee River.[72] In 1813, "a quite upstanding African Negro" defended himself against a beating by the vicious overseer, Samuel Talley, injuring Talley's hand.[73]

Black slaves sometimes turned despair and rage against themselves, seeking freedom from their realties by taking their own lives. Patience's husband, Gander, who was said to have drowned while bathing, may have committed suicide. This was the interpretation of one of the missionaries who was sent by Vann to investigate the scene: "[W]e found him [Gander's body] without injury and had reason to think that he was tired of life and shortened his life on purpose."[74] When Renee's husband, Ned, learned that he and his family were to be sold, he attempted suicide by cutting his own throat. Ned immediately lost the use of his vocal chords but did not die from his injury for three more months.[75] In 1813, an enslaved woman from Africa also succeeded in taking her life by slitting her throat, hoping, perhaps, for freedom in the next world.[76]

In addition to signaling their rejection of slavery through harsh words, subtle deeds, forceful threats, and suicide, enslaved men and women on the Vann plantation attempted escapes. In 1804, three slaves ran away from James Vann, and whites in the neighborhood feared an impending theft of their horses.[77] When Ned tried to kill himself upon hearing of his family's sale, three of his sons made the different choice to run away. A few years later, Renee and Ned's son Sam (who had perhaps returned or been captured after a prior escape) was under threat by Nancy Vann, James Vann's sister, because "he had treated Jim Brown's overseer very badly; indeed, he had threatened his life." According to Renee's frenzied report, Nancy had enlisted a group of Indians to murder Sam, but he eluded capture. "[H]e had gotten away from the plot of the Indians. . . . [H]e had led a horse away from Vann's estate and a young negro woman who is his wife."[78] In 1812, Nancy Vann lost a whole group of slaves who used her attendance at a Cherokee ball game to make good their escape.[79]

Isaac, the Henry Bibb of Diamond Hill, ran away from the Vann plantation on at least four separate occasions. Henry Bibb was a slave from Kentucky who wrote his autobiography, now a classic in slavery studies, after the last in a series of escapes from his multiple owners. Bibb could not abide captivity under any circumstances. He wrote: "Among other good trades I learned the art of running away to perfection. I made a regular business of it, and never gave it up, until I had broken the bands of slavery."[80] These were sentiments passionately shared by Isaac. In July of 1802, soon after seeking English literacy lessons, Isaac ran away in the dead of night "when Mr. Vann and his overseer weren't at home." Isaac "took a female slave and one of his master's horses with him. A couple of Negroes hurried after the runaways and brought the Negro woman and the horse back, but they couldn't catch Isaac." When Isaac realized that the woman with him, most certainly his wife, had been captured, he returned "of his own free will" and sought reconciliation with Vann through the missionaries. The next fall, Isaac stole a horse and ran again, sending a message to his master by way of "a Negro who lives at the cowpens." Isaac warned Vann that "if anyone dared to pursue him he would shoot at him because Mr. McKee had given him his weapon." Mr. McKee, the white blacksmith on Vann's estate, lost his job as a result of Isaac's threat and was forced by Agent Lovely to "leave the country within 10 days." The missionaries reported that this was Isaac's third escape.[81]

Elsewhere in the extended black community that radiated out from Diamond Hill, slaves employed a variety of means to ease their suffering, seek retribution, or secure their freedom. In 1805, a black man named Paul wrote to Agent Meigs with a complaint about the influential Chief Doublehead. Paul asserted that his former master had granted him freedom on his deathbed, and that many white witnesses could attest to this fact. Paul then charged that Doublehead had stolen Paul's substantial property through information obtained from the widow of the deceased. Paul itemized the seized items (including a cleared lot, horses, cattle, skins, saddles, kettles, and a fur), which he totaled at a value of $1,038, and wrote: "[T]o Col. Meigs — I looks for the restitution of my property confident that he will do this endeavour to see the property of a slave returned to himself."[82] In 1809, the wife of Five Killer traveled through Diamond Hill in search of her enslaved black woman who had run away.[83] In 1818, James Vann's cousin passed by with an escaped slave who had just been recaptured.[84] Turning to arson, a common tactic in slave rebellions, a woman owned by Peggy Scott Vann's sister, Sally McDonald, burned down her mistress's house in the nearby town of Oothcaloga. When the news spread that McDonald's home was on fire, the missionaries rushed to the scene, and "they found the house completely burned down. Her own Negro woman had set it on fire, after carrying the bed out."[85]

The many examples of bold and creative resistance on Diamond Hill and in surrounding areas demonstrate both the suffering and daring of black slaves. Seeing friends and relatives stand up for themselves, attempt escape, and commit suicide was a feature of everyday life in the black community of Diamond Hill. This pattern of resistance had the effect of instilling pride in group identity, even as it underscored the recurring experience of loved ones lost.

The Slaves' Cultural World

In the midst of intensive social interaction among Afro-Americans, Africans, and Afro-Cherokees on Diamond Hill, core aspects of African cultural systems were shared, learned, and preserved. John Michael Vlach explains this culture-making process that occurred on large plantations, writing: "[S]paces that slaves claimed and modified for their own domestic purposes provided them with their own sense of place. In these locations they were able to develop a stronger sense of social solidarity, a feeling of community that would serve as a seedbed not only for resistance but also for the invention and maintenance of a distinctive African American culture."[86] In addition to creating a black community, slaves on Diamond Hill reinforced for one another an adaptive black cultural identity rooted in the memory of African values and practices. The incorporation of enslaved men and women directly from Africa in the early years of Vann's estate served to freshen and sustain aspects of community life that were African derived. In this way, black experience on Diamond Hill again reflected black life on white-owned plantations across the South. In the late 1700s and through the first several years of the nineteenth century, a decreased yet steady importation of slaves into the United States meant that African-born people with fresh cultural roots were present to ground the cultural foundation of the American-born slave population. In 1800, when Vann was developing Diamond Hill, 19 percent of the U.S. slave population was African-born. By 1810, that number had grown to 21 percent before declining to 12 percent in 1820. The presence of men, women, and especially elders from Africa ensured the preservation of, first, African ethnicities and, later, of a "black" racial and cultural identity in slave quarters across the South. It was not until around 1830 — long after James Vann's death — that ethnically diverse

African lifeways had cohered into an amalgamated African and American cultural form.[87]

Given these numbers, it is not surprising that classic works of scholarship in slavery studies have made the case that "the American slave was able to retain many African cultural elements and an emotional contact with his [or her] motherland."[88] Out of the root material of African beliefs, customs, and values, slaves in North America and the global African diaspora forged distinctive black cultures that incorporated Euro-American and American Indian elements. The feelings of identity, self-worth, and social meaning created by an African-oriented culture "bound slaves together and sustained them under brutal conditions of oppression."[89] In grounding the argument that black American slaves both retained and reinvented aspects of African practice, historians and anthropologists have charted a number of features in slave community life specific to the cultures of West and Central Africa from which the majority of American slaves were taken. Among these are the retention of African languages, words, and names; spiritual worship expressed through dance, especially the "ring shout" ceremony; belief in supernatural signs and omens; drum and fiddle playing; and respect for elders and ancestors. In the black community on Diamond Hill there is clear evidence of African-language use and drum playing, strong evidence of indigenous African spiritual and folk beliefs, and indirect indication of elder respect. This large plantation in the Cherokee Nation was a place where the slaves' African past lived on in memory and practice.

Vann's purchase of slaves from Africa at least until 1805 meant that indigenous languages were spoken by Africans and heard by American- and Cherokee-born blacks on the Vann plantation. Patience spoke in her African tongue, as did Pompey, a man who also behaved "in the African manner." The missionaries classified Pompey among the group of "Africans who can still speak only a little English."[90] Crawje, a slave owned by James Vann's daughter, Delilah McNair, was also among this group. In the missionaries' eyes, Crawje was "a poor ignorant heathen from Africa and did not even understand English." An interpretive inversion of the missionaries' Eurocentric view would indicate that Crawje practiced an African indigenous spirituality, was rich in the cultural knowledge of her homeland, and was fluent in an African language. But when Crawje died, her relative Betty "wailed terribly according to the custom in this country," an indication that even as black slaves carried on African ways of being, they also adopted practices of the surrounding Cherokee society, resulting in a rich cultural blend. Similarly, some elderly African slaves who had been on the Vann place for at least a decade adapted their African-language use to develop what seems to have been an African-Cherokee creole. Missionary Anna Rosina Gambold described "two old women . . . turned of eighty" whose "language is very unintelligible, being a mixture of African and Indian."[91]

In addition to language, spiritual life was an identifiable arena in which African cultural values persisted among the slaves on Diamond Hill. In early America, black slaves on the whole adopted Christianity only in slow fits and starts, beginning haltingly with the mid- and late-eighteenth-century evangelical revivals. Not until the middle of the nineteenth century did the majority of blacks enthusiastically embrace Christianity.[92] The slaves' religion, then, for a long time reflected African "cosmologies," described by religious historian Yvonne Chireau as "a proliferation of ideas—ranging from concepts of divinity to theories concerning cause, effect, and the responsiveness of spiritual forces to human will—[that] have informed expressions of black American religion and magic."[93] Whereas many white slaveholders showed little interest in converting slaves before the 1820s–40s, slaves owned by the Vanns had ready and regular access to the Moravian Church's Christian mission complex as early as 1801.[94] Vann family members were scarcely interested in church attendance, but they did not dissuade their slaves from participating in the Moravians' Sunday services. Several slaves owned by the Vanns and neighboring Cherokees took advantage of the missionaries' presence, visiting the complex to work for pay, ask for food, and listen to sermons. Few, however, became regular or serious churchgoers. The missionaries reported frustration at the slaves' lack of Christian devotion, and not until 1827 did the Moravians notate the successful conversion of a black slave, their "first-fruit of the local Negroes," the African-born Suniger Jacob, baptized Christian Jacob.[95] Sam Kerr, a black traveling preacher, visited the Vann slaves to exhort blacks toward Christian belief, but, although he was sheltered in the quarters, he seems not to have attracted a following.

Like many slaves across the United States, especially through the eighteenth century and even into the nineteenth, blacks on the Vann estate "tenaciously held onto the supernatural belief of their African ancestors."[96] They retained faith in signs, omens, and witches, all aspects of "the rich tradition of folk belief and practice, including conjure, herbalism, ghost lore, witchcraft, and fortune-telling, [which] flourished in the slave quarters." Betty, for example, described by the missionaries as "an African woman, a quiet and unusually diligent Negro woman," reacted out of her African heritage when her house burned down. "A deeply rooted superstition," the missionaries reported, "caused her not to hurry and put out the fire even though she saw it right away in the distance. Betty claimed that in her country such appearances of fire are often created by witchcraft, and if one looked, it would all disappear. She said she believed it would be just so with her house."[97] This faith in "the power of the supernatural" was a feature of slave communities derived from an African spiritual source and heightened by Euro-American and Native American folk beliefs.[98] For Betty and other members of the black community on Diamond Hill, living in a broader Cherokee context in which witchcraft was also an accepted reality likely reinforced African beliefs in a supernatural world beyond the purview of Christianity.

Adam and Milly, American-born slaves who lived at the mill with a number of slaves from Africa, also believed in the efficacy of supernatural forces. They feared that "they were cursed by someone" because "they had been ill for a time." Adam and Milly saw witchcraft or conjure as the cause of their sickness and sought "spiritual power as a force for self-defense." They went in search of what Yvonne Chireau calls a "spiritual professional" who "bridged the physical realm and the invisible world." In the words of the Moravian missionaries, the couple turned to "an old Indian woman from whom they sought help." The woman, the missionaries reported, "reinforced this opinion" that Adam and Milly had been cursed.[99] The missionaries saw the couple's self-diagnosis as foolishness and the Indian woman's response as "trickery." Their suggestion that Adam and Milly seek a medical remedy indicates a divergence of cultural viewpoints. Adam and Milly's African-oriented perspective in which spiritual and material realms overlapped pointed them toward a supernatural cause, a view shared by the Cherokee woman. The couple's turn to this woman in their time of need is an indication that no black spiritual leader, conjurer, or root worker was available to them on Diamond Hill. In the absence of such a figure, Milly and Adam created a new option, reaching out to a Native American woman whom they hoped could help.

African-inspired spiritual life on Diamond Hill was also evident in dance accompanied by music, a praise form "integral . . . in the worship of the gods and the ancestors" in West African cultures.[100] The black community on Diamond Hill participated in dances throughout the year, especially on weekends and during the Christmas season. The missionaries often recorded notations like: "In our neighborhood the Negroes danced through the entire night" and "the Negroes danced the entire day."[101] Though many of these gatherings were strictly secular in nature, some surely had religious significance. The use of the drum by Diamond Hill slaves indicates religious dance, since drumming was a feature of African worship that helped to move dancers toward ecstatic possession by ancestor and godly spirits. Because drums were such an important aspect of African culture, they were "by and large forbidden to the slave in the United States."[102] Again, a broader Cherokee cultural context may have insulated African cultural practices. Cherokees also appreciated and celebrated the rhythm of drums, and drumming was never banned on Diamond Hill.

The playing of the fiddle on Vann's plantation also suggests religious dance, since the violin was used in the Mali Empire to "summon the ancestral spirits" in times of worship. Most fiddle playing in southern slave quarters was reserved for secular festivities, but some had spiritual ramifications.[103] On the Hopeton plantation in Georgia, for instance, "above twenty violins [were] silenced by the Methodist missionaries." But because the slaves at Hopeton "were not given to drink or intemperance in their merry-making," it is likely that their violin playing had a religious rather than secular impetus.[104] One example from Diamond Hill intimates that fiddle playing also had religious significance there. A group of slaves who had been invited to a dance in the quarters attended a Moravian Christmas service instead. In repudiation of the black dance, "a young African . . . took his violin, which he otherwise had used on such occasions, stomped on it with his feet, and threw it into the fire!"[105] While it is possible that this African man on the verge of Christian conversion was rebuking secular dance, it could be that he sought to destroy an artifact central to the practice of his African faith.

A final indication that slaves here danced as a form of religious observance comes from the disapproving interpretation of the Moravians, who recorded: "[I]t was very unpleasant during our worship service . . . to hear the Negroes' despicable worship of the devil. There was the continuous thunder of musket, drumming, screaming, and dancing that lasted until late in the night."[106] In their choice of language, so much like the language used by European travelers who encountered religious services in Africa that were foreign to them, the Moravians revealed their understanding that something spiritual in nature was taking place in the slave quarter. Because the Moravian missionaries did not attend the black dances they so despised, no written description of devotional dance exists for the Vann plantation. It is therefore impossible to verify whether blacks on Diamond Hill performed the "ring shout," a religious dance identified by scholars as the chief expression of African-derived religious worship in the American slave quarters.[107] It stands to reason, though, that enslaved blacks here, as elsewhere in the slaveholding South, would have engaged in this essential praise form.

The fact that the historical record reveals so little about black culture in the quarters likely stems not only from Moravian disdain but also from the slaves' value of cultural secrecy. In an attempt to protect the practices that were dear to them but often forbidden by white masters, enslaved blacks carried out these practices in the stillness of night and the secrecy of woods.[108] Although James Vann did not intervene in his slaves' religious life, blacks on the plantation may also have striven to seclude themselves from the Vanns, overseers, and missionaries to hold religious gatherings. One example from the Moravian diary hints at this possibility. When a visiting preacher tried to host a church service for slaves inside James Vann's home, members of the black community refused because "the Negroes did not want to go into Mr. Vann's house for the service."[109] This was a notable rejection, given that enslaved blacks *did* enter Vann's house to participate in secular drinking parties. The lack of direct description about black religious observance, which certainly took place on Vann's estate, raises parallel questions. We cannot know, for instance, what folktales were told in the slave quarters, what pet names were used for relatives, or what spiritual songs were sung. But the faint sketch provided by Moravian missionaries gives a strong indication that a good deal of what we would recognize as "black culture and black consciousness" flourished on Diamond Hill.[110]

Other aspects of black slave culture that had a basis in African values are suggested but not fully revealed on the Vann plantation. When the sixty-seven-year-old Grace arrived on the grounds, she garnered immediate respect from other enslaved women, suggesting the functioning value of respect for elders, who were viewed in the African context as being closer in the life span to revered ancestral spirits.[111] As one of the oldest black women on Vann's land, Grace would come to perform a community role specific to African women. Anthropologist Stanlie James has explained that the function of what she calls the "othermother," or a woman who takes responsibility for children not her own, was common in polygamous West African societies. This role continued and perhaps grew in African American slave communities in which children were often separated from their biological families. James argues that othermothering was a form of cultural work that extended loving care beyond that for individual biological children to an entire enslaved community. By James's definition, the "community othermother," typically over forty years old, was considered wise in experience, commanded respect from others, and was able "to critique the behavior of individual members of the community and to provide them with directions on appropriate behavior(s)."[112] This definition aptly describes Grace's interaction with members of the larger black female community, who quickly accepted her care and advice.

The slave quarters of Diamond Hill housed a black community steeped in cultural values and practices inspired by an African homeland. The beliefs, behaviors, and interactive styles exhibited by blacks there mirror those of African-influenced slave communities in other parts of the early-nineteenth-century South. There is a strong indication, too, that being enslaved in a Cherokee context provided insulation and reinforcement of particular African-based practices. This has proven to be the case in other slaveholding societies of the African diaspora, where, for instance, a wide array of Catholic saints created a functional rubric for the memory and worship of diverse African gods. In places where the dominant culture had features in common with the slaves' own culture, African practices were less likely to fall under attack and more likely to be preserved.[113]

Thus, in a similar way that French-influenced New Orleans created a "permissive" environment for the practice of the African-based voodoo religion, the indigenous American Cherokee context permitted the expression and productive reinvention of African ways of life.[114] Cherokees believed in a distant divine being who created humankind, as well as in worlds of animated spirits below and above the earth. The ancestors of black slaves also believed in a High God, in lesser gods who had a series of special domains and purposes, and in a spatial division of planes where spirits and humans dwelled.[115] Enslaved blacks regularly engaged in ritual dances and drumming, as did their Cherokee captors. Like many members of the Indian society in which they were enslaved, blacks on Diamond Hill believed in a powerful supernatural world that involved "magical control," positive conjurations, and the dangerous misdeeds of witches.[116] (It is probably not coincidence that Adam and Milly, who thought they had been struck ill by spiritual forces, approached a Cherokee elder for help in 1811, a moment when Cherokees were themselves experiencing a traditional spiritual revival.) If, as anthropologist Melville Herskovits has argued, a notable number of Africans captured for the slave trade were priests in the cult of the river spirit, their reverence for the spiritual power of water would have resonated with Cherokee beliefs in the sacred cleansing power of rivers and springs.[117] Like most ethnic groups in West African societies, Cherokees practiced polygamy. This meant that the black men on the Vann plantation who had more than one wife were living in domestic arrangements common to those of their ancestral home and to the dominant society in which they now resided.[118]

It is quite possible and even probable that the combination of all of these parallels resulted in a supportive environment for the nurturance of an African-inspired cultural matrix among Cherokee-owned slaves. Diamond Hill was a place where the slave population was large enough to sustain a black community *and* where the dominant Indian society held features in common with African societies. Enslaved people in this location were therefore able to develop a unique black lifeworld rooted in memories of Africa, adapted to a new indigenous American context, and insulated from the intense acculturative pressures of the white slaveholding South.[119]

Overlapping Social Worlds

Enslaved Africans, Afro-Americans, and Afro-Cherokees on Diamond Hill lived in an African-influenced black community. This was the centering core of their existence, the basis of their sense of identity, the compass for their daily rhythms. The quarter was a physical place *and* a cultural home-base, a nurturing point from which black men, women, and children set out to meet an oppressive "world of work."[120] It was, as Ira Berlin has phrased it, "the heart of African American life in the countryside."[121] But beyond this central sphere of black community life, slaves moved into a second circle of interaction — the social sphere of Cherokees. The Vann plantation was a site of intense and frequent relations across the boundary lines of race as well as class. Blacks moved relatively comfortably through particular Cherokee social spaces, and certain Cherokees were often welcome in the space of the quarters.

As in other locations in the slaveholding South, social interactions between Cherokees and blacks here had their beginnings in childhood. Enslaved children were playmates of James Vann's children, as well as the Cherokee boys and girls enrolled at the Springplace Mission school. Joseph Vann, a favored son of James, was a "pure mischief" maker in the eyes of the missionaries. While attending the school, little Joe wrestled a baby bear, shot at pigs and misled dogs, and hid after his fits of misbehavior. Joe also enticed other children to participate in his antics. Once, when the pupils had received permission to visit the elder enslaved woman Grace, they instead followed Joe to the Conasauga River. Along the way, Joe and the other Cherokee boys convinced Grace's young son, George, to join them. Instead of searching for blackberries, as the boys later claimed, they "went swimming in the water."[122] Mary Vann, a daughter of James, was also a disappointment to her missionary teachers. James finally pulled Mary out of school because of her "naughty behavior" and made plans to have her study sewing with her stepmother, Peggy Scott Vann. But rather than remaining indoors to take her sewing lessons, the missionaries reported, Mary "spends most of her time now in the company of Negroes."[123] Jesse, the son of Peggy Vann's uncle, Cherokee statesman and slaveholder Charles Hicks, ran away from the mission school for a spell and was found "staying in the neighborhood with Negroes."[124] One father of another mission school pupil complained that instead of "constantly hav[ing] his book in front of him and learn[ing]," the boy "plays with Negro children so much."[125]

This was a pattern on Diamond Hill. Black and Indian children often played in the woods, and black and Indian boys played junior stickball games, a competitive Cherokee lacrosselike game known as the "little brother to war."[126] Enslaved children spent time in the mission schoolhouse after hours, discussing ideas with the Cherokee students. Cherokee children also snuck away from school to watch the dances in the slave quarters, a practice the missionaries condemned to the same extent that they condemned their pupils' attendance at traditional Cherokee ceremonies. In January of 1806, for instance, the missionaries complained: "The children had been lured to watch the Negro dance. Brother Byhan, however, went and brought them back home."[127]

As black and Cherokee children matured on the Vann plantation, their social lives continued to intersect. Unlike many southern plantations, where passage into adulthood meant an effectual social separation between elite whites and enslaved blacks, men and women in the Diamond Hill slave community socialized with Cherokee adults of both the poorer and the planter classes.[128] Blacks attended Cherokee stickball games, major sociocultural events in Cherokee communities that trained young men for the physical challenges of warfare. On one occasion, the missionaries indicated that "the Indians and Negroes had organized a big ball game in the neighborhood" together. A year later, they wrote: "Many Indians on their way to a *general ball play* pour-[ing] in from all corners and borders of the nation to Coosawattee, traveled by here. . . . A few came to our spring to find a root that is supposed to bring a ball player success and good luck. Also the Negroes from our neighborhood were also [*sic*] invited; the nightlong dance was held this evening."[129] Soon after this general stickball game took place, a black man and a Cherokee man organized a "Horse Racing" that drew a large Indian crowd.[130]

Blacks also frequented parties in the homes of wealthy Cherokees. Wali Vann, James's mother, was fond of what the missionaries deemed "heathen amusements." She often hosted parties in her home, and she invited enslaved blacks to participate. Wali was particularly fond of the elderly Grace and made special arrangements to have Grace attend her festivities. On one occasion, Wali "had another dance and had also invited [Grace] and said she even would pick her up on a horse." The missionaries disapproved of Grace's participation, especially because she was a professed Christian. They wrote in their diary that Grace had "let herself be misled by the old Vann woman to attend entertainment." When the missionaries confronted Grace about her behavior, she told them that "she had been afraid to oppose Mother Vann, who was her mistress."[131] It is quite possible that Grace meant these words, was struggling with her faith commitment, and feared affronting her master's mother. It is just as possible, though, that she offered this reason as an excuse to the intrusive missionaries for behavior she wished, if ambivalently, to engage in.

Cherokees likewise spent time in the slave quarters, openly attending dances and visiting with families with no apparent social stigma from their Cherokee peers. When a Cherokee man named No Fire went looking for one of his wives in the aftermath of an argument, he found her "in a Negro's house," where she had probably sought out friends.[132] The Moravian diary and letters are peppered with mentions of "Negro and Indian dances," occasions that caused the missionaries great distress. Grace's husband, Jacob, was the host of some of these gatherings, throwing "Indian dances . . . in his house often."[133] In the summer of 1811, the missionaries described what seems to have been a booming block party: "[M]any Indians stopped in at our place. . . . [W]e finally learned that they were invited by a Negro woman in our neighborhood to a dance, which lasted the whole night. . . . Late at night our former pupil Tlaneneh came into our yard with his relatives. . . . Afterward they went into the neighborhood to the dance. As Tlaneneh said, they were invited. We had cause to suspect that he had actually come here to talk our children [pupils] into going there as well."[134] During the Christmas holiday in 1814, one of the missionaries observed in a letter, "[w]ild Shouts and heavy stomps could be heard . . . while Cherokees and Negroes danced," and another lamented in the diary, "The Negro and Indian dance in our neighborhood causes us heartache." Three days later, the missionaries added, "The Negro and Indian dance is still continuing in our neighborhood at night. May God have mercy!"[135]

In times of illness, blacks and Cherokees sometimes turned to one another for aid. In some instances, enslaved blacks were assigned this duty by their masters, such as when Pleasant nursed the critically ill Peggy Scott Vann and when an unnamed slave woman was sent to care for Charles Hicks.[136] The reverse could also be true, such as when Peggy Vann secured a "Cherokee doctor" to treat an ill enslaved man with "red and white corals" thrown "into a vessel of water." But at other times, the exchange of health care was independently motivated. When Adam and Milly feared they were cursed, they sought help from an old Cherokee woman. The traditional healer Earbob cured Pleasant's mysterious ankle pain, most likely at her request. And an enslaved man named Bob "perform[ed] the operation" of bleeding an Indian who was ill.[137] The Moravian diaries do not record the sharing of medicinal herb treatments among blacks and Cherokees on Diamond Hill, but it is likely that such information exchange did occur.[138]

The nearly one hundred enslaved blacks on Diamond Hill moved through separate yet intersecting worlds that made up a rich cultural and social universe. Africans, Afro-Americans, and Afro-Cherokees created a life for themselves in the quarter, where black community and cultural ways were anchored in African memories and reinvented in the context of Cherokee America. Ceaselessly defending their humanity, and dragging scraps of experiential joy from the "slough of despond"[139] that was slavery, these men, women, and children lived lives rich in spirit. Despite the harshness of bondage, they nourished intimate relationships and created cultural meaning in a social space of their own.

Beyond this central zone of close-knit relations in the quarter, enslaved blacks engaged in a broader Cherokee social arena, in which they observed and participated in Indian communal and cultural events. Just as essentially, enslaved blacks dwelled in a "world of work," where Cherokee masters and white overseers dictated their schedules, extracted their labor, and threatened them with separation from loved ones in order to maintain discipline. Navigating the sorrows and pleasures, intimacies and exigencies of bonded life in this native locale was the daily trial and rare triumph of African-descended slaves owned by the Vanns.

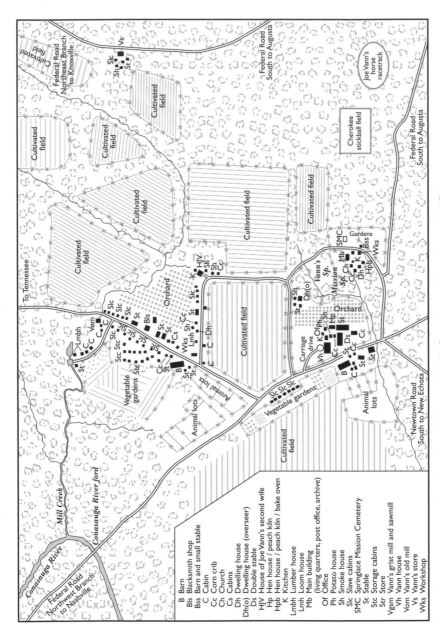

Vann plantation conjectural map based on a diagram at the Chief Vann House. From Rowena McClinton, ed., The Moravian Springplace Mission to the Cherokees, vol. 1 (Lincoln: University of Nebraska Press, 2007). Used by permission of the University of Nebraska Press.

B   Barn
Bls   Blacksmith shop
Bss   Barn and small stable
C   Cabin
Cc   Corn crib
Ch   Church
Cs   Cabins
Dh   Dwelling house
Dh(o) Dwelling house (overseer)
Ds   Double stable
HJv   House of Joe Vann's second wife
Hp   Hen house / peach kiln
Hpb   Hen house / peach kiln / bake oven
K   Kitchen
Lmbh   Lumber house
Lmh   Loom house
Mb   Main building
       (living quarters, post office, archive)
Of   Office
Ph   Potato house
Sh   Smoke house
Slc   Slave cabins
SMC   Springlace Mission Cemetery
St   Stable
Stc   Storage cabins
Str   Store
Vgsm   Vann's grist mill and sawmill
Vh   Vann house
Vom   Vann's old mill
Vs   Vann's store
Wks   Workshop

CHAPTER 4

A House Divided

We often wish that we were at least ten miles further away from Vann's, so that we would not hear the cruelty and tyranny which is practiced in that house. — Moravian Springplace Mission Diary, September 13, 1805

A house divided against itself cannot stand. — President Abraham Lincoln, Illinois Republican State Convention speech, 1858

The Mistress's Plantation Map

Just as black slaves on Vann's plantation knew their surroundings in ways particular to their experience of bondage, Peggy Scott Vann, the young mistress of Diamond Hill, would have had a contingent relationship to her plantation environs. Because of gradual changes in men's and women's roles among members of the Cherokee slaveholding elite who had begun to adopt some aspects of Euro-American gender ideals, Peggy stood in a position of disempowerment relative to her influential husband. Throughout Cherokee early history and into the first years of the nineteenth century, newly married Cherokee men customarily relocated to the homesteads of their wives. As a result, most Cherokee women continued to enjoy the proximity, support, and social protection of their birth families after marriage. But when Peggy married James Vann and settled on his estate, she did the exact opposite, separating from her maternal kin's home-place and the immediate circle of their care. Although her older sister, Betsy Scott, had also been married to Vann for a time, Betsy soon left the relationship, leaving Peggy behind as Vann's sole wife.

There are indications in the Moravian diary that Peggy's relocation to her husband's home — a consequence of Cherokee interaction with Euro-American settlement patterns as well as the disbursement of Cherokee farms in the aftermath of the Revolutionary War — had an isolating effect. While her husband traveled for business, Peggy often stayed behind on a plantation surrounded by wilderness and peopled mainly by black slaves. James forbad Peggy to entertain strangers in his absence, and visiting her closest relatives, who lived in distant towns, was an undertaking Peggy rarely initiated until after James's death. With black slaves to work the fields, Peggy was displaced from the agricultural labor that had long shaped Cherokee women's identity and economic independence.[1] And exacerbating her spatial isolation was the relational distance Peggy would have felt from her in-laws in a cultural context in which a spouse's relations were not viewed as intimates. Although her husband's mother and sister lived on the estate, Peggy was not as close to them as she would have been to her own clan members.

Adrift in an alienating social environment that turned the expectation of Cherokee marriage on its head, Peggy must have eagerly awaited the frequent visits of her maternal uncle, Charles Hicks, a close associate of James's who traveled to Diamond Hill on political business. Peggy also found company in the slave quarters, where she formed a bond with Caty, a young black woman who had grown up in the Cherokee Nation but died prematurely in 1808. While James Vann might have seen Diamond Hill as a place of material comfort and psychic retreat to which he returned after taxing missions of political negotiation and business enterprise, Peggy may have experienced that same plantation as a space of containment as well as privilege. The large wood house that James had built, the sprawling, productive, fertile grounds, might have been at times for her a gilded cage.

Peggy's reality of spatial enclosure and effective separation from kin placed her in a precarious situation. Like plantation mistresses of the Euro-American South, and unlike most other Cherokee women who remained within their families' protective circles, Peggy was exposed to the daily vicissitudes of her spouse. And in a Cherokee plantation environment that saw "rising paternalism and female suppression as male planters took on white ways," James Vann began to take advantage of Peggy's social vulnerability through acts of abuse and intimidation.[2] When Vann was inebriated, an occurrence that happened more and more regularly in the first few years of the 1800s, he often struck out at Peggy, who became a primary victim of his unpredictable rage. On one such occasion the missionaries recorded, "We heard horrible things he had done again last night. Especially he mistreated his wife so badly it can not be repeated." Although Peggy was "suffering greatly physically," Vann returned the next day and "was so angry that he immediately knocked his wife to the floor. She then fled with Vann's mother."[3]

This extended attack on his wife was not an isolated incident. Vann, the missionaries reported, had lately begun to behave in a manner that was "malicious." He acted, they wrote, "as if he had lost his mind. No one's life was safe because he was in the house shooting, burning, and ravaging." When they tried to orchestrate an intervention by having Brother Wohlfahrt speak to him, Vann "jumped out of bed, took the bottle, and drank as in a rage. He said that it was his house, and he could drink, dance, fornicate, and do whatever he wanted in it; it was not anyone's business." The missionaries despaired of the situation, praying that Jesus Christ might "free him from Satan's chains which bind him so tightly."[4] Their prayers, however, seem to have gone unanswered. For between the years 1805 and 1809—the economic and political zenith of James Vann's administration—Vann terrorized Peggy, his mother, Wali, and black slaves on the premises, turning Diamond Hill into an epicenter of domestic violence.

Peggy suffered her husband's frequent abuse at the same time that she witnessed his punishment of black slaves like Demas, a man James had dragged out of bed and chained inside of the Vann family home for suspected theft.[5] Peggy must have realized, as Demas lay shackled beneath her floorboards, that these two forms of domestic abuse—violence against wives and violence against slaves—were interrelated. Both the systematic reduction of blacks to chattel in Cherokee country and the contraction of Cherokee women's roles to that of "proper" wives had come in the wake of American conquest. Following the Revolutionary War, the United States had introduced a civilization program that instructed Cherokee men to abandon hunting and take up management of family farms, relegated Cherokee women to a diminished domestic sphere, and fostered plantation-based race slavery to replace and expand women's agricultural work. This directive set in motion a restructuring of power relations. It elevated Cherokee men as heads of their households; it precipitated a decline in Cherokee women's economic and political standing, and it created a new class of subjugated people within the Cherokee Nation: African-descended slaves. And even as American colonialism refashioned relations within Cherokee families and on Cherokee farms, U.S. officials placed pressure on Cherokee leaders, exacerbating internal differences and encouraging factional conflict. Hence, the space of the "domestic" in Cherokee life—within homes, on farms, and even within the national leadership—was undergoing dramatic rearrangement and reinterpretation at the very moment that Peggy Scott joined James Vann on Diamond Hill. The subjugation of Cherokee women to Cherokee men, of black slaves to Cherokee owners, of Cherokee leaders to American authority was all of a piece.

These shifts in Cherokee life in the early nineteenth century had a profound and immediate impact on the subset of women who were positioned among the political and economic elite. For it was their (often mixed-race Euro-Cherokee) families that first responded to American gender ideals and took advantage of novel opportunities for economic advancement. While many Cherokee women in remote interior and mountain towns gradually faced such changes, women like Peggy Vann were the first to encounter gendered vulnerabilities linked to the exigencies of American colonialism. Although he did not take up all of the white settlers' practices, her husband was among a set of men who first adopted Euro-American ideas about commerce, slavery, and gender roles, which included an elision of women's independence and authority. She had moved with him to an isolated plantation and trading center far away from her family. And to make matters worse, her husband had become a heavy drinker who provided alcohol to other Cherokee men assembled on his grounds. This combination of decreased regard and increased isolation for women and access to an inhibition-reducing substance for men created a threatening environment for Peggy Vann, other women of the Cherokee slave-holding class, and some poorer Cherokee women whose location placed them and their families within reach of these harmful external influences.

Like his adoption of chattel slavery, the violence that James Vann perpetrated against his wife would prefigure a growing trend in some sectors of Cherokee society. Based on admittedly limited ethnographic evidence, it seems that Cherokee women were not regular victims of domestic violence prior to the nineteenth century. Few outside observers had access to the intimate spaces of Cherokee homes in the seventeenth and eighteenth centuries, making the question of whether domestic violence regularly occurred before extensive contact with Europeans difficult to answer. But despite a paucity of information, a circumstantial and contextual review of available sources suggests that the traditional configuration of gender relations in Cherokee society warded against a prevalence of domestic abuse. Not only did Cherokee women participate fully in economic life through their labor as agriculturalists, food gatherers, and preparers of animal skins, but they also owned their family homes and household implements. Cherokee women were free to choose their own sexual and marriage partners, though they did heed the advice of older clanswomen and were likely influenced by the wishes of family members with regard to beneficial matches. Once married, Cherokee women tended to remain near maternal relatives, creating networks of protection if domestic violence should become a threat. Divorce was also easily attained for women, who simply had to place a husband's belongings outside of the cabin door to signal his rejection.[6] In contrast to Euro-American societies in which women were dependent on men economically and separated from their parents upon marriage, Cherokee women would have had few barriers to leaving, or rather, expelling, abusive spouses. In a synthesis of the documentary and ethnographic literature, anthropologist Raymond Fogelson concluded: "It seems clear that Cherokee women enjoyed notable freedom from, and with, men. They possessed considerable power, which they exercised within the household and in other selected domains."[7]

Of the early documentary accounts written by European traders and travelers in Cherokee country, two directly address the issue of domestic violence. English botanist William Bartram, who published his observations of Creeks and Cherokees in 1789, included the lengthy comment: "[Y]ou may depend upon my assertion that there is no people any where who love their women more than these Indians do.... They are courteous and polite to the women.... I never saw or heard of an instance of an Indian beating his wife or other female, or reproving them in anger or in harsh language. And the women make a suitable and graceful return; for they are discreet, modest, loving, faithful, and affectionate to their husbands."[8] Bartram's observation must be read with a degree of skepticism. He wrote of his travels in a romanticized style that naturalized Indians as part of a primitive landscape. In a well-known example, he included a sexually laden temptation-in-the-garden scene in which he and his white male companions cannot control their "passions" when they come upon a group of beautiful "Cherokee virgins" gathering strawberries into baskets.[9] But even if Bartram does not make for the most reliable of witnesses in every detail, his assertion that Cherokee women were not victims of spousal abuse becomes more convincing when read alongside other primary sources. Trader Alexander Longe wrote in 1725: "[T]he women rules the roost and wears the breeches and sometimes will beat their husbands within an inch of their lives.... The man will not resist their power if the woman was to beat his brains out."[10] Like Bartram's, Longe's testimony is problematic. Longe strains credulity when he charges that Cherokee women abused their husbands to the point of death, but his emphasis on men's willingness to be harmed rather than to do harm, together with Bartram's comment about men's tenderness toward women, indicates that most Cherokee women did not experience violence at the hands of their husbands.[11]

Based on Longe's account, historian Theda Perdue concludes that "men apparently never tried to dominate their wives" in this earlier period. But starting in the early 1800s, a pattern of abuse of Cherokee wives becomes discernible in the written record. Perdue demonstrates that between 1813 and 1838, missionaries and U.S. officials cited incidents of alcohol abuse in tandem with incidents of violence against women.[12] As early as 1805, Moravian missionaries began to chronicle spousal abuse on Diamond Hill. And certainly by the 1820s, when Cherokee women had also lost political power through the ratification of a Cherokee constitution that denied them the right to vote, violence against women in the home had become amply documented.[13] At the site of Diamond Hill, and in the social circles that congregated there, additional evidence supports the proposition that a pattern of domestic violence in some pockets of Cherokee society emerged in the early nineteenth century. As in the rest of the U.S. South, where patriarchal domination left women vulnerable to physical abuse, heavy drinking was a predominant cause of this violent turn in gender relations.[14]

A series of notations by the Moravian and Boston-based American Board missionaries indicate that Cherokee men in James Vann's cohort and beyond beat and even murdered their Cherokee spouses, often under the influence of alcohol. In 1813, for instance, a Cherokee woman named Naki who lived one and a half miles away from the Springplace Mission reported that "[h]er otherwise very good and sober husband, The Trunk, had gotten drunk and chased her out of the house." Six days later, The Trunk (a relative of Peggy Vann's), "in his drunkenness . . . mistreated his wife very horribly and would have killed her if Harry, a Negro, who was also present, had not torn her from his anger and bound him. Then she fled with the children into the woods." Back in Naki's cabin, "horrible excesses were being carried out by the drunken Indians." One of Naki's older daughters was also nearly attacked, but she "found a chance to disappear and hide herself in the woods."[15] In another example two years later, a man named The Tyger "threatened to beat his good wife and little son." The Tyger's son prevented this by ushering his father to the slave quarters and asking a black man to monitor him. After the incident, The Tyger's son commented to his father: "I must protect my mother from you, when you are drunk." The missionaries concluded that although The Tyger and his wife normally "live[d] together on the best terms, . . . [h]is strong passion for brandy . . . causes his good-natured wife grief."[16] In 1807, a group of Cherokee women added their own voices to a growing critique of Cherokee men's alcohol-induced aggression. That autumn, when the Vanns hosted the annual payment from the U.S. government for ceded lands and hundreds of Cherokees from the Cherokee Upper Towns gathered at Diamond Hill, several women lamented to the missionaries that "their men loved whiskey too much and when they were drunk, they were very angry."[17]

Of all the incidents of domestic violence in early nineteenth-century Cherokee country, James Vann was the most documented perpetrator. His simultaneous status as one of the largest slaveholders in the nation might not have been coincidental to this fact. As master of his Diamond Hill plantation domain, Vann began to take on some of the recognizable characteristics of white southern masculinity. Although he did not aspire to an orderly plantation environment and never achieved the respectability of southern white patriarchs, Vann did gamble frequently, drink heavily, and physically abuse his wife and slaves in ways that were tolerated in the white South. He subjected his wife to acts of violence too terrible for the missionaries to record. His abuse of Peggy was so severe that a visitor "who had arrived [in 1808] . . . could not say enough about how horribly Mr. Vann treated his good wife in his drunkenness."[18]

Vann also showed signs of emotional abuse toward female family members. A primary example is the illness and death of Peggy Vann's favored slave, Caty. Corrupt as this mistress-slave relationship might have been, Peggy expressed feelings of intense affection for Caty, "her dear Negro woman [to] be remembered by her in her last days."[19] In 1820, the year that Peggy died, missionary Anna Rosina Gambold wrote in a eulogy: "In 1808, a Negro woman belonging to her, departed this life . . . which made a deep and lasting impression on her mistress."[20] When Caty died in her sleep, Peggy was forlorn. She asked the missionaries to make a coffin for Caty and conduct a proper burial ceremony. Peggy wished to have Caty, "whom she really loved dearly," buried in her own garden. In the face of Peggy's obvious attachment to Caty, and despite Peggy's wishes for a sentimental burial, James intervened to ensure Caty's degradation and Peggy's further heartbreak. The garden burial Peggy imagined was not to be. Instead, James "gave secret orders to dig the grave outside on the place of the skulls where three Negroes who had been executed in such a horrible way were buried, and of which Mrs. Vann learned nothing until this morning when the funeral procession was to start, which was a real stab in the heart for her, but she did not dare to say anything against it."[21] Peggy was so attached to Caty that Caty warranted a mention in Peggy's own eulogy. The premeditated emotional cruelty that James Vann directed toward his wife greatly affected her, but according to the missionaries, fear of him kept her silent. During Caty's burial, "Many tears, especially by Mrs. Vann, were shed."[22]

Notable in this example of James's emotional abuse and in other examples of Cherokee men's physical abuse previously described, is the way in which black slaves were drawn into incidents of violence against Cherokee women. In the case of Caty and Peggy Vann, James lashed out at his wife through the medium of Caty's lifeless body. In the examples of The Trunk and The Tyger, black men were enlisted to protect Cherokee women from their dangerous spouses. The violent acts perpetrated by Cherokee men, especially those who were slaveholders, highlighted the connection between Cherokee women and black slaves, both of whom were vulnerable to brutal treatment in varying moments and to varying degrees.[23]

On Diamond Hill, black slaves shared a state of heightened vulnerability with Peggy Vann and other women of the Vann family. In the inebriated condition that led him to serially strike his wife and shoot at his mother with a pistol, Vann rampaged through the slave quarters, setting cabins on fire at will. And while his wife and slaves bore the brunt of his unfettered aggression, Vann also lashed out at nearly anyone present on his plantation grounds. He fought with his Indian drinking companions, tied up and lashed a former overseer for allegedly stealing pigs, and would have shot his clerk, Valentine Geiger, if Geiger had not "tore the flint from his pistol."[24] Vann's frighteningly erratic actions led his own mother to choose "not to live close to [him] any longer."[25]

Black chattel slavery and the plantation environment likely encouraged James Vann's violent tendencies, giving him permission to act out his rage, especially against those who had no rights or protection. For in the southern plantation setting that Vann had chosen to reproduce, violence against slaves was commonplace, a "disposable brutality" that contributed to a larger "toleration of [white] male violence." In his travels through the plantation South, Frederick Law Olmsted observed that male slaveholders, who lived as the virtual lords of their domains, were wont to develop undue faith in their own opinions, exaggerated belief in their own authority, an intense feeling of personal pride, and a lack of "ordinary restraints and means of discipline." To these characteristics Olmsted added a readiness to resort to violence in conflicts that might be resolved differently in a nonslaveholding society. Southern historian Clement Eaton has also noted that "the Southern plantation and the autocratic control over negro slaves left a strong imprint upon the personality of the Southern aristocracy."[26] The habit of owning other human beings, the ability to lay them low, instill fear, and coerce obedience, could affect slaveholders' character and render them vulnerable to the worst excesses of human kind. This psychological effect of slave ownership was so potent, in fact, that slavery studies scholar David Brion Davis has labeled it a core characteristic of slavery. A key facet of slavery, then, a central aspect of the system's makeup, is the dehumanization of another person that transfers a sense of perverse superiority onto the slave owner. This sense of superiority won through the debasement of others could permeate a slaveholder's identity and color his (or her) way of being in the world.[27] Even as Vann rejected some aspects of southern slaveholder culture, he incorporated and replicated this base feature.

A man already plagued by impulsivity and selfishness, James Vann indulged in excessive violence in a plantation climate that fostered it. And violence against the weak (which, of necessity, reinforced a system of coerced labor) was spreading contagiously on Diamond Hill. James's mother, Wali, his sister Nancy, and even his wife, Peggy, all themselves victims of Vann's abuse, viciously punished enslaved black women and girls, as did white women in southern households. In one instance, Wali Vann "beat Grace's daughter horribly on the way home." On another occasion, Nancy Vann had Renee "greeted with a beating and threatened that she might be sold" when Renee tried to take up for Nancy's daughter, Ruth. And when the missionaries determined that Nan, "the Negro girl" they had borrowed from the Vanns, was unsatisfactory, "Mrs. [Peggy] Vann had her fetched home . . . and on her arrival gave her a large number of lashes along with a strong reprimand."[28] Although their gender made the Vann women vulnerable to a male head of household's excesses, their race, Cherokee nationality, and privileged class status empowered them to mistreat black slaves. Violence against women on this Cherokee plantation and violence against owned people of African descent were linked through the imposition and adoption of American ideals of civilized agricultural society. Members of both these groups were left open to assault by Cherokee men whose status had been elevated through acceptance of a patriarchal plantation system. And yet, even in a context that rendered both groups vulnerable, black slaves, deprived by their status of "human dignity, respect, and honor," faced the ultimate exposure.[29]

Four Women

In 1805, one of the most dramatic years of Diamond Hill's early history, an event transpired that seems, at first rendering, like a fateful clash between men. But although this surface interpretation is an accurate one, the contest between James Vann and the white and black men who defiantly robbed him reveals the interrelated dynamics of gender and race on the plantation. Just as Peggy Scott Vann's experience on Diamond Hill can also be viewed as a story about plantation slavery, the theft of James Vann's cash fortune by working white men and male slaves can also be seen as a story about the gendered subjugation of four women. These four women — one white, one black, and two Cherokee — appear as minor actors in the unfolding narrative of events, but an analysis of their treatment reveals the interrelationship between race and gender oppression, as well as the ultimate privilege of white manhood in an Indian nation subject to the United States.

Reports of the robbery of 1805 began in late August while James Vann was away on a business trip to the Tellico, Tennessee, blockhouse (or trading factory). The missionaries recorded in their diary:

> Last night *on the 28th* four of Mr. Vann's Negroes ran away again. Before they went, however, they robbed their master of all of the money he had in the house, about thirty-five hundred dollars. They also emptied a chest full

of silk and cotton scarves. They took away some of Mrs. Vann's things and Mr. Vann's clothing and three pistols with them. The chest with the gold was under the bed where Mrs. Vann and a white woman were sleeping. The money chest was found empty in the woods this morning and they had left one single dollar in it. Early today everyone went after the thieves but came home again in the evening without results.[30]

Meanwhile, Nicholas Byers, a factor at Tellico, wrote to Agent Meigs express mail from the blockhouse apprising him of the same set of facts: "I haste to inform you by request of Mr. Vann who is now here, that he has just had tidings of his house being robbed of a trunk containing *all* his money. [A]nd three of his negroes are missing and supposed to have committed the robbery with accomplices of bad white people that have been lurking about in the neighborhood."[31] Back at the Springplace Mission, the Moravians dreaded James Vann's reaction to the news. Black slaves, his human property, had stolen themselves along with the entirety of his gold and cash fortune, leaving behind, as if underscoring their triumph, one single dollar bill. The missionaries worried: "Now all of us are waiting in horrified anticipation about what will happen when Vann comes back home. A few months ago about seven hundred dollars were stolen from him, and afterward he behaved himself so that everyone had to flee. How will it be then, when he hears that all his money is gone?"[32]

The black men who so blatantly defied James Vann did not even want the loot. Bob, Isaac, and Peter had plotted, instead, for their freedom. A black woman named April who was said to have aided the men may have been Isaac's wife. For Isaac, described as "self-righteous" by the missionaries, this would be a fourth attempt at liberation.[33] The scheme began when Bob, Vann's stable hand, was in search of wayward horses in the company of John Spencer, a long-term white visitor at the Vann house. In the course of conversation, Bob told Spencer that "he would wish his master would sell him." Spencer told Bob that if Bob helped him, he would "clear him" of Vann's ownership. Spencer then brought Isaac into the fold, explaining in his confession: "I got in with Negro Isaac and propost to him that if he would help me to Rile Mr Jas Vann and takes Vann money, that I would git him to a country where he should be free[.] Negro Peter came to me after I propost the affair to Isaac and told me that he would Rile his master and take the money [and] I would git him free."[34]

On a night soon after the plans were laid, Spencer gave Peter a "New Rifle, to kill his master." The plan had evolved from theft alone to theft and murder, perhaps to ensure the black men's freedom as well as Spencer's clean getaway. The group of black men who would do the deed had grown by one and now included Ned or Sam. Spencer also enlarged his circle of nonblack accomplices. He enlisted Joseph Boring, a former overseer of Vann's, promising that after Vann was dead, he would have Bob select the finest horses among Vann's holdings for Boring's benefit. Spencer was also vaguely in cahoots with John Falling, the Cherokee husband of Nancy, James Vann's sister. Spencer and Boring, who would not do the actual deed, planned to "divide the money between [them]" and "the Negers for thire share should be free."[35]

The plan was to murder Vann before the burglary was undertaken, but after two aborted attempts, Vann remained alive. The thieves then decided to strike instead while Vann was away. Since Peter was familiar with the Vann family's habits, he was selected to lead the way into Mrs. Vann's room at night. On a trial run through, Peter had discovered that "Mrs. Vann sleepd so sound she would not awake [a]s [he] has been in the room where the money is and got some whysky & open'd a trunk & took a silk [handkerchief] out of the trunk, and feeld under the bed For the trunk where the money was."[36] But, according to Peggy Vann, the break-in did not occur as planned. She charged that she awakened and that the robber then showed her a stick and said he was "prepared to beat her to death along with another woman sleeping with her, if they had just made a sound."[37] Peter and the black men with him stole away from the house. Bob then took command of the operation, hiding the money in the stable where he worked "in the slotte among the oates." On the second day, Spencer moved the money to another location. Peter, Isaac, Bob, and the fourth black accomplice, now on the run, stopped by Boring's spring in search of "something to eat." Later that day, Spencer told Boring that "it was all done now but one thing and that was to kill Mr. Jas Vann, and that he would do it in a day's time."[38]

But Vann would survive this lethal ambush, and sixteen days after the robbery had taken place, he saw to it that Isaac, Bob, and a third slave were captured. The men confessed to the crime and charged that Spencer had "forced them to steal from their master." After Spencer was apprehended, he confessed "under torture," naming Boring as an accomplice. Vann organized a manhunt for Peter, who was still at large and reported to have a weapon. Meanwhile, James Vann began executing the guilty slaves. Vann reserved the most brutal treatment for Isaac, perhaps because Isaac had always been so boldly defiant of Vann's authority. The missionaries wrote: "Mr. Vann wants to burn alive his Negro Isaac, who robbed him. He is out for his blood; he called all the Negroes together to watch it and learn an example from it as well." Just over a week later, Bob was executed by pistol shot. The fourth black accomplice may have somehow avoided capital punishment, as the manner of his execution is not recorded. The black community of Diamond Hill, forced to witness Vann's revenge and suffer Vann's random whippings while the manhunt for Peter continued, must have been shaken to its core. In late October, Peter was captured, beaten, and "locked up in chains" under Vann's house. Peter did not repent of his actions; instead, he appeared "insolent as if he was not afraid of anything." In early November, Vann had Peter hanged.[39]

At least three women, and perhaps a fourth, whom Vann suspected of involvement in the robbery, also suffered from his quest for revenge. Vann "punished very harshly a Negro woman [April] who had taken part in the robbery." He also tortured a young white woman whom he suspected. This woman, who had probably been the one sharing Peggy's bed on the night of the break-in, was likely to have been Vann's mistress or a household servant. A Moravian witness wrote in a letter to Agent Meigs: "At the time Vann's money was stolen He put the persons he suspected to torture, amongst others a young White Girl by the name of Crawford." Vann tied the girl up by her thumbs, and when she did not confess, he tied her up by her toes. When she was finally released, the girl could hardly walk. She hobbled to the Springplace Mission, where she hid beneath a bed. But Vann, who was in "a great passion," sent an enslaved man to find her. The man "carried her back [to Vann] in his arms."[40] What happened to the girl when she was returned to Vann is not recorded. In all probability, her torture continued. Nor do the missionaries note the punishment, if any, suffered by Peggy Vann, who was also in the house when the theft occurred and therefore a likely target of her husband's fury. Nancy Vann, whom James later suspected of tangential involvement, would face her own penalty down the line when Vann had plans to "force [her], through shameful means, to turn [the money] over."[41]

Black men were executed for their part in the robbery scheme. A black woman and a white girl were beaten and tortured, and Cherokee women were threatened with assault. But the white men who masterminded the entire affair were protected from harm by the U.S. government. After extracting confessions from the first black men he captured, Vann had John Spencer and Joseph Boring detained. He chained them in his home and held them as prisoners while he awaited the counsel of several Cherokee chiefs. Vann explained to the missionaries that "[i]n four days the chiefs would meet at his place" to determine whether "the white people had to die." Chiefs Chuleoa and Sour Mush arrived at Vann's plantation, along with a third unnamed chief and six other Cherokees. After a day's deliberation, the nine advisers "wanted to execute the prisoners." But before they could carry out this judgment, Agent Meigs intervened. He declared by letter that "they should not dare kill the white people."[42] Instead, Meigs wanted Spencer and Boring delivered to him, at which point Meigs would replace Vann's stolen fortune and reimburse him for transport costs.

Vann was enraged by this decision, concluding from it that U.S. citizens could violate Cherokee people on Cherokee land with governmental impunity. He sent a letter along with the remanded prisoners, telling Meigs: "[W]ee are all here dissastisfied that wee shall not punish a whiteman when he steels and maks Plots with Negros to kill aney man that has property in this Nation."[43] Vann's clerk, Valentine Geiger, also wrote to Meigs in protest: "It is well known that Mr. James Vann is one of the first class of man in the Nation, and by his hospitality is taken in by a villain of the states of these united states." Geiger posed a rhetorical question in his letter: what if he, a white man, should choose to live in the Cherokee Nation for the rest of his life and a "villain or a heigh way robber comes to my house & takes all I possess." Geiger then argued that he would not be able to pay the transportation and legal costs of sending the thieves to U.S. territory for trial. He conjectured that this requirement that white lawbreakers be tried in the United States for crimes committed in Cherokee country "is great encouragement for thives to come and steal in the Nation."[44] Return Meigs did not see the situation in quite the same way. The white men would remain in his protective custody. But enslaved black men and women, and even a poor white girl of probable ill repute, would attract no attention, receive no protection, from an agent of the United States.

The U.S. agent made clear distinctions between Euro-American men and others who might be subject to Vann's attacks, but Vann himself did not. Under the influence of alcohol, raging emotion, and a plantation climate permissive of violence against the weak, James Vann was an equal-opportunity abuser. Vann was willing to kill white men, just as he was willing to kill black men, though he realized that harming whites made him vulnerable to U.S. state retribution and therefore sought agreement from Cherokee chiefs. As for his slaves, over whom Vann had complete jurisdiction, no such approval was necessary. Vann likewise evidenced little gradation in his treatment of women of various racial backgrounds, suggesting that he saw his personal authority as extending beyond the black people he owned to the Cherokee and white women with whom he was intimate. Vann attacked black women, white women, and even Cherokee women within his own family. His behavior in this regard was silent testimony both to his transformation into a southern-style patriarch in the realm of gender relations and to the growing consent of these restructured gender expectations among his male slaveholding peers. It is noteworthy, in this latter regard, that Charles Hicks, Peggy's maternal uncle, did not, as far as the missionaries record, ever intervene to protect his niece from abuse, a duty that would have been his solemn obligation in a traditional system of Cherokee clan revenge.

The Duel

For the women in James Vann's family, the first months of 1806 foreshadowed another tumultuous year. James continued to drink to excess and project a demeanor so threatening that "[w]hite people also [tried] all sorts of ways to keep him in a good mood and to pacify his restless conscience." One white companion tried to wean Vann from alcohol and "did not even allow him a glass of wine per day." When Vann appeared morose without his brandy, the friend "got his violin, played it, and held a dance or told him funny stories." Still, the missionaries prognosticated, "this cure would not last because of what it consisted."[45]

In January, before Vann departed for a business trip to New York, he threatened his sister Nancy's new husband, John Falling, of whom he disapproved. John Falling then came to Diamond Hill under the cover of night to collect his wife and her belongings, taking her "to his place apparently out of fear of her brother."[46] Several months later, word reached Vann that Falling had issued him a "challenge." John Falling and James Vann, Cherokee men both, understood the meaning of this unusual invitation. Falling had challenged Vann to a duel, that high ritual of Euro-southern masculine culture in which gentlemen engaged to defend their honor. James's travels across Tennessee, Georgia, and South Carolina had exposed him to the manners and mannerisms of white southerners, as had his interactions with Moravians and white laborers at home and the influence of his own white southern father. James also kept an English-language library that provided potential insights into Western cultural practices. He, like John Falling, recognized the duel as "the means by which honor was upheld, as a mark of status and a claim of leadership" in white southern male society. Among southern gentlemen, a call to duel could scarcely be refused, except for reasons of striking differences in age or rank, or the excuse that one's family could not spare the would-be combatant. Vann, never one to shrink from a fight, accepted Falling's challenge. A means of settling disputes that had been transported to white southern culture by aristocratic British and French officers in the Revolutionary War would be taken up by the slaveholding class of the Cherokee Nation.[47]

That evening, as Diamond Hill residents were settling in for sleep, Wali Vann pounded on the missionaries' door. When the Moravians let James's panic-stricken mother in, "she collapsed with loud sobbing" and exclaimed, "Jemmy has killed Falling." James and John Falling had agreed to duel, Wali explained, and the two men had met at the set time and place. "When they had gotten as close as possible," Wali said, "they fired at the same time and Falling's charge hit against Vann's rock wall, so that the fire hit it and at the same time Vann's charge went through Falling's chest and threw him dead to the ground."[48] Wali Vann feared for her son's life, for revenge-seeking members of Falling's clan would now target him. Earlier that day, Falling's brother had already made an attempt at murder. After witnessing the duel, the brother "hid himself behind the trees and took aim at him," but Vann escaped unharmed. One of Vann's longtime adversaries, Chief Doublehead, was a member of Falling's clan and would surely take this opportunity to avenge his relative as well as to act out his own personal vendetta.[49]

Wali also grieved for her daughter Nancy, who learned of the outcome of the fight from her remote location at Falling's house and was said to be distraught. Wali wanted to send for her daughter and have her brought home to Diamond Hill, but "[t]he Negroes and Indians [were] afraid to go there because they fear[ed] for their lives." In the aftermath of the duel, Wali and Peggy Vann wrung their hands and cried. The women were in a "pitiable state . . . such a state of constant fear that even a rustling leaf frighten[ed] them. The desire to eat and sleep [was] almost foreign to them, and they looked like people condemned to death." Women in the Vann family and blacks and Indians who lived on the grounds worried at the thought of Falling's family seeking vengeance. Even Little Isaac, a black child owned by James, was threatened by Falling's relatives, "who aimed a flint gun at him" when he followed his master's instructions to locate Falling's body.[50]

For his part, James Vann remained "quite composed," even "cold-blooded" throughout the affair. He "knew well that his life was once again in danger . . . and spoke about matters concerning his last will and testament." Nevertheless, he boasted: "I am not so easy to be killed." Vann seemed unmoved by the death of his brother-in-law, the distress of the women in his family, and the danger everyone on Diamond Hill now faced. Perhaps it was James's utter self-centeredness that led Sam Kerr, the visiting free black preacher, to criticize Vann in the presence of Vann's mother. "[H]er son," Kerr reportedly said, "behaves himself like a childish boy and not at all like a *man*."[51]

Kerr's harsh assessment of Vann, in which the word "man" was emphasized in the original, was an indication of the multiple and even competing masculinities that circulated through the Cherokee Nation in this early-nineteenth-century moment. As an elder black man, Kerr accused the reckless Vann of lacking in a quality of manhood that Kerr would have respected; in issuing a "challenge," John Falling dared James Vann to live up to white southern standards of elite manhood. And both of these incidents took place as Cherokee men of Vann's social class abandoned hunting, a former marker of Cherokee masculinity, to engage in and oversee agricultural labor, a former marker of Cherokee femininity. As Cherokee masculine identity was being transformed in this changing colonial context, Vann may have turned to violent behavior all the more. For, in addition to hunting, warfare had been the purview of Cherokee men in the main, bringing honor and distinction to its skilled practitioners. With the Cherokees' final submission to U.S. military power after a long guerrilla war, and with the return of most men from their shrinking hunting grounds, the practical meaning of Cherokee manhood was under assault. For James Vann, filling the role of punitive plantation patriarch and carrying out excessively aggressive acts may have been part of a larger process of remaking masculine identity.

After John Falling was buried, Nancy, who appeared "very frail and cried a lot," visited the missionaries with her child, Ruth, and a stepdaughter. She said she planned to move back home to Diamond Hill once she had harvested the crops in Falling's field. The traumatic turn of events that had left Nancy widowed and James a target for execution drew the Vann women closer together. Wali, Nancy, and Peggy were now often found in each other's company. Meanwhile, James Vann resumed his traveling with a bodyguard, declaring that he was unafraid. When he was at home, Vann "surrounded" himself with "loaded weapons," surely an intimidating scene for Peggy and Wali, both of whom had been victims of James's violence in the recent past.[52]

In addition to taking precautions of self-defense, Vann set about righting his political relationships in the aftermath of the duel. He gave his version of the conflict with Falling at a meeting of Cherokee chiefs, who "excused the former even though the relatives of the *latter* [were] still after revenge."[53] Valentine Geiger, Vann's clerk, wrote a letter to Agent Meigs asking him to intervene on Vann's behalf by affirming the chiefs' decision. Although Meigs condemned the Cherokee "customs [of clan revenge] which have descended down to them from their ancestors from time immemorial," he declined to step in.[54] The month after Vann's reprieve by the chiefs, he bestowed gifts of jewelry, scarves, and English spelling books on the Moravian missionaries and their children, thanking them for being "his most honest friends." If Vann offered words of solace to the sister whom he had widowed, their exchange has not been preserved in the historical record. Toward the end of the year, Vann received welcome news from the Cherokee Council. He was "made a counselor chief at the last talk in Oostanaula and had been taken in protection from these chiefs against all the pursuits of his enemies."[55] Despite the jeopardy and state of fear that he had brought on his household, Vann's political career had progressed in the aftermath of the duel. Now, as a council member and "chief" in the Cherokee Nation, his influence would be even greater.

Although Vann threatened to harm his sister Nancy for suspected involvement in the 1805 robbery, he never directly addressed the conflict that had prompted the duel and resulted in Falling's death. A month before Falling had issued his challenge, he was accused of stealing from Vann by a member of the Cherokee Council. Although Falling's involvement in the robbery of 1805 had been leaked by Falling himself, to defend his honor, Falling wanted to duel. Missionary John Gambold explained the whole affair in a private letter to a friend in Salem:

> You know that a year ago Mr. Vann was robbed rather grossly and that he wreaked vengeance on the black part of the thieves, but that he got back the larger part of his money. Now a short time ago his brother-in-law John Falling said when he was drunk that more than $800 of this money had been deposited with him, this was brought out at a talk in Estenally last month [and] a delegate of the Council informed J. F. that he should immediately return this money to Mr. Vann, The former, however, denies steadfastly that he said such a thing or that he has the money. . . . We feel sorriest for poor Nancy Vann, J. F.'s wife, she is really sitting between two fires."[56]

Gambold wrote that Falling had participated in the burglary and hidden the cash "under a stone or rock, and this was actually the cause of the duel with J. Vann in which he lost his life." Over a year after the crime, Nancy Vann purchased an enslaved man named Jim with what her daughter Ruth Falling described as "Uncle Jim's money, which her grandmother had buried in the earth." Ruth continued: "This is why [the money] became so filthy and black that the mother and grandmother first had to carry it to the water and clean it before they could spend it." According to Ruth's testimony, Nancy and Wali knowingly benefited from the theft of James's fortune. It seemed that two of the Vann women — subject to James's nontraditional form of male authority and abuse — had developed an agenda for their own revenge. Years before, Nancy's brother had stolen a slave that she had inherited from their father, and he had done so "by force."[57] Through the vehicle of the robbery, Nancy and her husband sought to recover the value of this human property. Nancy used the pilfered funds to purchase a new slave for herself.

The robbery of 1805 and duel of 1806, major happenings in the history of

Diamond Hill, revealed not only contests for wealth and standing between Vann and other men but also the subjection of black slaves and Cherokee women in the context of plantation slavery. Slavery was a push factor in each of these events — from the four black men who committed the crime to earn their freedom to the stolen slave of Nancy's that led Falling to take part, resulting in his eventual death through duel. In the unfolding of these disruptive occurrences, the vulnerability of Cherokee women, poor white women, and especially enslaved black men and women becomes apparent. In the end, nearly everyone on Diamond Hill suffered for his or her involvement — real or suspected — in the heist and subsequent duel. Isaac, Bob, and Peter lost their lives in public executions that terrorized the slave community. A black woman, possibly Isaac's wife, suffered beatings and perhaps the loss of her spouse. A young white girl was abused, and in all likelihood, so was Peggy Vann. Nancy Vann was threatened and widowed. Peggy and Wali Vann were traumatized by fear. But James Vann, a man with a cat's nine lives, lived another day and recovered the bulk of his massive cash fortune.

Expanding Circles of Violence

In the first years of the new century, Diamond Hill's residents suffered wave upon wave of internal strife. James Vann himself was the principal perpetrator of domestic violence on his plantation grounds, as he murdered enslaved blacks, beat female family members, killed his brother-in-law, and picked drunken fights with friends. In 1806 and 1807, Vann would also rally a group of like-minded men to undertake politically motivated acts of violence in the broader national domestic sphere.

Vann had long been an adversary of Chief Doublehead of the Lower Towns, for reasons both personal and political. Doublehead and Vann were rumored to have clashed in an altercation at Cavet's Station during the Chickamauga rebellion, and Doublehead was accused of killing his pregnant wife, a sister of one of Vann's former wives.[58] In addition, Vann and Doublehead held opposing positions regarding strategies for national progress and cessions of Cherokee land. Doublehead was well known as a cooperator with U.S. officials, who accepted bribes in exchange for shifting Cherokee policy toward the U.S. agents' desired ends, especially regarding land sales. Although James Vann kept an eye out for entrepreneurial opportunities, he believed the Cherokee Nation was stronger with its territory intact, and he therefore never advocated land cessions.

In 1805, a conflict over land had heightened the animosity between Vann and Doublehead. Doublehead influenced a minority of chiefs who agreed to sell the last tract of Cherokee hunting grounds. Vann attended the treaty session in Washington, DC, but deeply opposed the measure. When Vann learned that Doublehead and his close allies would receive personal tracts of land in exchange for their support of the sale, he was incensed. He "regarded [Doublehead] as the betrayer of the interests of his nation; and told him so at Washington. High words ensued and dirks were drawn; but the parties were separated & no blood was shed."[59] Although Vann had the opportunity in Washington to accept payment in land as a bribe, he refused.

In the aftermath of this devastating land sale, Vann led what historian William McLoughlin has called the Cherokee Rebellion of 1806–10. This movement was a "revolt of the young chiefs," in the view of Doublehead and his allies who were targeted by the rebellion. The so-called young chiefs were men who had not yet gained the status of major, elder chiefs but wielded influence nevertheless. Because he was "very influential and wealthy" as well as "shrewd and determined," Vann emerged as the natural leader of this group, which also included Charles Hicks (the uncle of Peggy Vann) and The Ridge (a wealthy slaveholder and friend of James Vann). The group that came to be known as "Vann's party" orchestrated an attack on a white wagon caravan trying to pass through Cherokee country, appointed themselves as monitors of government surveyors laying a new boundary line, and opposed a U.S.-backed plan of removal to Arkansas. The party also plotted to assassinate Doublehead, a scheme that was carried out in 1807.[60]

As Vann gained prominence as a nationalist rebel chief, his former supporters in the U.S. Department of War increasingly viewed him as an adversary. Agent Meigs, who had previously praised Vann for his influential advocacy of the federal road, now wanted Vann arrested. And Vann's pattern of assaulting white Americans who visited his home and establishments, sometimes by invitation, gave Meigs just the opening he sought. In 1808, Vann had shot a Georgian who was dining at his home and stabbed a Tennessean at his Chattahoochee ferry. Although Vann had offered restitution to the injured men, Meigs had Vann arrested. Meigs plainly stated his political motive in a letter to the governor of Tennessee: "If Vann is properly brought to Justice, it will have a very good effect, will silence his partizans — negociations with the Cherokees will be conducted with ease."[61] But because the white victims refused to press charges, Meigs was forced to release Vann, who received a hero's welcome by his political party.

In addition to the campaigns carried out by his rebel group, Vann found a second forum for organized violence. In 1808, the Cherokee Council passed a law establishing a national police force called the Lighthorse Brigade, which was charged with suppressing "horse stealing and robbery of other property." Lighthorse officers had the authority to identify, judge, punish, and even execute criminals, and they were protected from clan revenge by law. Unlike Cherokees' long-standing means of curbing antisocial behavior through persuasion, exclusion, and clan retaliation, in order to consolidate control and decrease tensions with white settlers, the nation was now sanctioning state-enacted corporal punishment. Although Vann was not a salaried captain, lieutenant, or private in this force, he rode along with the Lighthorsemen in his district, meting out punishment as he saw fit.[62]

Violence Out of Bounds

By the early 1800s, Cherokees felt their familiar world beginning to collapse around them. The national territory was steadily shrinking, despite efforts by politically powerful men like Vann to protect it. As a result of lost hunting grounds and agricultural fields wasted in the Revolutionary War and its aftermath, people were going hungry. The U.S. president and his agents urged Cherokees to abandon their own ways and adopt "civilized" manners of life, to give up hunting and clan revenge, to adopt large-scale agriculture and domestic arts. Meanwhile, violence was increasing and taking new forms. As an early adopter of plantation slavery, James Vann owned, used, and abused black slaves in a manner that few Cherokees would have recognized in the 1700s. For women like Peggy Vann, this mounting violence penetrated the space of the home. Her husband assaulted female intimates and black slaves alike, killed his brother-in-law in a duel, rode with the Cherokee Lighthorse brigade, and attacked whites and Indians who crossed him. Women in the Vann family also became complicit in this rising culture of violence, lashing out against vulnerable black women and girls whom they viewed as property. Beyond Vann's grounds, Cherokee men beat their wives under the influence of alcohol, and Cherokee police officers, for the first time in the nation's history, were authorized to apply harsh corporal punishment. These forms of abuse departed dramatically from long-standing Cherokee practices. In the eighteenth century, Cherokee men did not commonly strike their wives, and the Cherokee police, first established in 1797, did not punish fellow Cherokees.[63] What is more, Cherokees who did harm others in this earlier period were subject to a fundamental principle held sacred by all — the ethic of clan protection. Being in a family, belonging to a clan, was the main measure of security that any individual Cherokee needed. If a person was unduly harmed, she or he could be certain that a clan member would seek righteous retaliation, thereby restoring community balance.

But in the first years of the nineteenth century, balance was illusive as James Vann and his fellow Cherokees stood at the crux of cultural change. New mechanisms and forms of violence were burrowing into Cherokee society while the old system of clan protection was weakened by U.S. disapproval and Cherokee leaders' desire to meet external expectations. Violence against women is a primary example in which this shift is visible. A Cherokee woman, who in the past could expect an uncle or brother to retaliate if she were abused, now had diminished familial protection due to the decline of clan retaliation. Her level of security therefore decreased even as her husband's access to alcohol and guns, which exacerbated the likelihood and peril of domestic violence, increased.

James Vann's duel with John Falling is another example of diversifying violence at a moment of cultural shift. In this, the only recorded duel in Cherokee history, Falling was motivated to preserve his honor by white southern norms of masculinity. Vann assented to this novel form of dispute settlement, but in the aftermath of the duel, Falling's family did not. They rejected the ethos of the duel and sought to apply the system of clan revenge. Cherokee Council members then tried to protect Vann by overturning the Fallings' right to vengeance. In this case, two deadly but culturally distinct forms of violence, the southern duel and Cherokee clan retaliation, were employed simultaneously for a time, multiplying the possibility for widespread harm. And undergirding this proliferation of violent formats was the plantation slavery environment that sanctioned and encouraged the dehumanization and wanton abuse of less powerful human beings.

In the early 1800s, a critical moment of cross-cultural reckoning in Cherokee society, James Vann, a man predisposed to recklessness and fervor, adopted multiple forms of violent action. As the ordered system of Cherokee clan revenge began to give way and Euro-American rituals and technologies of violence penetrated Cherokee society, Vann faced a smorgasbord of brutal options. He could duel people, shoot people, beat people, and whip them, and be confronted with fewer cultural checks than would have been the case a century before. As traditional Cherokee means of maintaining order weakened, and Cherokee men, especially those in the slaveholding elite, began to adopt practices of gender and state violence more common to Euro-American society, residents of the Cherokee Nation were suspended in a deadly cultural limbo. More people were vulnerable to unbounded violence, and fewer protections remained to ward against it.

During a visit with Peggy Vann at the Moravian mission, an elderly Cherokee chief warned of his people's acquiescence to white cultural influence. Chief Koychezetel (also known as Warrior's Nephew) told a story in which the sky people, spirit beings and messengers from God, chastised the Cherokees' changing way of life, which included the adoption of extracultural forms of violence. In telling the tale, Koychezetel quotes the sky people's leader as saying:

> God is dissatisfied that you so indiscriminately lead the white people onto my land. You yourselves see that your game has gone. You plant the white people's corn. Go and buy it back from them and plant Indian corn and pound it according to your ancestors' ways. Make the people go away. The mother of the nation has left you, because all her bones are being broken through the milling. She will return, however, if you get the white people out of the country and return to your former way of life. You yourselves can see that the white people are completely different from us. . . . Also your mother is not pleased that you punish each other severely. Yes, you whip until blood flows. Now I have told you what God's will is, and you should tell others.[64]

In the vision related through this spiritual tale, the consequence of Cherokee acceptance of Euro-American ways — Euro-style farming and milling, abandoned hunting, bloody violence, white settlement — was utter desertion by "the mother of the nation." The story chastised those who would hear it, warning that Selu, the first woman and magical Corn Mother who had given birth to the Cherokees across the mists of time, no longer recognized her descendants.

CHAPTER 5

House of Prayer

So Vann's famous house, which . . . had become pretty much a Sodom,
is now standing vacant and the Negroes are left to themselves.
—Letter from missionary John Gambold to Charles Gotthold Reichel, 1811

Here Lies the Body

In the aftermath of conflict after conflict, the residents of Diamond Hill must
have hoped for respite. But dramatic lightning storms in the spring of 1808
portended this was not to be. At the end of April, "an unusual number" of
strong storms arose, dropping lightning bolts that felled three trees close to
the Springplace Mission barn. The first tree, an oak, "was so completely shattered that only the stump remained." Two peach trees "were also struck down,
and the field was full of splinters of wood, many of which were as big as fence
posts." May brought a continuing slate of storms, and at high noon on the
24th, three storms converged: "It stormed, rained, and hailed so heavily that
the houses shook, and there was a terrible roaring. . . . The houses, although
the doors and windows were closed, were littered all the way to the dividing
walls with hail the size of bird eggs, which the wind blew in from the chimney.
Toward evening the most beautiful rainbow we have ever seen presented itself
and young and old were delighted at the sight."[1]

The storm cycle wreaked havoc on the Vann estate but ended with a bril-
liant sign of hope. The murder of James Vann, which would occur the following winter, had the same effect—forcing change at the Moravians' school,
causing chaos for long-suffering slaves, and ushering in a new beginning for
Vann's battered wife.

In early February of 1809, James Vann set out on a task to which he was
most dedicated—capturing and punishing horse thieves in the company of
the Lighthorse Brigade. James wanted his favorite son, Joseph, to accompany
him. And although "the boy cried and did not want to go along," his father
"forced him to go."[2] Later that month, when father, son, and an enslaved servant departed on a similar outing, only two would return. On February 21, the
missionaries related the "horrible news of *Mr. Vann's murder.*" Vann had "gone
here and there in the country holding the strictest trials, he had an Indian shot
who did not give himself up willingly." After this extreme treatment of an al-

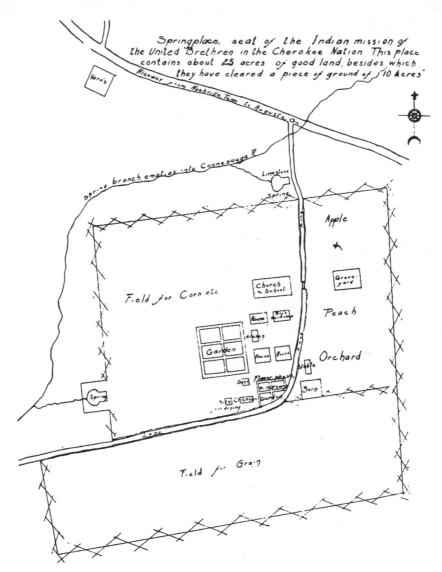

Springplace, seat of the Indian mission of the United Brethren in the Cherokee Nation This place contains about 25 acres of good land, besides which they have cleared a piece of ground of 10 acres

Vann's

Highway from Nashville Tenn to Augusta Ga

Spring branch empties into Connesauga R

Limestone

Spring

Apple

Grove-yard

Field for Corn etc

Church & School.

Peach

House

Garden

Orchard

House

House

Stable

Spring

Flower plots

Barn

Chicken

Toge

Field for Grain

Springplace Mission diagram, early 1800s.
Courtesy of the Chief Vann House.

leged thief, Vann made his way to Buffington's inn and tavern, where he sent his son upstairs to bed, drank himself beyond all reason, and fell into a war of words with a group of former friends whom he "treated extremely contemptuously." Late that evening, "when Vann was at the table, which stood across from the open door, a shot was fired from outside and hit him directly in the heart." "Thus fell this man," the missionaries recorded, "who had for so long been feared by many, but loved by a few, in his forty-first year." Although the perpetrator was never sought or captured, the missionaries thought, and most historians have agreed, that Alexander Saunders, the former friend whom Vann had so rudely insulted, committed the crime.[3]

Immediately after the shooting, Vann's slave swept up the sleeping child and led him to safety on Vann's Chattahoochee plantation. This heroic man who may have saved Joseph's life, who could have stolen Vann's money and made his own escape, goes unidentified in all of the original accounts of the incident. Back at the tavern, less honorable men stole the clothes of Vann and his son, "as well as other valuables including his pocketbook containing a large sum of money in banknotes." By the time Vann's widow heard the news and arrived to claim his body, "Vann had already been buried in the woods close to the road."[4]

The community at Diamond Hill was shaken to its core by this dreadful turn of events. With James Vann's passing, everyone's place on the plantation shifted, social relations tilted askew, and no one knew what to expect from a now uncertain future. "Everything around us looks very confused," missionary John Gambold wrote, "all hearts are filled with terror of death, and with fear, and with apprehension of the things which follow."[5] The women in the Vann family fell into immediate, inconsolable grief. The missionaries observed that "Mrs. Vann and her parents-in-law, [were] almost half-dead from shock." They wrote, further, of Peggy's reaction: "Her husband, despite all of the suffering that he often caused her, was now a genuine heartache." Peggy expressed this heartache in her own words, saying: "I had only *one* husband and remained true to him even under the most difficult trials, and his death hurt me indescribably." She had married James Vann as a teenage girl and lived her entire adult life on Diamond Hill. She loved and missed her intolerable husband and at the age of twenty-six could not yet see the promise of a life without him. The missionaries tried to reach Vann's home to comfort Peggy, but they "could not get there because of the loud wailing that prevailed in the house." To the missionaries, Peggy and her in-laws were engaged in unintelligible "heathen mourning" practices, but Peggy and her family found comfort in the familiar rhythms of Cherokee ways. In her hour of need, Peggy's relatives traveled from near and far to be with her. Her mother, sisters (including a former wife of James), cousins, and brother all made repeated visits to Diamond Hill.[6]

While Peggy lost herself in grief, her mother-in-law began to close ranks against the foreign missionaries. To comfort Peggy, and perhaps to feel closer to the memory of her deceased son, Wali moved into the main house. "His mother, who stayed here the first three weeks with Mrs. Vann to keep her company, conducted herself like a real heathen," John Gambold wrote, "and together with the other female relatives who came here from time to time, she observed the Indian mourning customs faithfully with loud wailing and kept her daughter-in-law hemmed in so closely that it was impossible to get near her with any comfort on our part." When John and Anna Rosina Gambold finally managed to pay Peggy a visit, Wali rejected them on cultural grounds: She "expressed herself in a very offensive manner . . . and then explained that they were *Indians*, and they did not understand [the missionaries'] teachings." Wali spoke "maliciously" to the missionary couple, accused them of having designs on James's fortune, and said she would no longer allow her daughter-in-law to house, feed, and care for pupils attending the mission school.[7]

Wali's rebuke was just one of the trials the missionaries faced in the aftermath of James's death. Without his powerful patronage, Cherokees grew suspicious of the outsiders' presence. Rumors spread among the towns that the Cherokee schoolchildren would be "picked up by the white people and would be taken into the settlements since Mr. Vann was no longer living." Parents began to withdraw their children from the school. A second set of rumors charged that the school had been closed and the missionaries were mistreating children who remained by denying them food beyond one meal a day. Although Agent Meigs had requested and received one hundred dollars from the secretary of war to support the teetering school, by the end of the year, Anna Rosina Gambold lamented: "[A]fter our neighbor Vann's horrific death, it first seemed, and later was actually planned, that our small school, the only work wherein we still serve Him at this time in the Cherokee Nation, might be destroyed! Most of the children, specifically those whom Mr. Vann took in for room and board, had to move home to their people, and the beautiful Passion Week was celebrated with only three!"[8]

Even more so than the missionaries, black men and women owned by James Vann were aware they faced a future of harsh uncertainty. With their master's death and the impending redistribution of the Diamond Hill estate, they might be separated from their families or sold off to an unknown place. At the same time, some members of the black community saw in Vann's death an opportunity for increased latitude; they refused to work and ignored the missionaries' counsel to carry out their tasks as before. "At the news of their master's death," the missionaries recorded, "some of the Negro people in our neighborhood became unrestrained, some of them completely confused, so that nothing could be done with them." Blacks on the plantation were "much upset and part unruly," to the extent that the overseer pondered breaking his contract and moving on to Natchez, Mississippi.[9]

Tangible fear, mounting anxiety, and increasing chaos permeated the slave quarters, and individual reactions as well as group interactions evidenced the strain. Grace, who had formerly been an observing Christian, began to miss church, drink heavily, and speak impudently to the missionaries. The missionaries intuited that Grace's "heart ha[d] become distant from the Savior since her master's death."[10] Having seen her family sold at the bankruptcy of her former master, Grace knew full well how a change in the circumstances of a slave owner could affect the security of his slaves. Perhaps she abandoned religious faith following Vann's death because she had lost hope in a stable future for her loved ones.

Other members of the black community turned against one another in a prolonged period of internal discord. Five months after Vann's death, the missionaries recorded: "[T]hese wretched people have lived for some time in horrible trouble and strife; one hears almost daily about their fighting and even bloody battles among themselves." Certainly, internal conflict was not new to members of the black community. Like any population living in close quarters, they had experienced their share of animosities, jealousies, and rivalries over the years. But this 1809 reference to daily, bloody fights among blacks was the first to be made by the missionaries. In the vacuum left by Vann's authoritarian management, members of the enslaved community seemed to be jockeying for power and position. Following Vann's murder, the missionaries began to hear reports of a sharp division between African-born and American-born slaves, manifested by Afro-Americans insulting and excluding Africans. In this caustic environment of separation and strife, Grace and Jacob, the elderly couple whom Vann had placed in charge of his mill and whom many other blacks admired, suffered a brutal challenge to their seniority.[11]

In July of 1809, while Grace was bandaging a black baby who had been burned in boiling water, her husband fell into a fight with another slave over a long-running point of contention. Jacob grabbed a stick and was prepared to beat the man with it, but Grace intervened, and Jacob "threw the stick away." The wife of the man who had avoided a beating went with a friend to find an administrator of Vann's estate. They accused both Grace and Jacob of attempted murder. The administrator, James Brown, along with two white men, seized the elderly Jacob, who was "tied to a post and wretchedly beaten." A witness to her husband's treatment, Grace "fled out of fear and horror first into the woods, and afterward to [the missionaries'] kitchen." Although Peggy Vann and the Gambolds pleaded on Grace's behalf, the overseer and one of his relatives arrived the next morning "with clubs and ropes." They dragged Grace from her hiding place, tied her to a tree, and lashed her eighty times. At sixty-eight years old, Grace nearly died from this savage attack. The missionaries insisted that Grace and Jacob's fellow millworkers had prompted this punishment because of "envy and hatred" toward the older couple and resentment of Jacob's supervisory role. They had taken advantage of James Vann's passing, which provided an opening for structural change among the enslaved community. Because Brown was a stranger to the plantation and did "not know the character of the Negroes here," he was easily manipulated by the rival group of slaves, who appealed to an outside, controlling authority to seek retribution and divert existing hierarchies.[12]

Grace healed slowly from her wounds. When Anna Rosina and John Gambold accompanied Peggy Vann to visit her, they "found the poor old woman in great physical pain but very uplifted spiritually." Grace could barely speak due to her condition, but she quietly expressed a renewed connection to Jesus Christ from her sickbed. Later, Grace explained that while she had been tied to the tree, it seemed as though an invisible someone spoke, reminding her of the Son of God's suffering. This voice, perhaps an angel's, perhaps a delusion brought on from intolerable pain, sustained Grace through the beating and restored her Christian faith.[13]

The assault on Grace and Jacob would not be the only atrocity visited upon enslaved blacks by the superintendents of Vann's estate. In 1810, administrators David McNair and James Brown "found it necessary to sell some of them." The sold slaves' final destination would be the Mississippi River town of Natchez, where large-scale Euro-southern cotton plantations thrived.[14] A bustling slave port since 1720, Natchez had passed from French to Spanish and finally to American hands in 1795. Soon thereafter it became a cotton production center that fed on the importation of thousands of slaves. Natchez-area planters built row upon row of iconic estates characterized by "mansion residence[s]" and "appropriate dependency buildings." Their goal "was a simple one from which few slave masters deviated in the first sixty years of the nineteenth century: to grow cotton, in order to buy more slaves, in order to buy land, in order to grow more cotton."[15] In 1853, travel writer Frederick Law Olmsted described the Natchez region in a chapter titled "The Exceptional Large Planters," writing: "I found the country beautiful . . . and the land almost all inclosed in plantations, the roadside boundaries of which are old rose-hedges. . . . On many of the plantations, perhaps most, no residence is visible from the road, and the negro quarters, when seen, are the usual comfortless log huts." In his interviews with Natchez-area slaveholders and overseers, Olmsted collected a catalog of crimes against humanity, including gruelingly long workdays, whippings and lashings, capture by dogs, close surveillance, and sale of slaves away from their communities.[16] Those slaves targeted for the Vann administrators' scheme would join the million blacks who were being transported to the southern frontier during the height of one of slavery's ugliest eras: the domestic slave trade that Ira Berlin has termed the Second Middle Passage. Slave testimonies from this era collected by Edward Baptist record the deepest of sorrows — mothers stolen away while their children slept beside them, children tricked into slavers' wagons with the lure of candy, and slaves taking new names like "Remember Me" and "Sophia Nobody" to mark their feelings of desolation and isolation.[17] Slaves on the Vann estate had these and other trials to confront when they were abruptly sold off to a bleak and distant land.

This heartless relocation of masses of people was a "criminal assault on family and personal identity," and Vann slaves had surely heard tell of the horrors of life "down the river." When Big Jenny learned that she was among the group to be sold, she "cursed, swore, and repeatedly wished her soul to eternal damnation." Meanwhile, her husband was already "lying in chains." When "Old Negro Ned" found out that he and his family were on the list, he attempted suicide and later died from his wound. Three of his sons ran away, and their mother, Renee, was left with an incomprehensible weight of grief. Patience, the African woman who had lost her feet in a forced march to the plantation, begged to be allowed to live with her new husband at the mill, only to learn that he, too, was being sold. With Ned and Renee's boys on the run and Ned wasting away from his self-inflicted wound, a white slave trader arrived at Diamond Hill, and "[t]he Negroes, who [were] supposed to be taken to the Natchez, were driven in a wagon." This was a dim day for those whose fates were so forcefully sealed, the dearly departed and the left-behinds. "The power of darkness," the missionaries wrote of the event, "was quite oppressive around us."[18]

A Room of Her Own

The cruel disruption of black lives was one pivotal aftershock of James Vann's death. The second was the Christian conversion and personal rebirth of Peggy

Scott Vann. The first Moravian missionaries to arrive at Diamond Hill in 1801 described James Vann's young wife as distant and removed. Although Peggy had been polite and generous, as her position as the lady of the house required, she was not receptive to intimate social interaction or to disclosures about the missionaries' faith. She kept to herself in those early years and rarely attended events hosted at the Springplace Mission. Peggy's rather cool orientation toward the Moravians began to change in the aftermath of James Vann's fatal shooting of his brother-in-law in a duel. Peggy, along with her female in-laws, was traumatized by this turn of events, and the missionaries described the women's distress as an "opportunity" for evangelism. When Anna Rosina Gambold visited Peggy the day after the duel, "she found Mrs. Vann still crying and very upset about her husband because his life was being threatened severely by the relatives of the deceased. Sister Gambold took the opportunity to have a heart-to-heart talk with her, for her to know the Savior and find comfort in His Word." Days later, John Gambold also visited with Peggy and "Mother" (Wali) Vann. At the end of the month, Anna Rosina again visited at Peggy Vann's, where she also found Wali and Peggy's stepdaughter, Delilah McNair. Slowly, with their words of spiritual comfort, the Gambolds drew Peggy in. The missionary couple's persistence at this time of emotional need bore fruit by the last Sunday of that month, when Peggy, her mother-in-law, her daughter-in-law, and several of their slaves all attended the sermon. "Mother Vann and Mrs. Vann," the missionaries recorded in their diary, "seemed to be very touched and cried a lot." By June, the newly widowed Nancy Vann was also attending sermons in the company of her mother, while Peggy and Wali had begun to visit the missionaries in the evening.[19]

The Gambolds were successful in forging emotional connections with Peggy and her in-laws during their moment of intense fear and grief. The missionaries offered reassurance in their tales of a divine Christ who was personal, loving, and real, and their efforts produced the hoped for result. The Vann women, emotionally raw and vulnerable, opened themselves to the missionaries' presence and teachings for the first time. The Gambolds wrote to friends at home: "Mrs. Vann and the old mother are also much more attached to us since this occurrence. They come frequently to the Sunday services, visit often and urge us to visit them and the former shows a great change. She used to be quite stiff and unfeeling, and now she seems soft, and . . . indicate[s] through her tearful eyes and affectionate hand-clasps her love for us." During the summer following the duel, Peggy began to visit the mission school and serve as an interpreter and mediator between the missionary teachers and Cherokee parents.[20] That next fall, when Peggy was at the mission helping to sew a quilt, she gave the Moravians a first indication that she viewed them as friends and spiritual guides. As Peggy was preparing to leave one day, "Sister Gambold said to her, 'We would like to always have you near us[.]' [Peggy] shook her hand and said with tears in her eyes, 'I hope *one day* to be *where you* will be.'" By Christmas of that year, the missionaries joyfully recorded, "[W]e really enjoyed the company at Mrs. Vann's, because we could see clearly and feel anew that she seeks and likes the Savior and is not without the feeling of His love in her heart."[21]

The series of tragedies that befell Peggy Scott Vann and her family had created successive openings for a deepening of Peggy's relationship with the missionaries. At the deathbed of her favored slave, Caty, in 1808, Peggy was indelibly moved by the missionaries' ministrations and Caty's acceptance of Christ. Her husband's death just three months later was the final catalyst for Peggy's own conversion. Again, the missionaries saw in Peggy's emotional turmoil an opportunity for underscoring their message. They "repeated [their] visits with the distressed Mrs. Vann and each time tried to give her a few words of comfort from the gospel." In April, Peggy told the Gambolds: "I could not have withstood the troubles I have met if I had not been supported. I always think I am still not clever enough for closer community with you, but this is what I really desire." In May of the following year, after participating in a Sunday service, Peggy emphasized once again the importance of having been supported through traumatic experiences: "I have often been helped in the greatest distress, I know it, I had a Helper. . . . Yes, it was He! Without Him, what would I be? I would not have made it!" That day, Peggy proclaimed that she had received the grace of God to accept his son as her savior and friend. On August 13th of 1810, Peggy was baptized in the presence of the missionaries, her mother, her sisters, her uncle Charles Hicks, and her slave, Candace, who "cried very loudly during the proceedings." Because she was the first Cherokee to formally convert to Christianity, the missionaries described her as "the first fruit of the Cherokee Nation, our dear Peggy Scott, widow of James Vann." Contemplative, reserved, and dressed "completely in white," Peggy received the baptismal name Margaret Ann. Much like the elderly Grace who had heard the voice of an angel while tied to a whipping tree, Peggy came to communion with the Christian God through heartache and suffering. The wounding she had witnessed and withstood on a slaveholding plantation located in a colonized Indian nation had led her to the heartfelt conviction that Jesus was one's most trusted friend.[22] In him, she sought and found comfort from a world of distress, a relief she later expressed in a personal letter: "The dismal Clouds of Night must vanish, when Joys divine my Heart replenish, while I recline upon Thy Breast: Ah then I find on Earth my Heaven! Such Comforts to all those are given, who seek in Thee their Peace & Rest."[23]

Once Peggy began her Christian journey, she dedicated herself to her new-found faith with an uncompromising passion. She developed an intimate friendship with Anna Rosina Gambold, whose steadfast kindness had made an impression over the years. Most evenings, Peggy could be found sitting with Anna Rosina before the mission fireplace, listening to moving accounts of missionary endeavors around the world. In good weather, Peggy often brought gifts of blueberries or beans to her Moravian friend; often, Peggy spent entire nights in Anna Rosina and John Gambold's company. Following her baptism, Peggy had begun to study English under Anna Rosina's tutelage, "chiefly in order to enjoy more spiritual fellowship with the members of the [Salem] Congregation," and now she read her Bible fastidiously and wrote about her faith.[24] She also rejected Cherokee cultural practices of which the Gambolds disapproved. When relatives of her deceased husband came to invite her to a ball play, Peggy "turned this down with revulsion." She refused to wear and began to trade away her "former heathen jewelry like earrings, silver bracelets, and such things." She harbored hopes that her blood relatives would also convert and began to tell them "the story of the Creation and the Fall of the first people, the Son of God's Incarnation, sufferings, death, Resurrection, and Ascension." She said of her fellow Cherokees, "Oh, we are a poor, needy nation. Our countrymen go around in their ignorance!" and she steadily endeavored to alter this by becoming a witness for Christ. Letters that Peggy penned to her brothers and sisters in the Moravian Church attested to her spiritual transformation and adoration for Jesus, as well as her dedication to evangelism. She wrote: "I gave myself in that happy hour over unto him to live unto him alone in this World. I have no other Care in this World, but to love my dear Savior, and I daily pray, that I may love him more and more. . . . I make use of every opportunity to speake [sic] to my Country People of his Love to men and of His Death and Sufferings."[25]

Peggy's personal transformation did not sit well with many of her fellow Cherokees. Now that Peggy had accepted the Euro-Christian faith of the Americans, she was a cultural outlier in her community. Her in-laws felt rejected when she refused to engage in social events, and they suspected the missionaries of trying to siphon off James's wealth through the cultivation of Peggy for their cause. "Mrs. Vann . . . was in quite an oppressive situation," the missionaries wrote, "since she had to put up with all sorts of bitter insulting language from some of her husband's relatives. This . . . was just because she had left their presence and does not want to participate in their amusements; she seriously seeks *our* company." Peggy's in-laws and other Cherokee neighbors teased her unmercifully about her new religious habits, and Peggy even suspected that they had sent a white man to ridicule her for reading the Bible. The same suspicion that Peggy had once held toward the foreign missionaries who misunderstood and maligned Cherokee cultural practices was now being leveled at Peggy. Her deceased husband, who never believed in Christianity, had nevertheless opened the door to religious proselytizing by inviting the missionaries to live among Cherokees on his grounds, and now Peggy had taken them and their message into her heart. Other Cherokees, who were highly suspicious of white American intentions, judged Peggy harshly. In their view, she had accepted alien people and a foreign worldview that seemed both preposterous and contemptuous of the Cherokees' way of life. "Oh these relatives!" Peggy is quoted as having said, "[H]ow much ill will they bear me! . . . They are trying to wear me out so that I will pull away from you [missionaries] to escape the evil gossip."[26] Peggy weathered these critiques by turning to the Lord. Once she had become "enemies" with her in-laws due to her "close connection" with the missionaries, Peggy comforted herself with the thought: "What do I have to fear from *humans* if I have *Him* for a *Friend*?"

Peggy also found solace in a novel independence that followed James's death and her attachment to the Moravians. When James was alive, she had not been allowed to receive strangers in his absence; she had not been able to properly bury the slave woman to whom she felt close. Now Peggy directed her own personal affairs in a cabin that was hers alone. Ten months after James's death, Peggy moved out of the big house. "She was tired of the wild occurrences in her former house and therefore had asked the administrators to let her leave there and help her prepare a small hut about a mile from here." Peggy arranged for her husband's former store building to be relocated to the new site and set about arranging "this and that in her house." The missionaries visited Peggy there and wrote that "[a] precious feeling of joy prevailed in the cabin," where they all sung hymns and dined together. Following Peggy's move, the missionaries wrote: "So Vann's famous house, which since Peggy's moving away had become pretty much a Sodom, is now standing vacant and the Negroes are left to themselves." With none of the Vann family members living in the big house, it stood unoccupied and unmonitored. For a brief moment in time, before the estate administrators tightened their oversight, blacks enslaved by the Vanns may have enjoyed a bit of freedom in luxurious surrounds. Perhaps they slept in James Vann's bed and served themselves on his dishes. Perhaps they were the ones, at last, to lean back on the high front porch and view the blue-tipped mountains.[27]

Peggy, in the meantime, underwent a change of her own, transforming herself from mistress of Diamond Hill to head of household for a working farm. She reclaimed her maiden name and called herself Peggy Scott, an action attributed by the missionaries to an "Indian custom." Along with her relative The Trunk, who had come to help her, Peggy and the enslaved black woman Candace set about clearing land. The plantation mistress the missionaries had once described as "shy and reserved" now "lifted very large trees, as she [was] an unusually diligent and competent person." As much as she loved the Moravian missionaries, Peggy disliked most other Euro-Americans, and she "had learned not to allow any of the white people, from whom she had always protected herself, to approach her house." "Mrs. Vann," the missionaries wrote, "is not inclined to marry again. But she herself is a very industrious and skilled person, spins, knits, and sews, weaves [for] herself and for others and in addition together with her negress she also does plantation work, cuts down the biggest trees and makes fence rails and fences, etc., and with it all is happy." Peggy named her new home Mountjoy, perhaps after a place that her friend and spiritual mentor, Anna Rosina Gambold, had fondly recalled from a missionary journey to Ohio back in 1803.[28]

In the aftermath of her husband's death, and through the vehicle of Christian conversion, Peggy Scott renewed her life and took charge of a small farming household. She reveled in her home-place and warmly welcomed others to share it. For her birthday that first year, a "lighthearted and cheerful" Peggy hosted a small party and "decorated her little house with greenery and flowers and also used the little paintings and verses that she had received . . . so that it really was a beautiful sight." Never having had children herself, she began to take in young relatives and other Cherokee children in need. By the end of 1811, Peggy had enjoyed her first communion and adopted the care of "one Indian boy and four Indian girls," whom she educated at the mission school. But Peggy did not, and could not, accomplish this turnabout alone. Her newfound independence rested on the bondage of others. In addition to her slave Candace, Peggy had successfully negotiated with Vann's estate administrators to acquire "a Negro and a Negress, in addition to her own Negress and little girl, who can be very useful to her on her plantation." Because of the unpaid service of Candace, Will, Hanna, and their children, Peggy gained the luxury of living on her own.[29]

At least as early as 1806, James Vann knew his life was threatened. He anticipated his own death after the duel with his brother-in-law and again after the
assassination of Chief Doublehead, which he had helped to plan. Fear of the
inevitable led Vann to choose "the white man's law," as a historian of Georgia
once put it, and file a will in the Jackson County Courthouse near his Chattahoochee plantation.[30] Vann's will has garnered the attention of scholars of
Cherokee and Georgia history for decades, in part because he was one of the
first in his nation to use such a legal mechanism, in part because of the content of the will itself, and, finally, because of the swift and critical reaction by
Vann's family and the Cherokee Council. In 1808, the very first year that the
Cherokee Nation adopted a written code of law, James Vann filed a legal will in
the state of Georgia. The crux of Vann's last will and testament was as follows:

> 1st I do hereby give & bequeath unto my beloved wife PEGGY Daughter of
> the late WALTER SCOTT dec'd all my household furniture.
> 2nd All the rest & residue of my property which I shall or may die possessed
> of, be that whatsoever it may & wheresover it may, I give and bequeath unto
> my natural son JOSEPH to have to hold forever.[31]

In a dramatic break from Cherokee custom, Vann had left the bulk of his property — two plantations, two stores, two ferries, a mill, 115 slaves, and tens of
thousands of dollars worth of cash to a single, minor son.[32] Other Cherokee
people had adjusted their way of life in response to changing times and the
pressures of the U.S. civilization program. They were plowing fields, spinning
thread, centralizing government, and adopting a legal code, but even at a moment of mounting cultural change, James Vann's will was shockingly out of
step. In a cultural milieu where matrilineal family lines were still valued and
respected, Vann had left nothing to his mother or sisters. In a community that
cherished children, Vann had left nothing to his several other recognized sons
and daughters. Even his daughter Mary, who lived in the house with James
and Peggy, was deprived of her inheritance. And Peggy, who had departed
from Cherokee practice by leaving her family's farm and moving into a home
that was owned by her husband, was shown to be especially vulnerable in this
document. Although James had freely appropriated Peggy's valuable personal
property (in the form of black slaves) in the early years of their marriage, he
did not return this wealth to her upon his death. Peggy's exposure to the economic whims of her husband was visible in the will in which she only received
the household furnishings.

Members of the Cherokee Council were so affronted by Vann's will that they altered it after his death by way of legal fiat. In April of 1809, the council met and issued the following decision: "Upon a full consideration of the Writing of JAMES VANN dec'd purporting to be a Will & also a decree of the Chiefs and Warriors in Council revoking, annulling & setting aside said writing determining that the same is not agreeable to the rules & regulations of the said Nation & it being their wish that the property should be divided among all the children of the said JAMES & his widow. It is ordered that the property be disposed as is directed by the said Council."[33] The council members then underscored the ethical point behind their decree: "[I]t appearing from the face of the Will that all the property was left to one child named JOSEPH VANN but the Chiefs think that all the children are of one father who ought to receive some share of the property & also the widow who ought to share alike with the other Children and to remain in the house as long as she pleases & no doubt JOSEPH VANN will agree in opinion with the Chiefs when he comes to the years of maturity."[34]

The Cherokee Council allowed the executors to reserve the "greatest share" for Joseph while ensuring that Mary Vann, Robert Vann, Lilly McNair, Sally Vann, Jimmy Vann, and Jesse Vann all received proceeds from the Chattahoochee property. Because Peggy now had the right to live in the main house for as long as she liked, the council members added an expectation of culturally appropriate generosity: "The Chiefs & warriors expect that PEGGY will treat the people well as usual when they come to your house."[35]

The councilmen's decision was firm enough to effectively redistribute James Vann's fortune but vague enough to ensure ongoing conflict within the family. John Gambold, who was asked by the administrators to help manage Vann's estate papers, recorded much of the internal wrangling in a series of letters to the home church in Salem. Gambold disclosed that Vann had cheated his sisters out of their inheritance of female slaves, who had since had offspring, and "[n]ow these two above-named sisters came and demanded them from the Executors said negresses and their children, a total of 18 persons." Meanwhile, James's mother "demanded restitution" for cattle her son had stolen from her inheritance from her brother. Although Wali was "hard to satisfy," she "finally received a pair of Negroes to her entire satisfaction." Against the administrators' wishes, Peggy chose not to remain in the family home but instead made use of Vann's former store building, which she renovated into living quarters. She did, however, seek legal possession of two estate slaves, based on the accusation that, contrary to Cherokee custom, James had grafted her private property onto his estate holdings. "Good friends have now seen to it," Gambold wrote, "that she has been compensated for some of it from the Estate." In addition to acquiring an older "mulatto" boy named John, by decree of the council, Peggy received "one Negro husband and wife, whom she could select herself, also a pair of horses, 4 cows with calves, etc." But because the enslaved couple had had a child since the council's mandate, the legal transfer of the couple's child became a point of contention. It is no wonder that the original executors of Vann's estate, George Paris and Richard Rowe, resigned in June of 1809, leading to the appointment of James Brown and David McNair, and making John Gambold the sole person with consistent familiarity with the particulars.[36]

By the time of James Vann's death, his family was so heavily entrenched in black chattel slavery that human property both caused and remedied the bulk of their disputes. With more than one hundred slaves in his possession, valued at over $30,000 in the early 1800s, James Vann's enormous wealth was concentrated in human property.[37] When this famous Cherokee family negotiated the details of their inheritance, they wrangled, in essence, over black people's lives.

The Earth Moves

The period following James Vann's death was a time of great instability for Diamond Hill residents. The Moravian Springplace Mission lost support in the Cherokee community due to the absence of its influential patron. As enrollments declined, Charles Hicks (Peggy's uncle and James's political ally) stepped in and offered to advocate for the missionaries before the Cherokee Council. The fragile mission soon found its student body replenished by the children of "some of the most respected people in the nation."[38] Peggy Vann became a Christian, moved away from the home where she had lived with James since 1805, and made a new life for herself on a rugged plantation a mile away from the mission. Africans, Afro-Americans, and Afro-Cherokees on the Vann estate experienced an extended moment of danger and possibility. Some members of their community were sold away to Mississippi planters; others were redistributed to the nearby homes of Peggy, Wali Vann, Nancy Vann, and James's daughter Delilah (Lily) McNair. Most would remain on the central plantation, finding ways to take advantage of the chaos created by their master's murder, and awaiting the changes their next owner, the young Joseph Vann, would bring.

Even as Cherokees, blacks, and whites struggled to regain their footing on the grounds of James Vann's former estate, the larger community of the

Cherokee Nation entered a time of radical reorientation. For the thirty-plus years since the American Revolution, Cherokees had fought to survive as an independent people in a context of ongoing warfare, land loss, and coercive dictates from the U.S. government. A series of unsettling events in 1811 and 1812 left many Cherokees in a state of extreme insecurity and led them to question the compromises they had made in pursuit of national survival. The summer of 1811 ushered in a severe famine that threatened the lives of many; the long-standing principal chief, Black Fox, died; white intruders poured over Cherokee borders; the price paid for furs and pelts plummeted; and the Shawnee leader Tecumseh traveled to nearby Creek country to urge southern Indians to join in an international revolt against white expansion. Many Cherokees feared that they were sacrificing the essence of Cherokee identity by "work[ing] and think[ing] like white men," only to face more hardship. They sought to revitalize their sense of self-knowledge and to ensure a better future through spiritual revival.[39]

In January of 1811, a dramatic spiritual vision spread across the Cherokee settlements. Three Cherokees, a man and two women, had been walking near Rocky Mountain, a hill in the northwest Georgia vicinity of the Vann estate, when they heard a tremendous roaring in the sky, like an unnatural thunder. Before their eyes, a group of Indians emerged from the clouds bearing a message from the Great Spirit. The Great Spirit was displeased that Cherokees had taken up white farming methods and milling technologies, had abandoned indigenous corn varieties, had allowed whites to people their land, and were punishing one another with violent policing tactics. The Great Spirit urged Cherokees to return to their traditional ways; if they did not, harm would befall them, culminating with abandonment by the Mother of the Nation, the Corn Mother, Selu. The message of this vision spread swiftly across the entire nation. The first three witnesses told their town chiefs, who carried the story to the council meeting in February. That same month, Chief Koychezetel (Warrior's Nephew) brought the message to Peggy Scott and others in the area of Vann's estate.[40]

Even as Cherokees had made concessions in a context of colonial subjugation, they had not fully abandoned their own spiritual and cultural worldview. Cherokee Council members therefore took this warning seriously, and in May of 1811, they issued a sharp statement to Agent Meigs, directing him to remove all white people from Cherokee country, including missionaries, skilled workmen, and whites with Cherokee spouses. In doing so, they held the U.S. government to a promise made in the Treaty of Holston to secure the Cherokee borders from America's roving citizenry. Individual Cherokees seeking vigilante justice acted independently of Meigs's compliance, and in one case, three Cherokees set fire to the home of a white settler family. Other Cherokees followed suit, threatening to burn out the whites who did not leave voluntarily. In one instance, four Indians related "through a Negro, who can speak Cherokee," that a particular white family must leave the nation within three days. Reaction to this state of affairs was heated on the Vann estate. Peggy had long been troubled by the unlawful presence of white intruders. She had once been verbally insulted by a white man who approached her house and then cursed and raged at her. "It is indescribable what kind of repulsive white people come to this country!" missionary Anna Rosina wrote after the incident. Although Peggy was "terrified" at the thought that her beloved Moravians would depart, she supported the value of Cherokee people maintaining control over their lands.[41]

Most enslaved blacks on the Vann estate agreed wholeheartedly with the edict and began to plan ahead for a future devoid of whites. They knew of the Cherokee Council's decision and had heard (perhaps through Pleasant, the missionaries' slave) that James Vann's son-in-law had been by the mission and "confirmed the news that at the Indians' request the government of the United States had given an order to drive all white families, including single males, out of the Cherokee Nation." U.S. soldiers had already entered the country and were causing "terrible devastation" as they expelled whites by force. The soldiers had orders to destroy fields, orchards, and possessions of those whites that refused to leave. A visiting soldier had told the missionaries: "All buildings in Cherokee country not designated by the Indians, as well as all fences, boards, and so on that belong to white people, will be set in flames, and the fruit trees will be cut down to their roots." Upon learning of these occurrences, black slaves recognized an opening for greater economic autonomy. They quickly sketched a plan whereby they would take over and divide the land currently occupied by the mission. The missionaries wrote: "[T]here was once again much noise in our neighborhood concerning our moving out of the country. The Negroes were especially busy dividing our fields and gardens among themselves." Planning ahead, some blacks were especially desirous of inheriting Pleasant's garden, which must have been a fine work of agricultural art. For her part, Pleasant would have been pleased to let her garden go. She was "almost beside herself with joy" at the news of the Moravians' impending departure. If they were forced to leave, she would be able to return home to North Carolina, where she had probably left family behind.[42]

The missionaries were of mixed minds. They noted in their diary that "for years the Indians had already indicated that those whites who had come into the country without a profession and settled down should leave with their possessions. . . . However, instead of complying, more of them moved in." Still, the Moravians empathized with the targeted whites: "As glad as we are to see and hear that the Indians finally have become active about freeing their country of people who bring them more harm than good . . . we still could not help but feel pity for these our poor white fellow humans." The missionaries' alarm rose when they soon realized that neighboring Cherokees intended to see *them* go as well: "[P]eople who otherwise are so well disposed towards us had hinted that we would not be allowed to stay in this nation . . . because the order to drive out applies to all white people with no exceptions." But the missionaries would receive a reprieve, and the slaves a disappointment, when the Cherokee Council amended their edict to exclude "useful whites," such as teachers, intermarried whites, and skilled laborers.[43]

Even as the Moravian missionaries found a modicum of security, tumultuous events continued to roil across the Cherokee Nation. That summer, a terrible drought and famine struck, and Wali Vann, who was greatly saddened by "the starvation in the country," told stories about hungry children dying from the ingestion of poisonous roots. A Cherokee woman visited Peggy to spread the news that the people of her town had sought out "a certain famous rainmaker . . . because of the long drought." After her townspeople had carefully followed the protocol set out by the rainmaker, the woman was confident that he had called the slate of rains that finally arrived in late July. In August, a celestial comet cut through the sky. And in mid-December, the earth began to shake.[44]

A series of three earthquakes, among "the most powerful in U.S. history," began on December 16th in the Mississippi River town of New Madrid, Missouri. From there the shocks spread to the south and east. Severe damage ensued as far as 250 miles beyond the New Madrid seismic zone epicenter, and far to the east, Cherokee towns buckled from the quakes.[45] On December 16th, the missionaries recorded the first set of tremors: "[T]wo shocks from an earthquake were felt. The houses shook and everything in them moved. The chickens fell to the ground from their resting places and caused a frightful crying." The quakes continued into January and February of 1812, alarming Cherokees, who saw these natural events as warning signs from the Great Spirit. Shoe Boots, a successful farmer and slaveholder whose life companion was an enslaved woman named Doll, explained to the missionaries, with Peggy as his interpreter, that God was incensed with the white people: "Many Indians believe that white people are responsible for this," he said, "because they already possess so much of the Indian land and want even more. God is angry about this and wants to scare them through earthquakes to put an end to this. *All* the Indians believe very much that *God* allowed the earthquakes to happen."[46]

As if God had not spoken clearly enough, amid the series of earthquakes, "there was an extraordinary appearance in the sky." At nine o'clock in the evening on February 13th, a total eclipse curtained the moon. "[I]t was as if [the sky were] covered with a black scarf," the Moravians reported. "In the west was a small white stripe on the horizon and from the east shone a red light, which lit everything outside like a full moon." Cherokees passed on prophecies and apocalyptic dreams about these signs from God that condemned the white presence. Charles Hicks wrote in a letter, "The people in my neighborhood are unusually distressed because of the earthquakes, and I believe fear and horror has spread throughout the entire nation." Meanwhile, fears of a foretold hailstorm spread across the mountain towns, and residents "fled and tried to creep into caves in the cliffs to be out of danger." "At the current time," the missionaries wrote, "there is really much ferment in the nation along with a dark heavy feeling. . . . It is indescribable to what foolish fables these poor blind heathens listen."[47]

The Moravians dismissed the Cherokee visions and interpretations as heathen superstition, as did Christian convert Peggy Scott. Instead, they felt that they alone "saw only too clearly." The missionaries' view, rooted in what could rightly be called a different belief system of spiritual superstition, was that Satan, "the evil enemy," sought to mislead "the poor heathens" by "warn[ing] them against the teaching of the white people, which is that Jesus the crucified is their only legitimate Lord and Master." While the Moravians labored to show the Cherokees their version of truth, news of the foretold, vicious hailstorm continued to circulate, and "Indians dug out dwellings in the ground to escape it." An old woman related that a "conjurer" had said: "In three months' time . . . the moon would become dark again, then would hailstones as big as 'hominy blocks' fall."[48] Wali Vann had also heard tell of this vision. She related that "God revealed to an Indian that a great darkness would arise and was supposed to last three days. During this all the white people and also those Indians who had clothing or household items in the style of the white people would be carried away along with their livestock. Because of this, they should put aside everything that was similar to the white people and what they had learned from them, so that God would not mistake them in the darkness and carry them away with them."[49] When local Cherokees asked the pupils at the mission school if the hail would certainly come, the students expressed doubt and assured the questioners that the missionaries "knew more than the Indians about such things." "However," the missionaries wrote, "we knew nothing . . . no human could know what God had decided to do."[50]

The missionaries' humble statement of ignorance proved prescient. On May 17, three months after the hailstorm prophecy began to circulate, the missionaries wrote: "At noon there was a terrible thunder and hailstorm. The hail, some of which was as big as hazelnuts, was driven through the chimney and roof so often that the houses were completely covered with it inside. Much in the garden was damaged by it." They praised "our merciful God for His gracious prevention of greater damage."[51] For several days, Cherokee country was cloaked by a darkened sky. By whatever means they had had at their disposal, spiritual or meteorological, the Cherokee prophets had predicted this storm, though on a much more destructive scale. That summer, spiritual revivalists answered the slate of compelling signs with an equally dramatic act. Agent Meigs wrote: "[T]o appease the Anger of the Great Spirit which they conceive is manifest by the late shocks of the earth . . . they have revived their religious dance of an ancient origin."[52]

The return of the ghost dance marked the height of the Cherokee spiritual and cultural revival of 1811–12. But soon, other events would cause an eclipse of the human kind. The Redsticks, traditionalists and spiritual revivalists of the Muskogee Creek Nation who had also been inspired by Tecumseh and The Prophet, commandeered weapons and laid siege to a Euro-Creek homestead, giving the U.S. military an excuse to declare war. The Creek War of 1813–14, in which nearly a thousand Creeks lost their lives to Andrew Jackson's army, was now under way. "In the end," wrote William McLoughlin, "the spiritual fervor of the revival was turned aside by the excitement of war."[53]

Meanwhile, the residents of Diamond Hill faced new and trying circumstances. Although the Cherokee Council at first refused to answer the American request for military aid against the Creeks, they later "decided to concede to the government's desire."[54] Leading Cherokees of James Vann's ilk, like his close friend The Ridge, Shoe Boots from Etowah town, and fathers of Springplace Mission pupils, volunteered to fight against the Muskogee Creek rebels. Enslaved blacks on Diamond Hill confronted the new and brutal regime of white overseer Samuel Talley, who not only "whip[ped] them quite mercilessly sometimes for little things, sometimes with no reason at all," but also terrified black parents with the threat that he would send their sons and "all the rest of the estate Negroes except for the old ones and those who were sickly" to fight for the U.S. military. The Moravians, for their part, spent an evening with General Andrew Jackson while he was en route to the conflict zone and described Jackson and his companion as "upstanding, dear men."[55]

CHAPTER 6

In My Father's House Are Many Mansions

We are experiencing little pleasure in our neighbor and former pupil Joe Vann. His house is not dissimilar to a den of thieves.

—John and Anna Rosina Gambold in a letter to Reverend Van Vleck, 1817

Going to the Chapel

Peggy Scott's commitment to her newfound Christian faith was heartfelt and absolute. The spiritually effusive letters she sent to Moravians in Salem attested to her personal transformation, as did the many attempts she made to share the gospel with her fellow Cherokees. Peggy viewed her role as evangelist to her people as a special charge: "It is given to me," she once explained, "to tell them *why* the Son of God suffered thus." Peggy often praised the Lord, expressed her deep love for Him, and wondered at her fortune to have been found and saved. "I am the greatest sinner," she said after taking Communion one summer evening. "How can even I come to such great grace? How indescribably great is the love of our Savior indeed! Oh, I do love Him!"[1]

Although her Cherokee neighbors viewed Peggy's religious conversion with skepticism, white observers marveled at the change in her. On one occasion, a respected Marylander named Thomas Chase visited the Springplace Mission and commented that "Margaret Ann [Peggy's baptismal name] . . . had become through grace a true Christian woman." Another visitor to the mission, General David Meriwether from Georgia, commented that Peggy was "a wonder and a visual proof of God's grace" whose example was evidence that God would enlarge "a congregation for Jesus out of the heathen." Anna Rosina Gambold was taken by delighted surprise when, upon looking for Peggy one day, she "saw her in a corner of the field, covered with her large silk scarf, on her knees." Anna Rosina then "hurried away so as not to disturb the praying woman." She would later write that Peggy lived a "truly edifying Christian life, led in the faith of the crucified Son of God."[2]

After James Vann's death, Peggy's religious devotion led her to leave the plantation big house and move into her own home nearby. She gained, through this move, an independent style of life that helped her to heal from

The north side of the Vann House, shaded by a spruce tree.
Courtesy of the Chief Vann House.

the abusive relationship she had experienced with her husband. She managed her own farm, took in Cherokee children, learned to read and write in English, and regularly translated for Cherokees at the mission. Her life was full, and, the missionaries observed, she was content never to marry again. But the same devotion to God and her earthly godparents, the Gambolds, that had helped Peggy find her own place in the world after the death of her husband, also left her subject to a new form of authority. Following her conversion in 1810, Peggy would submit to the will of God, as interpreted by John Gambold and the Moravian Church, in ways that would forever alter her life and the lives of her slaves.

Within three years of James Vann's death, a comfortably situated former white overseer of Diamond Hill, Joseph Crutchfield, began to court Peggy Scott.[3] In 1811, Crutchfield began making appearances at Springplace Mission services. By the summer of 1812, he had "spoken to . . . Peggy numerous times about marriage," but with undesired results. And Crutchfield was not the only man who had noticed the attractive, propertied widow. A Cherokee man had "already sent her two express messengers with marriage offers." Frustrated by his lack of progress and certainly aware of the competition, Crutchfield "turned to Brother Gambold in this matter." John and Anna Rosina Gambold had been keeping well abreast of the developments and "believed [they] would have to grant this matter further consideration." They had already met with other ministers at the church missions conference and discussed Peggy's situation, which, to their minds, was tenuous at best. Although it was the traditional role of Cherokee women to supervise homes and engage in agricultural work, the Gambolds saw this charge as too great for Peggy. They could "well see that she [would] not be able to manage her household as a widow in the long run," and they thought she should remarry. They greatly preferred Joseph Crutchfield, "known as an honest, diligent, and sober man" who was "serious about salvation," to the other suitor, whom they feared might "use violent measures to obtain his goal."[4]

Peggy, however, was reluctant to consider either man's proposal. She told the missionaries that "it was extremely difficult for her to think about coming out of her lonely situation wherein the Savior had done so much indescribably for her." Although she really did not wish to remarry, Peggy chose "to put herself completely under the guidance of the Savior and the advice of His servants." In the end, Peggy was willing to submit herself to the will of God, as interpreted by the church. The matter of her potential marriage was taken up by the Helpers' Conference (a council of elders) in Salem. They concurred with John Gambold and approved "the marriage of Indian Sister Margaret Ann Scott to Mr. Joseph Crutchfield." Four days later, the wedding took place at Mountjoy before an audience of gathered relatives and missionaries.[5]

It must have been a shock to Peggy to find herself remarried within a week of expressing disinterest in it, but she accepted this life change with grace. As the years passed and her new husband accepted Christ, her marriage to Joseph Crutchfield proved much happier than her marriage to James Vann had been. Peggy had in Joseph a partner in faith as well as in life's daily requirements. The year following their wedding, on Joseph's birthday, Peggy hosted a breakfast celebration and presented Joseph with a note: "My dear Joseph!" the note began, "The God of all Grace, who hath called unto us His eternal Glory by Christ Jesus . . . make You perfect, establish, strengthen, settle You."

Joseph had promised John Gambold that his chief interest in marrying Peggy was to know the Lord through her. Perhaps this was true. It was also the case that through this union, Joseph acquired the benefit of Peggy's enslaved property, the $500 cash she was paid from the Vann estate, and the comfort of her Mountjoy home on Vann's former grounds. The relatives of James Vann, including his mother, Wali, with whom Peggy had grown close, resented Joseph Crutchfield's intrusion. For years they attempted to divest Peggy of slaves she had gained from the Vann estate and to force the Crutchfields out of the area, leading the couple to defend themselves before the Cherokee Council. This marriage did not, in the end, return Peggy to a miserable state of matrimony, but it did reflect a new authority in her life. Against Peggy's expressed desire, John Gambold and the leaders of the Moravian Church had advanced and sanctioned the whole affair. When the Gambolds began to exert a similar influence over Peggy's treatment of her slaves, blacks in her household would suffer dearly.[6]

At the time of her marriage to Joseph Crutchfield in 1812, Peggy owned seven black slaves: Candace, whom she had purchased for $200 from the Vann estate out of funds the estate owed her, and Candace's baby daughter, Virginia; two children born of the deceased slave Caty (one of whom lived with Peggy's mother); Will and Hannah, a couple whom Peggy was permitted to select as part of her inheritance from the estate; and John, a "suffering" "mulatto" boy who had been sent to James Vann's relatives before Vann's death.[7] Peggy had not come to own these individuals by chance but by thoughtful selection and legal struggle. She carefully chose those she would possess from among scores of blacks on the Vann estate.

Similarly to the way she had once attached herself to Caty, Peggy developed a companionable fondness for Candace, evident by her inclusion of Candace in her baptismal celebration and her desire for Candace's company at mission services. Candace's own Christian faith strengthened the women's bond, and Peggy saw to it that Candace's daughter Virginia, and later Deborah, received formal baptisms in Peggy's home. Peggy also chose Will and Hannah, an African couple described by the missionaries as "good-natured, diligent and loyal and — for Africans not unskilled people." One of the few existing original documents from the Vann estate papers focuses on this couple. In 1811, the Cherokee Council affirmed Peggy's legal right to "Will and Hanah [sic] both African . . . as slaves for life" and to "their future offspring." Because the administrators took several months to finalize the transfer, Hannah had delivered a son, Butler, by the time she and her husband came into Peggy's possession and before the council had rendered their decision. Peggy had repeatedly attempted to purchase the baby, who was eight or nine months old when Will and Hannah moved to Mountjoy, but the estate administrators refused. Allowing Peggy to buy the child would be financially unfeasible, they argued, since "they could get more for it in 8 to 10 years." The child, now in his fourth year, would have to be returned to the Vann estate. Will and Hannah were "completely inconsolable" now that Butler "was going to be torn away . . . by force." They had showered their son with as much love and attention as was possible in their circumstances, and he was "very well raised so that one could really take joy in him." Even Peggy was "very fond of the little child" and had "faithfully cared for him because he was sickly." At the end of a protracted tussle, Peggy succeeded in keeping Will and Hannah's family together. The Cherokee Council decided that "the Negroes should have already been turned over to Peggy before the child was born." In the next few years, Butler would be joined by a baby brother, Matthew, and baby sisters, Magdalena and Rose.[8]

Peggy Scott was neither a proto-abolitionist nor an African colonizationist.[9] She was a woman who had grown up in a slaveholding family, had married into a plantation lifestyle, and never expressed doubt or concern about buying and owning people of African descent. She did, though, develop close relationships with enslaved black women and harbor tender feelings for enslaved black children. Her relationship with blacks before her conversion to Christianity was complex in its contradictions, but straightforward in its lack of moral encumbrance. In her early years as a plantation mistress, Peggy was not concerned about the religious lives and sexual activity of the Vann slaves. She never commented on their moral failings and was likely uninterested in the subject. Peggy enjoyed the company of her favored slaves. She spent time with them socially and cared for them in periods of illness. She felt close to Caty, who had grown up in Cherokee country and knew little of white American culture or the Christian faith, a characteristic, in fact, that probably made Caty a more attractive companion for Peggy in those early years.[10] At the same time, though, Peggy had power over Caty and her other human possessions, extracted their labor by compulsion, and never outwardly questioned the ethics of this dynamic. Although Peggy felt personally attached to particular individuals, her relationship to her slaves was fundamentally exploitative. With the addition of Christian conviction, this relationship would change for the better and for the worse.

Testimonies of formerly enslaved African Americans give dual assessments of Christian slave owners. Harriet Jacobs, author of the classic narrative *Incidents in the Life of a Slave Girl*, for instance, exposed Christian slaveholders as cruel tyrants who used particular biblical passages to justify their inhumane practices, even as she praised one kindhearted female slaveholder as an example of "Christian womanhood."[11] Peggy Scott's acceptance of the Christian faith and submission to the Gambolds as her earthly godparents had a similarly bifurcated effect on the lives of blacks on her farm. Soon after James's death, as she developed authority over her own household, one of Peggy's first decisions was to give her adult slaves Saturdays off. This would permit them to earn money for themselves on Saturday and preserve Sunday for church attendance. Although churchgoing was mandatory in this new arrangement, and other "places" and "amusements" were strictly forbidden, Candace, Will, and Hannah were pleased with this change. Sunday services did not extend all day, and they now had virtual autonomy on the weekends.[12]

Other, corrosive consequences of Peggy's conversion were by no means welcome to the trio. Before becoming a Christian, Peggy had been accustomed to thinking of blacks in particular, though contradictory, ways—as property to be acquired, as laborers to be rewarded or punished, and in special cases, as close companions. She had not, however, thought of black adults as minors or wards over whom she had moral authority. This would begin to change through the example and at the urging of John and Anna Rosina Gambold. The missionaries, who disapproved of parties and drinking, advised Peggy on how she should respond to her slaves' involvement in such activities. In addition to praying about the matter, "she should explain to her Negroes in a motherly manner the great sins in which they participate . . . and should seriously forbid them from taking part in such harmful entertainment again." The Gambolds were suggesting that Peggy refashion her relationship to Candace, Will, and Hannah as one of "maternalism." As with the paternalistic ideology of slavery in the white South, in which male owners should act as fathers to the plantation community, exercising patriarchal authority over their slaves in an organic, familial racial hierarchy, Peggy should see herself as her slaves' moral mother. She should set out rules of proper behavior and strictly enforce them for the good of her dependents. When Peggy heard this advice from the Gambolds, "she promised to do this and seemed completely calmed." The Gambolds later gave similar advice to a slaveholding Cherokee woman who was considering a Christian life. When the woman expressed doubts that upon becoming a Christian "she might not be able to treat her Negroes friendly all the time" as would be expected, the missionaries reassured her by explaining that "it was the Christian's duty to punish evil in her servants, as well as in her children."[13]

In 1816, when relations between Peggy and her slaves reached a point of crisis, the Gambolds' model and continuing counsel dictated the outcome of events. "[U]p to this point," the missionaries wrote, "things were as respectable as one can expect it among slaves." But on January 1, 1816, Candace, a single woman who had chosen to separate from her husband back when she had been owned by James Vann, gave birth to a baby girl. The Gambolds were appalled at Candace's behavior and sickened by the "sinful origin" of the baby. They were even more incensed when they learned that Will, Hannah's husband, was the father. The three adults were setting a "bad example" of a "disgraceful life style . . . before the eyes of the growing Negro children."[14]

The feelings of Hannah, Candace, and Will regarding this extramarital relationship were not considered by the missionaries. Perhaps Will and Candace had engaged in an illicit affair to which Hannah feelingly objected. It is also possible, though, that Hannah accepted the relationship. Both Will and Hannah were African-born; they had been accustomed to polygamous marriages in their homeland. And even on the Vann plantation of the early 1800s, African men were known to have two wives. Peggy's feelings about the relationship might also have been mixed. As a Christian, she now condemned sexual relations outside of marriage, but as a Cherokee girl, she had grown up in a cultural environment in which sexual choices for women were much more open and polygamy was commonplace. She herself had been a co-wife in the early years of her marriage to James. Whatever Hannah, Candace, or Will may have thought about the issue is not recorded, and was likely inconsequential to the Moravian missionaries. John and Anna Rosina Gambold had passed judgment and decided what was to be done. The Gambolds proclaimed in a letter: "Since these [parents] seem to be resolved to remain heathen and to keep with the freedom of the flesh, it can be seen in advance that they will be harmful to their children . . . so there is nothing left for Bro. [Joseph] & Sister [Peggy] Crutchfield to do than to sell their adult negroes, for which they have to wait for time and opportunity."[15]

Nine months after the baby's birth, the awaited opportunity arose. According to the Gambolds, Peggy and her second husband sold Will and Hannah because of their "pagan sinful living." The Crutchfields kept Magdalena and Matthew, the two older baptized children, with them. The eldest child, Butler, may have been sold with his parents or to an entirely different location. The couple's youngest child, Rose, who was still a nursing baby, was allowed to remain with her exiled mother "for a time." Soon after their parents' sale, both baby Rose and her older brother Matthew died of whooping cough. Rose, who had been baptized upon her birth in May of 1815, was buried in the mission cemetery adjacent to Diamond Hill, and remains there still. The fate of Will and Hannah, parents who had previously expressed depths of love for their children, is not recorded. Candace remained in Peggy's household without her fellow enslaved companions of many years. Her child with Will, Virginia, was baptized into the Christian faith because the missionaries could "hold nothing against the poor child for her sinful origin."[16] The moral crime of separating not one but two family units did not seem to register for the missionaries, or, perhaps, even for Peggy Scott Vann Crutchfield.

In 1816, the year that she sold Will and Hannah, Peggy set about bringing her slaves to moral enlightenment in a systematic fashion. She felt a keen responsibility for the "education and instruction of her baptized Negro children, whose preservation from harm lay very close to her and her husband's hearts." So in between visits to her ailing mother, who died that year, Peggy and her husband consulted with the Gambolds about organizing a forum for the black children's religious instruction. By October of 1817, Peggy, who had just gained English literacy six years before, had launched "a school" in her home for the enslaved children she and her husband owned. She instructed them daily with the aim of teaching them to read the Bible, and for this the Gambolds sent her "a few spelling books." Soon Peggy had begun including the mothers of her enslaved minors in the daily lessons.[17]

In January of the next year, black adults in the vicinity took the initiative to build on the opening Peggy's school provided. They lobbied the Moravian missionaries to hold a school for them. "The Negroes on Vann's estate came of their own accord," Anna Rosina wrote in a public letter, "and in greater or smaller parties, to our evening prayers, and staid with our children till bedtime; desiring to be taught the letters of the alphabet, in order to learn to read. We encouraged them, and gave them some spelling-books, and occasionally some instruction." When Peggy and her husband visited the American Board of Commissioners for Foreign Mission's Chickamauga mission to the Cherokees in Tennessee, they attended a Sunday school for black slaves and "returned with new enthusiasm" to expand their educational project. They intended to "begin a Sunday school immediately for the Negroes" of all ages, and because the Springplace Mission buildings were fully in use on Sundays, Joseph Crutchfield volunteered to cut and haul lumber for a new school building and meeting house, which he would also fund. Together, Peggy and Joseph, along with John Gambold's brother, Joseph Gambold, would take charge of teaching interested slaves how to read. Their intention "was made known to the neighboring blacks, who informed their friends at six miles distance; and the next Sunday above twenty came."[18]

While the new buildings were being constructed for this student body of twenty, the church-school convened in various and sundry locations—in the

Springplace Mission barn; in the home of John Gambold's missionary brother, Joseph Gambold; in the Cherokee students' dorm; and in the mission kitchen. A local white millwright, Joel Marshall, also joined the volunteer teaching staff, as did Michael, Pleasant's teenage son and the missionaries' slave, and Cherokee pupils at the mission school. Joseph Gambold, whose signature green eyeglasses perched on the tip of his nose while he read, was a particularly effective teacher, and after a few months, some of the slaves were "beginning to read quite nicely." That summer, when by chance three of the teachers took ill, training exercises continued. Anna Rosina had black students at her bedside reading and spelling out words to her, and Joseph Crutchfield lay on a blanket with students gathered around him, to whom he would recite the alphabet. Enslaved blacks responded to this new opportunity with "joy." Peggy's enslaved women Candace and the elderly Phoebe were "very much touched." Anna Rosina Gambold described the diversity of the black student body: "All are eager and desirous to learn: even two old women, who, by what can be conjectured, are turned of eighty, came and held their little spelling-books, till we told them, that it was to no purpose, as they were not even able to *see* the letters. They thought it was sufficient to hold the book in their hands! Their language is very unintelligible, being a mixture of African and Indian. One of Brother Crutchfield's Negroes, and old Frenchman, is nearly in the same predicament."[19] Africans, Afro-Americans, Afro-Cherokees, and even French-speaking slaves in the community pursued education with a passion. From the very young to the very old, Cherokee speakers to African-language speakers, they took full advantage of the rare opportunity they had helped to foster.

The slaves' Sunday school was a remarkable undertaking for Peggy and Joseph Crutchfield and the Gambold family, who were led by their Christian faith to teach enslaved blacks how to read the Bible for themselves. In few locations across the white slaveholding South would such a scene have been imaginable—of slaveholders banding together and giving their all for the education of slaves. Peggy's school provided a bountiful opportunity for blacks on the Vann estate to receive literacy education, which they might later turn to their own, nonreligious ends. Like the majority of Cherokees whom the missionaries had tried to reach, most enslaved blacks on Diamond Hill did not seek spiritual transformation. Only Grace and old Jacob, Candace, Phoebe, "Christian Jacob," and a handful of others actually committed themselves to regular church attendance or experienced religious conversion. Christian Jacob, an African man, along with several enslaved children, were the only blacks baptized by the Springplace missionaries. Blacks in the area, Moravian missionary Renatus Schmidt complained in 1822, "give no evidence of any effect of the gospel upon their hearts and lives." They, like most Cherokees, saw the Christian Mission as a resource for the development of practical skills that were needed for survival in a harsh and unpredictable world.[20]

But for Peggy Scott, who was unique among Cherokees in the early 1800s, Christian conversion and commitment shifted the contours of her life. In her openness to counsel from spiritual mentors whose notion of women's ability differed from Cherokee norms, she entered a second marriage that she had at first refused. In her yearning to be unfailingly pious, she separated herself from other Cherokees, causing friction between herself and her in-laws. As a slaveholder, she learned to demand strict adherence to Christian behavioral codes and to pass moral judgment on slaves who did not comply. The charge that Christian missionaries hastened native people's acculturation to Euro-American values is clear in Peggy's case. But even as Peggy relinquished bits of her former self to follow the guidance of the church, she also gained greater confidence, valuable abilities, and a new means of influence. Peggy learned to read and write as a result of her conversion. She then turned that prized skill to the betterment of her nation. In the years 1817–19, when the Cherokees faced unyielding pressure from U.S. government agents to sell their south-eastern lands and move to Arkansas, Peggy protested with her pen. She joined a group of Cherokee women who presented an antiremoval petition before the Cherokee Council, and she wrote personal protest letters to prominent Americans, including a U.S. government official, a Moravian minister, and a New England poet. Because she was an Indian member of the Moravian church, Peggy's writings received fairly wide circulation. She relied on Mora-vian go-betweens, such as her dear friend Anna Rosina, to pass on her letters to leading individuals. One of these letters appeared in at least two Chris-tian periodicals. The very same Christian faith that posed challenges to long-standing Cherokee beliefs created a platform for Peggy Scott, who boldly challenged U.S. mistreatment of the Cherokee Nation using writing skills and publicity channels derived from Christian missionary networks.[21]

Over time, in addition to her political advocacy, Peggy gained significant influence as a spiritual guide to other Cherokee women. Beginning with her own mother and sisters, and then reaching out to aunts, in-laws, and other women in nearby towns, Peggy spread the gospel to which she was so devoted. By 1819–20, she had gathered around her a circle of Cherokee women who turned to her to translate the missionaries' words, to read the Bible as a group, and to interpret the meanings of Christianity. For Peggy did not simply trans-late the speech of the ministers; she also, according to the missionaries, "added [her] own experimental comments upon it." After years of hearing Peggy's passionate, coaxing testimony, several Cherokee relatives and friends, and even her former mother-in-law, Wali Vann, had converted. The years 1819 and 1820 brought more converts to the Moravian Church than all of the Moravian missionaries' previous years in the Cherokee Nation combined. Much of that success was due to Peggy Scott, who labored tirelessly for the Lord and passed along what surely was a unique Cherokee Christian perspective to her fellow congregants.[22]

Passing as Indian

The slaves' Sunday school was an exceptional passage in Peggy Scott's life as a slaveholder. It was also a profound moment for one of its teachers, a young black slave who experienced the school as a catalyst for dramatic personal action. Michael was the baby boy born to Pleasant, the Moravians' slave, while she was en route to the Springplace Mission back in 1805. Pleasant was under the legal authority of head missionary John Gambold and his wife, Anna Rosina, as was her infant son. Michael's father was a white man, most likely his mother's former owner, but this is where the similarity between Michael and many other slaves in the white South ends. Deeming Pleasant to be unfit, Anna Rosina inserted herself into the role of surrogate mother and strove to raise Michael according to her moral and spiritual standards. Michael learned to read from Anna Rosina, and he regularly interacted with Cherokee students at the mission school. As the sole black child being raised at the mission complex, Michael's most constant companions, besides his mother and the missionaries, were Cherokee children. His educational preparation made it possible for Michael, at age twelve, to assist the teachers at the slaves' Sunday school as the only black instructor, as well as to independently tutor an enslaved child, Little Jack, at night.[23]

But at the same time that Michael stood apart from other enslaved blacks due to his residence at the mission station and the privileges that ensued there, his growing maturity meant the Moravians increasingly viewed him as a slave who should do manual labor. In 1818, as the Gambolds assigned Michael greater and more laborious tasks, they grew frustrated by his open intransigence. Michael, they felt, was a "naughty" child, who, although "big and strong for his age," did not want to work. "We still have our yellow Michael," the Gambolds wrote in 1818, "put him to work also where and how we can. Why [we] do not have more help in him I cannot make plain on paper, for that observation is needed of our whole situation, arrangements, and (his) entire nature." Michael had likely inherited his mother's pride and backbone; neither mother nor son accepted the notion that they should be slaves. But additionally, as the Gambolds intimated, their own "arrangements" had contributed to Michael's stance. He had grown up feeling virtually free and enjoying the privileges of the Cherokee boys around him. Now that he was an adolescent and the Gambolds willed him to think like a slave, Michael refused outright.[24]

. During his time in the slaves' Sunday school, in which he closely interacted with other enslaved blacks, Michael surely recognized the stark differences between his life and theirs, and at the same time glimpsed the future the Moravians had in store for him. The following year, on a day after heavy winds tossed about uprooted trees, drove the plowing horses wild, and endangered the lives of slaves at work in Vann's fields, Michael ran away. He was thirteen years old and by age and circumstance primed for rebellious behavior. Although Michael had returned home after a previous escape attempt that same year, the Gambolds observed that this time "he was resolved to force a removal from here." Michael had begun to ignore Anna Rosina's directions and responded "defiantly" when he was questioned about his lack of obedience. John Gambold, who was angered by Michael's insolence, beat him for what was probably the first time. "I was obliged to remind him of his duty with a stick," Gambold wrote in a private letter, "at which he resisted so fiercely with hands and feet that . . . the punishment became much more severe than originally intended; thereupon he threw himself on the ground and screamed that we wanted to beat him to death; I gave him a few more blows, told him to get up and go to work."[25]

Michael responded to John Gambold's abuse by running away again, but the Gambolds did not mention the beating in their mission diary entries. Instead, they attributed Michael's flight to a fight with his mother. Word came through Peggy Scott Vann Crutchfield that Michael had "presented himself as free and engaged himself for work about 12–15 miles further on." He spent the night in the home of the sister of a former pupil at the Springplace Mission and said he had been freed the winter before. He also "had his hair cut by an Indian and had his face painted so that he might pass for an Indian." Peggy commissioned a Cherokee man to track Michael down. Five days after the beating incident, the tracker found Michael "30 miles from here with a Half-breed, busy planting corn." Although Michael "took his knife out . . . in order to resist him," the man "took it away from him and by force mounted him on the horse and brought him back." Because the Gambolds did not know how "wicked slaves [were] broken," they "were convinced there was nothing left . . . but to sell him." They then "pray[ed] that the Savior might provide for [them] the possibility to do this." Soon they heard from Thomas Gann, an overseer of Joseph Crutchfield's distant plantation, that "he could easily get rid of the youth in Alabama Territory and presumably at a profit." The missionaries took Gann up on his offer, selling Michael for $500.[26]

Pleasant, who must have been paralyzed with fear as these events unfolded, "began to howl and scream" at the news. Her response, the missionaries reported, "was indescribable." Her son then shouted at Pleasant that he wanted to go and did not wish to stay with her. Michael, still not more than a child, lashed out at his mother, whom the missionaries had always criticized in his presence, and who had no power to protect him. Pleasant, heartbroken by the sale of her son, could bear neither his rejection nor the loss of him through sale. She cursed and raged at the missionaries, until John Gambold threatened her with violence, after which she was "quiet but very gloomy" and then fell into a depressed stupor, "like she was unconscious."[27]

The month following his sale to Gann, Michael received a pseudo-reprieve from what would have been an unknown fate in Alabama. David Ooaty (or Watie), a Cherokee man in the area, asked to purchase Michael, and this surprising turn of events could not have been coincidence. Ooaty was the father of Buck and Stand, two boys who had studied at the mission school and knew Michael well.[28] Perhaps the sons requested that their father intervene; or perhaps, given his limited options, Michael expressed a hope for this particular family to take him. Michael was said to be "joyful" about the transfer "because he is especially fond of his sons Buck and Stand." Pleasant, on the other hand, was enraged anew, wishing, perhaps, that her son were returning home instead. Michael, who had spent his childhood with Cherokee youths and had passed as an Indian to escape, was now ensconced in a Cherokee family with whom he felt close. Although he was not fully free, the true desire of his heart, Michael had at least found a lesser weight of servitude.[29]

The Gambolds' reaction to Michael's sale was to blame Pleasant repeatedly for the whole miserable chain of events. They blamed her poor parenting and her spiteful tongue and accused her of having tried to abort Michael while pregnant. They were never able to see, or at least to write, that Pleasant's life as a mother had been characterized by trauma. Her son was likely conceived by force; she was maligned in her efforts to raise him, and she had no power to save him from beatings or from sale. The Gambolds could not perceive the pain of Pleasant's experience or recognize the loving, damaged woman that she was. Peggy Scott, a slaveholder herself who had even aided in Michael's capture, *did* know something of systemic, pervasive trauma. Perhaps this is why she alone, of all the contemporary writers whose words are preserved in the Moravian Archives, found something good in Pleasant. She wrote in a letter to Moravians back in Salem: "You mentioned poor Pleasant in Your Letter. I can say, that I like her very well, and I am in the Hopes, that She may also yet be won for our dear Saviour."[30]

The House That Joe Built

In 1818, when Michael was fleeing the Springplace Mission and Vann estate, another young man was replanting roots there. Joseph Vann, now of age, had returned to Diamond Hill in 1817 to claim his plentiful inheritance. Joseph, "the second son," had been his father's favorite. James Vann had kept Joe close as a child, taking him along on business trips and Cherokee ball plays and having new sets of clothing made for Joseph's travels. Even after James's will was revised by the Cherokee Council, Joseph remained "the primary heir according to his father's wishes." While "[e]ach of the other children received eight Negroes and a number of horses and cattle," Joseph had reserved for him the bulk of the estate. He may have spent the nine years since his father's death with his birth mother, Nancy Brown, or in school in South Carolina, where his father had enrolled him in 1807. But now the boy who had once been fond of mischievous tricks, the darling of his tempestuous father, was back to manage his father's plantation at the age of nineteen. Noted as one of the most prosperous Cherokees in an 1809 census commissioned by Agent Meigs, Joseph stood to inherit 250 horses, 1,000 cattle, 150 swine, 10 plows, and 115 black slaves.[31]

It was not long before the residents of Diamond Hill saw in Joseph a reflection of James. Like his father, Joseph was shrewd, ambitious, avaricious, and often unfeeling when property was at stake. He was well educated, having attended two private schools in Georgia, the Springplace Mission, and a South Carolina school. He was handsome and so pale in skin tone that a visitor from South Carolina described him as "quite fair, almost white."[32] Dissatisfied with the limitations on his inheritance set by the Cherokee Council upon his father's death, Joseph sued his siblings and Peggy Scott's family for Vann estate property in the Cherokee courts. When his petitions failed, Joseph purchased $4,020 worth of slaves and other property from his sister, Mary Vann Stedman.[33] Joseph also used his ample wealth to invest in his primary personal amusement. He "set up a race tracking in his field" where crowds from Georgia and the Cherokee Nation came to watch horse races, placed bets as large as $500, drank brandy wine, and "rollicked all night."[34] In the years immediately following his return, Joseph married twice, having, like his father, multiple spouses. Joseph's wives, Jennie Springston Vann and Polly Black (in some sources Blackwood) Vann, were both Cherokee women.[35] Although Joseph avoided Christian worship, as had James, he supported his wives' desire to attend services at the Moravian mission and allowed his children to be baptized.[36]

By the age of twenty, Joseph took a firm hold of plantation management, monitoring his enslaved labor force and extending his cultivated acreage. In addition to "assign[ing] his Negroes to clear another eighty-acre field . . . for his plantation, which is already very large," Joseph immediately "took away his Negroes' freedom of being allowed to work on Saturday." He also disrupted dancing parties in the slave quarters, introducing a degree of paternalistic surveillance never practiced by his father. In these first two initiatives, Joseph frustrated the missionaries, who felt he was crowding them when he had land enough already and who wished the slaves to retain weekends off so they could attend Sunday services. Nevertheless, in 1819, Joseph directed his slaves to clear still more land, creating "enormous" fields. Joseph Vann did not exhibit the unpredictable violent tendencies demonstrated by his father, but he did employ corporal punishment of his slaves. For blacks on Diamond Hill, Joseph's exacting manner of oversight, backed by a threat of violence, created new forms of subjugation.[37]

Joseph's steps to tighten control over his slaves anticipated a repressive systemization of black slavery that soon would take place at the level of Cherokee national governance. In 1820 the Cherokee Council forbad slaves from trading property without their owners' permission, forbad slaves from purchasing or vending liquor, and authorized the organization of "patrolling" companies to monitor slave activity. In 1824 the council outlawed intermarriage between Cherokees and "negro slaves" and revoked slaves' ability to possess "horses, cattle, or hogs."[38] Just as Joseph Vann was growing into the role of the strict planter-manager, the Cherokee government was following suit, lending state support to slaveholders' authority. Even so, white missionary observers proclaimed Cherokee slaveholding practices to be lax. Renatus Schmidt, a missionary based at Springplace, wrote: "Our neighbor, Joseph Vann, has about an hundred. They are very well treated, and having very little to do, are rather wild."[39]

In May of 1819, Joseph Vann was honored by a visit from President James Monroe, who stayed over night in Joseph's home while conducting a tour of the southern states. Joseph's remembrances of the event are not recorded, but the Gambolds reported on the "pleasure of seeing the President of the United States," who had arrived "during heavy rain" and was visiting "in Vann's house." The president's large company overwhelmed the home Joseph's father had built, such that Monroe's son requested overflow sleeping quarters at the mission. With the inheritance of multiple slaves, business acumen learned from his father's example, sheer personal determination, and knowledge of the niceties of white society, Joseph Vann steadily increased his personal wealth and standing, earning the nickname "Rich Joe."[40]

Two months after the president's visit, and perhaps in partial response to it, Joseph embarked on a grand new venture. In the same letter in which they described meeting President Monroe, the Gambolds added in a postscript: "Our neighbor Joseph Vann is building a large brick house." Indeed, Joseph had enlisted a locally renowned white brick mason along with skilled white craftsmen to commence work on a splendid manor house. The bricklayer, Robert Howell, had built the brick home of Joseph's sister and brother-in-law, Delilah and David McNair. James and John McCartney, brothers who were employed as general contractors and carpenters, moved into the neighborhood with their families and settled in for a long-term building project. Joseph bargained down the cost of the project by ensuring that "his negroes [would do] the hawling." The McCartneys employed "yellow Jim" and hired a "black girl" to do specified work. Jim, who seems to have been formerly employed in James Vann's mill before running away and then returning to work for pay, must have possessed specialized skills. The unnamed slave girl, who was borrowed from Joseph, would have done domestic chores like cooking, cleaning, and carrying water to the construction workers.[41]

The manufacture of the bricks for Joseph's home became a topic of local lore. The bricks were said to have been specially imported from Savannah, Philadelphia, and even England.[42] But a young Irish American boy whose family settled near the Vann home in the early 1830s remembered the brickmaking differently. At the age of ninety-three, Reverend William Jasper Cotter recalled in his autobiography:

> The best master builder was engaged to make the brick and build the house. A skilled architect was engaged to prepare the plan, and when it was laid before Mr. Vann and the builder every mark of the profile was plain. It was a handsome, two-story brick building with beautiful surroundings.
>
> It would be difficult to say how many false stories have been told about that house. . . . The truth is that [the bricks] were made about four hundred yards from the house. I have seen the old brickyard where they were made.[43]

Enslaved black men fired the famed Vann House bricks, and the location where they worked is still identifiable in the fields behind the Chief Vann House State Historic Site. Significantly, the product of these black men's labor was to be found not only in the materials of the Vann family home but also in the building that housed the new Cherokee governmental offices. Unbeknownst to Joseph, in 1823 the McCartney brothers sold $82 worth of his bricks for the building of the Council House that was being erected in the capital city of New Echota.[44] Slavery, it could be said, was no longer just the enterprise of an odd, wealthy few but had become, by the 1820s, a cornerstone of Cherokee progressive society.

The crew made up of Howell, the McCartney brothers, unnamed black slaves, and unnamed Indian wood carvers labored on Joseph's house for a period of nearly two years. In 1821, they completed their major work, with additional tasks undertaken in 1823. They had created a handsome Federal and Georgian style home embellished with glass windows, venetian blinds, ionic columns, square pediments, sunk paneled walls, medallion cornices, carved Cherokee roses, scalloped bead board, newel posts, a garret with wainscoting, outdoor porticos, a mantel festooned with wood-carved snakes and lizards, and the pièce de résistance: a mystically suspended stairway that would become an architectural marvel generations later. The grounds were similarly impressive. To the north of the house, a formal decorative garden greeted guests and passersby on the federal road. To the south, the Vann family's private entrance spilled into working garden beds divided by a curvilinear brick walkway. To the east of the house was a functional courtyard, where slaves would have carried out all manner of outdoor work; 100 feet south of the courtyard was a stable. A separate kitchen, made of recycled wood that might well have come from James Vann's 1805 home, formed one edge of the courtyard ten feet east of the main house. Inside the kitchen, a thin interior wall might have marked off a slave's sleeping quarters. To the northeast, just beyond the kitchen, was a square building with windows that likely served as the plantation's office. And 140 feet east of the kitchen stood three adjoined foundationless structures; these buildings, some of the most poorly constructed on the compound, were probably slave cabins.

Levin Branham, an enslaved man who lived on the Vann estate as a boy in the 1850s described the place in his narrative: "The old Indian or Chief Vann house has a large spacious yard with many beautiful shade trees. . . . The front of the house which faces the south, has four white columns imitating white marble posts. The door to the entrance of the house has a large arch, hand carved and pegged, which was made by the Indians." New England traveler Benjamin Gold stayed overnight at Joseph's home in 1829 and described it as "a large elegant brick house, elegantly furnished." When wealthy white newlywed and plantation mistress Juliana Margaret Conner visited the Vann home in 1827, she gave the place a rather mixed review. She remarked first on the "fine large brick house—finished in a most extravagant style." However, Joseph's main color choices of red, gold, blue, and green did not suit Mrs. Conner's refined tastes. She pronounced the home "gaudily painted" in her reminiscences.[45]

Juliana Conner associated the glitzy home she visited with her host, Joseph Vann, but for decades in the twentieth century and into the twenty-first, Georgia state officials attributed the home's construction to Joseph's father, James. After half a century of misconception unwittingly created by 1950s restorers who read about James Vann's 1804 building project in the missionary records and assumed it referred to the extant house, we now know that Joseph Vann was the original owner. James McCartney, a principal builder of the home, sued Joseph Vann for construction costs in 1825. This rediscovered lawsuit, which spanned at least four years in the Tennessee courts, delineates and assigns a value to each and every act of labor that contributed to the erection of the brick manor house and outbuildings, confirming for researchers in 2007 that Joseph, not his father, had contracted for the construction.[46] The sixteen years and one generation difference between the previous date assigned to the Vann House and the corrected date is meaningful to any assessment of James and Joseph Vann's lives and legacies. James has been described by scholars, writers, and public history interpreters as nearly white in identity, cultural orientation, and actions—in large part due to his construction of an iconic, brick plantation house. The fact that James did not build this house reopens the question of his cultural identity and points historians toward a closer inspection of the many other aspects of his complicated life, which included rejecting Christianity, engaging in polygamy, maintaining Cherokee- as well as English-language fluency, and carrying out a valiant struggle to preserve Cherokee land rights. James Vann was a mixed-race Euro-Cherokee man who lived out practices from both cultural worlds but who always identified himself, and was identified by peers, as an "Indian."

Born at the turn of the nineteenth century, Joseph Vann came of age in quite a different era than his father had—after the ravages of the Revolutionary War and the postwar Cherokee rebellion, after the Treaty of Holston had dictated a plan for Cherokee civilization. Joseph grew up at a time when instead of waging armed resistance, Cherokee leaders like his father sought to centralize national government and to appease the U.S. government through change and negotiation as a form of self-defense. Joseph reached maturity and built his grand home on the cusp of the Cherokees' progressive political and cultural movement. In 1821–22, Cherokee intellectual Sequoyah (George Guess), would create a written form of their language. In 1828, Elias Boudinot (Buck Watie) edited and published the first edition of the *Cherokee Phoenix* national newspaper. In 1827, the Cherokee Nation ratified a constitution modeled in form after the U.S. Constitution. And at the very same time that Joseph was constructing his show-stopping house, the Cherokee Nation was building a new seat for their formalized central government — the city of New Echota.

Perhaps Joseph Vann meant to say with his miraculous floating staircase that he had risen to heights of wealth that others in the region, Cherokee or white, could only view with wonder. Perhaps he meant to signal with the construction of an office and formal garden that his was a place of serious business and bounded, manicured beauty. Perhaps he announced, through this entire dramatic venture, that his lifestyle placed him among the whitest, richest slaveholding elite. But these were not the only messages broadcast by the Vann verandahs. While Joseph's erection of a grandiose plantation home was certainly an indication of his family's incremental movement toward a Euro-southern elite sensibility, it was also in keeping with two key aspects of Cherokee nationalistic philosophy at the time — it demonstrated the achievement of high western "civilization" that Cherokees strategically hoped would gain American respect for Cherokee sovereignty, and it staked a bold claim of permanence on the Cherokee's southeastern landscape. Even as he occupied the lavish rooms of his finished brick home, Joseph was playing a leading role in the Cherokee government's project of national preservation and visibility. In the late 1820s, he would serve on the Cherokee National Committee (one of two representative legislative bodies) as clerk and later as president, a position formerly held by Principal Chief John Ross. Joseph would also become a delegate and signatory of the Cherokee Constitution.[47]

Certainly, due to changing times and the context of his upbringing, Joseph was even more acclimated to Euro-American cultural ways than James had been. This generational shift in cultural orientation is captured visually in the formal portrait of Joseph in tailored coat, velvet vest, and black bowtie that hangs in the dining room of the Vann House today. But even with his luxurious clothing, decorative china, and storied bricks, Joseph Vann, like his father before him, could not be classified as "white."[48] His father was Cherokee; his mother was Cherokee; his wives were Cherokee, too. And he was a wealthy Cherokee man living in an increasingly stratified, rapidly changing Cherokee society in which over three hundred other prosperous families shared aspects of his class status and lifestyle.[49] Although Euro-American socialite Juliana Margaret Conner commented on the lightness of Joseph's skin when she visited the Vanns on a nuptial tour in 1827, she did not mistake him for a white man. Vann's fine house, she reported in her travel diary, was characterized by "dirt and confusion." She found there "neither order or comfort" and was served "a miserable breakfast." The narrow standards of domestic order, cleanliness, and refinement that were culturally appropriate in her native South Carolina milieu were entirely absent on this Cherokee plantation. Juliana Conner was relieved to depart from the Cherokee Nation, where the women "reminded her of the sybils and witches of olden days" due to their "disagreeable" use of the Cherokee language, and where a "lazy and indolent people . . . would not take the necessary trouble to render their houses clean or comfortable." Conner, an ethnocentric and often elitist observer, classed Joseph Vann and his "much darker wife" among this latter group and not among the high-toned white gentlemen and ladies with whom she and her husband had also socialized in their travels. It mattered not that Joseph was an extremely rich, elegantly clothed, and culturally accommodating planter, distinct from most men in the Cherokee Nation. He, his dark-skinned wife, and "gaudy" abode missed by far the cultural mark of idealized whiteness.[50]

Home-Going

As Joseph Vann remade Diamond Hill, enlarging its fields and replacing its main residence with a home that still attracts attention more than one hundred and eighty years later, Peggy Scott Vann Crutchfield prepared for a major move of her own. The immediate vicinity of Diamond Hill must have grown uncomfortable for its former mistress as the young Joe Vann stretched his administrative wings. Meanwhile, the nearby town of Oothcaloga (or Oochgeelogy), thirty miles from Spring Place, was home to many of Peggy's newly baptized Cherokee women friends.[51] Peggy had inspired and encouraged these women on their spiritual paths, leading them in religious discussion and translating the missionaries' sermons. On one such occasion, Anna Rosina described an exchange among this circle of women that had formed through Peggy's evangelism:

> Sister Crutchfield expressed herself thus, "In our youth we lived for *ourselves*; and now, when we are old and almost powerless, we give the remainder of our days to *Him*. . . . He accepts us *when* and *how* we come and does not reject us as we have surely deserved. . . ."
>
> The others agreed with her. When our Sisters are together like this, it is

exceptionally instructive to hear their childlike and yet such solid expressions. Thus they spoke to each other about their baptismal names and each one's was important to her. Those who had forgotten what theirs meant in their language had it repeated through Sister Crutchfield.[52]

Peggy, who had long been criticized by other Cherokees because of her Christian conversion, found a deep joy in the like-minded company of these Cherokee women: her sisters Sally McDonald and Elizabeth Scott, her aunt Susanna Ridge, her mother-in-law Wali Vann, her stepdaughter and niece Delilah McNair, her sister-in-law Nancy Vann Talley, and others.

Early in 1820, Peggy and her husband, Joseph Crutchfield, decided to move to Oothcaloga, the hometown of wealthy Cherokees Susanna and Major Ridge. The Crutchfields made plans to build a residence and sent their slaves ahead to begin preparing the land. Because the women of Oothcaloga had asked the Gambolds to begin a new mission in their neighborhood, a request the Gambolds were seriously considering, Peggy had the hope of Anna Rosina being near her after the move. Joseph Crutchfield set about having a two-story house built that was thirty feet long and twenty feet wide, with two piazzas. The same bricklayer who had built Joe Vann's house crafted the Crutchfield's chimney. Between the main house and a spring were two smaller buildings. A third building, intended to be the residence of John and Anna Rosina Gambold, stood just to the west of the Crutchfields' main house. Their little complex in Oothcaloga was to be the heart of a beloved Cherokee Christian community, but Peggy, the spiritual light behind the spreading religious enthusiasm, would not live long enough to see it flourish.[53]

Peggy had been susceptible to bouts of serious illness at least since 1816, when she was so weakened by consumption that the missionaries feared for her life. Pleasant was "entrusted" with Peggy's care at that time, and Anna Rosina prepared a recommended home remedy to good effect. In January of 1820, Peggy took ill again. For weeks she suffered from physical weakness, worsened by a toothache, facial swelling, and a consumptive cough. She began to read *Memoirs of the Life of Miss. Caroline E. Smelt*, about the "instructive illness and blessed end" of a Christian woman from Georgia. During periods of brief revival in the illness, Peggy took trips to Oothcaloga, and her Christian friends and relatives visited Spring Place. By September, Peggy had begun to speak of her own death, saying her illness was sent by the Savior and urging her Cherokee sisters in Christ not to waste their good health when they could be sharing God's word with other Cherokees. Soon she became too weak to leave her home, and a string of relatives and friends came to visit at her bedside. By the middle of the month, Peggy was so weak that she could no longer translate for the missionaries. And in early October, just after moving into her new Oothcaloga house, Peggy began her retreat into death. Because she was too weak to travel, the missionaries held Communion early, in Peggy's bedroom.[54]

After a brief revival of energy, Peggy drew her last breath on October 18, 1820. The missionaries wrote on that day: "We have lost much in her; not only was she a reliable interpreter, but also a true evangelist among her people. Since she was always respected by them, her words also had weight." The day following Peggy's death, "[a] special phenomenon was seen in the air in a great part of this country. A bright light, in the form of a very great fireball, moved slowly from the northeast to the southwest, and was accompanied by a muffled

God's Acre Moravian cemetery grave marker. Photograph by Tiya Miles.

noise like distant thunder." Two years later, Connecticut poet Lydia Howard Huntley Sigourney described this comet and the scene at Peggy's funeral in her epic poem *Traits of the Aborigines*: "The evening after the funeral, a large meteor was observed, emitting vivid streams of light, and attended with an explosion of thunder. 'This,' said one of them, with their characteristic gravity, 'this is a warning to us. It signifieth that a good woman hath died.'" Peggy was buried in the Springplace Mission cemetery, or God's Acre, before a crowd of over one hundred people. Afterward, missionary Renatus Schmidt festooned "blessed Peggy's resting place with rose vines, carnations, and violets." The missionaries wrote in their year-end summary: "It also pleased our Lord in this year to pick the 'first flower' from His garden here . . . our dear Sister Margaret Ann Crutchfield. Her loss lies close to our hearts. We miss her very much and will miss her for a long time."[55]

After Peggy's passing, the blacks in her household underwent an upheaval much like the one they had suffered when Will and Hannah were sold. They were "distributed," with no details recorded, among Peggy's siblings. Meanwhile, John and Anna Rosina Gambold, having received approval from the home church, planned their move to Oothcaloga, where they would begin a new Cherokee mission. They packed their belongings and prepared to relocate to the poplar cabin Peggy and Joseph had built for them. But before their move, Anna Rosina took ill with "severe pressure in her chest." She passed away, presumably of a heart attack, on February 19, 1821. John Gambold had been deeply attached to his wife, a remarkable woman in many regards, who had left behind a comfortable life of teaching school in Bethlehem to marry John and travel to a fledgling Indian mission. "I will not try to describe how I felt," he wrote. "However, I must bear witness for my eternally faithful Savior about one thing. He granted me the grace to direct my tearful eyes toward him and to receive the comfort from the fullness of his grace that my deeply wounded heart so desperately needed." Anna Rosina Gambold was buried in the Springplace Mission cemetery, where one hundred people gathered to say farewell. Although the graves are unmarked at Springplace, a recent state archaeological dig revealed two gravesites unusually close to one another. These twin graves, a modern-day Cherokee Moravian visitor to the cemetery mused, must be the final resting places of Peggy Scott Vann Crutchfield and Anna Rosina Kliest Gambold, two memorable women whose souls were joined in their love for Christ.[56]

John Gambold, now in his early sixties, founded the Oothcaloga Mission without his beloved wife. He was sometimes "transported" in mind to "the grave of [his] unforgettable Anna Rosina," whereupon he "cried [him]self out" and called to a "hidden God." Feeling "completely alone in this country," John remained only because he believed he was doing God's will. Since Joseph Crutchfield had remarried and moved to Alabama, he sold the entire plantation to the Oothcaloga Mission. John Gambold remarried himself, to a Moravian woman named Anna Maria, and directed the new mission until his own death in 1827.[57]

Perhaps in his final years, John took comfort in the presence of Michael, the enslaved boy he had once beaten so unapologetically. Michael's owner, David Watie, lived in Oothcaloga, and Michael often traveled about with Watie or on his own. Michael married a woman named Hannah and had at least two children, Salomo Michael and Rosana. To John Gambold's certain delight, Michael returned in adulthood to the religious teachings instilled by his former Moravian owners. They recorded in their Oothcaloga Mission Diary: "We had a sincere talk with the Negro Michael. The Brothers baptized him as a child because he belonged to the mission in Springplace. It seems that the things he learned in school there during his childhood and what he heard about the Savior have not been erased from his heart." Michael had his son baptized at Oothcaloga eight months before Gambold's death.[58]

Michael's mother, Pleasant, remained enslaved at the Springplace Mission until old age rendered her feeble. The missionaries wrote in 1826: "Old Pleasant is so sickly that she can hardly take care of the cooking. May the savior help us!" In 1828 they concluded: "One must really include Pleasant in the expenditures, because she can no longer do much." Toward the end of a lifetime of exploitation, Pleasant might have found a glimmer of joy, at last, in the births of her two grandchildren. But even this potential for emotional satisfaction would be short-lived, for in 1829, after nearly twenty-five years in the Cherokee Nation, Pleasant was sent back to North Carolina. Moravian missionaries Gottlieb and Dorothea Byhan had had enough of her, now that she was "old [and] almost inept." They made plans to transport Pleasant by wagon, complaining that they could not "endure" her any longer. To her lasting honor, Pleasant never accepted the status of chattel, never allowed her Christian owners to lay claim to her pride of self. The Byhans complained, as the Gambolds once had:

> [Pleasant] seems to have distaste for God's word and doesn't want to hear anything like this. She never comes to services and she discourages those Negroes who sometimes want to come so that they do not come either.... She even says, as she has actually said, that she would not die yet because the devil was not ready for her. . . . Thus we cannot do anything but send her away.

Finally, the Byhans concluded with bitterness: "Either *she* had to give in or *we* did."[59]

Pleasant never gave in. She had served the inaugural Christian mission to the Cherokees longer than any other single person of the period. She died at the age of eighty "among the assets" of the Moravian Church in the same year that Cherokees began their forced march to Indian Territory. Pleasant was buried in the segregated "stranger" cemetery in Salem, North Carolina, where her remains still lie beneath the foundation of St. Philips, a historic, hallowed Afro-Moravian Church.[60]

Losing the House

As Joseph Vann's political prominence grew in the 1820s, he participated in the Cherokees' governmental centralization project. The creation of a constitution, the organization of three branches of government (and within them, two representative legislative bodies), and the building of a national capital were all actions intended to demonstrate the materiality and effectiveness of a Cherokee state. Cherokee leaders hoped the United States would recognize their political independence and territorial rights, but rather than inspiring this respectful reaction, the Cherokee Nation's bold move alarmed American officials. The federal government saw the Cherokees' innovation as a potential threat to the existing relationship in which the United States assumed oversight over the Cherokees and other Indian nations. President John Quincy Adams assured the southern states that the Cherokee Constitution would "not be recognized as changing any one of the relations under which they stood to the General Government."[61] Adam's successor in 1828, President Andrew Jackson, was a lauded Indian fighter and proponent of Indian Removal. The state of Georgia, which had long viewed Cherokee land as its rightful territory, responded immediately and negatively to the Cherokee assertion of sovereignty.

In December of 1828, Georgia passed a law, effective in June of 1830, extending its jurisdiction over Cherokee territory within the state's claimed boundaries. Georgia then enacted what amounted to a red code, extinguishing the Cherokee Council, forbidding Cherokees from convening "under pretext of authority from the Cherokee tribe," dissolving the Cherokee courts, deeming Indians incompetent witnesses to testify against whites in the Georgia courts, and expelling all unauthorized whites from within the Cherokee borders. In 1829, Georgia passed an additional law ordering all male missionaries on Cherokee premises to sign an oath of allegiance to the state.[62] Georgia gambled that the severity of these codes would separate the Cherokees from their missionary allies and force Cherokees to move to Arkansas to lands made available by the federal government. But the majority of Cherokees remained in their homes, and the majority of missionaries, including the Moravians, refused to sign the oath. Georgia's coup d'état, which coincided with the discovery of gold in Cherokee country, was followed by a reign of terror. Citizens of Georgia reveled in their government's unjust actions, all too eager to benefit from Cherokee people's suffering. Some white citizens, John Gambold once wrote in an angry, confidential letter, felt "enmity against the Indians" due to past wars, "[o]thers again hate the Indians merely for their mode of Living, so different from Ours: for their dark Colours, their Language, unintelligible to us & other alike frivolous Reasons; Others, indeed, the greater number of them, have no other Reason, than a desire to possess their Land."[63] Hostility, ethnocentrism, racism, greed — all of these base emotions fed Georgia's invasion of the Cherokee Nation.

As eager white gold miners elbowed their way into the Cherokee community of Dahlonega, the Georgia Guard arrested Cherokee leaders and white missionaries, shut down the *Cherokee Phoenix* printing press, and rudely harassed Cherokee women. Black slaves owned by Cherokees ran for their lives, as white Georgians entered the country and seized them as booty. Joseph Vann, who in 1831 had been elected to the high government office of president of the Cherokee National Committee, was among those detained. The *Cherokee Phoenix* newspaper reported that "Mr. Jos. Vann . . . who is a native" was arrested for unknown reasons when the Georgia Guard passed by Spring Place. Missionary James Trott, who was seized around the same time, described being "arrested . . . by a detachment of the Georgia Guard in a warlike manner" and then "kept in close confinement" in a "gloomy cell." He said that Vann and other leading Cherokees "were arrested for nothing, to be plain, some of whom were insulted and [ill] treated in various ways and then sooner or later set at liberty."[64] By 1832, when the U.S. Supreme Court ruled Georgia's legal takeover unconstitutional in the precedent-setting case *Worcester v. Georgia*, great damage had already been done.

In its outrageous illegal act — the creation of a police state in Cherokee territory — Georgia enjoyed total support from the newly inaugurated president of the United States. One of Andrew Jackson's first moves in office was to champion an Indian Removal bill. In May of 1830, the bill passed by a narrow margin, despite organized Cherokee opposition, widespread public protest by Christian activists in the North, and heated debate in Congress. It was now the federal government's policy that all Indian nations east of the Mississippi could and should be removed to the West. Georgia wasted no time in acting on this law. In 1832, the state set about devising a system for seizing and reassigning Cherokee lands and homes. Georgia established a lottery in which white residents could purchase chances to win 160 acres of Cherokee land (40 acres in gold country), complete with any structures on the lots. Although the state included language ensuring Cherokees rights to the lands that whites did not want, in practice, Cherokee families would be forcibly displaced. Under the protection of the Georgia Guard, teams of surveyors entered Cherokee territory, followed by eager white settlers hoping to spot the best lots. "This part of Indian country," the Moravians wrote in their diary, "will now be divided through the 'Lotterie' game to the residents of Georgia, and they also have legal power to take their winnings."[65]

At the Moravians' Springplace Mission, the lottery had immediate and dire effect. On the inopportune day of Christmas Eve 1832, Colonel William Bishop, head of the Georgia Guard, arrived with a legal document declaring him the purchaser of a lot encompassing the mission complex. Although Bishop, with "curses and oaths" meanly offered the site back to the Moravians for a price, the missionaries refused. Joseph Vann protested what he viewed as the wrongful seizure of his family's "improved" land. He "began a legal case through the Indian agent against the current resident of Spring Place . . . to get back the property which has been secured for him until now by law." But having no defense against the legal barriers to Cherokee landownership newly erected by Georgia, Joseph "forever gave up any future claims to Springplace." The Moravians were forced to relocate to Tennessee, and their hope of "being able to return to Spring Place disappeared forever."[66]

From their "temporary place of refuge" across state lines, Moravians witnessed the naked oppression of Indians. Cherokee congregants were losing their homes, "since all protection has been withdrawn from the poor Indians and they are vulnerable to the greed of whoever happens to be owner of their land." Church attendance by their beleaguered congregation shrank because the Cherokees' "external circumstances become increasingly oppressive through which they become increasingly impoverished. Robbed of their plantations and homes, they move from one place to another, while others who are more diligent exert great effort trying to cultivate anew on the Tennessee side."[67]

With the Moravian missionaries now displaced, diary reports on events at Diamond Hill became impossible, creating a gap in the historical record during the years leading up to Cherokee Removal. We can suppose, though, through contextual readings of the chaos and desperation faced by many Cherokees, that Joseph Vann, his wives and children, and all of those dependent on them, lived in a state of dread and instability. Joseph had already tried and failed to retain authority over the Springplace missionary compound. Surely he would have feared that his family's home might be next. The Vanns clung to their precious house for as long as they possibly could. But in 1833, when Georgia expanded its web of repressive laws aimed at Cherokee people, Joseph was caught off guard. A new law made it illegal for "any Indian, or descendant of an Indian, or white man the head of an Indian family, claiming the privileges of an Indian" to hire whites or slaves belonging to whites within Georgia's claimed boundaries. The penalty for infraction of the act was forfeiture of "all right and title that they may have to any reservation of occupancy within the limits" of Georgia. The land once occupied by Indians so charged would be issued to a new owner "as though such improvements had never been occupied by such Indian."[68]

Joseph Vann was known for employing white overseers and workmen. Emboldened by Vann's clear infraction of the new law, Colonel Bishop, owner of the Springplace Mission lot, claimed the brick manor home as his own. Spencer Riley, a constable who had lived on the premises and rented a room from the Vanns, challenged Bishop for possession. In testimony published in the *Georgia Journal* newspaper, Riley accused Bishop of seeking the lot for his brother. Bishop, Riley charged, had sent Mrs. Vann a note "in the absence of her husband," ordering the family to "quit the possession of the lot." Faced with a party of twenty armed men led by Colonel Bishop, Joseph and his family were forced to occupy one room temporarily and "at sufferance." The two white men then launched a gun battle over the property. When Bishop ordered Georgia Guardsmen to his aid, the soldiers shot Riley and ignited a log on the famous floating stairway. Joseph Vann, the ousted owner whose family huddled in the shadows, was told to "go up and extinguish the fire" to save his house for another man. "The affair at Vann's," journalist John Howard Payne wrote, "was one of still greater injustice, & barbarity as the contending parties had recourse to weapons of death."[69]

The Vann family, including Joe, three adult women, five boys, and six girls, fled from the suffocating smoke and emigrated across the Tennessee line. In his expulsion from Diamond Hill, the Springplace Mission site, and the Mill Creek complex, Joseph Vann lost not only his home but also 805 acres of cultivated land, functional businesses, barns, stables, and dozens of log cabins and domestic outbuildings. For three generations, the Vanns had occupied this rich plantation land, but this was the last Diamond Hill would see of its Cherokee owner and occupants. After the ouster of Joseph Vann, the brick home and grounds would be privately held by a succession of white Georgians for over one hundred and twenty years. A salvaged, partial newspaper clipping would later say of the Vanns' eviction: "Today the once beautiful and stately old Vann house stands at Spring Place with only the blue Cohuttas to tell of its romantic past. It was not until 1834 that the Vanns were driven from their home and beautiful Valley, where they had spent their lives."[70]

The Vann House viewed from the woods.
Courtesy of the Chief Vann House.

Bleak House

AN EPILOGUE

All I want in this Creation
Is a pretty little wife and a big plantation
A-way up yonder in the Cherokee Nation
— Popular Georgia song, 1820s

Moving West

When Joe Vann and his family were violently expelled from their plantation home, they shared the fate of fellow Cherokees. Their wealth, however, insulated them from the worst outcomes. Unlike many in their nation, the Vanns would not be homeless, for they were the owners of a second, fine estate. After fleeing Diamond Hill, Joe Vann and his family moved into a "hewed log dwelling house" with eight rooms and a porch on a 300-acre farm on the Tennessee River. Joe's Hamilton County home, acquired at a time that goes unrecorded, was not the architectural equal of the brick showhouse. Nevertheless, the plentiful estate supported a high standard of living. Joe still possessed thirty-five cabins, a mill, and a ferry, along with a large slave labor force that produced 3,200 bushels of corn, 500 of which were sold to yield $250 in income. Some of the women in the slave community were proficient weavers and spinners, contributing to the material comfort of the Vann family as well as to the Tennessee farm's potential profit. The family, which included five English-readers among them, would also continue to benefit from previous access to education. The Vanns would remain here at their Tennessee farmstead until a shift in federal policy compelled them to move again.[1]

The Indian Removal Act of 1830 placed unbearable pressure on the Cherokee Nation's political leaders. While some, like National Committee member John Ridge and newspaper editor Elias Boudinot, believed that expulsion was inevitable and argued that it was wise to sign a removal treaty on the best terms possible as soon as possible, others, like Principal Chief John Ross, urged continued resistance to the U.S. mandate. As internal dissension grew, U.S. officials turned the situation to their advantage. In the fall of 1835, John Schermerhorn, a representative for President Jackson, met with members of the minority faction who favored compromise. The result of the meeting was the Treaty of New Echota, a document that sanctioned Cherokee removal and established a target date within two years of the treaty's ratification. The treaty-making process had bypassed formal channels of Cherokee government, and the final product was rejected by most Cherokees. Joseph Vann, a leading elected representative, was probably away in Washington with John Ross's negotiating party at the time that the meeting took place. Ridge and Boudinot, his schoolmates from the Springplace Mission, had both signed the treaty, but perhaps Joseph would have followed in the footsteps of his willful father, refusing to sign away Cherokee lands. Despite the lack of formal approval by the Cherokee government, and regardless of a massive petition signed by thousands of Cherokees, the U.S. Congress ratified the Treaty of New Echota in 1836.[2]

After the passage of the treaty, Joseph Vann thought it best to relocate his family before the 1838 deadline. Like other Cherokees of means, Joseph traveled early to Indian Territory to select the most productive lands. He set his sights on acreage near Webbers Falls on the Arkansas River; then he returned to Tennessee to collect his human property. Vann transported at least forty-eight enslaved blacks west to his new estate.[3] His dramatic shipment of an intact labor force made an impression on the memories of Oklahoma residents interviewed by historian Marguerite McFadden in the early 1900s. McFadden reported: "It was quite a sight for the people around the falls when Joe Vann's property arrived by steamboat.... There were looks of astonishment and shouts of surprise as boat after boat came into view, some towing barges filled with men, women and children. As the boats drew near the shore the onlookers saw the barges were filled with black people, too many to count."[4] The fate of Vann's remaining sixty-odd slaves is not recorded. More than likely, they were sold to new white owners farther south. When the blacks still possessed by Vann arrived in Indian Territory, their primary task was to recreate his plantation enterprise from the ground up. This meant, first, clearing the land and preparing it for a cotton crop. Vann's grandson recalled in a Works Progress Administration interview that "by 1844, [Vann had] cleared 400 acres of fine bottom land, had built a big two-story double log home, and was considered the richest man in the Cherokee Nation."[5]

Nostalgic for the home he had lost so violently, Joseph Vann commissioned a near replica of his brick manor house. Although it lacked the sweeping verandahs of his former home, the western Vann estate still possessed a certain splendor. As in his Diamond Hill home, the walls were fancily painted in shades of red, blue, green, and gold, and hand-carved woodwork embellished the interior. After the plantation buildings were completed, Joseph transported his wives and children to the new location. Jennie Foster Vann is said to have traveled with her husband "in a carriage, stopping at various inns along the way." To Jennie would fall the new big house, where she "was established in what for those days was unbelievable luxury." Polly Black Vann, who arrived later, lived with her children in a house of their own nearby.[6]

While Joseph Vann, his wives, and children paid the steep psycho-spiritual price of exile, they did so with an economic edge that proved essential to the reestablishment of their family's wealth and status position in the West. The financial cushion that allowed the Vanns to relocate with relative ease was not shared by most Cherokees, who emigrated under grueling circumstances, losing thousands of lives in the process. The Vanns would not remain behind long enough to witness the by now emblematic scenes of mourning and destruction that characterized mandatory removal in 1838–39. They would not experience the separation of loved ones, the suffering in cramped holding camps, the forced march in fierce weather, the forlorn emptiness of cabins beloved—scenes which, in the words of a man who had hauled supplies for the Removal army, "melted to tenderness a heart of stone."[7]

A Sinking Ship

Joseph Vann prospered in the West just as he had in the South. While the majority of the Cherokee populace was ejected by the Georgia Guard, crowded into stockades, and forced to walk the Trail of Tears in the winter of 1838–39, Joseph Vann lived in incomparable comfort. He expanded the number of slaves he owned to figures that took on mythic proportions. Oral history accounts from the 1930s recall him as owning 300, 400, and up to 500 slaves. Joseph also indulged his habit of horse racing in Indian Territory. He built a fine stable and acquired a famous racehorse named Lucy Walker, described in oral accounts as "for a time the fastest quarter-mile horse in the world" whose colts sold for $500 each.[8] By the early 1840s, Joseph Vann had purchased his own side-wheeler steamboat in Cincinnati and brought it back to Indian Territory. At the time, his was the only steamboat registered in the Oklahoma region. He used the craft, named the *Lucy Walker* after his winning quarter horse, to transport cotton to Louisville, Cincinnati, and New Orleans.[9] Enslaved blacks grew Vann's cotton, loaded his cargo, and manned his vessel. And in 1844, when the *Lucy Walker* exploded in an accident deemed "a major world maritime disaster," a black man lived to tell the tale.[10]

The fateful trip occurred in October of that year, when Captain Holderman steered the *Lucy Walker* down the Arkansas River, to the Mississippi, and

The Lucy Walker *steamboat pictured in* Oklahoma's Orbit, *1961.*
Courtesy of The Oklahoman *Archives.*

finally, onto the Ohio. Accounts differ on why Vann took this particular trip. He may have set out on a routine journey to sell his cotton, or, as the most dramatic story goes, he was off to enter his horse in the Louisville racing event that preceded the Kentucky Derby. Once en route, the *Lucy Walker* picked up passengers from Mississippi, Virginia, Kentucky, Maryland, and Pennsylvania. Those who boarded were "[g]entlemen in their high beaver hats, cutaway coats, and checkered pantaloons," "ladies in crinolines," and a "general scattering of woodsmen and their families who were going down river, seeking new homes."[11] Many of the passengers reportedly boarded to travel to the horse races in Louisville. According to Vann's grandson, Edward Vann, Joseph accepted these additional passengers "more for the pleasure of their company than for profit."[12] All accounts agree that when Vann docked in Louisville, he had numerous wealthy passengers aboard, as well as black slaves, amounting to approximately 136 people in all. "The boat was a floating palace," the most embellished report exclaimed, "exhibiting opulent hospitality with respect to sleeping quarters, food and drink."[13]

While Joseph and his guests were "keeping up a continual round of drinking and celebration," Joseph is said to have noticed a swift steamboat pulling out from the wharf. Joseph's "unquenchable love of taking a chance" overcame him.[14] Since his captain had reportedly quit at the Louisville port, Joseph took command of the boat and vowed to beat the other steamer to New Orleans. In the account told by Edward Vann, as well as several others, Joseph ordered his black crew to stoke the engine with all available fuel, including "sides of meat" and "slabs of bacon." Vann's enslaved engineer refused to comply, warning Joseph that an excess of fuel would cause the boilers to explode. Unwilling to listen, Joseph threatened the slave "for the benefit of his Eastern friends" by pulling out "his old frontier 'hog leg' pistol and wav[ing] it under the Negro engineer's nose."[15] Under duress, the engineer and "fire boys" followed Joseph's command, and the boat swiftly advanced with the added fuel. The passengers aboard carried on gaily "[i]n full swing of a hilarious ball, to the tune of slave fiddlers and the inspiration of Joseph's Cherokee corn [alcohol]."[16] A great-great-granddaughter of Joseph Vann, Virginia Vann Perry, adamantly disputed this sensational version of events. "Those wild stories of gambling, drinking, [and] dancing were not true," she said. "He picked up church people on the way!" A nineteenth-century technical account in *Lloyd's Steamboat Directory and Disasters on the Western Waters* supports Perry's assertion, stating simply that the boat encountered mechanical problems four miles outside of New Albany, Indiana, and attempts at repair failed. When the water in the boilers emptied, the engine stopped. Three overheated boilers exploded, causing an immediate fire in the ladies' cabin.[17] The boat began to sink within a matter of minutes, and "fragments of the boat were found later on both the Indiana and Kentucky shores."[18]

Residents of New Albany, the closest city to the accident scene, rushed in to rescue survivors. Of the thirty who were saved, many were terribly injured. Fifty to sixty bodies were later recovered. The awful calamity of the *Lucy Walker* within its first year of operation made headlines in midwestern newspapers. Joseph Vann was among those who lost his life in "one of the worst steamboat disasters in American History."[19]

According to Edward Vann, the enslaved black engineer who had refused Vann's order jumped ship before the explosion occurred. "In went the side of meat," Edward Vann reported, "and over the side went the black engineer, the only survivor of the Lucy Walker explosion."[20] Despite the assertion made by Edward Vann and others in their accounts, this black crewman was not the sole survivor of the accident. It is significant, though, that this crewman's story takes center stage in Vann family and Oklahoma oral histories. In another of Vann's grandson's version of events, it is this single enslaved survivor who passed the story on to Joseph Vann's descendants, and it is his version that continues to be told. R. P. Vann explained to historian Grant Foreman in a 1932 interview: "My father was Dave Vann, a prominent member of the Cherokee Tribe. His father was the famous Joe Vann, who owned the steam boat *Lucy Walker* that blew up on the Ohio River in 1843. The only survivor of this explosion was an old negro who later lived at Ft. Gibson. He was an old slave who had worked for many years as engineer of the boat. Long after the explosion I met him at Ft. Gibson and he told me the story of the explosion."[21] R. P. Vann then recounts the familiar tale of a steamboat race, Vann's reckless order, the black engineer's refusal to obey, Vann's pistol waving, sides of meat thrown onto the fire, and a black engineer as the sole survivor of the resulting explosion. In the version told by his grandsons and repeated by white Oklahomans, Joseph Vann is a brazen pleasure seeker, his unnamed slave the knowing hero. This story has so powerful a hold on the public memory of Joseph Vann that contemporary descendant Virginia Vann Perry raised it of her own accord in an oral history interview. Although she personally disputes the notion that her forebear Joseph was "a drunkard and a wastard" who behaved irresponsibly on that fateful day, she acknowledges that "a black slave . . . came home and told the story that there was a race . . . and people accepted that was what it was."[22]

Former slave Lucinda Vann was a child at the time of the *Lucy Walker* explosion, but she vividly recalled the event and named the fabled black engineer: "The most terrible thing that ever happen was when the Lucy Walker busted and Joe got blew up. The engineer's name was Jim Vann. How did they hear about it at home? Oh, the news traveled up and down the river. It was bad, oh, it was bad. Everybody hollerin' and cryin'. After the explosion someone found an arm up in a tree on the bank of the river. They brought it home and my grandmother knew it was Joe's. She done his washing and knew the cuff of his sleeve. . . . Don't know what they ever did with that arm. Lord, it was terrible, Yes, Lord, Yes."[23] When Joseph Vann's now legendary engineer warned that the boilers would fail, Vann reportedly shot back: "If they do, we'll all go together."[24] His cocky prognostication proved more accurate than he knew. For in life and in death, the Vanns' experience intertwined with that of their African-descended slaves. A slave woman's storied identification of Joseph Vann's severed arm was the grim evidence of this intimacy. So critical is the presence of blacks to the story of the Vanns and their plantation that the tales we have about heir apparent Joseph Vann's last moments, those handed down to his grandchildren and preserved in the written record for posterity, are the tales of enslaved blacks. And so, in this final chapter in the history of Diamond Hill, members of that long-forgotten and long-suffering slave community have the last word.

Open House

A CONCLUSION

> If I had to live in a racial house, it was important, at the least, to rebuild it so that it was not a windowless prison into which I was forced, a thick-walled, impenetrable container from which no cry could be heard, but rather an open house, grounded, yet generous in its supply of windows and doors.
> —Toni Morrison, "Home," from *The House That Race Built*, 1997

All the Things That Make Us Proud

Ever since the 1950s, when local volunteers and the Georgia Historical Commission saved the crumbling Vann House from demise, the site has continued to inspire both community devotion and historical fantasy. Locals and tourists alike turn out for the site's signature annual events, like the wintertime Christmas by Candlelight celebration and the midsummer Chief Vann House Days festivities. In 2002, the Friends of the Vann House community group, the oldest of its kind in the state, approached the Trust for Public Land to launch an ambitious fund-raising campaign. Their goal was to raise $1.5 million to purchase eighty-five acres of land across the highway from the Vann House. This open acreage, which was part of the original Diamond Hill estate and had once supported outbuildings, was threatened by a trailer park development project. Even local schoolchildren got in on the fund-raising act, raising money for the purchase through their drama club. In 2003, drama and choral students at Northwest Elementary School, located in the Chatsworth school district, performed the play "Vann's Trail of Tears," a revival of a 1978 school production. Proceeds from the drama about "James Vann, a Cherokee Indian Chief with Scottish ancestry," benefited the land campaign at the historic site. After sustaining a multiyear campaign, the Friends of the Vann House coalition was successful in raising the necessary sum. In November of 2005, the Vann House hosted a land-acquisition ceremony to mark the tremendous accomplishment.[1]

In the same year that the Vann House coalition celebrated its victory, a housing development of two- to eight-acre "luxury estates" beginning in the $500,000 range was being advertised in nearby Forsythe County, Georgia. Named the Legends of Settendown Creek, this new residential community

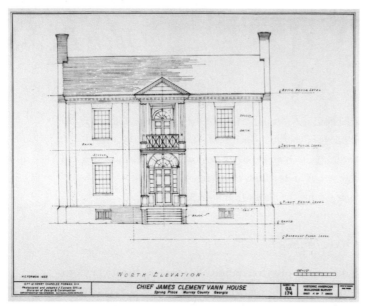

Architectural drawing of the Vann House, north elevation. Courtesy of Hargrett Rare Book and Manuscript Library/ University of Georgia Libraries.

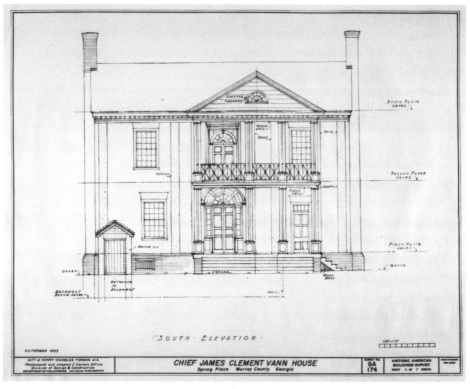

Architectural drawing of the Vann House, south elevation.
Courtesy of Hargrett Rare Book and Manuscript Library/University of Georgia Libraries.

Land Preservation Campaign card. Courtesy of the Chief Vann House.

highlighted Cherokee history as a chief selling point and rested on lore that prior to Indian Removal, "the Cherokees hid their treasures in the hills around Settendown Creek." Among the area's venerable Cherokee figures listed in promotional materials was James Vann, "a wealthy mixed blood Cherokee" whose "holdings extended to gold mines, land, slaves, and public buildings." By 2008, the Legends development was thriving with 144 home sites and an active home owners' association. The development's website continued to highlight a fanciful Cherokee history, alluding to a nearby "sacred temple" that had once stood "under the protective wing of the eagle" and telling of a "secret Cherokee treasure tunnel" that was marked by "cryptic maps."[2]

While luxury homes sprung up around fantastic legends of Cherokee history and heroes, longtime devotees of the Chief Vann House, many of them descendants of original state historical commissioners and community restorers, went about their labor of love. Nearly forty-five years after the initial dedication of the restored house museum, the grandson of a former Vann House preservationist donated seed money for the construction of an Interpretive Center on the grounds. The center was dedicated in July of 2002 and named for former Chatsworth mayor Robert E. Chambers, whose "finest hour" in life had been the 1958 dedication of the home.[3] I was in attendance at the dedication ceremony, observing and asking questions for research related to my first book about a mixed-race Afro-Cherokee family. I remember it as a scorching day in late July, when ice cubes melted straight away in tall glasses of southern sweet tea. The event was heavily attended, and the crowd spilled out beyond the doors of the Interpretive Center onto the green plantation grounds.

The program of speakers for the dedication included state officials, county officials, Cherokee principal chiefs and council members from the Cherokee Nation of Oklahoma and the Cherokee Eastern Band of North Carolina, Cherokee flutists and singers, a representative from the Trail of Tears Association, representatives of the Vann family and the Chambers family, and a well-known local minister. The speakers touched on a range of issues, including, most prominently, the economic success of James and Joseph Vann, the injustice of removal, and Cherokee perseverance through trying historical times. The Cherokee history of the site predominated, as well it should have. The role of Euro-American missionaries in the Cherokee Nation was also highlighted, correlating with the missionary history on the Vann estate. But as I listened closely to the speakers, taking copious notes, I was struck by the absence of any attention to African-descended slaves or Cherokee women. Although James Vann had built his home near his mother, Wali Vann, and with the partnership of his wife, Peggy Scott Vann, neither woman received a word of acknowledgment.[4] And although blacks were the largest population on Diamond Hill — numbering nearly one hundred people — they were rendered completely absent, absolutely invisible, in this museum dedication. Perhaps more egregious than the omission of black people's historical presence, many of the speakers celebrated the Vann family's wealth with no attribution of its derivation from black labor and no concern for those whose lives were diminished by enslavement. The local minister described James Vann as "a mover and shaker" who "enjoyed the finer things in life." This plantation, he said, was "the pride of the Cherokee Nation." A high-level state administrator said about the site: "James and Joseph Vann built this plantation and did all the things that make us so proud of this area."

The center's dedication ceremony patently exposed a troubling reality: the long and plentiful tradition of Vann House preservation and interpretation had fully excluded blacks and substantively discounted Cherokee women. At the time, this was the case not only in the speeches that so many attendees heard but also in the Vann House tour itself. And while black experience went unrecognized by Vann House supporters, the fruits of black suffering — Vann's splendid estate and accompanying wealth — were taken as a point of pride and celebration. In the light of a new century, the dedication of 2002 was playing a role in solidifying and carrying forward interpretive narratives of the past that idealized Cherokee history, highlighted Cherokee likeness to whites, under-

[handwritten in margin: 2002 dedication]

mined black history, and sidelined Cherokee women's lives. Jennifer Walford Vann, a young Vann descendant who recently studied anthropology and women's studies in college, was disappointed with her initial tour of the Vann House for these very reasons. "I did not get a strong sense of Cherokee culture," she said, "and I also did not get much of an impression about the lives of the African-Americans who lived there. It seemed like a very 'white man' experience since I also didn't get much of a feel for the lives of women there."[5]

Slavery, colonialism, and patriarchal power are sensitive and contentious issues across our nation. And of those, slavery is an especially thorny subject for many southern communities. Historian James Oliver Horton has demonstrated in his overview of slavery and public sites that "the South was a particularly explosive arena for issues of race and the interpretation of slavery." Horton's co-edited collection of essays titled *Slavery and Public History: The Tough Stuff of American Memory* is a virtual catalog of misrepresentations of the past skewed toward valorizing a white male nation and cloaking the gritty history of slavery. From the Liberty Bell to Mount Vernon, this catalog includes, time after time, first-person narratives of ugly battles among museum curators, historians, and members of the public over racialized representations of the past. Historian Fitzhugh Brundage, a foremost thinker on the subject of how southerners remember history, has questioned "prospects for an inclusive culture in the South" given "contemporary understandings of the southern past." He has asked: "Can the previously hidden memories of blacks, Latinos, and other marginalized groups be incorporated into the public life of the South?"[6]

The ideological and political deck seems stacked against the Vann House, the oldest architectural restoration project undertaken by the Georgia Historical Commission. Can such a venerable institution alter an entrenched interpretive vision? Can core narratives be revised to reflect a multiracial past and thereby foster a more democratic future? And will it take a virtual social tsunami to push a path toward change as has been the case at other historic sites? Given its geographical and cultural context, perhaps the Vann House, like so many other southern plantation museums, can never adequately confront the pains of our past that continue to haunt our present.

Or, perhaps it might. In the summer of 2008, I would find out as I traveled to the Vann House for the third time in a year and the last time before the completion of this book. Interpretive ranger Julia Autry had informed me the summer before that she and her fellow staff members hoped to stage a new exhibit on African American life at the Vann House. They would transform the cabin that had formerly been a site office and lately had been used for school group demonstrations into a space for black history. Autry's director, site manager Jeff Stancil, supported her in the project, and although funds were difficult to come by, through a well-timed appeal she had extracted a promise of $800 from the Department of Natural Resources. Over a period of less than twelve months, Autry and her part-time assistants, Rangers William Chase Parker, Ethan Calhoun, and Curtis King, created an exhibit from the ground up while maintaining their regular duties at the site. To complete this undertaking without professional curators, a luxury they could not afford, the rangers on staff had to become jacks-of-all-trades. Autry undertook documentary and photographic research, managed the practical organization of the plan, drafted reams of text for display, placed orders, and consulted with a small circle of scholars. Parker planned the layout with the use of a web-based design program and vividly imagined historical scenes that might arrest the public's attention. Parker and Calhoun, neither one of them trained craftsmen, constructed an elaborate brick stew stove and wooden cupboard for a kitchen scene that would feature Pleasant and her son. Together, Autry, Parker, and King tramped across fields and creeks trying to locate any sign of Vann's slave quarters. And in the long-standing Vann House tradition, community members dove right in. Tim Howard, president of the Whitfield-Murray Historical Society and past president of the Friends of the Vann House, assembled the loom that would signify black women's work in the weaving house. Brick mason Frank McCamey, who was in his seventies and had done brick restoration on the Vann House in the 1950s, taught Chase Parker how to lay bricks and helped with the stove construction. Jeff Stancil's wife, seamstress Rhonda Pearl Stancil, made plans to sew clothing for mannequins that would represent Pleasant, Patience, and Michael. No one from outside the Vann House, myself included, had suggested this massive undertaking. The decision had been internal, the commitment genuine, and the effort Herculean.

The resulting exhibit, titled "Patchwork in the Quilt: The Lives of Black Slaves and Free Blacks on the Vann Plantation," though still in preliminary form, would be unveiled just in time for a momentous occasion. On July 26th and 27th, the site would host its popular Chief Vann House Days, a festival to which hundreds of people flocked annually, including Cherokee artisans demonstrating and selling their crafts and historical reenactors who had camped on the grounds this time each year since the 1950s. On the second day of the festival, the Vann House would celebrate its fiftieth anniversary as a restored historic site. The anniversary, like the original opening it memorialized, was to be a standout affair. The Friends of the Vann House, who planned the event, had taken every detail into consideration, including the creation of a facsimile

Chief Vann House Days 2008
50th Anniversary Celebration

In commemoration of the 204th year of Chief Vann House and the 50th Anniversary of its restoration, the Georgia Department of Natural Resources and the Friends of the Vann House will sponsor **Chief Vann House Days on Saturday, July 26 from 10:00 a.m. – 4:00 p.m** *and a* 50th Anniversary Celebration on Sunday, July 27 from 2:00pm – 4:00pm.

As part of the festivities on **Saturday,** Cherokee & local craftsmen will demonstrate 19th century pottery, flute making, weaving, basket making, quilting, spinning, rug making, blacksmithing, storytelling, blowgun shooting, woodcarving, and much more. Special guests include Cherokee potter Shirley Oswalt from the Snowbird community in North Carolina and Cherokee flutist Tommy Wildcat from Oklahoma. Regular admission prices will be charges for Saturday.

Then **Sunday** will mark 50 years to the day that the Vann House was first opened as a state historic site. On hand to mark the occasion will be local politicians, historians, and other dignitaries along with Cherokee tribal officials. *ADMISSION IS FREE FOR SUNDAY!*

The Vann House museum will be open both days featuring a short film and interpretive exhibits on the Vann family and the Cherokee Nation. Park rangers will be on hand to provide tours through the Vann House and give information about Cherokee history. Regular admission prices will be charged on Saturday but Sunday is free admission.

The Chief Vann House is located three miles west of Chatsworth, Georgia at the intersection of Ga. Highway 52A and 225. For further directions or more information call 706/ 695-2598.

Georgia
STATE PARKS
& HISTORIC SITES

invitation that replicated the 1958 original. The best plans, it could be said, had been laid.

Still, as I traveled up a steep and winding highway to the mountain inn where I would stay with a colleague over the weekend, I worried. How would the crowd, sure to be made up of white southerners in the main, react to the new slavery exhibit? Would representatives from the Cherokee Nation of Oklahoma, including a supreme court justice from the very district where Joseph Vann had rebuilt his plantation, be open to the stories of people their historical forebears had once enslaved? Would one Vann House employee's fears that some enraged member of the public might try to burn down the exhibit cabin be realized in the dark of night?

July 27, 2008, dawned damp and misty in the Cohutta Mountains. Thin clouds cottoned the sky, threading themselves through distant peaks. Down below, in the valley where the Vann House sat, a rising sun began its slow baking of the southern soil. My colleague, historian Rowena McClinton, and I drove down the scenic byway and into the heart of Chatsworth. The little town's grand courthouse and modest shops and offices flowed into a district of small farms and distant residences, where cornstalks waved in the breeze and goats and horses lazily grazed. We approached the sign indicating our entrance into the historic township of Spring Place and passed the historical marker and preserved cemetery of the Springplace Moravian Mission. The iron gates of the Vann House were thrown wide in welcome; the parking area was packed. Visitors in historical garb exited their overstuffed cars. Children skipped about the grounds, sampling homemade fruit pies sold by a panel of local ladies. Friends of the Vann House volunteers stood at the entrance of the Chambers Interpretive Center, handing out programs, selling T-shirts, and distributing buttons that read, "I was Here July 27th 1958" to visitors who had attended the original dedication. There were a surprising number of representatives from this group in attendance, one of whom had handed Ranger Autry a faded newspaper clipping showing the woman, as a little girl, on the Vann House lawn during the initial opening. The crowd on this day, though still mainly made up of whites, was as diverse as I had ever seen it, with at least nine Cherokees from North Carolina and Oklahoma (including four council members), at least two Latino families, and eight African Americans in attendance.[7]

Everyone seemed to comment on the heat, gently taking the 1950s restorers to task for hosting their dedication on one of the hottest days of the year. The group then gathered beneath the shade of a generous white pine tree, and the ceremony began, just as it had fifty years before, with the ringing of a vintage Moravian Church bell. The program included representatives of the Friends of the Vann House, the Whitfield-Murray Historical Society, and the Cherokee-Moravian Historical Association, site officials, a state senator, Vann House donors, and representatives of the Cherokee Nation of Oklahoma. As a local white donor gave the invocation, offering thanks for "those who have gone before us — the noble Indian pioneers and our own forebears," I braced myself for a replay of the 2002 Interpretive Center dedication, in which Cherokees had been idealized, whites centralized, and African Americans ignored. But when Tim Howard, Friends of the Vann House treasurer and the third speaker on the program, listed families who had ties to the Vann House, he prominently included the Kemps, descendants of the black man Levi Branham who lived in the house as a slave of the white Edmond family after the Vanns' ouster. Troy Wayne Poteete, a justice of the Cherokee Supreme Court, flatly stated that Joseph Vann had rebuilt a replica of the Vann House in the West through the labor of black slaves. Site manager Jeff Stancil detailed the museum's recent work in relocating and restoring a common Cherokee farmstead to counterbalance the impression of excess wealth made by the Vann House, which represented the way only a few Cherokees would have lived. He then described the new slavery exhibit, calling the subject "an overlooked chapter of Cherokee history." Finally, Anna Smith, president of the Cherokee-Moravian Historical Association, offered a forthright benediction. She urged listeners that in "celebrating the spirit of this place," they were actually "celebrating the endurance of the Cherokee Nation." She emphasized that the Vann House was a "cultural crossroads," where Cherokees young and old, African Americans free and enslaved, and Moravians and other whites intercepted one another. She described the scene of the very first church service hosted by the Moravians, at which black slaves were the only ones who understood both the Cherokee and English languages. Smith allowed to the audience the unusualness of her benediction, absent, as it was, of prayer, but she hoped her feeling words had accurately captured the spirit of the site. After Smith had spoken, men in nineteenth-century dress fired off rifle shots, and the crowd was invited to enjoy refreshments on the lawn.

Anna Smith's benediction held a note of caution for visitors: this historic home was a place where the past should be taken seriously, with reverence reserved for all who had dwelled there. Later, as visitors toured the slavery exhibit cabin, they seemed to carry with them this somber weight of history. Visitors paused to read about the lives of Pleasant, Michael, and Patience, to gaze at photographs, to answer questions posed by their children. They allowed their eyes to linger on the over one hundred names of black women, men, and children who had worked and lived on these grounds. The Cherokee representatives from Oklahoma entered the cabin together and spent long moments there. I asked one member of their group what he thought of the exhibit. "It's wonderful," he replied. "Well, it's moving. People like to think and talk about Cherokees living this *Gone with the Wind* lifestyle, but who did the work? Somebody did the work."

The very different kind of work that Vann House employees undertook with this exhibit has only just begun. Can they overcome the hurdles that other historic sites have faced when trying to incorporate marginalized historical populations? Will they allow black slaves to have a presence not only in the segregated space of the cabin but also in the master narrative told by tour guides in the big house? Can they encourage visitors to spend as much time and thought with the slavery exhibit cabin and the restored Cherokee farmstead as they would in the ornate manor home? Would Cherokee women be given ample time in the standard main house tour just as black women's stories had been featured in the slavery exhibit?

It remains to be seen what will become of the Vann House effort to democratize the memory of its past, but there is cause for optimism. Although it had taken fifty years, change had found a way. It is difficult for Julia Autry, the main midwife and organizer of the exhibit, to step outside of the Moravian diary pages and leave in the past those enslaved blacks who have become in her mind, and in the mind of tourists, she hopes, all too human. But the next step Autry imagines for the expanded interpretation of the Vann House site is an investigation of the life and story of Peggy (Margaret Ann) Scott Vann Crutchfield.

The Way Forward

The Chief Vann House, like the state of Georgia and the U.S. nation in which it rests, is, in writer Toni Morrison's words, a "racial house." It was built as a plantation home, one of the foremost symbols of slavery in America, out of the fraught cross-racial dynamics of turn-of-the-nineteenth-century Cherokee and white relations. In commissioning a home of such gravitas and elegance, Joseph Vann signaled to all who would notice the dignity of his standing as a Cherokee planter and the permanence of the Cherokee Nation in the face of white intrusion. Building a "showplace" home like his was a whistle in the dark of colonial oppression, a means of demanding proper respect as a citizen of an Indian nation. It was, at the same time, a site of black oppression at the hands of those same Indians. A symbol of pride for the Cherokee elites whose backs were against the wall of removal was also a source of pain for blacks who lived there and labored in bondage.

So how do we live in this "racial house" that is the legacy of Diamond Hill and other plantation museums today, the legacy of our nation's deeply troubled past? Some have set their sights beyond the realities of interracial suffering and strife, preferring instead to dwell in a dreamscape of antebellum moonlit magnolias and, in the case of the Vann House, Indian mystique. But in doing so, they glorify a mythic style of plantation life that suffocated black slaves and signaled the Cherokee elite's desperate attempt at national survival. Toni Morrison's way, wise and studied, is to recognize the racial house for what it is and then rebuild it in the bright light of our discerning minds, so that every voice inside can be heard. The celebrated southern writer William Faulkner adopted a similar method in the aftermath of World War II, when he expressed a mission to "use words, in the re-arranging of the [national] house, so that all mankind can live in peace in it."[8]

After ten years of journeying with this particular house and the historical and contemporary people who made it, I can offer a direct point of view. The Chief Vann House is not an amusement park, not a fantasy farm, not a great escape, but is instead a local and national memorial, a place of suffering for enslaved African Americans *and* their Cherokee captors. We might then approach this place in a spirit of clear-eyed mourning, sensitive thoughtfulness, and quiet commemoration of a human will that endures. Working together — as students of history; lovers of old, magnificent buildings; southerners, northerners, westerners, foreigners, Cherokees, blacks, and whites — we can unwrap this grand old home's glittering facade, open wide its multistoried windows and doors, and allow the memories and meanings of all who dwelled there to flow through our understanding like a cleansing breeze. In the resonant words of southern writer Alice Walker, the way forward is with a broken heart.[9]

Acknowledgments

The most wonderful aspect of this book project is that I did not undertake it alone. Rather than feeling like a solitary scholar tucked away in some drafty garret, I was surrounded at every turn by the knowledge, warmth, input, and energy of colleagues, friends, and loved ones. I am deeply grateful to all of those, named and unnamed, who played a role in this narrative reconstruction of the people and place of Diamond Hill.

This book would not exist without the support of incredible Vann House staff members, volunteers, and researchers who contributed their extensive knowledge, source materials, and feedback at every step of the way: Jeff Stancil, Julia Autry, Rowena McClinton, Anna Smith, Jack Baker, Tim Howard, Don Shadburn, Sarah Hill, Ken Robinson, Rose Simon, George Fowler, Virginia Vann Perry, Nancy Carter Bland, Chase Parker, and David Gomez of the New Echota site.

I am also grateful to the staff and translators at the Moravian Archives in Winston-Salem and Bethlehem, without whose expertise and aid this project would have been literally impossible: Richard Starbuck, Nicole Blum, Grace Robinson, C. Daniel Crews, Elizabeth Marx, Julie Weber, and Lanie Graf. Thank you, also, to the memorably generous archivists and research librarians I encountered across the country, especially independent researchers Michael Wren and Jim Hicks; at the Georgia State Archives, Greg Jarrell, Joanne Smalley, and Amanda Mros; at the Gilcrease Museum, Kim Roblin; at the Oklahoma Historical Society, Phyllis Adams; and at the Connecticut Historical Society, Sharon Steinberg and Judith Johnson.

I am immeasurably grateful for the nine months I spent in luminous Santa Fe, New Mexico, at the School for Advanced Research. Without that oasis of time, this book would not have been written for years. Thank you to all of the SAR staff members and to the 2007–08 fellows, especially James Brooks, Rebecca Allahyari, Catherine Cocks, Laura Holt, John Kantner, Malena Morling, Silvia Tomaskova, Peter Redfield, Omri Elisha, Monica Smith, James Snead, Angela Stuesse, Tutu Alicante, Joseph Gone. Thank you, also, to the directors and administrators in American Culture (AC) and Afroamerican and African Studies (CAAS) at the University of Michigan, Philip Deloria, Kevin Gaines, Greg Dowd, and Judy Gray, for granting me leave, and to my longtime mentors, David Roediger and Jean O'Brien, for their support. I am deeply thankful to the readers for UNC Press, Joshua Piker and Leslie Harris, whose thoughtful and meticulous feedback improved this book immensely.

I am grateful to my above-and-beyond colleagues in CAAS at the University of Michigan for offering substantive feedback on the conceptualization and draft of the manuscript, most especially Magda Zaborowska, Warren Whatley, Kevin Gaines, Martha Jones, Xiomara Santamarina, Paul Anderson, Ruti Talmor, Elizabeth James,

Lori Brooks, and Devon Adjei. My colleagues Philip Deloria and Greg Dowd in Native American Studies (NAS) at Michigan also deserve a depth of gratitude for their unwavering support and invaluable advice on this project and various others. Thanks, also, to Michael Witgen and Andrea Smith in NAS, whose work has inspired me during this process. I am grateful to my research assistants Rachel Quinn, Kiara Vigil, and Alyx Cadotte, graduate and undergraduate students in American Culture at Michigan, who pushed this project forward in incredible, uncountable ways. For research funding, I owe a debt of gratitude to U-M's College of Literature, Science & the Arts, Rackham Graduate School, the aforementioned CAAS and AC, Arts of Citizenship, and the Center for Research, Learning and Teaching.

The double session titled "Indians as Southerners: Race and Slavery in the Native South," organized by Claudio Saunt for the Southern Historical Association's 2007 annual meeting, was fruitful for the revision of key aspects of this book. Thank you to Claudio Saunt, Barbara Krauthamer, Robbie Ethridge, David Chang, Malinda Maynor Lowery, Christina Snyder, and Brett Rushforth for their tough and serious engagement. To all other colleagues and friends who played a role in the birth of this book, those listed and those on the tip of my tongue, you have my sincerest thanks: my consummate UNC Press editor Sian Hunter, UNC Press's Beth Lassiter, Mary Caviness, and Mark Simpson-Vos, my academic soul sister Celia Naylor, Susan Ferber, Larry and Claudia Allums and the Dallas Institute of Humanities and Culture, Andrew Denson, Raymond Fogelson, Robert Warrior, Claire Potter, James Carson, Rayna Green, Theda Perdue, Dee Andrews, Maria Sanchez, Rebecca Scott, Martha Hodes, Paulina Alberto, Ariela Gross, David Scobey, Penny Von Eschen, Mary Kelley, Harriet Imrey, Gerald Gieger, Jean Clark and her friend at Old Salem, and the incredibly attentive anonymous reviewers at the University of Chicago, Oxford University, and University of North Carolina presses.

Dearest to my heart are the many family members on both my and my husband's side who continued to show me unbounded love and support throughout this process. To Joe, Nali, Noa, and Sylvan: you give my life a richness beyond thought and word. I love you.

RESEARCH PROCESS, METHODS, AND FINDINGS

Research at the Vann House

I first visited the Chief Vann House State Historic Site in the summer of 1998, while doing research on my dissertation about a mixed-race Afro-Cherokee family. In the early 1800s, the Shoeboots family, the subject of my research at the time, had lived a few towns away from the Vann family and had visited the mission complex located beside the Vann plantation. Touring the Vann House, a restored Cherokee plantation home, was a way for me to concretely imagine an era when wealthy and middling Cherokees had owned black slaves. Around the time that I visited the historic site, the staff was undergoing a major transition. The current director at the time of this writing, Jeff Stancil, had only recently taken charge in the winter of 1997, and the current chief interpreter ranger at the time of this writing, Julia Autry, had just stepped into her role in the winter of 1998.[1]

Before my visit to the Vann House that summer, I had immersed myself in readings about slavery in the Cherokee Nation and was aware of James Vann's status as a major Cherokee slaveholder. I was dumbstruck, therefore, when I was led through the Vann House by a very young part-time tour guide (a high school student, I supposed) who never once mentioned the topic of slavery or the presence of black slaves at the site. At the end of the tour, when I asked the guide about slaves at the Vann House, she became so flustered that she radioed the site office to seek assistance in answering my question. A novice to southern plantation home tours back then, I was shocked by the omission of black history, especially at a site where schoolchildren from surrounding towns and cities as far as Atlanta regularly visited to hear about their region's past. For the disregarded slaves of the past and impressionable children of the present, I felt a call to study the experience of blacks at this historic site and to make what I found available for public access and engagement. Multiple and in some cases adversarial communities, I thought, might gain from a broader interpretation of this plantation's history: Cherokees and members of other formerly slaveholding Indian nations and descendants of slaves held by them, members of the Moravian Church, southerners of all ethnoracial backgrounds, Native American and African American history buffs, old house enthusiasts, scholars, students, and the coalition of local residents who had cared for this site over the years. The pull toward a public history project became stronger, the picture of black life there even more vivid, when I delved into records of the Moravian Church's Southern Province, which had built the first mission to the Cherokees beside Vann's estate back in 1801. In my reading of the missionaries' diary and letters, an enslaved African American woman named

Pleasant became a larger-than-life figure in her outspoken criticism of the institution of slavery and her daily refusal to accept subjugation. Although I was still researching the Shoeboots family in the late 1990s when I encountered Pleasant, I began to keep a second set of notes on her appearances in the missionary records.

In 2004, after my book on the Shoeboots family was in press, I turned my attention to the Vann House project. My plan was to create a record of black history at the Vann House from which I would seek to publish one formal article for scholars as well as find alternative venues that were easily accessible to various publics. I began to study the missionary materials about the Vann House in earnest and to visit the site nearly once a year. I received funding from the University of Michigan's Arts of Citizenship Program, which supports projects that bridge academia and public culture, to create a website on African American history at the Vann House. In the course of attending Arts of Citizenship program workshops, however, I came to the conclusion that a website might not be as accessible as I hoped for the Vann House's most frequent guests, residents of small-town north Georgia and Cherokee communities. I then set about creating a brief historical booklet that could be made available at no charge to visitors to the site and could also be posted on the web for those with remote access. In 2004–05, the research and writing for this booklet was undertaken for credit by students in my undergraduate course titled "Blacks, Indians, and the Making of America."[2] Building from Moravian diary translations, WPA narratives of ex-slaves, and a list of classic secondary sources that I provided them, the thirty-plus enrolled students of diverse backgrounds researched and wrote individual papers on some aspect of black life on the Vann plantation. Over the course of the next spring and summer, I hired two undergraduate student editors, Alexandria Cadotte (Ojibwe) and Merwin Moss (African American) to help edit, truncate, and collate all of those individual essays into a handful of streamlined chapters for a twenty-eight-page final product. I served as overall editor, wrote a prefatory statement, invited Cherokee history scholar Rowena McClinton, Moravian Church archivist Richard Starbuck, and Vann House staff members to offer feedback on the draft, found a layout designer, and then had two hundred booklet copies made at Kinko's. I shipped a box of booklets to the Vann House in the winter of 2006, just in time for their popular annual Christmas celebration. The booklets were a gift to the Vann House and its visitors, to be given freely to anyone who had an interest in the subject. Meanwhile, I hired a webpage designer at the University of Michigan to post the booklet on the web.

Our little booklet and the spirit of collaborative research behind it worked some unexpected magic that Christmas season. Two weeks after receiving it, the director of the Vann House, who had been politely distant during my visits to the site, sent an effusive email praising the quality of the research and asking if they could produce more booklets since their supply was dwindling. This response was much more than I had hoped for. I gladly sent him the pdf file and made it clear that the material was theirs to reproduce as they wished. At the Moravian Archives in Winston-

Salem, when archivists read our booklet that relied on two different translations of the Moravian diary (one housed at the Georgia State Archives and one produced out of the Moravian Archives), they noticed gaps in some of their own translation work and realized that their translators were sometimes working from excerpts rather than complete original texts. This realization led them to correct their translations by returning to the original German script documents. (A copy of our booklet is currently available to researchers at the Moravian Archives as a computer file labeled "Vann—Africans, Tiya Miles.") Soon after the Christmas publication, I received a request from a Moravian organization based in Winston-Salem, North Carolina, the Cherokee-Moravian Historical Association, to reproduce the booklet yet again. Meanwhile, back at the Vann House, staff members were reading my students' work and looking at the history of their site from a new perspective.

Interpretive ranger Julia Autry was particularly moved by the sensitive subject matter contained in the booklet. Julia and I had first connected interpersonally during my visit to the Vann House in the summer of 2004, when I turned up with my husband and six-month-old twin daughters in tow. I recall that for the first time since I had been visiting the site, she threw the front doors of the visitor's center open upon my arrival and greeted me with relish, calling, "Bring me those babies!" from the entrance. It was during that visit that Julia told me, haltingly and through tears, that her own family's history of slaveholding in a nearby north Georgia town and the guilt such memories conjured for her had discouraged her from exploring black enslavement at the Vann House. In addition, a desire of the state of Georgia's Department of Natural Resources to keep the Vann House interpretation positively reinforcing for public consumption discouraged an acknowledgment of black slaves' experience there. But Julia was determined to move beyond those prohibitive feelings and to honor the memory of blacks owned by the Vanns, as a means, in some metaphysical way that I felt I understood, to make amends for her own family's past actions. Julia had been an avid and scrupulous reader of the Moravian diary translations since accepting her position at the Vann House years before. Now, with the head start provided by our booklet, she dove back into these records, searching for details about enslaved blacks. Julia Autry is the force behind the Vann House exhibit on black life that was unveiled at the fiftieth anniversary of the site in July 2008. She conceived the exhibit, sought approval from her director, applied to the state for funding, reached out to academic researchers for input, directed the contributions of eager Vann House college-age staff members, and brought the exhibit to life with her vivid imagination for context, image, and sound. A preexisting cabin adjacent to the Vann House is now the home of a slavery exhibit that describes a shared black experience and profiles the lives of two enslaved women, the outspoken Pleasant and the suffering Patience.

If Pleasant is the spiritual impetus behind this book project for me, Julia Autry is my earthly inspiration. My original plan to write a scholarly article on the black community to accompany the Vann House booklet blossomed through interaction with

Julia. During one of my visits to the site, Julia gave me a pointed look and said: "You know, there never has been a book written about the Vann House." With the encouragement of her less than subtle words, my intention to illuminate a single black community on the Vann plantation expanded into a plan to capture, to the extent that I was able, the entire swirling world of social life that unfolded there—black, brown, red, and white. This resulting book is a work of public history in the most basic sense of the concept. Its goal is one of public engagement and information-sharing toward the end of co-constructing a sense of the past that enriches rather than limits communities; and the process of its becoming was one of spirited collaboration between university professors, college students, local researchers, and staff members as well as supporters of a state-operated historic site.

My interaction with knowledge makers at, around, and connected to the Vann House took at least three different forms over the years that I worked on this project. At first, loosely borrowing an approach of anthropologists, I became an informal participant-observer in Vann House happenings. After my initial visit in 1998, I began to frequent the site nearly once a year, visiting seven times between 2001 and 2008 for periods of one day to one week. I attended the site under various circumstances, to witness special events, to take the tour in different seasons, and to interact with staff members, volunteers, and tourists. I traveled alone, with family, or accompanied by a fellow scholar, and once took the tour with a group of Cherokee and white history enthusiasts as part of a national conference sponsored by the grassroots Trail of Tears Association.

I was guided, in these visits, by the model of sociologists Jennifer Eichstedt and Stephen Small, who systematically studied 122 plantation museums and detailed their process and findings in the book *Representations of Slavery: Race and Ideology in Southern Plantation Museums*. Eichstedt and Small described a method in which they and their team of graduate students toured a house museum multiple times and refrained from asking questions during the first visit. In addition to taking notes on the standard tour "story," visual and aural aspects of the site interpretation, and the ways that tour guides interacted with them and other guests, they also analyzed printed materials like brochures, flyers, and postcards. They found in their study that most plantation museums adopted an approach of "social forgetting," in which the reality of enslaved black people's lives was ignored or marginalized in favor of romantic, "white-centric" tales of antebellum nostalgia, architectural glamour, Civil War tragedy, storied gardens, and colorful ghosts. At most of these sites, they argued, chosen modes of interpretation occluded the fact of slavery and "valorize[d] the white elite of the preemancipation South while generally erasing or minimizing the experiences of enslaved African Americans." In Small and Eichstedt's view, these sites operated within a "racialized regime of representation" that "produce and reproduce racialized inequality and oppression."[3] By treating slavery as a nonevent and signaling an inferiority of black experience relative to white elite experience, these plantation museums ushered visitors into a physical and psychic space where racial hierarchy is preserved, recreated, and normalized. Although my first visit to the Vann House was without the benefit of Eichstedt and Small's model, in successive visits I began to incorporate their approach of minimal interference with the way a tour unfolded and attention to multiple tiers of information. I was employing, it turns out, a classic model of museum studies/cultural studies investigation in which scholars attempt to interpret the "message" of museums through an analysis of text, exhibits, brochures, and other materials and the reception of that message by an audience.[4] I also applied Eichstedt and Small's conceptual frame to troubling aspects of Vann House interpretation that had already been apparent to me. In addition, working from the model they provided, I visited other plantations in Georgia, North Carolina, South Carolina, Kentucky, and Virginia to gain a sense of broader perspective. I found, in keeping with the conclusion of Small and Eichstedt's team, that the Vann House's interpretive avoidance of African American experience was not unique, but was instead a common feature of plantation museums across the South.

Through my regular appearances at the Vann House, often in the company of fellow researcher Rowena McClinton, a professor of history and translator of the Moravian missionary diary from German script to modern English, I came to know the Vann staff members and to develop a working relationship with them. Although they were not immediately or openly enthusiastic about my subject matter, Vann House officials never discouraged me. I had the opportunity, in these visits, to witness the dedication of the Moravian Springplace Mission cemetery that had recently been identified by state archaeologists and to observe special events like the opening of the new museum/visitors center in 2002.

In 2003, after the Vann House and its local support group, Friends of the Vann House, and the Trust for Public Land began raising funds to purchase a large parcel of land that was originally part of the plantation estate, Vann staff members sought my involvement for the first time. I drafted a statement about the importance of the site to African American history, which became part of the information packet presented to the governor. My slight involvement in this successful campaign furthered a sense of familiarity and trust with staff members and volunteers. In 2004, my third year of visiting the site for work on this project, Julia Autry made very special arrangements for me, my accompanying family members, and fellow researcher, Dr. McClinton. Tim Howard, local historian, middle-school teacher of Georgia history, former Vann House employee, and past president of the Whitefield-Murray Historical Society, gave us an extensive tour of the area, pointing out the boundaries of Vann's original plantation, taking us to what was believed to be an unmarked slave burial ground within the perimeter of the former Vann estate, showing us the natural limestone source from which plaster in the Vann House was made, and introducing us to "Willie" George Fowler, a local man who presented me with an aged brick from what he believed was a Vann House slave cabin hearth. (The brick, which sits on my desk as I write this, still bears the imprints of its maker's fingers.) We were also privileged to have a personal tour of Carter's Quarters, the private home of Vann House donor Nancy Carter Bland and former plantation of George Harlan, a Cherokee slaveholder in James Vann's social circle. James Vann's sister, Nancy Vann, had been married to Harlan for a brief time. In 1833, Mrs. Bland's estate had been owned by her great-great-grandfather, wealthy white slaveholder Farish Carter, who purchased it in the aftermath of Georgia State's lottery of Cherokee land. The grounds and buildings, which had seldom changed hands since the time of Cherokee occupancy, were stunningly intact. Although the main house had seen an addition over the years, the original plantation office, kitchen, springhouse, and slave quarters were still standing.[5]

This blossoming generosity of Vann House officials and local community members continued when I began research for the booklet project in earnest. Vann House staff opened their small library of source materials to me, mailed copies of primary documents, put me in contact with local historians and Vann descendants, and allowed me to reproduce images in their collection. In this same period, I began to use my regular visits to the Moravian Archives in North Carolina to research my own questions as well as queries of Vann House staff members who depended on the Moravian records for their ongoing interpretation of the site but were not as free to travel for research.

The years 2004 through 2008 marked a shift in my relationship with the two full-time and three to four part-time employees based at the Vann House. I ceased to be an observer standing at some distance from those with whom I was interacting, and I became a member of a research collective determined to help the Vann House achieve its utmost level of historical interpretation. I saw the employees and volunteers at the site as fellow knowledge producers whose interpretations could enrich my own. Vann House officials, and Julia Autry in particular, with whom I had many conversations and email exchanges, contributed to my research as fully as I contributed to the Vann House by providing them with difficult-to-access research material, written text for the land campaign, biographical information for a Springplace cemetery marker, and feedback on an exhibit in progress.

Together, Vann House employees and I arrived at tentative, yet exciting conclusions about the site. On one of my visits, director Jeff Stancil mentioned that Roane County, Tennessee, archivist and historian Robert Bailey had discovered in their archives and sent to Vann staff a theretofore unknown court case about the Vann home. Although Bailey had transcribed bits of the case, most of the aged cursive was nearly illegible. Thrilled with the possibility of a novel source, I offered to have the 100-page document transcribed, a project undertaken by one of my wonderful graduate student research assistants, Rachel Quinn. After Rachel had completed her work and I sent the transcription back to the Vann House, I began an analysis of the new material. The record was of an 1825 lawsuit brought against Joseph Vann by the hired builders of an elaborate brick house. This was peculiar, as the standard interpretation held that James Vann had built the brick house decades earlier. Upon reading the new material, I returned to the Moravian Archives and to all primary documents that mentioned James Vann's 1804–05 construction project. I found not only that James had different builders than the ones who had sued Joseph but also that no contemporary writer mentioned a building made of brick, which would have been quite noteworthy at the time. Simultaneously and in consultation, Vann House staff members and I reached the shocking conclusion that the Vann House had not been built by James Vann in 1804 at all but by his son Joseph in the 1820s. After we had all confronted the enormity of this finding, I visited the Vann House to walk the grounds with Rangers Julia Autry and Chase Parker in search of James Vann's 1804 home. Although our hypothesis is not conclusive and requires archaeological testing, we identified a site a few hundred yards east of the brick house that corresponds with descriptions in the written record regarding proximity to the federal road, the Moravian mission, and natural springs. The site is a flat, cleared hilltop on the original estate, facing a trench that was made by the 1803 federal road, on which a later house had been built by a Georgia resident. Just beyond this site in the woods, Rangers Parker and Autry identified the location of Vann's brickworks, where old bricks are still strewn about the forest floor.

In 2006 through 2008, my interaction with Vann House staff members took on yet another dimension. With the approval of the University of Michigan's Institutional Review Board, I began an oral history project that formalized my interaction with staff members as knowledge producers. The project aimed to identify a range of people with firsthand knowledge of the Vann House site and its history. I especially sought out employees, local historians and history buffs, Cherokee Vann family descendants whose names were provided to me by Vann House staff and local historian Don Shadburn, Cherokee historical researchers who frequented the Vann House, and descendants of freedmen and freedwomen formerly owned by the Vanns. The project usually began with a survey that asked five to seven simple questions about respondents' views of the Vann House and was followed up by more detailed email exchanges and/or in-person conversations, some more formal than others. In a few cases, the project began with an in-person interview or series of discussions that bypassed the survey stage. Through this process, I gathered a small set of thirteen responses from staff members, Cherokee researchers, Cherokee/white Vann family descendants, freedpeople/black Vann family descendants, and local and academic historians.[6] The comments of participants helped to broaden my knowledge base, correct my misinterpretations, and deepen my understanding of the nuanced relationship between the Vann House and its audiences.

My growing relationship with Vann House employees over the years was productive in the research process and a continuing source of personal delight. At the same time, though, as I developed a sense of responsibility not only to the black slaves who had once toiled on the Vann estate but also to the contemporary people who cared for this site, I faced new and necessary limitations on how I might write about my findings. My initial assessment of the Vann House representation of African American (as well as Cherokee) history had been sharply critical. I saw the site employees as participants in the act of "social forgetting" that was detrimental to present-day African American, Cherokee, and southern communities. Now, on the other end of a decade of personal interaction, I knew and cared about the people who had inherited a damaging line of interpretation begun in the 1950s, and I hesitated to expose them to undue censure. I could not betray the trust of well-intentioned people who had shared so much with me. My commitment to fully revealing crimes of humanity against black slaves of the past while honoring newfound relationships with white Georgians in the present led to a fragile balancing act between forthright analysis and respectful withholding.

Readers may find, as they assess the opening and closing chapters of this book, that my criticism of Vann House racial misrepresentation is directed toward a long-standing (at least as early as the 1950s restoration project) and widespread regional culture of white antebellum commemoration and Indian history fascination. This emphasis on a broad and long-term attribution for Vann House representational ills is not coincidental. In addition to being reflective of my views that occlusion of black history is a general rather than particularistic failing of southern plantation museums, and that nostalgic recollection of Native American history is a common rather than isolated aspect of American culture, this approach is protective of honorable people who have shown through word and deed a genuine commitment to valuing the full range of human experience at the Chief Vann House State Historic Site.

The Documentary Record

While I did engage in fieldwork activities associated with anthropological methods, the majority of my research for this book was historical and based on documentary evidence. In breadth, depth, and detail, the documentary record for Diamond Hill exceeds that of any other plantation site in the southern or western Cherokee territories. The establishment of a Christian mission beside Vann's estate, Vann's frequent intercourse with U.S. government officials, his role on the Cherokee Council, his use of American courts to protect his property, his children's use of the Cherokee courts to secure their inheritance, Peggy Scott Vann's religious letters, and the fame of the Vann home in the nineteenth century all resulted in the production of thousands of pages specific to the events, residents, and ancillaries of Diamond Hill. Records of the Cherokee Agency in Tennessee and the secretary of war include several letters to, from, and about James Vann and his clerk, Valentine Geiger. Additional letters to or from James and his son Joseph are scattered across collections of the Georgia State Archives in Atlanta and the John Ross Papers of the Gilcrease Museum in Tulsa. Between 1809 and 1838, Cherokee traveler John Norton, white newlyweds Juliana and Henry Workman Conner, white New Englander Benjamin Gold, and white resident William Jasper Cotter visited the Vann home and left chronicles of their impressions. (As far as I and my wonderful research assistant, Kiara Vigil, were able to uncover in his presidential papers, President James Monroe did not describe his 1819 visit to the Vann House in writing.) Records of the 1950s restoration process for the site and of later management policies have also been preserved in the Vann House library, the Georgia State Archives, and the Penelope Allen Collection at the University of Tennessee Libraries in Knoxville. Taken together with the voluminous records of the Moravian missionaries based there, these records document from a range of perspectives the key events, outcomes, and relationships that constituted social life on Diamond Hill.

At the same time, though, this wealth of material about James Vann, his family, and his estate must be viewed with a critical awareness of the power dynamics implicit in its production. Records about the Vanns and their establishment were generated in a colonial context in which Cherokees were compelled to negotiate with white Americans in order to protect their national independence and personal security. Cherokees' position of relative weakness shaped the kinds of records that were created in this era, the form written materials took, the tone and linguistic modes in which Cherokees wrote, and the likelihood that certain materials would be preserved over others. Most of James Vann's extant letters pertain to business contracts with the encroaching U.S. government or to the protection of Cherokee citizens and lands. Whatever personal letters he may have written, whatever business dealings he may have engaged in with Cherokees, did not survive to be archived. Moravian missionaries, whose records were essential to this project, carried out their work under the auspices of not only their church but also the U.S. Department of War, which funded the missionary effort in the hope of civilizing and pacifying the Cherokees. Peggy Scott's personal letters, rare among materials on Cherokee women of the past, were created in the aftermath of her conversion to Christianity and obscure rather than reveal her sense of self prior to the missionaries' cultural imperialist influence. Most existing writing by members of the Vann family is in the form of letters sent from Diamond Hill to U.S. or church officials. In contrast, records sent to the plantation from friends or family members, letters sent from the Vanns to intimates, and records about Vann's business affairs that he would have kept close at hand have yet to be found. It is not difficult to imagine that many of these records may have been lost or destroyed in the tumultuous period when the Vanns were forced to flee their home in the aftermath of the Georgia land lottery and the Indian Removal Act.

The longer I worked with these materials in the course of researching and writing this book, the more the records on Diamond Hill seemed implicated in "an era dominated by the alien politics and policies of a predatory colonial regime."[7] As a result, I arrived at a particular conceptualization of my source materials. I came to conceive of the records on James Vann and family as making up a *colonial archive*, since most were produced at the behest or as a result of U.S. military, political, economic, and cultural subjugation of the Cherokees. An external sign of the colonial nature of these materials was their archival home in U.S. government records and the holdings of early evangelizing churches. I was unable to find, in the course of my research, an independent collection of personal papers of the Vann family. In death, as in life, their world was enclosed by foreign institutional entities. As a point of contrast, I was struck by the papers of Farish Carter, the wealthy white slaveholder who purchased a plantation formerly owned by Vann's Cherokee associate George Harlan. As the only nearby planter whose wealth would have rivaled the Vanns', Carter seemed fitting for a counterexploration of the state of documentation for slaveholders in the area. According to his great-great-granddaughter, Carter's massive quantity of personal and business papers had been deposited at the University of North Carolina at Chapel Hill's library.[8] Carter's papers—intact, plentiful, ranging from private to business affairs, and donated to an institution of higher learning—seemed a perfect contrast to the scattered, incomplete, government-controlled records of Cherokee James Vann. In contrast to Vann's colonial archive, Farish's seemed to me a *citizen archive*, revealing of the relative racial privilege bestowed on its producer in his lifetime. The records of Farish Carter's and James Vann's estates signal the racial difference that separated even mixed-race, wealthy, slaveholding Cherokees from white elite southerners. This conceptualization of the colonial versus the citizen archive meant that even as I sought to rebuild Diamond Hill from the written sources, I was compelled to keep at the foreground of thought the price paid for those records' existence and the barriers to full understanding of Cherokee life inherent in them.

The Vann colonial archive is marked by a plethora of church records. By a wide margin, writings produced by members of the Moravian Church dominate the documentary record on Diamond Hill. Church historians have commented on the Moravian penchant for record keeping, which stands out among Christian denominations. Moravian records related to Cherokee history, housed at both the southern (Winston-Salem, North Carolina) and northern (Bethlehem, Pennsylvania) headquarters of the Moravian Archives, consist of a variety of forms. Missionaries to the Cherokees who lived beside Vann's estate kept a daily diary of occurrences in their local neighborhood and in the Cherokee national context to inform members back home and around the world of the challenges and progress of their evangelical task. Of these missionary diarists, Anna Rosina Kliest Gambold was the most prodigious. A keen observer of her world and a writer of some talent, Anna Rosina Gambold was the primary author of the Springplace Mission Diary between the years 1805 and 1821. Since their first mission establishment on St. Thomas, West Indies, in 1732, Moravian missionaries wrote detailed reports on local events, spiritual struggles, and conversion successes for church members back at home, but Anna Rosina's diary entries stand out for their attention to human social relations, to climatic and natural events, and to the exquisite ephemera of daily life.[9] Unlike other diarists at Springplace before and after her, and unlike her husband, John Gambold, who penned the Oothcaloga Mission Diary, Anna Rosina noticed the domestic and emotional struggles of Cherokee women and recognized black people as individuals. Without her democratic eye, we would know little about everyday life on the Vann plantation and virtually nothing about the names, experiences, and personal relationships of black slaves. In fact, one indicator that Anna Rosina had died and another missionary author had taken charge of the Springplace diary is a marked inattention to the presence of blacks after 1821. In 1836, Heinrich Gottlieb Clauder, a missionary at Springplace, made note of Anna Rosina's unusual contribution to the Cherokee mission record: "The voluminous journal of Mrs. Gambold, is written in the German language & is full of anecdotes, sometimes even of thrilling interest, particularly those in reference to the celebrated James Vann, & his contemporaries. . . . It is to be regretted that Mrs. Gambold had no biographer, & even astonishing that she was not her own, as she was passionately fond of her pen & wrote about almost every thing, excepting herself."[10]

Anna Rosina Gambold was one of approximately fifteen Moravian men and women who worked as missionaries in the eastern Cherokee country over a thirty-seven-year period prior to Cherokee Removal. In addition to keeping collective diaries, these missionaries wrote personal letters to friends and church officials. Their personal letters tended to record events of the diary in greater detail, to expose the missionaries' private views, to detail Vann family conflicts and finances, and to chronicle the Cherokee political scene. After her conversion, Peggy Scott, the former mistress of Diamond Hill, contributed letters of her own to this body of preserved writings. The church's publication on missions, *Periodical Accounts*, reported on and summarized the work of missionaries everywhere, including the Indian nations. These articles often provided a third description (following the diary and letters) of events that took place at the Moravians' Springplace and Oothcaloga Cherokee missions. The church body overseeing missionary activities met for conferences at which the views and concerns of missionaries were notated in the minutes, and the governing council of elders recorded decisions about the formation and continuation of mission stations. These records from one church consist of a variety of authorial voices and amount to a multiplicity of accounts rather than a unitary narrative. Some German-to-English translations of the Moravian materials are viewed by scholars as being more reliable than others, with greater trust assigned to the work of in-house Moravian Archives translators and historian Rowena McClinton than to Carl Maelshagen, the 1950s translator commissioned by the Georgia Historical Commission.[11] In my use of these documents, I privilege the McClinton and Moravian Archives translations, double-check translations against one another when possible, and footnote which translation I am working from for any given assertion.

In addition to the Moravian materials, a second set of missionary records produced by the Brainerd Mission of the Boston-based American Board of Commissioners for Foreign Missions (ABCFM), creates yet another record. The ABCFM missionaries founded the second mission to the Cherokees in present-day Tennessee. From this location, ABCFM missionaries had repeated contact with Moravian missionaries and converts. They viewed the longtime Moravian couple John and Anna Rosina Gambold as missionary elders, kept a diary of local and national happenings, and sometimes described people and events that coincided with life on Diamond

Hill. ABCFM missionaries also wrote letters about their daily life and transcribed documents from Cherokee Council meetings to which they were privy. Leaders from the New England office visited the southern missions and kept travel diaries of their observations. Peggy Scott visited the ABCFM mission to witness her sister's baptism and, later, gave Cherokee vocabulary lessons to ABCFM missionary Daniel Butrick, one of the few Christian missionaries to learn the language.

There are clear limitations to these ample missionary records beyond their origination in a problematic context of "western cultural proselytization."[12] Although white missionaries were dutiful scribes, they had only marginal access to the intimate circles of Cherokee and black societies. Over the decades that missionaries lived with Cherokees, their degree of access increased, but at a time when white Americans craved Cherokee land and disrespected Cherokee sovereignty, white outsiders could never be free from suspicion. Even the most dedicated missionaries who developed close relationships with individual Cherokees were political and cultural outsiders in relation to the centers of Cherokee life. From their post on the edge of the Vann estate, Moravian missionaries had an up-close and wide-angle view of unfolding events, but their view differed markedly from the perspective generated in the interior rooms of Vann family homes and the private spaces of slave cabins. The records that were produced from the pens of James, Peggy, and Joseph Vann are also of a restricted nature, dealing with financial exchanges, property transmissions, political negotiations, and religious sentiment rather than the internal relationships of family and cultural life. While it is possible to glean bits of information about intimate matters and Cherokee cultural ways in these letters — like Peggy Scott's gift of baskets to fellow Moravians — such extractions are few and far between. With one exception that I could pinpoint (a letter by a freed slave seeking assistance from the Cherokee agent), most records representing the voices of enslaved blacks in the preemancipation period were filtered through the interpretation of whites, who recounted black actions and motivations in their own statements and diaries. This was the case in the instance of the 1805 robbery, in which enslaved men's participation was detailed in their white co-conspirators' confessions.

Added to the problems of access to private social relations and a difference of standpoint and perspective, missionary sources pose questions of reliability regarding their presentation of Cherokee views and behaviors. Can Euro-American Christian missionaries be relied on to faithfully represent aspects and meanings of Cherokee life? Volunteers came to the mission field with culturally based, preconceived notions about Indian backwardness and heathen spirituality. Their judgmental and ethnocentric views come through in the language and tone of their writings and create an initial challenge for readers seeking Cherokee, rather than Euro-American, points of view. Like the travel diaries produced by European and American men in the eighteenth and nineteenth centuries, these records, in the words of historian Nancy Shoemaker, "say more about the Europeans who did the describing than about the people being described." However, Shoemaker offers a rationale for reading certain sources produced by whites in the interest of Native American history, arguing that "conversational" records — those that reproduce interactive talk between white and Indian parties — can reliably preserve native views when carefully interpreted.[13] Shoemaker shows that in Indian speeches and formal exchanges between Indians and whites, Indian voices as recorded by whites differ by national affiliation and language groupings, indicating that whites did not invent a monolithic Indian voice. Furthermore, she notes the frequent indictments of white behavior in these written talks, accusations that Euro-American authors would surely have left out if they were inventing Indian speech simply to serve their own interests. The Moravian missionary diary includes many extended segments of quoted, conversational speech by Cherokee speakers, set off from the rest of the text by punctuation marks. Some of the Cherokee speakers spoke their words in Cherokee, others in English, but all of their speech was recorded in German. The language of this quoted material has been standardized by the missionaries and later translators, so it does not carry with it Cherokee words or speech rhythms. However, the quoted material does include turns of phrase and concepts specific to Cherokee culture and sentiments harshly critical of white Americans. In addition, shorter passages of quoted speech by black slaves in the diary directly indict the Gambolds as well as the Vanns for their activities as slaveholders. Although missionary records cannot present a complete or fully intimate view of Cherokee or African American life, they do provide spaces for native and black voices to emerge. Read alongside other primary sources and contextual material that foreground Cherokee and black perspectives, these missionary records are vital to the reconstruction of a multiracial history of Diamond Hill.

The written records on Diamond Hill in the nineteenth century are complemented by transcribed oral sources. The WPA Federal Writers Project of the 1930s collected interviews with former slaves who had been owned by children of James Vann in Indian Territory and recalled events of their own parents' and grandparents' lives as well as the lives of Vann family members. WPA employees also interviewed descendants of James Vann, Cherokee historians, and white Oklahomans who recalled tales about Vann family history. These interviews are housed at the Oklahoma Historical Society as well as published in collections of Oklahoma and Black Indian slave narratives, edited by T. Lindsay Baker and Julie Baker and Patrick Minges, respectively.[14]

Interpretive Approaches

In my analysis of these source materials, I was inspired and guided by modes of interpretation anchored in both literary and historical studies. The work of Native American literature scholars Robert Warrior and Daniel Heath Justice was fundamental to how I read specific documents as well as the larger Vann plantation scene. I was influenced by the evocative metaphor of roads and homes prominent in Warrior's book *The People and the Word: Reading Native Nonfiction*, a work in which

Warrior reads political documents as well as narrative nonfiction as literary texts. Here Warrior reprises an argument from his previous writings, in which the image of an Osage writer in his isolated "little house" represented Warrior's vision of "intellectual sovereignty" in Native American literary studies—a vision in which native intellectuals could be home-based, influenced by the work of other native thinkers, and protected from an outside world of imposed thought disconnected from home and nation. In his book, Warrior extends this image with the addition of roads branching to and from the lone Osage cabin. These roads, in Warriors words, highlight "the importance of the ways that ideas travel great distances." He argues that while ideas need "rootedness and stability" to develop, they also blossom in the light of intellectual exchange.[15]

Warrior's notion of a simultaneous rootedness in home-place and mobility across space and "intellectual trade routes" settled in my mind around two major motifs in the history of Diamond Hill—the wood house of the Vann family that long predated their brick home, and the federal road that James Vann helped to make a reality.[16] With Warrior's framework in mind, I saw the earlier Vann home, built near the place where the family's Cherokee town had been burned down by white militiamen, as a sign of stability and cultural rootedness rather than a sign of cultural accommodation with which the brick house was associated. At the same time, I saw Vann's support and use of the federal road as representative of his desire to travel away from home and enter into a range of exchanges with people from different backgrounds. Warrior's concept of home and roads nudged me toward an understanding of Diamond Hill history that did not force a choice between a cultural separatist or fully assimilationist interpretation of Cherokee slaveholding society.

Reading the work of literary scholar Daniel Heath Justice helped me to fine-tune this understanding and fix it within the specific location of Cherokee cultural and intellectual history. In *Our Fire Survives the Storm: A Cherokee Literary History*, Justice outlines and conceptualizes the tradition of Cherokee writing in English as one of "cultural continuity." Justice rejects the charge of cultural assimilation commonly ascribed to Cherokees and prefers the notion of acculturation as "the adaptation of certain Euro-western ways into a larger Cherokee context, thus changing some cultural expressions while maintaining the centrality of Cherokee identity and values."[17]

Out of this conviction, Justice develops a matrix for interpreting Cherokee literature and culture that is historically based and intellectually flexible. He describes what he calls a "Chickamauga consciousness," a defiant stance rooted in the eighteenth-century Chickamauga resistance to American forces led by Dragging Canoe, and a "Beloved Path" based on the method of "accommodation and cooperation" modeled by stateswoman Nancy Ward in the same period. He argues that although Cherokee society embraced a dichotomous strategy for managing peace and war, with separate chiefs and councils to lead decision making in periods of unrest, Cherokees did not maintain a hard and fast line between modes of strategic action. Rather than insisting on strict dichotomies, the Cherokee way emphasized "balance and complementarity," allowing for a permeability of paired categories, such as modes of war and peace, and paths of resistance and accommodation. Justice sees both Cherokee history and the literature produced out of it as flexible and multi-faceted, incorporating of Euro-American cultural elements in a context of colonial imposition, capable of regeneration and self-transformation, and ever protective of the sacred heart of distinctive Cherokee peoplehood. Through Justice's conceptual-ization of permeable duality together with Warrior's metaphor of home and roads, I began to see James Vann and his estate in a different light. The assumption held by many of my conversation partners that James Vann's style of life and act of slave-holding turned him into a virtual white southerner did not hold. Vann could be Cherokee and also adopt chattel slavery, one of the worst abuses of Euro-American culture. Slaveholding was not necessarily a proxy for whiteness but could be seen as an aspect of cultural accommodation that coincided with a persistent Cherokee identity. In the interpretation of source materials offered in this book, this conclu-sion of simultaneous cultural duality is evident. In the end, I saw James Vann as a shrewd, talented, alcohol-addicted, damaged, sometimes hard-hearted man who successfully adapted to a newly imposed Euro-American regime of power, chiefly by becoming an expert materialist and entrepreneur. Meanwhile, Vann maintained a Cherokee-centered political stance, rejected Christian conversion, and continued in many ways to participate in Cherokee-grounded ways of life.[18] Vann's unique story of extreme financial success did not preclude his Cherokeeness but instead highlighted the flexibility, duality, and adaptability of Cherokee identity at the turn of the nine-teenth century.

A major aspect of this project was the interpretation of the lives of enslaved blacks based at Diamond Hill. Since this would be the first close study of black plan-tation life in an Indian nation, I sought to bring the fullness of black experience alive, to make it real and vibrant, and to reveal it as an essential aspect of the history of this place and its owners. Because the primary sources of black experience were in-direct, originating mainly in missionary accounts, legal papers, and business records, I relied heavily on secondary sources for analytical direction and historical context. I turned first to newer works in historical and archaeological slavery studies that traced in nuanced detail the varieties of enslaved experience across time and space, that emphasized the brutalities of bondage as well as the pleasures of daily life, that traced the role of gender in life as lived and in the conceptualization of Africans as fit for slavery, and that ferreted out material evidence of diasporic African cultural ways in practice.[19] Next I turned to classic works in the history of slavery studies, those produced in the 1970s and 1980s that dealt with fundamental questions of culture, community, and resistance.[20] The interpretation of black life on Diamond Hill in this book reflects all of these influences and rests fundamentally on findings about enslaved experience produced by other scholars. The revelation offered here is not, therefore, in the specific aspects of black labor, family, and cultural life that have been traced in previous scholarship, or even in the cultural incorporation of indigenous ways described by other scholars of Afro-Native history. Rather, the contribution I hope to make to the field of slavery studies is a picture of enslaved black life in an Indian nation that is closely linked both culturally and experientially to black life in other locales. Black slaves on the large plantations of Indian country experienced the particularities of indigenous national and cultural contexts, but they were also part of the larger story of transatlantic rupture, prolonged suffering, creative resistance, cultural persistence, and emancipatory longing that characterized black life elsewhere in the U.S. colonies and states.

In addition to modes of interpretation inspired by Native American literary studies and grounded in historical slavery studies, this project borrows conceptually from the approach of microhistory, "the idea that intense reflection on a single event, place, or life might yield insights across scales of time and place." As the editors of *Small Worlds: Method, Meaning, and Narrative in Microhistory* explain, attention to "event, biography, and local vantage" not only affords intimate understanding of small slices of the past but also "reveal[s] factors previously unobserved" by "offering insights into phenomena and patterns that may lie outside of macrohistorical narratives or flatly contradict them."[21] *The House on Diamond Hill* adopts a tight analytical frame — the spatial borders of Diamond Hill, Vannsville, and to some extent, surrounding Cherokee communities. It focuses on one place within a period of approximately fifty years and chronicles the people who dwelled there with as much intimacy as the documentary record allows. The close-study approach of this book positions Diamond Hill as a small world unto itself, but not as an isolated historical case. Instead, a project such as this implies and invites comparisons with previous findings in Afro-Native and slavery studies, revealing Diamond Hill as yet another star in the galaxy of native slaveholding, and revealing native slaveholding as yet another galaxy in the universe of American slaveholding. We learn through focused attention on this single plantation world that both diversity and consistency characterized the peculiar institution across the borders of the U.S. nation and its internal colonies. We can conclude, as the result of this study, that two principal arguments in the historiography of black slavery in American Indian nations apply in some instances, but not all, and vary in degree of applicability in specific cases.

The first of these arguments, which we might call the leniency thesis, emerged in the second phase of Afro-Native historical studies in the 1970s and early 1980s. At that time, scholars like Rudi Halliburton, Theda Perdue, and Monroe Billington engaged in comparative analyses of white and Indian slaveholders, weighing the relative treatment of blacks in a way that historian Barbara Krauthamer fears was "a perverse endeavor of attempting to compare the extent to which enslaved people were exploited."[22] Some scholars argued in those early works that Indians were harsh slaveholders, or that treatment was equivalent. Others argued that Native Americans, as a category, were kinder slaveholders than whites, that slavery in native nations was relatively permissive, and that black slaves did not attempt escape. The last of these arguments, which Krauthamer summarizes below, took root in the historical imagination. She writes: "Accepting the premise that Indians lacked an awareness of and interest in the accumulation of property, historians concluded that, because most Indian slaveholders did not force their slaves to raise commodity crops on large plantations, they practiced a mild or benign form of slavery." The resulting leniency thesis positioned native people as lenient slaveholders and could be read to imply that black slaves of Indians led lives of relative ease. Krauthamer concludes: "Such reductive formulations . . . have no explanatory weight and are deceptive, replicating the racial hierarchies of the nineteenth century and obscuring the array of conditions and contingencies that informed Native people's attitudes toward and practices of slaveholding, property ownership, and commodity production."[23]

Slavery in the Cherokee Nation was indeed a diverse practice that varied depending on place, time, personality, and economic orientation. The Diamond Hill experience, while not representative of most Cherokee lifestyles, characterizes what many blacks in the Cherokee country of the early 1800s went through. And on the Vann plantation, blacks experienced profound and sustained suffering. They were the objects of violent victimization and emotional terror at the hands of James Vann, his overseers, the administrators of his estate, and even Moravian missionaries. Their lives were harsh and uncertain. Their treatment was often inhumane. A microhistorical investigation of a place like Diamond Hill exposes these realities, providing new material for the ongoing comparison debate and raising additional challenges to the universality of the leniency thesis.

A second argument that has emerged more recently as a result of the "cultural turn" in slavery studies, finds that blacks owned by and related to native people sought and attained cultural likeness with their indigenous owners. This second "Indianization" thesis, emergent in the work of Celia Naylor, Barbara Krauthamer, Gary Zellar, David Chang, and in my own first book, takes cultural identity into account and seriously considers the imprint of the indigenous national contexts in which some black and Afro-Native slaves found themselves.[24] However, this line of argumentation can be read to suggest that blacks in Indian nations were fully separate and distinct from blacks in the United States, a conclusion that may contribute to a sidelining of Indian-owned slaves in the larger slavery story. The tools of microhistory, which allow for sustained analysis of a single location, reveal the world of the large Cherokee plantation as an incubator of black cultural life, indicating that the Indianization thesis must be balanced with a recognition of ongoing African-influenced cultural practices. These qualifications of and amendments to major arguments in the study of Cherokee and southern Indian slaveholding emerge and take on concrete form in the context of microhistorical study, which affords a fuller, multidimensional view of a single location in the interest of better understanding broader historical phenomena and processes.

In addition to enabling intensive analysis of specific case studies, microhistorical approaches privilege biographical investigation with the rationale that single lives make up the larger social groups and networks that propel and are propelled by historical forces. Attention to the biographies of James Vann in particular, of Peggy Scott, Joseph Vann, Anna Rosina Gambold, Pleasant, Grace, Isaac, and others in this study of Diamond Hill reveals the layered and contingent nature of individual existences, the force of personality that drives historical events, and the impact of political, economic, and cultural change on the formation of personalities. We learn through prolonged concentration on the intertwined biographies of a small set of Diamond Hillians that external challenges, internal struggles, incredible strengths, and heartbreaking failures shaped the people who made our history.

BLACK SLAVES AND FREE BLACKS ON THE VANN
PLANTATION, Compiled by Julia Autry and William Chase Parker,
Chief Vann House State Historic Site

During the year 2007–08, in the midst of their research on slave life on the Vann plantation, Vann House staff members compiled a chart of all blacks, enslaved and free, who resided on Diamond Hill and in adjacent households of the Vann extended family. Their research was based on Moravian missionary diary entries and letters, Cherokee Nation Agency and Supreme Court records, and consultation with a small group of historians and Moravian specialists. Their completed chart, on exhibit at the Vann House site, is edited and reproduced below. Where the surname "Vann" is listed in the category of slave owner, the reference is to slaves on the Diamond Hill plantation owned by James or Joseph Vann. Blank cells in the chart represent categories for which information is unknown.

Slave Name	Spouse	Children	Owned By	Place of Origin	Location
Adam	Betty and Milly	Louis	Vann		mill
April			Vann		
Ben	Chloe		Vann, Jack Rogers		
Betsy			Wali (Mary) Vann		
Betty (Old)	July		Vann and loaned to Sour Mush	Africa	Vann's cow pen
Betty	Adam	Louis	Vann		mill
Bob			Vann		stables
Bonaparte			Vann		mill
Butler			Vann, raised by Peggy Vann Crutchfield	Spring Place	
Caesar			Vann, Nancy Vann		mill
Candace	Will	Deborah, Virginia	Peggy Vann Crutchfield		
Caty			Vann	Cherokee Nation	weaving house
Charlat			Mary Vann Stedman, Vann		
Chloe	Ben		Vann		mill
Clarissa			Vann and Crutchfield	Virginia	mill, Mountjoy
Crawje			Delilah Vann McNair	Africa	McNair's
David	Minda	John	Vann		
Deborah			Peggy Vann Crutchfield	Mountjoy	
Demas			Wali (Mary) Vann		mill

Skill	Comments
agriculture	His wife, Betty, died Apr. 12, 1809. Their son Louis died Feb. 24, 1812.
	On Nov. 5, 1805, she was beaten but not killed for her part in the Aug. 28 attempted murder of James Vann and the theft of $3,500 from Vann's home.
	Robbed Vann's store at Big Water in Jan. 1807
	Attended to Mother Vann (Wali) and helped at the mission at times.
	Elderly. In 1801 Betty and July lived at Vann's cow pens some 25 miles from Springplace, an area so remote they were mostly cut off from other people. She was stooped with age and spoke little English.
	Betty died Apr. 12, 1809. Her son Louis died Feb. 24, 1812.
stable supervisor	Killed on Sept. 17, 1805, for a robbery and attempted assassination of James Vann that occurred on Aug. 28. John Spencer (a white man) gave Bob a gun to murder James. Ultimately, the conspirators stole $3,500, but Vann was not at home at the time and was not killed.
	Attended services from time to time from 1809 to 1819.
	His parents were given to Peggy Vann before he was born so he was not considered Peggy's. The overseer Samuel Talley took him away on May 1, 1813, when he was only 4 years old, but he was later returned.
	Can read and speak Cherokee. Retrieved a horse that was stolen from the missionaries in Aug. 1814 (so he was not sold to the Natchez territory with his father and brothers in 1810).
	Present at Peggy Vann's conversion ceremony. Has her children baptized.
	Ridiculed by the overseer for her religious beliefs. Much loved by Peggy Vann Crutchfield, who took care of Caty when she was ill. Died Nov. 7, 1808.
	Charlat and 9 members of her family were purchased by Joseph Vann in 1829 for 10 cows, 5 horses, and a wagon.
	In 1806, had a stillborn child, who she buried herself.
kitchen	Youngest daughter of Grace and Jacob.
	African. Spoke no English. Relative of Old Betty. Died on Feb. 19, 1811.
agriculture	David was described by the missionaries as "mulatto." Son John died May 19, 1809.
	Born Feb. 14, 1811. Baptized Feb. 24, 1811. Injured by a falling ladder in 1817.
laborer	In 1807, James Vann and his mother, Wali, fought over Demas to the point where James actually tied him up and took him, but he returned three days later. In 1813, was described by the missionaries as Wali's "eldest Negro." His children were at Hightower (about 50 miles away).

Slave Name	Spouse	Children	Owned By	Place of Origin	Location
Dick			Vann, Robin Vann		
Dully	Luckey				
Dully (Young)					
Erline			Mary Vann Stedman, Vann		
Gander	Jene and Patience		Vann		mill
George			Vann, Crutchfield, Hicks	Virginia	mill, Mountjoy
George			Mary Vann Stedman, Vann		
Grace (Old)	Jacob (Old)	Lydia, Clarissa, George	free	Virginia	mill
Hagar	Isaac		Vann, McDonald		
Hannah	Will	Magdalena, Mila, Rose, Matthew, Butler	Vann, Crutchfield	Africa	Mountjoy
Hannah	Michael	Salomo Michael, Rosanna	David Watie		Oothcaloga
Harry			Peggy Vann Crutchfield	Tennessee	Mountjoy
Hunter			James Brown, Vann, Sally Vann Nicholson		
Isaac			Vann		
Isaac	Hagar		Vann, McDonald		Chickamauga
Isaac (Little)			Vann		

Skill	Comments
laborer	Plowed the Springplace Mission fields in 1815.
laborer	Along with Turkey Cock, made beams for the missionaries.
	8 years old on Apr. 5, 1818.
	Erline was the 1-year-old granddaughter of Jenny and Jerry and with them was purchased by Joseph Vann in 1829 along with other members of their family for 10 cows, 5 horses, and a wagon.
laborer	Known as James Vann's favorite slave. Drowned in Mill Creek July 9, 1806.
laborer	Beaten by the overseer Samuel Talley in Dec. 1813 for helping Mr. Nicholson.
	George and members of his family were purchased by Joseph Vann in 1829 for 10 cows, 5 horses, and a wagon.
sews	A close friend of Mother Vann (Wali). Attended dances at Wali's home. Would often carry a switch to church to swat the children (and some adults) who misbehaved.
	Helped the missionaries with household chores for a time before being sold to McDonald. Requested that the missionaries hold services in Chickamauga (about 40 miles away).
	4-year-old son Butler taken away on May 1, 1813, but the Cherokee Council later returned him to her. Infant daughter Rose died on Oct. 12, 1816. Her 3-year-old son Matthew died Nov. 25, 1816.
	Her son Salomo Michael was baptized at the Oothcaloga Mission in 1827, and in 1829 her daughter Rosanna was baptized at Springplace.
	Saved the wife of The Trunk on Mar. 21, 1813.
	Elderly. Could read. The missionaries gave him a Bible in 1814.
	Spoke Cherokee and translated between Cherokees and whites. Played the fiddle for dances. Ran away on several occasions but always returned. Burned at the stake on Sept. 16, 1805, for a robbery of $3,500 and an attempted assassination of James Vann that occurred on Aug. 28.
	Lived in Chicamauga (40 miles away) but attended service at the mission from time to time.
tracker, hunter	Was threatened when he was sent to look for the body of Falling after Falling's duel with James Vann in May 1806. Tracked cows and pigs for Vann and missionaries.

Slave Name	Spouse	Children	Owned By	Place of Origin	Location
Jack					
Jack (Little)					
Jacob (Christian)			Vann	Africa	
Jacob (Old)	Grace (Old)	Lydia, Clarissa, George	Vann and Crutchfield	Virginia	mill
Jarry	Jenny	Sally, Charlat, George, Roseanna	Mary Vann Stedman, Vann		
Jem					
Jene	Gander		Vann		mill
Jenny	Jarry	Sally, Charlat, George, Roseanna	Mary Vann Stedman, Vann		
Jenny			Vann		weaving house
Jenny			Nancy Vann	Virginia	
Jenny (The Big)			Vann		
Jerry					
Jim			Vann		mill
Jim			Old Harlan, free in 1814		
Joe				Africa	mill
John			Vann	Spring Place	mill
Johnson			Vann		
Judith			George and Jenny Brown Fields		
July (Duly)	Betty		Vann and loaned to Sour Mush	Africa	Vann's cow pen

Skill	Comments
	Attended services at Springplace in 1818–19.
	This little boy attended a service at the Springplace Mission in March of 1818. Was often tutored by Michael at night.
	Born in Africa. Was called Suniger Jacob but was later renamed by the Moravians and known as Brother Christian Jacob. Was a skilled carpenter. Died on Dec. 8, 1829, and was buried in God's Acre.
mill supervisor	Purchased in Virginia along with his family. His wife, Grace, was free but accompanied her family to the Cherokee Nation. He was a skilled mill worker and supervisor.
	Joseph Vann purchased Jarry and members of his family from his sister in 1829 for 10 cows, 5 horses, and a wagon.
	Enjoyed Christmas verses.
	The slaves started a rumor that her nagging Gander was the reason he drowned.
	Joseph Vann purchased Jenny and 9 members of her family from his sister in 1829 for 10 cows, 5 horses, and a wagon.
spinning	Chloe was her mother-in-law. Broke the missionaries' cotton card and was afraid to tell them.
	Was raised Catholic in Virginia. Elderly. Attended a dance in Dec. 1818.
	James Brown and David NcNair (executors of Vann's estate) sell her to the Natchez territory in 1810. She became so hysterical at the news that they restrained her with chains.
	Wanted to become a "good boy" like the children at the Springplace Mission school. Vowed to stop cursing.
mill worker	Helped the missionaries slaughter pigs.
	Referred to by the missionaries as a "humble" man.
	Testified that he saw Gander before he drowned.
	At his mother's insistence, John was baptized May 16, 1809, before he died three days later.
	Missionaries visited him when he was ill in Jan. 1828.
	Lived about 12 miles from Springplace but came to services on occasion.
stock hearder	Elderly. In 1801 he and Betty lived at Vann's cow pens some 25 miles from Springplace, an area so remote they were almost entirely cut off from other people. He was African but spoke a little broken English. Lost his toes to frostbite. He wanted to learn to read but could not see well, and the missionaries had no glasses for him.

Slave Name	Spouse	Children	Owned By	Place of Origin	Location
Kerr, Samuel (Old)			Vann? Free in 1806. Ethiopia	South Carolina	
LeRoy					
Louis			Vann	Spring Place	mill
Luckey	Dully		Vann		mill
Lucy			Peggy Vann Crutchfield		Mountjoy
Lydia			Vann and Crutchfield	Virginia	mill, Mountjoy
Magdalena			Peggy Vann Crutchfield	Spring Place	Mountjoy
Maggy			Peggy Vann Crutchfield	Mountjoy	Mountjoy
Matthew			Peggy Vann Crutchfield	Mountjoy	Mountjoy
Michael	Hannah	Salomo Michael, Rosanna	Moravians and David Watie	Born "somewhere in Virginia"	Springplace Mission at Watie's
Mila			Mother Vann (Wali), Peggy Vann Crutchfield	Spring Place	Spring Place
Milly	Adam	Louis	Vann		mill
Milly			free but kidnapped		
Mima		Nancy	Vann		
Minda	David	John	Vann, Delilah Vann McNair		mill/McNair's
Moley			Wali (Mary) Vann		mill
Moses			Vann		mill
Nancy					
Nanny					

Skill	Comments
	Elderly. Ethiopian but grew up in Lancaster, PA. Could read. Knew the Vanns well (once owned by them?). Came for a "last visit" in the summer of 1806 and told Mother Vann (Wali) that James Vann should start acting like a man. Devout Christian. Attacked by a goat while visiting and healed at the mission.
	A young boy in 1808.
	Died at age 8 on Feb. 24, 1812.
	Described by the missionaries as "newly arrived" in 1808.
	Was a friend of young Phoebe and Candace, who were also slaves at Mountjoy.
	Regularly attended services at the mission with her parents, Grace and Jacob.
	Born Jan. 15, 1812.
	A child. On Mar. 6, 1817, her clothes caught fire, but she was saved by Peggy Vann Crutchfield.
	Baptized Aug. 29, 1813. Died Nov. 25, 1816.
laborer	Born en route from Bethlehem, PA, to Springplace in 1805. As a teen often quarreled with his mother, Pleasant. Sold to David Watie in 1819 and was moved to Oothcaloga (25 miles away). Has his son Salomo Michael baptized at Oothcaloga in 1827, and his daughter Rosanna was baptized at Springplace in 1829.
	Had an infant child that died in Oct. 1818.
	In 1811, she and her husband, Adam, thought they had been cursed and sought the help of a medicine woman.
	Milly was free, but in 1815, she was kidnapped by a man who tried to sell her as a slave. She sought shelter with the missionaries until she could safely return home to her mother.
	In 1813, she was whipped nearly to death by the overseer Samuel Talley for little reason, according to the missionaries.
	Minda insisted that her sickly baby John be baptized before he died in 1809. Her family's cabin burned in Dec. 1810. By 1820, she was owned by Delilah Vann McNair.
	In 1806, this young girl told the missionaries she wanted to be baptized, but they advised her to wait until she could give her heart completely to the Lord.
	May have run away in 1810 rather than be sold to the Natchez territory.
	Attended services at Springplace in 1807.
	Young. Had scabies and was treated by the missionaries in April 1806.

Slave Name	Spouse	Children	Owned By	Place of Origin	Location
Ned (Old)	Renee	Caesar, Moses, Sam, Chloe, Simon	Vann, Nancy Vann	Africa	mill
Parley			Vann, Delilah Vann McNair		McNair's
Patience	Gander		Vann	Africa	weaving house
Patty			Wali (Mary) Vann	Africa	mill
Peter			Vann		
Peter (Young)			Vann		
Phoebe (Old)			Peggy Vann Crutchfield		Mountjoy
Phoebe (Young)			Peggy Vann Crutchfield		Oothcaloga
Phyllis			Wali (Mary) Vann		mill
Pleasant		Michael	Moravians	North Carolina	Mission
Polly			Wali (Mary) Vann	Africa	
Pompey	Rachel		Vann, Delilah Vann McNair	Africa	McNair's
Rachel	Pompey		Vann, Delilah Vann McNair	Africa	McNair's
Renee	Ned (Old)	Caesar, Moses, Sam, Chloe, Simon	Vann, Nancy Vann	Africa	mill
Rosanna			David Watie	Oothcaloga	Oothcaloga

Skill	Comments
miller	Was the foreman at James Vann's mill. Could read. In Nov. 1810, he slit his own throat rather than be sold to the Natchez territory. Three of his sons ran away. He did not die immediately, but the wound made him unable to speak. He died two months later on Jan. 20, 1811.
	On Nov. 24, 1807, George Fields "bled" Parley, who was very ill at the time. On Dec. 26, 1807, Parley, while drunk, scared the Springplace children with a knife. He was inquisitive about religion.
seamstress	From the Guinea area of coastal West Africa. Spoke little English. Imported to Charleston, SC, and purchased by Vann in 1805. Feet removed due to frostbite. Spouse Gander drowned in 1806; second spouse sold to the Natchez territory in 1810. Horribly beaten by the overseer Samuel Talley in 1813.
	She attended services at Springplace but told the missionaries her husband objected and would not let her come often.
	Killed on Nov. 5, 1805, for an attempted assassination of James Vann and the theft of $3,500 that occurred on Aug. 28. He was the last of several conspirators to be captured, and, according to the Moravians, he was defiant until the end.
	Wanted to become a "good boy" like the children at Springplace. Vowed to stop cursing.
	A missionary letter refers to Mrs. Crutchfield and her oldest Negress, Phoebe.
cook	Was 16 years old in April 1819. Often snuck into the woods to pray and had a powerful religious vision while there. She was a cook for the road builders at Oothcaloga, where the Crutchfields later built a house. Suffered from dementia before her death at Oothcaloga on June 7, 1819.
	Delivered a stillborn child in Oct. 1819.
cook/laborer	Delivered Michael on the way to Springplace in 1805. Michael was sold to the Watie family in 1819 and was moved 25 miles away. Pleasant worked at Springplace longer than any other person, white or black.
	A friend to Patty. Spoke no English. Brought a sick child to the mission in 1819, and July (Duly) had to translate. The missionaries couldn't understand either because of their heavy African accents.
laborer	From Africa, he was mistreated by the American-born slaves. They refused to allow him to eat and instead gave his lunch portion to the dogs. He and Rachel desperately wanted to learn to read.
	She and her husband Pompey were given to Delilah Vann McNair after her father James's death in 1809. They returned to Springplace for a visit Christmas of 1818.
	After her husband, Ned, died in 1810 she was given to Nancy Vann. Attended the mission services very faithfully before Ned died but afterward couldn't come as often. She was heartbroken about this but continued to visit whenever she could.
	Was baptized at the Springplace Mission on Oct. 25, 1829.

Slave Name	Spouse	Children	Owned By	Place of Origin	Location
Rose			Peggy Vann Crutchfield	Mountjoy	Mountjoy
Roseanna			Mary Vann Stedman, Vann		
Ruben			Mary Vann Stedman, Vann		
Salomo Michael			David Watie	Oothcaloga	Oothcaloga
Sally					
Sally			Mary Vann Stedman, Vann		
Sally			Vann		
Sally			Mary Vann Stedman, Vann		
Sam			Vann, Nancy Vann		mill
Sambo					
Simon			Vann		mill
Syvets, Anthony			free		Springplace
Tabby					
Tom			Vann		
Toney					
Tony			Vann		mill
Turkey Cock			Vann		
Virginia			Peggy Vann Crutchfield	Mountjoy	Mountjoy
Washington			Mary Vann Stedman, Vann		
Will	Hannah, Candace	Magdalena, Mila, Rose, Matthew, Butler	Vann and Crutchfield	Africa	mill, Mountjoy

Skill	Comments
	Rose was born on May 1, 1815, and died on Oct. 12, 1816, and was buried in Springplace's God's Acre.
	Roseanna was purchased by Joseph Vann in 1829 along with members of her family for 10 cows, 5 horses, and a wagon.
	Ruben was the 9-year-old grandson of Jenny and Jerry and with them was purchased by Joseph Vann in 1829 along with other members of their family for 10 cows, 5 horses, and a wagon.
	Was baptized at the Oothcaloga Mission in 1827.
	Described by the missionaries as "mulatto." Was apathetic toward the missionaries.
	Sally was purchased by Joseph Vann in 1829 along with 9 members of her family for 10 cows, 5 horses, and a wagon.
laborer	Stopped by the Springplace Mission going to and from the fields.
	Sally was the 3-year-old granddaughter of Jenny and Jerry and with them was purchased by Joseph Vann in 1829 along with other members of their family for 10 cows, 5 horses, and a wagon.
	Nancy Vann arranged to have Sam killed in 1814, but he stole a horse and he and his wife ran to Captain James Blair, an Indian agent in South Carolina, for protection.
	Attended services at Springplace in July of 1814.
	May have run away in 1810 rather than be sold to the Natchez territory.
	Free in 1806. Described by the missionaries as "mulatto." Was a neighbor of the Springplace Mission from July to Dec. 1806.
	Attended services in 1816.
	In March of 1802, the Moravians sent him back to Vann because he did not perform to their satisfaction.
	Parley brought him to services in July of 1806.
laborer/animal tracker	Worked for Ned at the mill. Began aiding the missionaries in 1802 by clearing fields. Skinned a wolf for the Moravians in 1807. Helped to track a runaway pig.
laborer	Along with Dully, he made beams for the missionaries. He often helped the missionaries.
	Born at Mountjoy on Aug. 29, 1812, and was baptized there on Oct. 4.
	Washington was the 6-year-old grandson of Jenny and Jerry who with them was purchased by Joseph Vann in 1829 along with other members of their family for 10 cows, 5 horses, and a wagon.
laborer	4-year-old son Butler was taken away by Vann overseer Samuel Talley on May 1, 1813, but the Cherokee Council intervened to return him. Infant daughter Rose died on Oct. 12, 1816. 3-year-old son Matthew died Nov. 25, 1816.

THE MEMOIR OF MARGARET ANN CRUTCHFIELD
(PEGGY SCOTT VANN), Written by Anna Rosina Gambold

Toward the end of their lives, members of the Moravian Church write, or have written for them, faith biographies called "memoirs." These memoirs are preserved for each congregant and filed in the church archives. Although Peggy (Margaret Ann) Scott Vann Crutchfield was the first Cherokee convert to the Moravian Church and the Christian faith, up to the time of this writing, no memoir had been found for her. Moravian archivists, researchers, and translators concluded that Scott had never written or authorized this traditional form of religious prose. In contrast, a memoir has been known to exist for her uncle Charles Hicks, and it is stored in the Moravian Southern Province church archives.

Peggy's missing memoir became an object of scholarly longing as I conducted my research on this book. I set out to locate it with one tip in mind that I had received along the way from Cherokee-Moravian researcher Anna Smith. If a memoir ever had existed for Peggy, Smith told me, Anna Rosina Gambold would have written it. In one fortuitous Google search, I located a text by Gambold that I had never seen cited in the Cherokee or Moravian literature. The piece was titled "Margaret Ann Crutchfield, A Cherokee Convert," and it was compiled in a book of essays by and about people of color edited by the abolitionist Abigail Mott. Gambold's piece in Mott's collection perfectly adheres to the form and content of Moravian memoirs, and I am certain it is Peggy Scott's missing faith biography. The whereabouts of the original document are unknown to me at this time. A copy of the work, as published by Mott, appears below for the benefit of all who have an interest. Readers might note, as I did, the attention given to Peggy's close relationship with an enslaved black woman (Caty), as well as Peggy's modest admonition to Anna Rosina Gambold not to speak a word of her remarkable life.[1]

MARGARET ANN CRUTCHFIELD,
A CHEROKEE CONVERT.

Written by the late Mrs. Gambold, wife of the Moravian Missionary at Spring Place, in the Cherokee Nation.

1. OUR late beloved sister, Margaret Ann, was born August 20, 1783. Her father, Walter Scott, was agent in the nation under the British government; and her mother, Sarah Wilburn, was a sister of brother Charles Renatus Hicks.

2. Her first husband was the celebrated Cherokee chief, James Vann; during whose lifetime, she evinced an affection for the missionaries in her neighbour-

hood at Spring Place; and, as often as it was in her power, attended our meetings: not without evident concern for her soul.

3. In 1808, a negro woman belonging to her, departed this life in the faith of our crucified Saviour; which made a deep and lasting impression on her mistress. February 19, 1809, she had the great grief to lose her husband by means of a violent death. The three years of her widowhood proved the most important period of her life. By the gracious operations of the Holy Spirit on her heart, she learned to know her natural sinfulness.

4. The opinion she had harboured of herself, as being superior to other of her countrywomen, now presented itself to her in a most hideous form, so that she shuddered at the sight of her wicked heart, and felt and acknowledged herself the greatest sinner among them. She cried incessantly for mercy and pardon; and amidst floods of tears sought and found her Saviour.

5. In July, 1812, she again entered the marriage state, with our now widowed brother, Joseph Crutch-field, a cousin of her former husband. His becoming, after some time, a member of our church, and walking by our Saviour's grace, hand in hand with her in the narrow way which leads to life and bliss, rendered the days of their union a truly blessed period.

6. Four years since, she was frequently ailing and her husband, with us, feared greatly that we should have to part with her; we therefore removed her from her farm on Mount Joy to this place, where she abode during the winter months. By the blessing of our Lord upon the simple means used towards her recovery, she was enabled, in the following spring, to return home; and thinking herself perfectly restored; undertook, as before, the management of her extensive domestic concerns.

7. However, from too great exertions, and frequent colds, her consumptive cough returned, and increased to such a degree, that she was under the painful necessity of relinquishing her wonted activity, and betaking herself to rest. Now, her chief and most agreeable employ, was reading in the New Testament, and the hymn book of the Brethren's church.

8. Last spring we again took her to Spring Place, to her great joy. As riding on horseback apparently proved of benefit to her, she made repeated visits to her friends and relatives at Sogh-ge-lo-gy, and elsewhere, testifying of the Saviour's love to all poor sinners — of his all-sufficient atonement; and of the great happiness we enjoy, even here on earth, in his blest communion. When last with them, she addressed her Indian sisters thus: "My dear sisters, this is perhaps the last time that I shall visit you. I beseech you, most earnestly, consider our poor people, who as yet sit in darkness, and know not our dearest Saviour. O speak to them of his love, his sufferings, and death on the Cross! O be active in his cause, he deserves it of you! If it were his holy will, I would gladly stay longer here, only for the purpose of speaking more for him, and of showing *more* the way to him," &c.

9. These words she spoke amidst a flood of tears; and all the sisters wept, prom-

ising by the Saviour's grace, to follow her maternal injunctions. She arrived here in great weakness of body on the 2d September, 1820. She was now no longer able to edify herself by reading, therefore she was very thankful when we read or sung for her.

10. The frequent visits she received from her numerous friends and relations, were improved to the best purpose on her part. The Saviour and his love unto death, even the death of the cross, were, to the last, her chief delight, and the topic of her conversation. Having been honoured to be his messenger of peace to many of her people, this honour humbled her the more; and she ofttimes was at a loss how to express her sense of the high obligations she lay under to her Saviour, for favouring the vilest wretch, as she deemed herself to be, thus highly, only lamenting, that she was not able to do *much more* for her gracious Lord.

11. Since the 7th September, she kept her room — On the 16th October, in the presence of a number of friends, whom she solemnly enjoined to give themselves to our Redeemer, she received the last benediction, after a fervent prayer and thanks to him, for what he had proved to his handmaid, the first fruits of the Cherokee nation, during the ten years of her christian life. The feelings of the divine presence on this occasion is beyond description.

12. On the 18th, towards night, she was in great bodily pain. We sung by her bed as usual, and implored our God to shorten the sufferings of this dear bought soul; during which time, with a loud voice, she incessantly besought his coming soon. "Come, come, my dearest Saviour! hasten, oh, hasten, and take me home! I long, I long to be with thee! Thou canst not come too soon." This paroxism of bodily sufferings lasted about half an hour, upon which she fell, as it were, into a sweet slumber; and during our singing some appropriate verses, her longing soul almost imperceptibly left the emaciated body, and went into the arms of her dearest Saviour.

13. Much, very much might be said of her truly edifying Christian life, led in the faith of the crucified Son of God. Yet, in obedience to her repeated most solemn injunctions to her husband, we must stop here, fearing that the little we have said, might not be agreeable to the wishes of our departed sister — for these were *her* words: "I know assuredly that my name is written in heaven. When I am gone, I pray you say *nothing* of me, but let my name on earth perish with my body."

Notes

Source Abbreviations

ABCFM — American Board of Commissioners for Foreign Missions

Cherokee Agency Records — Records of the Cherokee Agency in Tennessee, Bureau of Indian Affairs, National Archives and Records Administration, Washington, DC

GC — General Correspondence

GDAH — Georgia Department of Archives and History, Morrow, Georgia

GHC — Georgia Historical Commission

GHCR — Georgia Historical Commission Records, Georgia Department of Archives and History, Morrow, Georgia

MAS — Moravian Archives, Winston-Salem, North Carolina

MMD — Moravian Mission Diary, Georgia Department of Archives and History, Morrow, Georgia

MSMC — Rowena McClinton, ed. *The Moravian Springplace Mission to the Cherokees*, 2 vols. (Lincoln: University of Nebraska Press, 2007)

Payne Papers — John Howard Payne Papers, Ayer Collection, Newberry Library, Chicago, Illinois

SCDAH — South Carolina Department of Archives and History, Columbia, South Carolina

SPMD — Springplace Mission Diary, Cherokee Mission Papers, Moravian Archives, Winston-Salem, North Carolina

SPML — Springplace Mission Letters/Correspondence, Cherokee Mission Papers, Moravian Archives, Winston-Salem, North Carolina

VH — Vann House

VHL — Chief Vann House State Historic Site Library, Spring Place, Georgia

VHOHP — Vann House Oral History Project, Conducted by Tiya Miles, Fall 2006–Fall 2008

Prologue

1. Interview with William Chase Parker, May 10 and June 3, 2007, VHOHP.

2. "Christmas Program Sets New Attendance and Revenue Records," *Friends of the Vann House Newsletter*, Winter 2009.

3. "Vann House Volunteerism Passed down through Generations," *Vann House Staff Notes*, Winter/Spring 2006.

4. Julia Autry, conversation with Tiya Miles, December 2006, Spring Place, GA.

Introduction

1. The structure of the restored Vann House columns was a point of ongoing contention between architect Henry Chandlee Forman and the builders, since Forman insisted they be built of the very finest materials. Forman argued that "the 48 columns on the outside of the Vann House are the most important and most conspicuous objects of the building" ("Memorandum to the Members of the Georgia Historical Commission," Sept. 27, 1954, GHCR, GC folder).

2. Lela Latch Lloyd, *If the Chief Vann House Could Speak*, inside front cover, v, 100, 2, xi. See also Howard and Loyd, *Vann House Speaks Again*; Penelope Allen, "Leaves From the Family Tree," *Chattanooga Sunday Times*, July 26, 1936; Whitfield-Murray Historical Society, *Murray County's Indian Heritage*, 13; and Helen McDonald Exum, "Showplace of the Cherokees," *Chattanooga News-Free Press*, Apr. 25, 1971, UTK-MS-2033, Penelope Allen Collection, 1801–1984, University of Tennessee Libraries, Knoxville.

3. Jewett to Murtagh, July 31, 1968, GHCR, VH folder.

4. "Traveling Northwest Georgia?," GHC brochure, circa 1950s–60s, GHCR, VH folder.

5. See, for instance, Allen to Gregory, Aug. 1, 1958, GHCR, VH folder; Robert E. Chambers Interpretive Center Dedication Program, VHL; and Robert E. Chambers, foreword to Lela Latch Lloyd, *If the Chief Vann House Could Speak*.

6. "The Chief Vann House," Oklahoma Historical Society, Oklahoma City.

7. This interpretation of the derivation of the Diamond Hill name was made by archaeologist Ken Robinson, whose Wake Forest University team excavated segments at the site in March 2005 and unearthed several quartz crystals (Ken Robinson, email correspondence with Tiya Miles, Dec. 21, 2006).

8. Shadburn, *Unhallowed Intrusion*, 30.

9. James Vann's first home on Diamond Hill would have been a modest log cabin. Specific information about Vann's second home, built in 1804–05, does not exist. Although Vann House officials believe they have identified the location of the house in a high clearing behind the current Vann House building, archaeological work has yet to be undertaken there. James Vann's second home may have resembled the large log home with multiple glass windows built around 1797 and occupied by Cherokee leader John Ross in present-day Tennessee. See "Scholars Track History of John Ross House," *Chattanooga Times-Free Press*, Mar. 4, 2007.

10. For more on the house museum movement in the South, see Yuhl, "Rich and Tender," and Brundage, *Southern Past*, 204–9. For more on Cherokee, North Carolina, see C. Brenden Martin, "To Keep the Spirit of Mountain Culture Alive."

11. Bandy to Cumming, no date, GHCR, VH folder; GHC to Cumming, May 22,

1958, GHCR, VH folder. The principal chief of the Cherokee Nation named Bandy ambassador for her work on behalf of Cherokee sites and bestowed her with a formal certificate. See "Mrs. Bandy Made Ambassador to the Nation of Cherokees," *The Dalton* [full title obscured], no date, GHCR, VH folder. See also Bandy to Cumming, no date, GHCR, VH folder; and Exum, "Showplace."

12. "Vann House Plan to Be Discussed," *Atlanta Journal*, Oct. 5, 1951; Harold Martin column, *Atlanta Journal*, Oct. 7, 1951, quoted in Chief Standingdeer Tribe brochure, no date, GHCR, VH folder; "Formal Opening of the Chief Vann House" program, July 27, 1958, GHCR, VH folder; Chief Standingdeer Tribe brochure.

13. In 1951, Senate Bill No. 75 established the GHC, which would remain active until 1973, when its projects were transferred to the Department of Natural Resources. See "Georgia Historical Commission," No. 496, Senate Bill No. 75, *Georgia Laws 1951*, GHCR, GC folder; and Gilmore, "Georgia's Historic Preservation Beginning."

14. Smith to Alexander, Nov. 25, 1952, GHCR, GC folder; "Site Information," GHCR, Data Summaries folder.

15. "Historical Commission Given Fund," *Atlanta Constitution*, Sept. 11, 1952, GHCR, GC folder; Pratt and Pratt, *Guide to Early American Homes South*, 110.

16. Designer: Gregory to Cumming, May 6, 1958, GHCR, VH folder; Alice Richards, "Dalton's Mrs. B. J. Bandy Pens Letter, Gets Results," newspaper name not given, no date, GHCR, VH folder; furnishings: Gilmore, "Georgia's Historic Preservation Beginning," 9, 11, 13, 14, 15; Bandy, foreword to *Early Georgia*; "Formal Opening of the Chief Vann House" program; family items: "Papers of Webbers Falls Founder Given to Museum," *Tulsa Daily World*, July 8, 1958, Vann Perry Collection, VHL; "Cherokees to Relive Glory of Past at Rites in Georgia," *Tulsa Daily World*, July 27, 1958, Vann Perry Collection, VHL.

17. Bandy to Cumming, Thursday (no other date), 1958, GHCR, VH folder; "Vann House Dedication, Sunday, 2 p.m.," *Chatsworth Times*, July 24, 1958, Bandy Scrapbook, VHL.

18. Attendance number (8,000): Exum, "Showplace"; attendance number (5,000): "Thousands Gather," *The Dalton News*, July 30, 1958; Mary Well, "Chatter," *Chatsworth Times*, July 31, 1958, Bandy Scrapbook, VHL; "Thousands Gather on Vann House Hill as State Dedicates Its Newest Museum," *The Dalton News*, July 30, 1958, Vann Perry Collection, VHL.

19. "Traveling Northwest Georgia?"

20. "Chieftain's Trail," VHL.

21. Boudinot, "Address to the Whites," GDAH. The address also appeared in *The North American Review* 23, no. 2 (1826): 470–74.

22. Allen, *Cherokee Nation*, 5–6.

23. Chief Vann House State Historic Site attendance chart, December 2007, courtesy of the Vann House.

24. VHOHP, email interview with William Chase Parker, May 2007. Although people from different racial backgrounds do visit the site, as Parker contends, my

observations clearly indicate that the vast majority of visitors are white and that visitors of color, especially African Americans, make up only a small minority of tourists there. The greater number of black visitors seems to be children in school groups or mixed-race or adopted black children accompanied by white parents.

25. This assertion is based on observational notes taken and interviews with Vann House tourists conducted by the author. For details on this research process, see Appendix 1.

26. Pratt and Pratt, *Guide to Early American Homes South*, v.

27. Jonathan Daniels in 1938 quoted in Brundage, *Southern Past*, 183.

28. Brundage, *Southern Past*, 184; also see p. 222 on escape from modern life.

29. Kropp, *California Vieja*, 3–4.

30. Brundage, *Southern Past*, 209.

31. Horwitz, *Confederates*, 386; Adams, *Wounds*, 6. Observers of southern identity comment on the role of historical attachment and romanticism as "a talisman against modernity" (Horwitz, *Confederates*, 386) and a means of assuaging present-day racial concerns.

32. Adams, *Wounds*, 17.

33. Seebohm and Woloszynski, *Under Live Oaks*, 16–17.

34. For more on the South as an internal, regional "other" within the United States and its comparison with the Caribbean islands, Europe, and the "Orient," see Cobb, *Away Down South*, intro, chap. 1. Also see Cox, *Traveling South*, 8–9, 144.

35. Adams, *Wounds*, 17.

36. Deloria, *Unexpected Places*, 3–7. I use the term "expectation" here in the manner defined by Philip Deloria as an ideological and materially effectual set of understandings about a group that function as both "products" and "tools" of domination. See ibid., 3–4.

37. *Georgia 1800–1900*, 200; Jim Wood, "The Editor Says," *Fayette County News*, May 19, 1965, GHCR, VH folder; Malone, "Cherokees Become a Civilized Tribe," 12; governor's remarks quoted in "Vann House Dedicated"; Denson, "Ancestors," 14.

38. hooks, "Revolutionary 'Renegades,'" 189; Green, "Tribe"; Deloria, *Playing Indian*; Naylor-Ojurongbe, "'Born and Raised.'"

39. Deloria, *Playing Indian*, 3.

40. Shoemaker, *Strange Likeness*, 31.

41. Jewett to Murtagh, July 31, 1968, GHCR, VH folder. I am grateful to James T. Carson, whose paper "Time and Memory in the American South," presented at the American Society for Ethnohistory conference in Williamsburg, VA, in 2006, followed by a long conversation, inspired my thinking about the notion of an ancient South.

42. Blight, "Epilogue," 348.

43. Bachelard, *Poetics*, 7, 5, 6.

44. Ibid., 7; Julia Autry, conversation with Tiya Miles, December 2006, Spring Place, GA.

45. de Baillou, "Chief Vann House," 3.

46. VHOHP, telephone interview with Virginia Vann Perry, Aug. 2008; VHOHP, email interview with David Cornsilk, July 2008. Perry, who lives in Muskogee, Oklahoma, stated that she has visited the Vann House several times and regularly participated in Vann family reunions at the house. When she first visited many years ago, she was especially interested in those features she had heard about, such as the hanging staircase "that was quite a phenomenon at the time" and vivid paint colors. She has since researched aspects of the Vann House and Vann family lore and determined for herself which stories should or should not be "credited with the truth."

47. de Baillou, "Chief Vann House," 3.

48. Elizabeth Fox-Genovese uses this term to refer to a southern household of twenty or more slaves in *Plantation Household*, 32.

49. Malone, "Cherokees Become a Civilized Tribe"; Malone, *Cherokees of the Old South*, 1–2, 31; Starkey, *Cherokee Nation*, 19–22; Woodward, *Cherokees*, 3–4.

50. Ridge to Gallatin, Feb. 27, 1826, in Perdue and Green, eds., *Cherokee Removal*.

51. Harmon, "American Indians and Land Monopolies," 16.

52. Justice, *Our Fire*, 6; Justine Smith, "Resistance Disguised as Fundamentalism," 1; Hatley, *Dividing Paths*, 233. Perdue, *"Mixed-Blood" Indians*, 35, 68–69.

53. Justice, *Our Fire*, xv.

54. Celia Naylor (*African Cherokees*, 11–12) poses a strong counterargument to the case that I am making here (and have made in other writings). Naylor argues that rather than being foreign to Cherokee society, black slavery was culturally familiar since it was preceded by existing Cherokee practices of captive-taking and the resulting bondage of unfree people. While I agree with and appreciate Naylor's point that holding some people against their will in a subjugated status was not new to Cherokees and that Cherokees "did not simply emulate European American versions of slavery," I distinguish between the capture of people of just any racial group, including other Indians, who were usually either ritually killed or adopted into families, and the purchase of people from only one racial group who were unlikely to be adopted into families and were expected to be held as property for life. It is this latter, particular form of slavery that I refer to as being a development stemming from European contact.

55. Philip Morgan found in his study of the eighteenth-century Chesapeake and Low Country that it was not uncommon for whites to attend events where slave musicians performed; nor was it uncommon for blacks and whites to drink together in public houses of entertainment. It was unusual, however, for planters to host slaves at drinking parties. He gives one example of this occurring in 1716 in Virginia, and the party seems to have been held out of doors. See his *Slave Counterpoint*, 413–15.

56. Berlin, *Generations*, 59, 73, 76.

57. Parish, *Slavery*, 51 (Parish is paraphrasing James Oakes in this statement); Oakes, *Ruling Race*, 191.

58. Philip Morgan, *Slave Counterpoint*, 18.

59. Hatley, *Dividing Paths*, 233. Hatley notes here that wealthy and mainstream Cherokees were different but not fully separate from one another. While most

farming Cherokees used Cherokee elites as a buffer between themselves and whites, this Cherokee majority still had to confront change. One example is that even as mainstream Cherokees retreated to interior and mountain spaces to avoid white encroachment, they began to set up farmsteads similar to those of their white neighbors.

60. Oakes, *Ruling Race*, 153.

61. Justice, *Our Fire*, 6.

62. What I am calling "communal economics" Tom Hatley describes as "a strong current of economic commonality" (Hatley, *Dividing Paths*, 12). Journalists and memoirists who wrote about the Vann House prior to the mid-1950s sometimes attributed the building of the structure to Joseph Vann, rather than to his father, James. These attributions were often a result of confusion about first names. It is interesting, though, that these early writers were correct and that the Georgia Historical Commission's official literature on the house in the 1950s and later created a mistaken consensus about James Vann's role as builder of the home, making the pace of change on Diamond Hill seem faster than it actually was. The early writers who attributed the brick home's construction to Joseph still cited the erroneous 1804 date.

63. Other fine treatments of Cherokee women's history exist, but none of these sustains an intimate focus on women of this class. See, for instance, Perdue, *Cherokee Women*; Hill, *Weaving New Worlds*; and Perdue, "Catharine Brown." Owen's *Cherokee Woman's America* is a postemancipation autobiography of a woman from the slaveholding class. Her narrative is illuminating in many ways, but beyond a brief description of the family's black "nurse," called "Granny Jenny," Owen rarely mentions slavery. Interestingly, Owen credits the 116-year-old "Granny Jenny" with remembering the stories of Owen's family that were passed down to Owen (47). Jenny becomes the source and conduit of this slaveholding family's history.

64. Hill, "Weaving History," 133–35.

65. See Naylor-Ojurongbe, "'Born and Raised'"; Krauthamer, "In Their 'Native Country'"; and Miles, *Ties That Bind*.

66. Joyner, *Down by the Riverside*, 1–2.

67. Philip Morgan, *Slave Counterpoint*, 559.

68. Walker, "Beyond the Peacock," 47; also cited in Seebohm and Woloszynski, *Under Live Oaks*, 19.

Chapter One

1. Secretary of War Dearborn to Agent Meigs, May 5, 1808, Cherokee Agency Records; McLoughlin, *Cherokee Renascence*, 131.

2. Lowrey to Meigs, Feb. 8, 1808, Cherokee Agency Records. Lowrey is also spelled Lowery and Lowry in the original sources.

3. McLoughlin, "James Vann," 40; Meigs to Dearborn, Mar. 24, 1808, Cherokee Agency Records; *MSMC*, vol. 1, July 26, 1805.

4. "Georgia Gazette Riddle for July 21–25, 2008."

5. Payne Papers, 2:43–46; Malone, *Cherokees of the Old South*, 60.

6. Meigs to Dearborn, Mar. 24, 1808, Cherokee Agency Records.

7. Byhan to Benzien, July 22, 1806, SPML.

8. Payne Papers, 2:43–46. While Payne places Vann at age forty-four at his death, the Moravians said he was forty-one. See *MSMC*, vol. 1, Feb. 21, 1809, 302.

9. Norton, *Journal*, 68. The time of night and details about the boy, Joe Vann, are described in *MSMC*, vol. 1, Feb. 21, 1809, 302.

10. Gambold to Benzien, Feb. 23, 1809, SPML.

11. McLoughlin, *Cherokee Renascence*, 151.

12. Payne Papers, 2:46.

13. McLoughlin, "James Vann," 39.

14. Wilkins, *Cherokee Tragedy*, 36–37.

15. Shadburn, *Unhallowed Intrusion*, 23.

16. Pommer, *Curse*; Julia Autry, conversation with Tiya Miles, December 2006, Spring Place, GA.

17. *MSMC*, vol. 1, June 6, 1805, 55–56.

18. Waldram, *Revenge*, 272–73.

19. Fogelson, "Analysis of Cherokee Sorcery," 123.

20. Alan Kilpatrick, *Night*, 18; Fogelson, "Analysis of Cherokee Sorcery," 124.

21. *MSMC*, vol. 1, July 26, 1805, 61.

22. Bell, *Chief James*. Shadburn uses very similar language to describe Vann's personality in *Unhallowed*, 24.

23. Bell, *Chief James*, 10.

24. McLoughlin, "James Vann," 41.

25. Blackhawk, *Violence*, 5; Deloria, *Unexpected Places*, 15–51; Andrea Smith, *Conquest*.

26. Mooney, *Historical Sketch*, 21–24.

27. Blind Savannah and Wild Potatoes are different English translations for the same Cherokee clan. There were seven Cherokee clans in all: Wolf, Deer, Bird, Red Paint, Blue or Panther, Wild Potatoes or Blind Savannah, and Twisters or Long Hair. See Gilbert, *Smithsonian Institution Bureau of Ethnology Bulletin 133*, 203–4.

28. Payne Papers, 2:43–46.

29. Brown, *Old Frontiers*, 390; Ehle, *Trail of Tears*, 44–45; Smith to the Secretary of War, Sept. 27, 1793, 468, American State Papers, Documents, Legislative and Executive of the Congress of the United States, 1789–1815, vol. 4, Indian Affairs; Philippe, *Diary*, 74; Mooney, *Historical Sketch*, 65; Wilkins, *Cherokee Tragedy*, 25–26. The earlier sources either do not name James Vann as being present at all during this attack or attribute the main action to Cherokee John Watts.

30. Justice, *Our Fire*, 37; McLoughlin, *Cherokee Renascence*, 20.

31. Smith to the Secretary of War, Sept. 27, 1793, 468.

32. Brown, *Old Frontiers*, 390. The family name Cavet (of Cavet's Station) is spelled multiple ways in various sources: Cavet, Caveat, Cavitt, Cavett.

33. Ehle, *Trail of Tears*, 44–45.

34. I borrow the term "biomyth" from black feminist theorist Audre Lorde, who describes her autobiography, *Zami*, as a "biomythography." I use the term here to convey the sense of a life story that has mythological elements. See Lorde, *Zami*, cover.

35. Bell, *Chief James*, 10.

36. McLoughlin, "James Vann," 39.

37. See the introduction, note 36, regarding my use of the term "expectation." See also Deloria, *Unexpected Places*, 3–4.

38. Quoted in Fogelson, "Analysis of Cherokee Sorcery," 126.

39. *MSMC*, vol. 1, Apr. 4, 1809, 311.

40. Fogelson, "Analysis of Cherokee Sorcery," 127.

41. Cumfer, *Separate Peoples*, 46.

42. Meriwether, *Expansion*, 177, 181.

43. John Vann to Thomas Brown, Dec. 7, 1742, Miscellaneous Records, Volume EE, 344, SCDAH.

44. Meriwether, *Expansion*, 160, 185.

45. Hatley, *Dividing Paths*, 98; Meriwether, *Expansion*, 162.

46. Easterby, ed., *Journal of the Commons House of Assembly, 1746–1747*, 45–50. Also see Robert Goudy v. John Vann, SCDAH.

47. Easterby, ed., *Journal of the Commons House of Assembly, 1745–1746*, 19–20.

48. Meriwether, *Expansion*, 196; Alden, *John Stuart*, 28.

49. Easterby, ed., *Journal of the Commons House of Assembly, 1745–1746*, 207–8; Deposition of James Maxwell, Esq., May 4, 1751, and James Francis to Governor Glen, Apr. 14, 1752, in McDowell, ed., *Documents Relating to Indian Affairs*, 116–18, 250–51; Meriwether, *Expansion*, 122. For more on Ninety Six, the town where John Vann lived, see Hatley, *Dividing Paths*, 85, and George, "Ninety Six Decoded."

50. Hatley, *Dividing Paths*, 182.

51. Meriwether, *Expansion*, 122.

52. Hicks, "Vann Family." John (the trader) Vann (James Vann's grandfather) was the son of John Vann (James Vann's great-grandfather). John (the trader) Vann had a brother named Edward Vann; both men appear in scattered references in the records of the South Carolina Archives. The Vanns' eighteenth-century genealogy is difficult to trace with certainty. Although I found Hicks's genealogy to be the most detailed, clear, and persuasive, it is not a fully confirmed or uniformly accepted account. I was not able to corroborate the name of John (the trader) Vann's wife or daughters. I was able to corroborate that John (the trader) Vann had a son named John Vann. See John Briant to John Vann, SCDAH. Note that James Vann's mother Wali Vann's first name is spelled multiple ways, such as Wa-li or Wah-li, in various sources. The notion that Wali Vann was half Cherokee (rather than "fully" Cherokee) is a matter of present-day dispute. The Vann House site interprets Wali as having had two Cherokee parents based on Vann, comp., "Vann Generations," 1, VHL, which names her as "WahLi (Polly Otterlifter)." "Vann Generations" gives Joseph Vann's (James Vann's father's) name as "John (alias Joseph) Vann," 3.

53. The South Carolina governor at the time was William Henry Lyttelton. See Hatley, *Dividing Paths*, 119–20, and Mooney, *Historical Sketch*, 26, 32–34.

54. Mooney, *Historical Sketch*, 34. For more on the effects of this war on the Cherokees, see Hatley, *Dividing Paths*, 155–66.

55. Mooney, *Historical Sketch*, 35.

56. Petition of Jo. Vann for 150 Acres, in Candler, ed., *Colonial Records of the State of Georgia*, 256, 404–5. Due to discrepancies and gaps in available records, concrete information about James Vann's parents' marriage and James's birth is lacking. Joseph Vann (James's father) came into Georgia in the early to mid-1760s, probably after the Cherokee War. Georgia colonial records place Joseph Vann on the Savannah River by 1766, with a wife and three children, but Moravian records indicate that James Vann was not born until 1768. According to Moravian accounts, James Vann was born in Georgia more than twenty-five miles away from the site of his future plantation and he showed the missionaries his birthplace in 1801. See "An Extract from the Journey of the Brethren Abr. Steiner and Th. Schweiniz," Oct. 15, 1801, MMD. The name Schweinitz is spelled Schweiniz in this Maelshagen translation.

The Moravian diary gives James's age as forty-one at his death in 1809, which would date his birth to 1768. See *MSMC*, vol. 1, Feb. 21, 1809, 302. In "Vann Family," Hicks gives James's birth year as 1766, one year off from John Howard Payne's assertion of James being forty-four upon his death in 1809. Neither of these dates is absolutely certain, though the Moravians' date was probably the closest to being accurate. The Cherokee name for James, Di-ga-lo-hi, is given in Hicks, "Vann Family." Hicks's updated, online version of this genealogical report gives the spelling as Ti-ka-lo-hi. As far as I could determine, the name does not appear in the other sources I examined. See *MSMC*, vol. 1, May 15, 1806, 103.

The Vanns originated from South Carolina, after having emigrated from Scotland. South Carolina documents indicate the presence of numerous Vann family members in the Edgeville and Abbeville districts in the mid-1700s through the mid-1800s. These are likely to have been members of the extended Vann family, but it is difficult to determine exactly where they fit into Cherokee James Vann's family tree. It is possible that a man named James Vann listed as owning a plot of land on Red Bank Creek in South Carolina in 1805 is Cherokee James Vann, but I do not believe this is the case, since this plot of land does not emerge in discussions of Cherokee James Vann's will, and since a South Carolina James Vann is listed as being involved in legal transactions in this same area for decades past Cherokee James Vann's death. See, for instance, South Carolina Judgment Roll, 1758; General Assembly Petition, Nov. 28, 1843; and John Pope, State Plats 2 (Red Bank River), Mar. 21, 1805, all in SCDAH.

57. Quoted in McLoughlin, *Cherokee Renascence*, 69.

58. Meigs to Crawford, Secretary of War, Apr. 14, 1816, Letters Received by the Secretary of War, Microfilm 221, Reel 70, National Archives and Records Administration, Southwest Branch, Fort Worth, Texas.

59. McLoughlin asserts the 15 percent figure in *Cherokee Renascence*, 69.

60. Gambold to Van Vleck, Apr. 22, 1816, SPML.

61. Perdue, *"Mixed-Blood" Indians*, 23. Cynthia Cumfer also argues that Cherokee women married white men to bring powerful allies into the community. See Cumfer, *Separate Peoples*, 35. Fay Yarbrough demonstrates that over time Cherokee women's agency in choosing intermarriage diminished. See Yarbrough, *Race and the Cherokee Nation*, 10, 11, 46, 62, 127–28.

62. Perdue, *"Mixed-Blood" Indians*, 25.

63. Gambold to Reichel, Aug. 4, 1810, SPML.

64. Philippe, *Diary*, 77.

65. Mooney, *Historical Sketch*, 73.

66. Meriwether, *Expansion*, 173; McLoughlin, *Cherokee Renascence*, 31.

67. McLoughlin, *Cherokee Renascence*, 3, 6.

68. Quoted in ibid., 3.

69. Meriwether, *Expansion*, 164.

70. McLoughlin, *Cherokee Renascence*, 19; O'Donnell, *Southern Indians*, 13; Mooney, *Historical Sketch*, 35.

71. M. A. H. Corners, Historical Traditions of Tennessee, MS, captivity of Jane Brown and her family, 1851, 12, Ayer Collection, Newberry Library, Chicago, IL.

72. Hagy and Folmsbee, eds., "Lost Archives," 122; McLoughlin, *Cherokee Renascence*, 19; Cumfer, *Separate Peoples*, 28.

73. Alden, *John Stuart*, 283; as the employee of Augusta merchant Andrew Mc-Clean, Vann had been appointed interpreter to the Cherokees but then was fired from this post (ibid., 292 n. 36); Ramsey, *Annals*, 120–21; Brown, *Old Frontiers*, 6; Bell, *Chief James*, 20.

74. Quoted in O'Donnell, *Southern Indians*, 13.

75. Hagy and Folmsbee, eds., "Lost Archives," 123.

76. O'Donnell, *Southern Indians*, 13.

77. Mooney, *Historical Sketch*, 35.

78. Taylor, *Divided Ground*, 8.

79. O'Donnell, *Southern Indians*, 37. For more on Indians and the American Revolution, see Calloway, *American Revolution*.

80. O'Donnell, *Southern Indians*, 41, 43.

81. Ibid., 43–49.

82. O'Donnell, "Southern Indians," 51.

83. Testimony of Two Cherokee Chiefs Relating to Nancy, A Cherokee Woman, Oct. 28, 1808, Cherokee Agency Records.

84. Narrative of Nancy, A Cherokee Woman, Nov. 24, 1801, Cherokee Agency Records.

85. Block, *Rape*, 81.

86. Ibid., 81, 84.

87. After a struggle that went on for seventeen years or more, neither Nancy nor her children achieved freedom at the behest of the Cherokee agent. For more on her case, see Miles, "Narrative of Nancy."

88. Richard Rowe, Nov. 28, 1829, Cherokee Boundary Papers, Record Group 75, Microfilm 234, Reel 73, National Archives and Records Administration Southwest Branch, Fort Worth, Texas. Rowe's relation to Vann is given in MMD, Oct. 1800.

89. McLoughlin, *Cherokee Renascence*, 19–20.

90. Ibid., 21; Treaty with the Cherokee: 1785, The Avalon Project at Yale Law School, New Haven, CT.

91. On the meaning of Echota town as a place of refuge, see Oochgeelogy Mission Diary, Nov. 20, 1827, MAS; the building of New Echota town is described in Gambolds to Benade, Oct. 16, 1823, SPML.

92. O'Donnell, *Southern Indians*, 52.

93. Corners, Historical Traditions of Tennessee, captivity of Jane Brown and her family; also recounted from the perspective of the Brown son, Joseph, in Ramsey, *Annals*, 509; Brown, *Old Frontiers*, 273.

94. A brief letter suggests that Vann may have been sought to help broker a peace in the post–Revolutionary War conflict. Governor Blount of Tennessee wrote to Leonard Shaw: "Speak to James Vann, and tell him, I depend on his exertions to restore peace and good order, which is the earnest wish of the United States" (Blount to Shaw, Jan. 8, 1793, 440, American State Papers, Documents, Legislative and Executive of the Congress of the United States, 1789–1815, vol. 4, Indian Affairs). The legendary attack on Cavet's Station during which Vann and Doublehead are said to have clashed took place eight months later, suggesting that Vann was involved in both peacemaking and war-making activities, as were some leaders in the Chickamauga resistance. For an alternative analysis of the Chickamauga resistance movement that attends to their peacemaking efforts and economic initiatives, see Cumfer, *Separate Peoples*, 54–55.

95. McLoughlin, *Cherokee Renascence*, 59.

96. Bell, *Chief James*, 33.

97. Ramsey, *Annals*, 272. A 1786 letter mentions "[a] Cherokee half breed by the name of Joe Vann" who gives information about the shooting of white intruders. This Vann could have been either Joe, as the name suggests, or his son James, as the racialized description suggests. See T. Barnard to Edward Telfair, Esq., Governor, Aug. 22, 1786 (Flint River), GDAH.

98. McLoughlin, *Cherokee Renascence*, 25.

99. Gambold to Reichel, Mar. 27, 1809, SPML; also in Gambold to Van Vleck, Sept. 26, 1821, SPML.

100. Gambold to Reichel, Mar. 27, 1809, SPML.

101. McLoughlin, *Cherokee Renascence*, 59; Cumfer, *Separate Peoples*, 29. McLoughlin and Cumfer both date this preservationist orientation of the Upper Towns to 1777.

102. Cumfer, *Separate Peoples*, 107.

103. It need be said that Vann was at odds with other leaders of the Upper Towns, such as John Lowrey, who advanced different versions of accommodationist prac-

tices. See Lowrey to Meigs, Feb. 8, 1808, Cherokee Agency Records; and Dearborn to Meigs, May 5, 1808, Cherokee Agency Records.

104. Justice, *Our Fire*, 15–16.

105. Gambold to Reichel, Nov. 19, 1805, SPML.

106. Lowrey to Meigs, Feb. 8, 1808, Cherokee Agency Records.

Chapter Two

1. Hicks, "Jennie Conrad Taylor Aniwaya," 1–3; Gambold, "Margaret Ann Crutchfield," 94; Betty, Peggy, and Sally Scott to Charles Goodwin, May 13, 1808, SCDAH. A reference to Walter Scott's salary as Cherokee agent appears in Shaw, *British Administration*, 187.

2. *MSMC*, vol. 1, July 2, 1810.

3. McLoughlin, *Cherokees and Missionaries*, 14.

4. Hawkins, "Benjamin Hawkins' Trip Across Georgia," 121, 122; Hill, "Weaving History," 119. Sally Waters's position as James Vann's aunt was confirmed by Cherokee historian and genealogist Jack Baker (conversation with Tiya Miles, July 2008, Springplace, GA).

5. Gambold to Reichel, Aug. 4, 1810, SPML.

6. MMD, Dec. 1801; "An Extract from the Journey of the Brethren Abr. Steiner and Th. Schweiniz," Oct. 8, 1800, MMD.

7. Norton, *Journal*, 68.

8. Gambolds to Van Vleck, June 12, 1820; Gambolds to Herbst, Nov. 10, 1810; Gambolds to Benzien, Dec. 19, 1810, SPML.

9. Gambolds to Brother Pete, Oct. 17, 1817, SPML.

10. Gambolds to Herbst, Nov. 10, 1810; Gambold to Benzien, Mar. 7, 1811, SPML. A power of attorney document refers to Peggy Scott and her sisters, Betty, Polly, and Sally, daughters of the "late Indian Trader" Walter Scott, as possessing "a certain tract of land of one hundred acres on Savannah River." The women had inherited this land from their father in 1802 and collected rents from it. James Vann and Charles Hicks were both witnesses to the appointment of Charles Goodwin as the sisters' attorney. Furthermore, this document, together with others in the South Carolina Archives, indicates that members of the nuclear Scott family and members of the extended Vann family had ties to the same area in the Edgefield District of South Carolina. See Betty, Peggy, and Sally Scott to Charles Goodwin, May 13, 1808, SCDAH. Mildred E. Whitmire cites this document in *Noland's Cherokee Diary*, 84, 90. See also Gambold, "Margaret Ann Crutchfield."

11. "An Extract from the Journey of the Brethren Abr. Steiner and Th. Schweiniz," Oct. 9, 1800, MMD.

12. Adair, *Adair's History*, 239, 240.

13. Jeremiah Evarts, "Letter from the Corresponding Secretary to the Prudential Committee," May 29, 1822, *Missionary Herald* (July 1822).

14. Norton, *Journal*, 66, 67.

15. Description of horse, no date, GDAH.

16. A. R. Gambold to Mrs. Benzien, July 22, 1806, SPML; *MSMC*, vol. 1, July, 2, 1810, 368–69.

17. Hamilton, "Minutes," 16:35.

18. Philippe, *Diary*, 75.

19. Alexandra Harmon ("American Indians and Land Monopolies," 4) argues that even as the Five Tribes (including Cherokees) valued collective landownership, they also had a habit "with ancient origins" of "growing crops on separate family plots." Although James Vann's actions placed him on the extreme margins of Cherokee agricultural practice, Harmon's observation suggests that the root of his enterprise — individualized agricultural pursuit — was not wholly foreign to Cherokee cultural practice.

20. Cynthia Cumfer (*Separate Peoples*, 121) points out that, paradoxically, the increase in white settlement in and around Cherokee territory created new markets for Cherokee farmers to sell their crops.

21. Range, *Century*, 4–6, 11–12.

22. Diagram of James Vann's plantation, about 1805, VHL; Norton, *Journal*, 66; Byhan to Gottlieb, Oct. 31, 1802, SPML; slave cabins with dirt floors: *MSMC*, vol. 1, Aug. 3, 1806, 119. Vann's mill was nearly completed by June of 1803, according to James McNare, who assisted in its construction. See Potter, ed., *Passports of Southeastern Pioneers*, 106.

23. Vannsville was the name of Vann's mercantile station adjacent to Diamond Hill. Because Vannsville was a trading center rather than a residential area, an 1809 Cherokee census numbered its population at 3. See McLoughlin, *Cherokee Renascence*, 169. Today, the area where Vann's plantation sits is known as historic Spring Place.

24. During the construction of a dam that would have flooded the area in 1954–55, Vann's Chattahoochee River tavern/inn was surveyed and relocated to the New Echota State Historic Site. See Caldwell and Caldwell, "Preliminary Report on the Vann House," National Anthropological Archives, Smithsonian Institution, Washington, DC.

25. Goulding, *Woodruff Stories*, 68–69.

26. Wohlfahrt to Benzien, Feb. 3, 1805, SPML; Vann to Meigs, June 20, 1804, Cherokee Agency Records.

27. David Brion Davis, *Inhuman Bondage*, 184.

28. Worth of Cherokee slaves: McLoughlin, *Cherokee Renascence*, 171, based on the Cherokee census of 1809. Example of approximate worth of Cherokee cabins: Polly Vann's houses at Vann's mill valued at $10, $12, $40, $60, in Valuations under the Treaty of 1828 Emigrations, 1833 and 1834, no. 69, Polly Vann, University of Tennessee Digital Library Database, University of Tennessee, Knoxville.

29. Gambold to Reichel, Mar. 27, 1809, SPML; McLoughlin, *Cherokee Renascence*, 181.

30. Baptist, "'Stol' and Fetched,'" 262; Berlin, *Generations*, 168.

31. The Cherokee Agency distributed a number of passports to whites relocating to Mississippi in the early 1800s; many of these travelers brought family members, slaves, and household furnishings. See Potter, ed., *Passports of Southeastern Pioneers*, 90, 91, 104, 119, 120.

32. Perdue, *Slavery and the Evolution of Cherokee Society*, 4–8; Perdue and Green, *Columbia Guide*, 60. While the indigenous ancestors of Cherokees, members of Mississippian chiefdoms in the southern Appalachian region, maintained hierarchical societies that likely included the longer-term bondage and subjugation of people we would describe as slaves, "Cherokees" (a nation that coalesced out of the remnants of these ancestral groups by the end of the 1600s) were not known to engage in such practices. Instead, Cherokees had relatively egalitarian social arrangements and an even distribution of property across households through the eighteenth century. Before the introduction of European racial slavery, Cherokees were unlikely to hold unfree people among them in large numbers or for long periods of time. See Perdue, *Slavery and the Evolution of Cherokee Society*, 4, 8; and Rodning, "Reconstructing the Coalescence of Cherokee Communities," 157–58, 172–73. Celia Naylor (*African Cherokees*, 7–12) offers a persuasive interpretation, different from my own, of the link between Cherokee war captives and Cherokee ownership of black slaves.

33. David Brion Davis, *Inhuman Bondage*, 3.

34. Descendants and genealogists of the Geiger family concur that this Valentine Geiger, Vann's clerk, was probably from Pennsylvania originally, having been descended from German immigrants. Another Valentine Geiger lived in Charleston in the early 1800s and worked as a merchant (Harriet Imrey, email exchange with Tiya Miles, Nov. 30, 2007; and Gerald Gieger, email exchange with Tiya Miles, Nov. 30, 2007).

35. Fisher, *American Instructor*, title page, iv. Moravian missionaries recorded seeing this book in Vann's library along with an unread New Testament and a navigational book. See "An Extract from the Journey of the Brethren Abr. Steiner and Th. Schweiniz," Oct. 10, 1800, MMD. On Geiger, see Hatley, *Dividing Paths*, 85. On Churchwell, see Gambold to Reichel and Benzien, Nov. 10, 1805, SPML.

36. Meigs to Hawkins, Aug. 2, 1803, Cherokee Agency Records.

37. Meigs to Dearborn, Oct. 25, 1803, Cherokee Agency Records. Before the agreement to build the road was reached, Vann purchased a wagon, angering the Cherokee Council members, who thought he had accepted a bribe. See McLoughlin, *Cherokee Renascence*, 77.

38. Meigs to Dearborn, Oct. 25, 1803, Cherokee Agency Records.

39. Ibid., Nov. 3, 1803.

40. Lovely to Meigs, Nov. 4, 1803, Cherokee Agency Records.

41. Evarts, "Letter."

42. Saunt, *New Order*, 155; Ethridge, *Creek Country*, 148, 155; Joel W. Martin, *Sacred Revolt*, 88; Braund, *Deerskins*, 184–85; Hawkins to Silas Dinsmoor, Apr. 15,

1797, in Hawkins, *Collected Works*, 122–23. On slaves on Hawkins's model plantation, see Hawkins, *Collected Works*, 10.

43. Cumfer, *Separate Peoples*, 26.

44. Byhan to Reichel, Dec. 5, 1806, SPML. William McLoughlin explains that the term "chief" was elastic at this moment in Cherokee history. "Young Chief" was sometimes used disparagingly by established Cherokee men to refer to prominent young men who rebelled against Cherokee leadership in the first few years of the nineteenth century. At the same time, "chief" was used to identify an influential, usually older person who was elected to the Cherokee Council. Over the course of the first decade of the nineteenth century, James Vann was described as a chief indirectly in the first usage in the writings of other Cherokees and directly in the second usage by Moravians referring to acts of the Cherokee Council. He was referred to as a chief in an ambiguous usage in a Cherokee Agency passport in 1805. His status shifted to one of recognition by the Cherokee Council as a chief in 1806. See McLoughlin, *Cherokee Renascence*, 111; Doublehead to Meigs, Oct. 3, 1806; Lowrey to Meigs, Oct. 23, 1806, Cherokee Agency Records; and Potter, ed., *Passports of Southeastern Pioneers*, 64–65.

45. McLoughlin, *Cherokee Renascence*, 125. The other most powerful man was Doublehead, also a chief in council.

46. Dearborn to Meigs, May 5, 1808, Cherokee Agency Records.

47. Norton, *Journal*, 68.

48. Sensbach, *Separate Canaan*, 19–24.

49. Ibid., 25–29, 43–45; Crews, *This We Most Certainly Believe*.

50. Crews, *Faith and Tears*; McLoughlin, *Cherokees and Missionaries*, 45–47; Payne Papers 5:49–52.

51. Sensbach, *Separate Canaan*, 37.

52. "An Extract from the Journey of the Brethren Abr. Steiner and Th. Schweiniz," Oct. 7, 1800, MMD.

53. Ibid.

54. Ibid., Oct. 15 and 16, 1800.

55. Vann offered to purchase Brown's (no first name given) plantation buildings and fields for the Moravians and then to sell it to them at no mark-up. When Abraham Steiner and Gottlieb Byhan arrived in 1801, they found that Vann had kept most of Brown's cultivated fields for himself, leaving only one for the mission. The Moravians named their mission Springplace, which had also been the name of Brown's farm. The town that grew up around the area is spelled Spring Place. See Schwarze, *History*, 56, 58, 63 n *, 65; and Hamilton, "Minutes," 15:9,10.

56. Payne Papers, 5:49–52.

57. Meigs to Reichel and Benzien, Dec. 29, 1802, Cherokee Agency Records.

58. MMD, Dec. 1801.

59. Schwarze, *History*, 63.

60. Steiner to Benzien, Aug. 18, 1801, SPML.

61. MMD, Jan. 15, 1801.

62. Ibid., Dec. 20, 1801, June 15, 1801.

63. Byhan to Reichel, Aug. 16, 1802, SPML.

64. MMD, June 30, 1801.

65. Ibid., Mar. 12 and 22, 1802, Jan. 1802. For more on the incorporation of fences and locks in southern Indian nations, see Saunt, *New Order*.

66. MMD, Aug. 1803.

67. Payne Papers, 5:49–52.

68. Vann to Steiner, June 15, 1803, SPML.

69. Hamilton, "Minutes," 15:29.

70. Vann to Steiner, June 15, 1803, SPML; Crews, *Faith and Tears*, 5.

71. Wohlfahrt to Benzien, Feb. 3, 1805, SPML.

72. Vann to Meigs, Dec. 28, 1801; Meigs to Vann, Jan. 28, 1802; Vann to Meigs, Feb. 5, 1802 (emphasis added), Cherokee Agency Records.

73. Vann to Meigs, May 3, 1802; Meigs to Vann, June 17, 1802, Cherokee Agency Records.

74. Vann to Meigs, Mar. 26, 1803, Cherokee Agency Records.

75. Meigs to Dearborn, Oct. 25, 1803, Cherokee Agency Records.

76. Ibid., quoted in McLoughlin, "James Vann," 52.

77. McLoughlin, "James Vann," 52.

78. Wattle and daub was also an African architectural method. Archaeologists studying Georgia coastal slave quarters have identified these earthen dwellings and categorized them as African in derivation. See Joseph, "African-American Life in Georgia," 104.

79. Hatley, *Dividing Paths*, 233.

80. MMD, June 1801.

81. Ibid., May 1802.

82. Ibid., Feb. 1802.

83. Ibid., Jan. 1802, July 1803, June 1803; SPMD, June 5, 1803.

84. MMD, July 1803; Hamilton, "Minutes," 15:22.

85. SPMD, July 20, 1803; also described in MMD, Aug. 1803.

86. Hamilton, "Minutes," 15:25.

87. SPMD, Aug. 31 and Sept. 1, 1803; Byhan to Reichel, Sept. 2, 1803, SPML.

88. Hamilton, "Minutes," 15:26–27.

89. SPMD, Jan. 14 and 16, 1804. Schneider later returned to Salem and oversaw the city's waterworks and forestry programs. See Fries, ed., *Records of the Moravians*, vol. 6, 2779.

90. Wohlfahrt to Benzien, Oct. 30, 1804; Feb. 3, 1805, SPML.

91. MMD, May 1802.

92. Byhan to Benzien, Apr. 7, 1805, SPML.

93. Vlach, *Back of the Big House*, 5.

94. SPMD, Aug. 15, 1805; Dec. 20, 1805.

95. Byhan to Benzien, Apr. 7 1805, SPML.

96. SPMD, May 29, 1803.

97. Vlach, *Back of the Big House*, 3.

98. *MSMC*, vol. 1, June 5, 1805, 55.

99. MMD, June 1801.

Chapter Three

1. Vlach, *Back of the Big House*, 77. The portrait of slave life in this chapter is drawn from Diamond Hill sources ranging between 1805 and 1829, a stretch of time that would be classified as the early antebellum period within two broad periods of American slavery separated by the Revolutionary War era: the colonial period (until 1770) and the antebellum period (1800–1865). See Kolchin, *American Slavery*, 28.

2. Norton, *Journal*, 68; Olmsted, *Cotton Kingdom*, 31.

3. Camp ("Pleasures of Resistance," 88) adapts this term from Edward Said's work.

4. Parish, *Slavery*, 67.

5. On the mill slave cabins, see Valuations under the Treaty of 1828 Emigrations, 1833 and 1834, no. 69, Polly Vann, University of Tennessee Digital Library Database, University of Tennessee, Knoxville. Vann House staff members have estimated a three-mile distance to the mill slave quarters. William Cotter, a resident of the area in the 1830s, wrote that Vann's slave quarters at Mill Creek were four miles away from the main house. See Cotter, *Autobiography*, 70.

6. Norton, *Journal*, 68. The year James Vann died, his son Joseph is listed as having 115 slaves. See McLoughlin, *Cherokee Renascence*, 174, table 6. See also Index of Black Slaves and Free Blacks on the Vann Plantation, VHL; and Appendix 2.

7. Vlach, *Back of the Big House*, 6.

8. Eaton, *Waning*, 26.

9. Norton, *Journal*, 60, 67–68; McLoughlin, *Cherokee Renascence*, 71, 73. Norton does not name the other largest slaveholder.

10. In 1823, commissioners from the state of Georgia presented a claim to the Cherokee Council for $80,000 for slaves stolen by Cherokees during the Revolutionary War. See J. R. Schmidt to Benade, Oct. 13, 1823, SPML.

11. Specific examples from Cherokee Nation records indicate a small exchange in slaves across national lines. The famous warrior Shoe Boots inherited slaves from a Creek. See Wilkins, *Cherokee Tragedy*, 61. Louis Philippe (*Diary*, 96–97) described an incident in which Cherokees stole slaves from a wealthy Euro-Chickasaw man (George Colbert) married to a Cherokee woman.

12. Major Wm. L. Lovely Account with James Vann (for 1804–1805), Cherokee Agency Records.

13. *MSMC*, vol. 1, May 1, 1813, 533.

14. Byhan to Benzien, Oct. 30, 1804, SPML.

15. Wohlfahrt to Benzien, Jan. 24, 1804, SPML.

16. Vann to Hooker, Esq., Nov. 5, 1802, Extract, Cherokee Agency Records.

17. *MSMC*, vol. 1, Mar. 9, 1805, 48.

18. It is important to note here that the vast majority of Cherokees did not engage in slaveholding or identify with the Cherokee planter class. (In 1835, 7.4 percent of Cherokees owned black slaves. See McLoughlin, *Cherokee Ghost Dance*, 228.) In addition, southern Indians who first adopted black slavery may have done so for reasons other than those espoused by white farmers and planters. Katja May has theorized, for instance, that in a context of U.S. pressure for Indian men to shift from hunting to farming and for Indian women to limit agricultural labor in favor of domestic work, placing black bondsmen in the fields was a way that Creeks could use black slavery to support the Creek cultural practice of keeping Indian men out of the fields to avoid pollution of the crops. See May, *African Americans and Native Americans*, 38–41.

19. Oakes, *Ruling Race*, 191.

20. *MSMC*, vol. 1, Sept. 22, Oct. 1, Nov. 7, Nov. 9, 1808, 282–84, 289; Gambold to Reichel, Sept. 30, 1808, SPML; Gambolds to Reichel, Nov. 9, 1808, SPML.

21. Hall, *Slavery*, 80–81; Gomez, *Country Marks*, 40; *MSMC*, vol. 1, Nov. 25, 1810, 393; June, 7, 1811, 435; and Wohlfahrt to Benzien, Feb. 3, 1805, SPML. The *Louisa* and *Hiram* slave ships originated in Rhode Island and sold Africans in Charleston between July and December of 1805. See Slave Voyages Database, Voyage 36812 and Voyage 36815. It was common practice for slaveholders not to furnish slaves with shoes for most or all of the year and to provide wooden brogans (heavy work shoes) in the winter months. See Camp, *Closer to Freedom*, 84–85.

22. Slave names: Berlin, *Generations*, 54; *MSMC*, vol. 1, July 9, 1806, 114.

23. *MSMC*, vol. 1, Nov. 25, 1810, 393; July 9, 1806, 113–14; June 7, 1811, 435; June 28, 1812, 492; May 11, 1813, 537; Gambolds to Van Vleck, May 12, 1813, SPML.

24. Berlin, *Generations*, 161–63.

25. *MSMC*, vol. 1, Apr. 3, 1808, 257; Sept. 22, 1808, 282; Gambold to Reichel, Apr. 28, 1808, SPML.

26. Gambolds to Van Vleck, May 14, 1819, SPML.
Before the mid-1700s evangelical awakenings, few black slaves experienced Christian conversion. The first significant inroads of Christianity into enslaved black communities did not occur until 1790–1830, with the development of the black church. For more on the long-standing disinterest in Christianity on the part of many black slaves, see Gomez, *Country Marks*, 245–56.

27. According to Jon Sensbach, "White Moravians had no moral objection to the institution of slavery." But they did believe that Christianity required "more humanitarian treatment of slaves." In the earliest years of Moravian history in North Carolina, the Moravian leadership frowned on the individual ownership of black slaves, fearing competition for white laborers, although the church itself could own blacks. Over time, church leaders permitted Moravians in outlying settlements to own slaves, and in the 1820s and 1830s, Moravians in the town of Salem could do

the same. The Moravian Church of North Carolina made its first purchase of a slave in 1769. See Sensbach, *African-Americans in Salem*, 10–11; and Crews, *Neither Slave nor Free*, 2–7. C. Daniel Crews, historian and director of the Moravian Archives Southern Province, has a slightly different view from Sensbach, arguing that Moravians "shunned the practice" of slaveholding at first. Enslaved blacks could become church members and worship alongside of white Moravians in the eighteenth century. By 1789, however, white Moravians began to espouse the principle of racial segregation, which they enacted in the early 1800s. By 1815, they had separated worship services and segregated burial grounds. See Crews, *Neither Slave nor Free*, 3–7.

28. Protocol of the Helpers' Conference, Apr. 10, 1805, MAS.

29. Ibid., Sept. 12, 1805; "Reports of the Christian Ludwig Benzien."

30. Protocol of the Helpers' Conference, Mar. 1805, MAS; Simon, "Saved."

31. McKinley, "Anna Rosina," 67–70; Gambold, "List of Plants"; Sigourney, *Traits*, 280.

32. Reichel, Benzie, and Peter to Meigs, Sept. 16, 1805, SPML.

33. Gambold to Benzien, Oct. 24, 1805, SPML.

34. "Letters from Christian Lewis Benzien to Members of the Unity Elders Conference, 1805 [A Few Extracts Translated]," Dec. 21, 1805, 2827, MAS.

35. Moravian letters suggest that Pleasant did not wish to birth this new baby, suggestive, if true, of sexual assault and the likelihood that she had a preexisting family. The Gambolds write judgmentally that Pleasant tried to hide her pregnancy, claiming she only had dropsy, and that she attempted to procure a medicine that she knew could harm the fetus. It must be noted that the Gambolds made these accusations in a letter in which they tried to justify their beating and sale of Pleasant's teenage son. See Gambolds to Van Vleck, May 14, 1819, SPML.

36. Gambold to Benzien, Sept. 28, 1806, SPML.

37. Hamilton, "Minutes," 16:50. For a keen analysis of motivations for descriptions such as this one of enslaved women by their mistresses, see Glymph, *House of Bondage*, 66–67.

38. Gambolds to "My dearly beloved Brother and Sister," May 20, 1811, SPML.

39. Byhan to Schultz, Jan. 14, 1828, SPML.

40. Camp, *Closer to Freedom*, 94.

41. Wohlfahrt to Benzien, Jan. 24, 1804, SPML; Gambolds to Reichel, Nov. 19, 1805, SPML.

42. Figures for the eight richest families (defined as owning ten or more slaves) are adapted from William McLoughlin's table 6, compiled with Agent Meig's 1809 census figures, in *Cherokee Renascence*, 170, 174. The 1835 census figures are taken from McLoughlin, *Cherokee Renascence*, 233, 234, table 1-A, 240.

43. Parish, *Slavery*, 5. David Brion Davis summarizes that "over half the slaves in the American South belonged to owners who held twenty or more slaves; one-quarter belonged to productive units of more than fifty slaves" (*Inhuman Bondage*, 198). Peter Kolchin (*American Slavery*, 100–101) emphasizes that most slaves lived on modest holdings where owners held fewer than fifty slaves but that holdings tended

to be higher in the Georgia and South Carolina low country and along the Mississippi River.

44. Norton, *Journal*, 147.

45. Senegambia: Gomez, *Country Marks*, 40; Suniger (Christian) Jacob: SPMD,
Mar. 28, 1817, July 29, 1827, Dec. 8. 1829; Schmidt to Schultz, July 2, July 30, 1827,
SPML; Crews, *Faith and Tears*, 55; Tjamba/Kassenti: Beltran ("Tribal Origins," 287)
locates the Kassenti in the Dagomba territory north of the Ashanti in West Africa.
Although Suniger appears to be a Dutch name, indicating a Dutch slavery back-
ground for Jacob, Johnson ("West African Reflection," 79) mentions the Kassenti
as one ethnic group transported to the Danish West Indies. Dagomba in Ghana:
Warren Whatley, email exchange with Tiya Miles, Nov. 10, 2008.

46. *MSMC*, vol. 2, July 3, 1814, 25.

47. MMD, Apr. 1802; *MSMC*, vol. 1, Jan. 31, 1805, 43; *MSMC*, vol. 1, Mar. 5, 1805,
47.

48. SPMD, May 28, 1802.

49. *MSMC*, vol. 1, July 16, 1806, 115.

50. SPMD, June 1 and 11, 1802.

51. Coyeetoyhee's complaint of having his slaves forcibly taken from him by a man
called Col. Brown, Dec. 23, 1815; and Glass letter to Meigs, relating to Negroes taken
by Col. Brown, Jan. 22, 1814, Special File 104 (claims for losses suffered by Cherokee
Indians, 1811–24, particularly during the War of 1812), Special Files of the Office of
Indian Affairs, 1807–1904, Microfilm M574, National Archives and Records Administration, Washington, DC. Although a group of prominent Cherokee men supported Coyeetoyhee's case with a letter to Meigs, there is no indication that Sarah
and her children were returned to the Cherokee Nation. The names of Coyeetoyhee's
and Sarah's children were Jenny, Lucy, Takinney, Nawchoee, Tennenolee, Wahkuck-
tiskee, and Ammayeuhah.

52. Gambold to Schultz, Oochgeelogy, Aug. 22, 1826, SPML.

53. Meigs to McNair and Taylor, Sept. 12, 1819, Cherokee Agency Records.

54. Ibid. It is not clear where Sarah Saunders Vann fits in the Vann family tree.
She is not noted as the wife of any of the known sons of James Vann. The last name
Saunders is also spelled Sanders in the available sources. The Saunders/Sanders
family line in Emmet Starr's "Old Families and Their Genealogy," includes a Sallie
(often a nickname for Sarah) Sanders who had no recorded husband or children.
The links I am making here are purely speculative in nature—but this Sallie Sanders
could have been the Sarah Saunders Vann of the Cherokee Agency record. It is
possible that an intimate relationship with a black or Afro-Cherokee man would
have gone unrecorded in family genealogy. This Sallie of Starr's "Old Families" was
a fourth-generation Sanders, the child of Thomas Sanders and Nannie Sonicooie,
the grandchild of Alexander Sanders and Peggy Sonicooie. Several members of the
Saunders family were involved in Cherokee constitutional convention work, as was
Joseph Vann. Alexander Saunders was the former good friend of James Vann believed

to have been involved in James Vann's death. These last details are further indications that Sallie (assumed in this scenario to be the same as Sarah of the Cherokee Agency record) would have had links to Diamond Hill through her family connections. See Starr, *History of the Cherokee Indians*, 51 (constitutional convention), 303 (key to genealogy), 374–76 (Sanders family; "Sallie" appears on 376). Saunders/Sanders search: *Census Roll, 1835, of the Cherokee Indians*, 38, 39, 45. George, John, and Sam Saunders of Talking Rock, who would have been Sallie's contemporaries in the Saunders family, owned a total of twenty-four slaves (p. 39). Tom Sanders, perhaps Sallie's father, is listed as living with two boys, three girls, and two adult women in 1835 (p. 45).

55. For more evidence on sexual relations between Cherokee owners and black slaves, see Minges, ed., *Black Indian Slave Narratives*; Naylor, *African Cherokees*; Yarbrough, *Race and the Cherokee Nation*; Miles, *Ties That Bind*; Miles, "Narrative of Nancy."

56. Gambold to Reichel, Aug. 6, 1806, SPML; *MSMC*, vol. 1 Aug. 3 and 10, 1806, 118, 121; *MSMC*, vol. 1, Aug. 6, 1806, 120–21. There are several interesting stories about free blacks in the Springplace Mission Diary. In 1815, a free woman named Milly sought refuge at the mission because she and her child had been kidnapped by a white man (see *MSMC*, vol. 2, Jan. 9, 1815, 54). Another free black woman married to a white man came to seek placement for her children at the mission school. She was told the school was for Indian children only (see *MSMC*, vol. 2, Apr. 2 and July 21, 1816, 111, 126).

57. *Laws of the Cherokee Nation*, Nov. 1, 1819, Nov. 11, 1824, 8–9, 39.

58. Gambold to Benzien, July 1, 1802, SPML; *MSMC*, vol. 1, June 8, 1806, 108.

59. Penningroth, "My People, My People," 172.

60. SPMD, Oct. 14, 1803.

61. *MSMC*, vol. 1, Dec. 26, 1805, 78. Cherokee laws bear out this conclusion, since no law forbade slaves' possession of firearms prior to Removal.

62. *MSMC*, vol. 1, Dec. 25, 1806, 152; *MSMC*, vol. 1, Dec. 26, 1806, 153.

63. Camp, *Closer to Freedom*, 69–70, 84, 78–83, 75–76, 87–89.

64. *MSMC*, vol. 2, Nov. 9, 1817, 185.

65. Naylor, *African Cherokees*, 52.

66. J. Gambold to Benzien, June 28, 1806, SPML; A. R. Gambold to Mrs. Benzien, July 22, 1806, SPML.

67. A. R. Gambold to Mrs. Benzien, July 22, 1806, SPML.

68. Gambolds to Benzien, May 25, 1806, SPML.

69. *MSMC*, vol. 1, May 11, 1806, 101.

70. A. R. Gambold to Mrs. Benzien, July 22, 1806, SPML.

71. *MSMC*, vol. 1, Oct. 15, 1806, 136.

72. MMD, Jan. 1807; *MSMC*, vol. 1, Jan. 10, 1807, 158.

73. *MSMC*, vol. 1, May 12, 1813, 537.

74. Byhan to Benzien, July 22, 1806, SPML.

75. *MSMC*, vol. 1, Nov. 24 and 25, 1810, 393; Jan. 20, 1811, 409.

76. *MSMC*, vol. 1, Nov. 15, 1813, 570.

77. SPMD, Oct. 18, 1804. Moravian records describe these departed slaves as having "run away." They do not indicate whether such escapes were meant to be temporary, as in acts of truancy, or permanent, but contextual circumstances indicate that most of these runaways did not plan to return.

78. *MSMC*, vol. 1, Sept. 25, 1814, 37.

79. *MSMC*, vol. 1, July 11, 1812, 494.

80. Bibb, "Narrative," 14.

81. SPMD, July 22 and 29, 1802; SPMD, Sept. 27, 1802; MMD, Sept. 1802.

82. Negro Paul to Meigs, July 29, 1805, Cherokee Agency Records.

83. *MSMC*, vol. 1, May 10, 1809, 314.

84. *MSMC*, vol. 2, Aug. 30, 1818, 236. The diary identifies this cousin as Wali Vann's sister's son.

85. Oochgeelogy Mission Diary, Apr. 14, 1822, MAS.

86. Vlach, *Back of the Big House*, 236.

87. Gomez, *Country Marks*, 4, 18, 20, 23, table 2.5.

88. Blassingame, *Slave Community*, 48.

89. Stuckey, *Slave Culture*, ix.

90. Pompey: *MSMC*, vol. 1, Nov. 4, 1810, 390.

91. Crawje: *MSMC*, vol. 1, Feb. 20, 1811, 414; Betty: *MSMC*, vol. 1, Feb. 20, 1811, 415; two old women: "Extract of a Latter [*sic*] from Anna Rosina Gambold."

92. Kolchin, *American Slavery*, 143. Berlin, *Generations*, 74, 117–18, 193–94.

93. Chireau, *Black Magic*, 37. See also Raboteau, *Slave Religion*, 4.

94. Kolchin, *American Slavery*, 55–56; Berlin, *Generations*, 206–7.

95. Schmidt to Schultz, July 30, 1827, SPML.

96. Chireau, *Black Magic*, 33.

97. *MSMC*, vol. 1, Dec. 29, 1811, 464.

98. Raboteau, *Slave Religion*, 275; Blassingame, *Slave Community*, 114; Chireau, *Black Magic*, 43, 56–57.

99. *MSMC*, vol. 1, Nov. 24, 1811, 458; Chireau, *Black Magic*, 7–8.

100. Raboteau, *Slave Religion*, 15; Stuckey, *Slave Culture*, 25; Philip Morgan, *Slave Counterpoint*, 581.

101. *MSMC*, vol. 2, Jan. 1, 1815, 53; Dec. 25, 1816, 142.

102. Raboteau, *Slave Religion*, 65; Philip Morgan, *Slave Counterpoint*, 582.

103. Raboteau, *Slave Religion*, 222.

104. Quoted in Stuckey, *Slave Culture*, 21.

105. *MSMC*, vol. 2, Dec. 25, 1818, 255.

106. *MSMC*, vol. 1, Dec. 24, 1805, 78.

107. Stuckey, *Slave Culture*, 16; Raboteau, *Slave Religion*, 68–72.

108. Raboteau (*Slave Religion*, 212–18) relates that black slaves referred to these secret wooded places as "hush harbors." Stuckey, *Slave Culture*, 24.

109. *MSMC*, vol. 1, Apr. 10, 1805, 50.

110. Levine, *Black Culture*.

111. Raboteau, *Slave Religion*, 12; Stuckey, *Slave Culture*, 87; Blassingame, *Slave Community*, 39.

112. James, "Mothering," 48.

113. Raboteau, *Slave Religion*, 59.

114. Ibid., 80.

115. Hopkins, *Down, Up, and Over*, 109–16; Creel, *Peculiar People*, 52–56; "God and Maker": Margaret Scott to Benziens, Feb. 13, 1811, SPML; "The Great Man in the sky": *MSMC*, vol. 1, May 20, 1810, 360; Hatley, *Dividing Paths*, 12; McLoughlin, *Cherokee Renascence*, 178; Mooney, *Myths*, 239–61, 311–49; Raboteau, *Slave Religion*, 8. The notion of parallel worlds of the living and the dead appears in Kongo and Yoruba belief systems. See Chireau, *Black Magic*, 37. See also on Kongo beliefs Gomez, *Country Marks*, 148–49; and Ferguson, "'Cross Is a Magic Sign,'" 118–19. Theda Perdue (*Slavery and the Evolution of Cherokee Society*, 42–44) discusses general cultural similarities (animal symbolism, disinterest in materialism, kinship, pre-European slavery forms) between Cherokees and African-descended slaves.

116. Hatley, *Dividing Paths*, 12. Belief in witchcraft is discussed in MMD, Jan. 15, 1801. Cherokee weather conjurations are discussed in *MSMC*, vol. 1, Mar. 1, 1812, 477; and Hatley, *Dividing Paths*, 12. See also Jack Kilpatrick, "Cherokee Conjuration."

117. Herskovits, *Myth of the Negro Past*, 106–7; also cited in Stuckey, *Slave Culture*, 15. Blassingame (*Slave Community*, 40) mentions slaves in South Carolina who believed springs and fountains were inhabited by a guardian spirit. Trader James Adair wrote about Cherokees: "They are also strongly attached to rivers, — all retaining the opinion of the ancients, that rivers are necessary to constitute a paradise. Nor is it only ornamental, but likewise beneficial to them, on account of purifying themselves" (Adair, *Adair's History*, 239). See Mooney (*Myths*, 24, 426) on the Cherokee "river god" and reverence for streams. For a discussion of rivers regarding the ceremonial immersion of infants, see Perdue, *Cherokee Women*, 32–33. Also see enchanted lake and whirlpool stories in Mooney, *Myths*, 321–322, 347.

118. The enslaved men Gander and Ben were both noted by the missionaries as having two wives. Gomez's description of Kongo gender relations (*Country Marks*, 144) is also relevant here, as Kongo practices of female agricultural work and male hunting, as well as communal landownership by clans, resonated with Cherokee practices.

119. Camp and Baptist, "Introduction," 5.

120. Vlach, *Back of the Big House*, 33.

121. Berlin, *Generations*, 75.

122. *MSMC*, vol. 1, Oct. 29, 1806, 137; Gambolds to Mrs. Benzien, July 22, 1806, cited in *MSMC*, vol. 1, 612 n. 61; *MSMC*, vol. 1, June 13, 1808, 270. Given Grace's age, George may have been a grandson or an adopted son.

123. *MSMC*, vol. 1, Sept. 30, 1806, 134.

124. *MSMC*, vol. 2, Jan. 6, 1816, 100.

125. *MSMC*, vol. 1, May 27, 1809, 317.

126. *MSMC*, vol. 2, Apr. 30, 1820, 352; Timberlake, *Memoirs*, 103; Perdue, *Cherokee*, 20.

127. *MSMC*, vol. 1, Jan. 1, 1806, 81; *MSMC*, vol. 1, Dec. 26, 1806, 153–54.

128. Blacks and whites in the nineteenth-century white slaveholding South did share a physical intimacy due to the living arrangements on some farms and small plantations and due to the need to have black slave labor close at hand. They also interacted socially in circumscribed ways. For instance, masters and slaves attended church together in the mid-1800s, most commonly with segregated seating in Protestant congregations. See Raboteau, *Slave Religion*, 208, 273. Masters sometimes hosted parties for slaves or observed slave festivities, in part to demonstrate their largesse or to monitor the slaves' activities. See Camp, "Pleasures of Resistance," 94–95. Blacks and poor whites, especially in urban areas, shared genuine social space to a much greater degree than blacks and wealthy whites, spending time together in what Victoria Bynum has called a "subculture of poverty" and an "interracial subculture." See Bynum, *Unruly Women*, 46–47; and Kolchin, *American Slavery*, 305, 416. However, positive social interactions between blacks and poor whites had significantly diminished by 1800. See Kolchin, *American Slavery*, 310. The relations between blacks and Cherokees on Diamond Hill mirrored some of these interactions, but they also stand out for the extent and kind of socializing that occurred between black slaves and members of the Cherokee slaveholding elite. As Ira Berlin indicates, white elites had begun to emphasize social distance from black slaves by the early eighteenth century. See Berlin, *Generations*, 59.

129. Gambolds to Van Vleck, June 21, 1816, SPML; *MSMC*, vol. 2, Sept. 21, 1817, 176.

130. Gambolds to Van Vleck, Dec. 29, 1817, SPML.

131. Grace and Wali: *MSMC*, vol. 1, Sept. 24, 1809, 332; *MSMC*, vol. 1, Sept. 8, 1811, 448; *MSMC*, vol. 1, Mar. 3, 1811, 418.

132. *MSMC*, vol. 1, Dec. 21, 1805, 77.

133. *MSMC*, vol. 2, Feb. 12, 1815, 56.

134. *MSMC*, vol. 1, Aug. 10, 1811, 445.

135. Gambold to Van Vleck, Dec. 28, 1814, SPML, cited in *MSMC*, vol. 2, notes, 510; *MSMC*, vol. 2, Dec. 25 and 28, 1814, 48–49.

136. *MSMC*, vol. 2, Dec. 6, 1816, 140; *MSMC*, vol. 2, Dec. 25, 1817, 192.

137. MMD, Oct. 1803; Schwarze, *History*, 121–22.

138. Celia Naylor-Ojurongbe ("'Born and Raised,'" 169–73) and Gary Zellar (*African Creeks*, 257) have found evidence in the WPA narratives and other firsthand accounts of Indian-owned black slaves in Indian territory becoming proficient in indigenous healing practices.

139. Bunyan, *Pilgrim's Progress*, 29.

Chapter Four

1. Tom Hatley (*Dividing Paths*, 233) discusses this contraction of Cherokee women's roles due to plantation slavery. He also offers the interesting interpretation that with the adoption of plantation slavery that placed blacks in the fields that had long been under Cherokee women's care, women maintained their traditional function of controlling the fates of captives. While I do not agree that Cherokee mistresses held this much control over the slave labor force, I appreciate Hatley's related insight that because of black slave labor, Cherokee men did not fully take over women's fields, and this may have been a (limited) "tactical victory" for Cherokee women.

2. Ibid.

3. *MSMC*, vol. 1, June 18 and 19, 1805, 57.

4. *MSMC*, vol. 1, Feb. 2, 1805, 43; *MSMC*, vol. 1, June 17 and 20, 1805, 57; *MSMC*, vol. 1, Aug. 13, 1805, 62.

5. Demas was a slave owned by Wali Vann. James accused Demas of stealing oxen, imprisoned Demas in his home, and then forced Demas to work in his fields. Demas was innocent of the crime. See *MSMC*, vol. 1, Feb. 11, 14, and 15, 1807, 166–68.

6. Perdue, *Cherokee Women*, 25, 44–46, 56–58; Perdue, *"Mixed-Blood" Indians*, 14–15, 23–24; Miles, *Ties That Bind*, 52–54. In an exception to most observations about Cherokee women's freedom in choosing sexual partners, eighteenth-century trader James Adair wrote that he once witnessed a woman punished for serial adultery by having to suffer a group rape by over fifty men. If this incident did occur, it is certainly an extreme and anomalous example of gender violence in the 1700s. See Adair, *Adair's History*, 153.

7. Fogelson, "'Petticoat Government,'" 170.

8. Bartram, "Observations on the Creek and Cherokee Indians," 31.

9. Cox, *Traveling South*, 43–44, 53; Bartram, *Travels*, 357–58.

10. Longe, "Small Postcript," 30.

11. Perhaps another way to come at this question is to note the absence of domestic abuse in observational accounts. White male observers of Cherokee gender norms were quick to judge what they viewed as abnormal or "savage" behaviors. They did not withhold, for instance, their observation that Cherokee women were like "Amazons" because of their participation in warfare and council decisions, or their view that women did the majority of hard labor while Cherokee men enjoyed excessive leisure, or their sense that Cherokee gender roles were unnaturally reversed, or their conviction that Cherokee women possessed too much sexual freedom. See *MSMC*, vol. 1, Nov. 9, 1808, 289. These writers stood ready to record untoward relations between Indian women and men, in part because they viewed gender roles as a key indicator of the level of civilization a society had attained and an accurate measure of white and Indian difference. See Timberlake, *Memoirs*, 93 ("Amazons"); Adair, *Adair's History*, 153 (loose sexuality, "petticoat-government," "Amazons"); Philippe,

Diary, 71–73, 82 (loose sexuality, women's labor/men's leisure). These images of Indian women as promiscuous drudges are common in the writings of European men. See Shoemaker, introduction to *Negotiators of Change*, 2–3. Given this pattern, the fact that these writers did not document physical abuse of Cherokee women is a strong indication that they did not regularly observe it. For more on gendered interpretations of group difference, see Kathleen Brown, "Anglo-Algonquian Gender Frontier"; see also Jennifer L. Morgan, "'Some Could Suckle over Their Shoulder.'"

12. Perdue, *Cherokee Women*, 45, 179–80.

13. Carolyn Ross Johnston (*Cherokee Women in Crisis*, 77) argues that rates of both domestic violence and drunkenness increased in the aftermath of forced removal in 1838–39.

14. Bertram Wyatt-Brown (*Southern Honor*, 281) asserts that "alcoholics" tended to be "wife beaters" and that such behavior was probably more common in the South than in other regions. Victoria Bynum (*Unruly Women*, 83) also points to a societal "expectation" of drunkenness paired with spousal abuse in the South. For further examples of domestic abuse of white plantation mistresses, see Clinton, *Plantation Mistress*, 80–81; and Glymph, *House of Bondage*, 58–59.

15. *MSMC*, vol. 1, Mar. 15 and 21, 1813, 522, 524.

16. *MSMC*, vol. 2, June 18 and 19, 1815, 73–74. In 1815, Sarah Hicks, a Cherokee, was the victim of stranger violence. While walking through the woods, she was attacked by a "totally naked drunken Indian," who "struck her on her arms and shoulder with a thick cudgel" (*MSMC*, vol. 2, Mar. 26, 1815, 62).

17. *MSMC*, vol. 1, Oct. 24 and 25, 1807, 224–26. A family murder in 1817 was recorded by both Moravian and ABCFM missionaries. The Moravians wrote: "An Indian murdered his wife and three children. He had put the bodies in a potato cellar, shut the doors carefully, and went away" (*MSMC*, vol. 2, Feb. 10, 1817, 149). The ABCFM journal says: "An Indian on Highwasse [*sic*] river murdered his wife & children about a week since; supposed to be occasioned by a disagreement respecting removing over the Mississippi, he wishing to go, she not" (Phillips and Phillips, eds., *Brainerd Journal*, Feb. 13, 1817, 29). In addition to these examples of domestic violence, journalist John Howard Payne recorded that just prior to 1806, Doublehead, an adversary of James Vann's, had "married the sister of James Vann's wife" and "used her brutally." According to Payne, "Doublehead had beaten his wife cruelly when she was with child; and the poor woman died in consequence" (Payne Papers, 2:26–30). Also see note 58, this chapter.

18. *MSMC*, vol. 1, Jan. 16, 1808, 244. For more on southern planter norms of masculinity (gambling, drinking, violence), see Wyatt-Brown, *Southern Honor*, 281, 339–56; Clinton, *Plantation Mistress*, 105–7; and Fox-Genovese, *Plantation Household*, 200–202.

19. *MSMC*, vol. 1, Nov. 9, 1808, 289. The missionary recorder states that these words about Caty are "According to Mrs. Vann's own testimony."

20. Gambold, "Margaret Ann Crutchfield," 94.

21. Gambolds to Reichel, Nov. 9, 1808, SPML.

22. *MSMC*, vol. 1, Nov. 9, 1808, 289.

23. The Moravian diary indicates one example of domestic violence between black men and women in the slave quarters: "In a Negro house, where there was drinking until late in the night . . . one mistreated his wife by beating her in a quite barbaric way" (*MSMC*, vol. 1, Nov. 15, 1813, 569–70). The diary also includes one example of a Cherokee woman attacked by a black man. In 1815, Eley Hicks was at home alone when an enslaved "mulatto" entered, threatened to "cut [her] throat," and "tr[ied] to scare and abuse her." The man was startled by the cries of Eley's children and the footsteps of approaching neighbors. A group of Cherokees found the man at his master's house and "harshly punished" him. See *MSMC*, vol. 2, July 2, 1817, 166–67.

24. *MSMC*, vol. 1, Jan. 31 and Feb. 3, 1805, 43, 44.

25. *MSMC*, vol. 1, Feb. 15, 1807, 168. Wali Vann made this declaration after James had kidnapped the slave Demas.

26. Fox-Genovese, *Plantation Household*, 201; Olmsted, *Cotton Kingdom*, 555; Eaton, *Waning*, 27. For an enlightening discussion of southern violence and its relationship to slavery from the field of cultural psychology, see Nisbett and Cohen, *Culture of Honor*, 85, 1, 3.

27. David Brion Davis, *Inhuman Bondage*, 29, 32.

28. Glymph, *House of Bondage*, 33; *MSMC*, vol. 1, Aug. 25, 1813, 554; *MSMC*, vol. 1, Sept. 27, 1807, 216; *MSMC*, vol. 2, Aug. 1, 1817, 171.

29. David Brion Davis, *Inhuman Bondage*, 29.

30. *MSMC*, vol. 1, Aug. 28, 1805, 64.

31. Byers to Meigs, Aug. 28, 1805, Cherokee Agency Records; Potter, ed., *Passports of Southeastern Pioneers*, 82.

32. *MSMC*, vol. 1, Aug. 28, 1805, 64.

33. John Spencer or John Spring Confession, Sept. 14, 1805, Cherokee Agency Records; Mr. Joseph Boring Confession, Sept. 23, 1805, Cherokee Agency Records; on Isaac, see *MSMC*, vol. 1, Jan. 31, 1805, 43. April is named in MMD, Nov. 6, 1805, but in no other source. The Spencer confession lists Isaac, Bob, Peter, and a fourth man, Net, as the black men involved. Since no other "Net" is listed among the slaves of the Vann holdings, this was most likely a misspelling of Ned. However, the Boring confession does not name Ned and instead refers to Sam as the slave involved in the conspiracy who came to his home after the crime. Either Ned or Sam could have been the fourth black accomplice. A possible reason for the discrepancy could be that one of the Neds on the plantation, married to Renee, had a son named Sam. However, to the extent that we can infer from the missionary records the age and temperament of the two Neds owned by Vann, Chloe's husband Ned seems more likely than Renee's husband Ned to have involved himself in such a daring attempt.

34. Spencer Confession.

35. Spencer Confession; Boring Confession; Boring as Vann's overseer: *MSMC*, vol. 1, July 2, 1805, 59. In 1801, Joseph Boring had received a passport from Meigs to

travel through Cherokee territory on his way to Jackson County, Georgia; see Potter, ed., *Passports of Southeastern Pioneers*, 88. "Boring" is spelled "Bohring" in the Moravian diary.

36. Boring Confession.

37. *MSMC*, vol. 1, Oct. 20, 1805, 70.

38. Boring Confession.

39. Isaac and Bob: *MSMC*, vol. 1, Sept. 13, 15, 16, 28, 1805, 65–67; Peter: *MSMC*, vol. 1, Oct. 20 and Nov. 6, 1805, 70, 72; MMD, Nov. 6, 1805.

40. *MSMC*, vol. 1, Nov. 6, 1805, 72; Mrs. Wohlfahrt's narrative of Vann's treatment of a Miss Crawford, summer 1805, Cherokee Agency Records.

41. Gambold to Van Vleck, Sept. 26, 1821, SPML.

42. *MSMC*, vol. 1, Sept. 16, 21, 25, and 26, 1805, 66–67.

43. James Vann's letter sent with prisoners Spencer, alias Spring, and Boring, Sept. 27, 1805, Cherokee Agency Records.

44. Valentine Geiger's letter relative to a robbery on James Vann in September 1805, Cherokee Agency Records.

45. *MSMC*, vol. 1, Apr. 30, 1806, 98.

46. *MSMC*, vol. 1, Jan. 20, 1806, 83.

47. MMD, Oct. 1800; Wyatt-Brown, *Southern Honor*, 356, 167, 354. For more on the dueling ritual see Wyatt-Brown, *Southern Honor*, 350–56.

48. *MSMC*, vol. 1, May 15, 1806, 102–3. A rock wall, assumed to be the spot where Falling fell, is still intact at the Vann House Historic Site.

49. *MSMC*, vol. 1, May 15 and 16, 1806, 103–4.

50. *MSMC*, vol. 1, May 16, 1806, 104; Gambold to Reichel, May 30, 1806, SPML.

51. *MSMC*, vol. 1, May 15, 1806, 103; *MSMC*, vol. 1, Aug. 3, 1806, 118; Gambold to Reichel, May 30, 1806, SPML.

52. *MSMC*, vol. 1, May 31, 1806, 107; *MSMC*, vol. 1, July 9, 1806, 113.

53. *MSMC*, vol. 1, June 30, 1806, 112.

54. Meigs to Valentine Guyger [*sic*], June 6, 1806, Cherokee Agency Records.

55. *MSMC*, vol. 1, July 9, 1806, 113; *MSMC*, vol. 1, Nov. 26, 1806, 143.

56. Gambold to Benzien, Apr. 26, 1806, SPML.

57. Gambold to Van Vleck, Sept. 26, 1821, SPML.

58. Payne wrote that Doublehead had "married the sister of James Vann's wife" and "used her brutally" (Payne Papers, 2:26–30). Payne does not specify which wife of Vann is being referred to, but perhaps it is Jennie Doublehead Foster; also see note 17, this chapter.

59. Ibid. Vann, along with several other Cherokee leaders, was named in a group passport for travel to Washington, DC, "on their way to the seat of Government" in Oct. 1805. See Potter, ed., *Passports of Southeastern Pioneers*, 64–65.

60. McLoughlin, *Cherokee Renascence*, chaps. 4, 5, and 6, 105–6, 109–11, 124–27, 138; Doublehead's murder: *MSMC*, vol. 1, Aug. 12, 1807, 206.

61. Quoted in McLoughlin, *Cherokee Renascence*, 138–39.

62. *Laws of the Cherokee Nation*, Sept. 11, 1808, 3–4; McLoughlin, *Cherokee Renascence*, 139–40, 151.

63. McLoughlin, *Cherokee Renascence*, 45.

64. *MSMC*, vol. 1, Feb. 10, 1811, 411 n. 13, 637. McLoughlin discusses the role of this story in the Cherokee spiritual revival of 1811–12 in *Cherokee Renascence*, 178–80.

Chapter Five

1. *MSMC*, vol. 1, Apr. 28 and May 24, 1808, 261, 264.

2. *MSMC*, vol. 1, Feb. 8, 1809, 301.

3. *MSMC*, vol. 1, Feb. 21, 1809, 302. On Saunders as perpetrator: Gambold to Benzien, Feb. 23, 1809, SPML; *MSMC*, vol. 1, 628 n. 6; McLoughlin, *Cherokee Renascence*, 151; McLoughlin, "James Vann," 71; and Don Shadburn, interview with Tiya Miles, December 2007, Cumming, GA.

4. *MSMC*, vol. 1, Feb. 23, 1809, 303.

5. Gambold to Benzien, Feb. 23, 1809, SPML.

6. *MSMC*, vol. 1, Feb. 21 and 23, 1809; July 2, 1810; Mar. 17, 1809, 303, 368, 306.

7. Gambold to Reichel, Mar. 27, 1809, SPML; *MSMC*, vol. 1, Mar. 4, 1809, 304–5.

8. *MSMC*, vol. 1, Apr. 1, Aug. 28, Dec. 31, 1809, 310, 328, 341. Passion Week refers to the days between Palm Sunday and Easter Sunday.

9. *MSMC*, vol. 1, Mar. 4, 1809, 304; Gambold to Benzien, Feb. 23, 1809, SPML.

10. *MSMC*, vol. 1, Mar. 26, 1809, 308.

11. *MSMC*, vol. 1, July 9, 1809, 320. Pompey and Patience, both African-born, told the missionaries that African American slaves ridiculed and mistreated them. See *MSMC*, vol. 1, Nov. 4, 1810; June 7, 1811, 390, 435. Michael Gomez (*Country Marks*, 189–95) argues that examples of contempt for African slaves on the part of Afro-American slaves as described by white observers are sometimes misleading. In periods of the highest levels of importation of Africans, Afro-American slaves felt respect for their African peers. Expressions of disrespect or dislike for African slaves began to appear in the American-born black slave community by 1830, when numbers of African slaves had dwindled.

12. *MSMC*, vol. 1, July 10, 1809, 320–21.

13. *MSMC*, vol. 1, July 18, 1809; Aug. 6, 1809, 322, 324.

14. *MSMC*, vol. 1, Nov. 24, 1810, 392 n. 73, 635.

15. Ronald L. F. Davis, *Black Experience in Natchez*, 16, 18, 17.

16. Olmsted, *Cotton Kingdom*, 422, 415–34.

17. Berlin, *Generations*, 161; Baptist, "'Stol' and Fetched,'" 243–66.

18. Baptist, "'Stol' and Fetched,'" 259; *MSMC*, vol. 1, Nov. 24 and 25, 1810, 392–93. Big Jenny's husband was owned by the McNairs, Vann's daughter and son-in-law.

19. *MSMC*, vol. 1, May 16, 18, 25, 1806; June 8, 1806, 104, 105, 106.

20. Gambold to Benzien, June 28, 1806, SPML; *MSMC*, vol. 1, Aug. 29, 1806; Sept. 6, 1806; Sept 12, 1806, 126, 128, 129–30.

21. *MSMC*, vol. 1, Oct. 23, 1806; Dec. 25, 1806, 137, 152.

22. *MSMC*, vol. 1, Mar. 4, 1809; Apr. 9, 1809; May 31, 1810; Aug. 13, 1810, 304, 312, 362, 375.

23. Peggy's note to Joseph transcribed in *MSMC*, vol. 1, July 4, 1813, 544.

24. Gambold to Benzien, Sept. 14, 1810, SPML. The Gambolds reported to Rev. John Herbst, "Since her husband's death, she has made great effort to learn to read and write and got so far that she [wrote] a very sweet little letter in which she reported to the H.C.F.G. in Salem and described her heart's condition, especially since her baptism" (Gambolds to Herbst, Nov. 10, 1810, SPML). In an extensive footnote to her book-length poem *Traits of the Aborigines of America*, Lydia Howard Huntley Sigourney writes that Peggy Vann (Margaret Ann Crutchfield) was "taught to read and write by her benefactress," Anna Rosina Gambold. Sigourney and A. R. Gambold were correspondents. See Sigourney, *Traits*, 280–81 n. 10; and Gambold to Sigourney, June 7, 1824, Connecticut Historical Society, Hartford. A notation of Peggy's Bible reading is in Benzien to Scott, Nov. 15, 1810, SPML.

25. *MSMC*, vol. 1, Aug. 13, 1810; Aug. 23, 1810; Dec. 31, 1810; Aug. 23, 1810; Aug. 20, 1810, 376, 378, 401, 378; Scott to Benziens, Feb. 13, 1811, SPML.

26. *MSMC*, vol. 1, Apr. 1, 1810; Aug. 29, 1810; June 16, 1810, Aug. 30, 1810, 354, 365, 379–81.

27. *MSMC*, vol. 1, June 16, 1810, 365; Gambold to Reichel, Dec. 28, 1806, SPML; *MSMC*, vol. 1, Dec. 26, 1809, 340; Gambold to Reichel, Mar. 6, 1811, SPML.

28. Gambolds to Reichel, Sept. 15, 1810, SPML; *MSMC*, vol. 1, June 16, 1810; Aug. 29, 1810, 365, 380; Gambolds to Herbst, Nov. 10, 1810, SPML. Neither Vann House employees nor local historians have yet been able to locate Mountjoy. The fact that this name does not appear on any known Cherokee map as a town or settlement suggests that Peggy invented the name. Rowena McClinton has made the inference that the name Mountjoy was inspired by words written by Anna Rosina Gambold in her poem/travelogue of her missionary trip to Goshen, Ohio, with George Loskiel, for which she was employed as a recording secretary. She wrote: "Mountjoy's our halting place to-night" (Loskiel, *Extempore on a Wagon*, 11). Although Loskiel is listed as the author, scholars of Moravian history agree that Anna Rosina Gambold wrote this text.

29. *MSMC*, vol. 1, Aug. 20, 1810; Apr. 7, 1811; Dec. 31, 1811, 377, 424, 465; Gambolds to Herbst, Nov. 10, 1810, SPML.

30. Elrod, *Historical Notes on Jackson County, Georgia*.

31. Jackson County, Georgia, Early Court Records, 66–67. Interestingly, James Vann filed his will in the same year that Peggy Vann and her sisters assigned a new attorney to oversee their inherited property in South Carolina. It is possible that James Vann, who was a witness to the sisters' document, suggested that Peggy take this step as part of a larger process of legalizing the family's property holdings in the white courts. See Betty, Peggy, and Sally Scott to Charles Goodwin, May 13, 1808, SCDAH.

32. In addition to his more famous ferry on the Chattahoochee River, Vann had a ferry on the Hightower River. Richard Rowe, Nov. 28, 1829, Cherokee Boundary

Papers, Record Group 75, Microfilm 234, Reel 73, National Archives and Records Administration, Southwest Branch, Fort Worth, Texas: "From the shallow ford to the hightower is about 25 miles and the ford is about 40 miles below Vanns ferry on that river."

33. Jackson County, Georgia, Early Court Records, 65–66.

34. Ibid.

35. Ibid.

36. *MSMC*, vol. 1, Dec. 26, 1809, 340; Gambolds to Reichel, Nov. 18, 1810; Gambold to Reichel, Mar. 27, 1809; *MSMC*, vol. 1, May 1, 1813, 533 n. 47, 645; Gambold to Benzien, June 24, 1809, SPML. Beyond John Gambold's summaries, Vann's estate papers have not been preserved.

37. This $30,000 figure for the value of Vann's human property is based on a conservative calculation of one hundred slaves valued at $300 each. This calculation follows the formula of the 1809 statistical survey of the Cherokee Nation conducted by the Cherokee Agency, which used a $300 value per slave and concluded that the 583 slaves in the Nation at that time were valued at $174,900. See McLoughlin, *Cherokee Renascence*, 171. Joseph Vann inherited 115 slaves from his father in 1809. See McLoughlin, *Cherokee Renascence*, 174, table 6.

38. *MSMC*, vol. 1, Dec. 31, 1809, 341.

39. McLoughlin, *Cherokee Renascence*, 178–79.

40. *MSMC*, vol. 1, Feb. 10, 1811, 411; McLoughlin, *Cherokee Renascence*, 179–81.

41. *MSMC*, vol. 1, Aug. 29, 1810; May 2, 1811, 380, 429. In letters protesting Cherokee removal, Peggy Scott espoused a sovereigntist ethos. See, for example, "Letter from a Cherokee Woman," *Missionary Herald*, Apr. 1819. For a fuller discussion of Scott's political views, see Miles, "'Circular' Reasoning."

42. *MSMC*, vol. 1, Apr. 26, 1811; May 2 and May 5, 1811, 427, 430; Gambolds to "My dearly beloved Brother and Sister," May 20, 1811, SPML. The elderly Grace and her husband, Jacob, were two members of the black community who attended the Moravians services regularly and despaired to see the missionaries go. See *MSMC*, vol. 1, May 2, 1811, 429.

43. *MSMC*, vol. 1, Feb. 28, 1811; May 2, 1811, 416–17, 429; McLoughlin, *Cherokee Renascence*, 181–82.

44. *MSMC*, vol. 1, May 23, 1811, 433. Because of her Christian convictions, Peggy Scott was skeptical about the rainmaker's purported power (see *MSMC*, vol. 1, July 28, 1811, 442–43). The ABCFM Brainerd Mission Diary includes a description of Cherokee rainmaking protocols: "In making rain, seven men or women are chosen to represent the clan, who keep fast during the time the conjurer is about to obtain rain; and when the rain comes he sacrifices the tongue of a deer which is procured for that purpose. The conjurer himself observes a strict fast, with frequent bathing, during the time he is making rain. On such occasions, the conjurer speaks a language different from the present language of the nation, and which few understand" (Phillips and Phillips, eds., *Brainerd Journal*, Apr. 16, 1818, 55).

45. "Mississippi Valley — Whole Lotta Shakin' Goin' On."

46. *MSMC*, vol. 1, Dec. 16, 1811; Feb. 17, 1812, 460, 474.

47. *MSMC*, vol. 1, Feb. 13 and 23, 1812, 473, 475.

48. *MSMC*, vol. 1, Mar. 8, 1812; Feb. 29, 1812; Mar. 1, 1812, 479, 477.

49. *MSMC*, vol. 1, Mar. 8, 1812, 478–79.

50. *MSMC*, vol. 1, Feb. 29, 1812, 477.

51. *MSMC*, vol. 1, May 17, 1812, 489.

52. Quoted in McLoughlin, *Cherokee Renascence*, 183.

53. Ibid., 183–85.

54. *MSMC*, vol. 1, Aug. 17, 1813; Sept. 15, 1813, 552, 559.

55. *MSMC*, vol. 1, May 11, 1813; Nov. 7, 1813; May 18, 1812, 537, 568, 490. Jackson's companion was Captain John Strother.

Chapter Six

1. *MSMC*, vol. 1, Mar. 19, 1812; June 6, 1812, 482, 490–91.

2. *MSMC*, vol. 1, Aug. 9 and 14, 1812; Apr. 14, 1811, 496–97, 425; *MSMC*, vol. 2, Aug. 15, 1816, 128; Gambold, "Margaret Ann Crutchfield."

3. The Moravian missionaries describe Joseph Crutchfield as white in Gambolds to Schulz, Apr. 13, 1824, SPML. For more on Crutchfield see Rising, "Pioneer Sketch," 512–25.

4. *MSMC*, vol. 1, Oct. 13, 1811; July 4, 1812, 453, 493.

5. *MSMC*, vol. 1, July 4 and 9, 1812, 493–94.

6. Peggy's note to Joseph transcribed in *MSMC*, vol. 1, July 4, 1813, 544. In 1811, Peggy was owed $700 from the Vann estate, minus $200 for an enslaved woman (Candace) she had purchased from the estate and $50 she had already received for cattle James had taken from her. That left a debt due to her of $500. See Gambold to Benzien, Mar. 7, 1811, SPML.

7. Gambold to Benzien, Mar. 7, 1811, SPML; *MSMC*, vol. 1, May 1, 1813, 533.

8. *MSMC*, vol. 1, Feb. 24, 1811, 415–16; Gambolds to Herbst, Nov. 10, 1810; and Gambolds to Reichel, Nov. 18, 1810, SPML; council document regarding ownership of Vann slaves, May 5, 1811, in *MSMC*, vol. 1, May 1, 1813, 533.

9. In the 1820s some Cherokee slaveholders, as well as *The Cherokee Phoenix* newspaper, expressed support for emancipation and African colonization. For more on Cherokee slaveholders' views on African colonization, see Perdue, "Cherokee Planters." As a point of comparison, one wealthy Choctaw slaveholder, George Harkins, also criticized the institution of slavery; he felt that slavery made the children of Choctaw slaveholders self-indulgent and unwilling to work. See Kidwell, *Choctaws in Oklahoma*, 33.

10. Caty accepted Christ on her deathbed, and witnessing this transformation deeply affected Peggy in her spiritual development. Before that time, Caty had not known the Christian faith. Peggy's caretaking of Caty on her deathbed echoes a trope in white southern plantation mistress's diaries and letters. See, for example, Fox-Genovese, *Plantation Household*, 26, 35.

11. Jacobs, *Incidents*, 68–75, 99–100.

12. Gambold to Reichel, Mar. 6, 1811, SPML. In two other examples, Cherokee converts to Christianity improved their treatment of slaves. Peggy's uncle, Charles Hicks, gave his slaves Easter off, informing them that "[b]lacks as well as others, would be saved" (*MSMC*, vol. 1, Apr. 22, 1816, 114). Minda, the slave of Delilah McNair, Peggy's niece and daughter-in-law, spoke positively about her mistress's "blessed change of mind, which her slaves were also able to enjoy" (*MSMC*, vol. 2, Apr. 16, 1820, 350).

13. *MSMC*, vol. 1, Nov. 24, 1811, 458. The Gambolds were speaking to "old Mrs. McDonald" in this second exchange, with Peggy serving as translator (*MSMC*, vol. 2, June 17, 1818, 226–27).

14. Gambolds to Brother Simon, Mar. 18, 1816, SPML.

15. Ibid.

16. Ibid.; Gambolds to Brother Simon, Oct. 21, 1816; and Gambolds to Von Schweinitz, Nov. 26, 1816, SPML; *MSMC*, vol. 2, Oct. 13 and 27, 1816, 134–35.

17. *MSMC*, vol. 2, Jan. 11 and 21, 1816; Oct. 29, 1817, 102–3, 183; "Extract of a Latter [*sic*] from Anna Rosina Gambold."

18. "Extract of a Latter [*sic*] from Anna Rosina Gambold"; Gambolds to Van Vleck, May 2, 1818, SPML. As early as 1806, blacks owned by the Vanns and McNairs (James Vann's daughter and son-in-law) requested instruction from the Moravian missionaries in the form of oral readings from the Bible, but the endeavor did not move forward. See Gambold to Benzien, June 28, 1806, SPML.

19. Gambolds to Van Vleck, May 2, 1818; Gambolds to Van Vleck, June 11, 1818, SPML; "Extract of a Latter [*sic*] from Anna Rosina Gambold."

20. "Cherokee Mission," 235. By 1823, Baptist missionaries to the Cherokees were having greater success than the Moravians at attracting black slaves to the faith. Three slaves belonging to Wali Vann were baptized by Baptists that year. See SPMD, June 27, 1823.

21. Peggy Scott's letter, titled "Letter from a Cherokee Woman" and printed under the heading Specimens of Indian Improvement, appeared in the *Missionary Herald*, Apr. 1819, and in the *Religious Intelligencer*, May 8, 1819. Recipients of her letters were usually unnamed, but based on contextual analysis, they were likely to have been: Thomas L. McKenney, Superintendent of Indian Trade; Jacob Van Vleck, Moravian minister and president of the Provincial Board of the Southern Province; and the Hartford, Connecticut, poet Lydia Howard Huntley Sigourney. The text of the Cherokee women's antiremoval petition that Peggy helped to author is printed in two original sources: Hoyt, Hall, Chamberlin, and Butrick to Worcester, June 30, 1818, Papers of the ABCFM, Houghton Library, Harvard University, Cambridge, MA; and Gambold to Van Vleck, July 17, 1818, SPML. Copies of this statement can also be found in Perdue and Green, eds., *Cherokee Removal*, 132–33, and on the Women and Social Movements in the United States, 1600–2000, website, Center for the Historical Study of Women and Gender, SUNY Binghamton and Alexander Street Press, <http://womhist.alexanderstreet.com>. For

a detailed discussion of Peggy Scott's antiremoval writings, see Miles, "'Circular' Reasoning."

22. Scholars have argued that nineteenth-century Cherokee Christians combined aspects of the Christian faith with indigenous spiritual experience, such as prophetic dreams that included Cherokee spiritual symbols like water, and revised or original hymns that reflected a reverence for the spiritual power of nature and included symbols of Cherokee history. See Justine Smith, "Resistance Disguised." Cherokee practices and Christian beliefs also merged in the practice of communing with God out of doors. See Perdue, "Catharine Brown." Peggy Scott prayed in the fields, and it is quite possible that her interpretation of the Bible and sermons in the Cherokee language maintained layers of Cherokee cultural and religious meanings.

23. *MSMC*, vol. 2, Mar. 10, 1818, 209.

24. Gambolds to Van Vleck, May 2, 1818, SPML; "Extract of a Latter [*sic*] from Anna Rosina Gambold"; Gambolds to Van Vleck, May 14, 1819, SPML.

25. *MSMC*, vol. 2, May 4, 1819, 284; Gambolds to Van Vleck, May 14, 1819, SPML. Vann House interpretive ranger Julia Autry's insights contributed greatly to my interpretation of Michael's actions.

26. *MSMC*, vol. 2, May 5 and 6, 1819, 285; Gambolds to Van Vleck, May 14, 1819, SPML. The Cherokee man who Peggy commissioned to hunt for Michael was a neighbor, Tuhsiwalliti. See *MSMC*, vol. 2, May 9, 1819, 286.

27. Gambolds to Van Vleck, May 14, 1819, SPML; *MSMC*, vol. 2, May 12, 1819, 286–87.

28. Buck and Stand, cousins of statesman John Ridge, would both become famous men in Cherokee history. Buck (later Elias Boudinot) edited and printed the *Cherokee Phoenix* newspaper; Stand became a Confederate general in the Civil War.

29. *MSMC*, vol. 2, June 20, 1819, 299–300.

30. Gambolds to Van Vleck, May 14, 1819, SPML; Scott to Benziens, Feb. 13, 1811, SPML.

31. *MSMC*, vol. 1, Dec. 24, 1808, 294; *MSMC*, vol. 1, June 31, 1808, 266; Hicks, "Vann Family"; SC school: *MSMC*, vol. 1, Aug. 29, 1807, 210. Joseph also attended Gideon Blackburn's school. See *MSMC*, vol. 2, Aug. 1, 1814, 27–28; and *MSMC*, vol. 1, Aug. 20, 1810, 378. Another son of Vann's from the Tellico area, whose mother was deceased, was brought to receive his part of the inheritance but arrived too late. He received only a mare and foal. See McLoughlin, *Cherokee Renascence*, 174, table 6.

32. Joe Vann also attended Mr. Roger's school and a school near Vann's business partner, Captain Blair, in South Carolina. See *MSMC*, vol. 1, Mar. 24, 1806, 93; Aug. 29, 1807, 210. See also *Diary of Juliana Margaret Conner*, 82, Juliana Margaret Conner Papers, Southern Historical Collection, Manuscripts Department, Wilson Library, University of North Carolina, Chapel Hill.

33. Gambold to Van Vleck, Nov. 11, 1821; and Smith to Schultz, Sept. 18, 1826, SPML; Cherokee Supreme Court Records, no. 155, Nov. 10, 1828; and no. 213, Cherokee Collection, Microfilm 815, Tennessee State Library and Archives, Nashville.

34. Horse racing: Schmidt to Van Vleck, July 11, 1822, MMD; SPMD, Jan. 1, 1828; Feb. 2, 1829; Mar. 7, 1829.

35. Hicks, "Vann Family." Hicks records Joseph's marriages as having taken place around the years 1820 to "Jennie Springston" and 1822 to "Polly Blackwood." McFadden refers to the latter as Polly Black in "Saga of 'Rich Joe,'" 74.

36. SPMD, June 18, 1829; June 1, 1834. In 1824 Joseph's baby girl was baptized at Springplace, though her (unnamed) mother had not converted. See Schmidt to Benade, Apr. 12, 1824, SPML.

37. *MSMC*, vol. 2, Feb. 3, 1818; Jan. 4, 1819; Dec. 26, 1820, 204, 260, 397; SPMD, June 9, 1827.

38. *Laws of the Cherokee Nation*, Oct. 28, 1820, 24 (patrollers); ibid., Nov. 11, 1824, 38, 39 (intermarriage, property).

39. *Periodical Accounts Relating to the Missions of the Church of the United Brethren, Established Among the Heathen*, vol. 8, "North American Indians. Delawares, Cherokees," Feb. 19, 1822, 213, Moravian Archives, Bethlehem, PA.

40. Gambolds to Van Vleck, July 3, 1819, SPML; *MSMC*, vol. 2, May 25, 1819, 289.

41. Gambolds to Van Vleck, Feb. 7, 1820; May 12, 1820; and Aug. 22, 1820, SPML; James McCartney v. Joseph Vann, VHL.

42. Cotter, *My Autobiography*; "Vann Home Scene of Early History," Western History Collections, Cherokee Nation Papers, University of Oklahoma, Norman, OK.

43. Cotter, *My Autobiography*, 70–71.

44. James McCartney v. Joseph Vann, VHL.

45. National Register of Historic Places Inventory, 2, VHL; James McCartney v. Joseph Vann, VHL; Clemens de Baillou, "Archaeological Investigation and Excavation at the Chief Vann House in Spring Place, Murray County, Georgia. April–May 1953," GHC, VH folder; Branham, *Life and Travels*, 12–13; Benjamin Gold to Brother, Dec. 8, 1829, GA; Conner, *Diary of Juliana Margaret Conner*, 82.

46. James McCartney v. Joseph Vann, VHL. McCartney's ten-page itemized tally found the total cost of the home to be $4,965.25. The jury found for the plaintiff and, after taking into consideration partial previous payment, ordered Vann to pay McCartney $3,798.97. The jury later reduced the amount to an unspecified sum between $1,900 and $2,100 plus interest. Joseph must have appealed the decision because by 1829 the case was still pending in the circuit court. Recovered records do not reveal the final outcome.

47. Joe Vann as delegate to constitutional convention, as National Committee member and clerk: *Cherokee Phoenix*, Mar. 6, 1828; May 28, 1828; June 4, 1828; July 2, 1828; Nov. 5, 1828; Nov. 4, 1829 (resolution respecting permits for missionaries, which Joe favored); Nov. 11, 1829; Joe Vann elected as president of National Committee: *Cherokee Phoenix*, May 28, 1831.

48. The formal portrait of Joseph Vann was commissioned by the Georgia Historical Commission and painted by artist Frank Mack in the 1950s. According to Vann House staff members, Mack's work was said to be based on a drawing made of

Joseph before his death (photo print by W. Prentis Greene, no date, held at the Oklahoma Historical Society). See Julia Autry and Jeff Stancil, email exchange with Tiya Miles, Mar. 2009. Pottery shards from Joseph Vann's home were unearthed by archaeologists and are replicated in the Vann House dining room today. Glazed bricks were found on the premises, but the builders did not use them for any special purpose in the house. See "Inventory. Vann House Archaeological Material," no date, GHC, VH folder; and "Archaeological Investigation and Excavation at the Chief Vann House."

49. William McLoughlin (*Cherokee Renascence*, 169) gives this figure of "three hundred or so families . . . prospering most through acculturation" for the year 1809. By the time Joseph built his home, that number of well-off Cherokee families would have increased.

50. Conner, *Diary of Juliana Margaret Conner*, 82–84. It was not uncommon for travelers, such as Fanny Kemble, who married into a slaveholding Georgia Sea Islands family, to disparage white-owned plantation homes. Kemble and others commented on the disappointing state of disrepair and/or cleanliness at southern plantation homes, since many plantations did not measure up to idealized ideas of order. See Cox, *Traveling South*, 114–16. On her trip, Conner criticized white towns and public houses she encountered for lacking expected services, being disorderly, and falling short of her standards of cleanliness; however, she did not describe these places as "gaudy" or their inhabitants as "lazy." These qualities she reserved for Joe Vann's home and her portrait of the Cherokee Nation.

51. "Mission Among the Cherokee Indians in North America."

52. *MSMC*, vol. 2, June 26, 1820, 371.

53. Gambolds to Van Vleck, Feb. 7 and May 19, 1820; and Gambold to Van Vleck, Feb. 16, 1822, SPML. For more on Major and Susanna Ridge, see Wilkins, *Cherokee Tragedy*.

54. *MSMC*, vol. 2, Mar. 31, 1820; May 7, 1820, 346, 356; Gambold, "Margaret Ann Crutchfield"; *MSMC*, vol. 2, Sept. 2, 7, 9, 17, 1820, 382–85.

55. *MSMC*, vol. 2, Oct. 18, 19, 1820, 389; Sigourney, *Traits*, 281; *MSMC*, vol. 2, Oct. 22, 1820, 390; Gambolds to Von Schweinitz, Nov. 18, 1820; *MSMC*, vol. 2, Dec. 31, 1820, 398.

56. Schmidt to Van Vleck, Apr. 26, 1821; Gambold to Van Vleck, Aug. 8, 1821, SPML; Oochgeelogy Mission Diary, 1821, MAS; MMD, Feb. 20 and 21, 1821; twin graves supposition: Tiya Miles, conversation with Anna Smith, Mar. 1, 2007. A state archaeological report inspired the theory expressed by Ms. Smith. The authors found that the Springplace God's Acre was organized into subsections, which probably reflected a burial system common to other Moravian cemeteries in which people in the same sex, age, and marital status groupings (or choirs) were buried near one another. Anna R. Gambold and Peggy Scott were both married women at their deaths, making it more likely that they would have been buried in the same subsection. In addition, Figure 7 in the report representing the placement of graves shows two

graves (numbered 2 and 3) that are much closer together than any of the rest. See Serman, "Ground Penetrating Radar Survey," 2, 16, VHL.

57. Gambold to Van Vleck, Apr. 26, 1821; and Feb. 16, 1822, SPML. Gambold wrote that Crutchfield left to escape Peggy's relatives, who were seeking possession of the couple's property; Crutchfield took one black slave with him. See Gambolds to Benade, Oct. 16, 1823, SPML.

After the Moravians departed, the Oothcaloga home was retained by Peggy's uncle, Young Squirrel, and his children until 1832, when his possession was threatened in the state of Georgia's illegal lottery of Cherokee lands. Regarding Lots Nos. 209-141-142 in the 15 District 3rd Section, a letter to the Georgia governor notes: "The large house was built by Peggy Vann the old man[']s sister[']s daughter, which by consent of the Indians, the Moravian Missionarys occupied for the purpose of educating the Indians for some time . . . but long before the surveying of the land the missionaries left the premises." Young Squirrel appealed to retain the property. The outcome is not recorded. See J. M. C. Montgomery to His Excellency Wilson Lumpkin, re. Cherokee Affairs, Feb. 10, 1833, Cherokee Indian Letters, Talks, and Treaties, 1786–1838, 394, GDAH. The Oothcaloga home burned down in the 1980s, but the Oothcaloga cemetery, where John Gambold was buried, still remains.

58. John Gambold died on November 7, 1827, of pectoral dropsy. See *Cherokee Phoenix*, Apr. 24, 1828; Michael's faith: Oochgeelogy Mission Diary, Aug. 10, 1828, MAS; Michael's son's baptism: Oochgeelogy Mission Diary, Mar. 23, 1827, MAS; Michael's daughter was baptized at Springplace in 1829. See SPMD, Oct. 25, 1829.

59. Pleasant's illness in old age: SPMD, May 23, 1826; Byhan to Schulz, Aug. 17, 1826; Mar. 24, 1828, SPML; Pleasant "inept": Eder to Schulz, Oct. 25, 1829, SPML; Byhans about Pleasant: Byhan to Schulz, Oct. 20, 1829; Nov. 10, 1829; Dec. 1, 1829, SPML.

60. Pleasant arrived in Salem on November 15, 1829. See Byhan to Schulz, Dec. 1, 1829, SPML. Pleasant died on November 18, 1838. See Church-Book for the People of Colour in and about Salem, N.C., Commencing the 24th Day of March, 1822, MAS. Pleasant listed as an asset of the church in "Reports of Christian Ludwig Benzien." In April of 2006, the Southern Province of the Moravian Church issued an apology for its history of slaveholding; the Northern Province followed suit in June.

61. Quoted in McLoughlin, *Cherokee Renascence*, 409.

62. Prince, *Digest of the Laws of the State of Georgia*, 278–80; McLoughlin, *Cherokee Renascence*, 424, 439; Starkey, *Cherokee Nation*, 107.

63. Gambold to McKinney, Jan. 7, 1817, SPML.

64. *Cherokee Phoenix*, May 18, 1831; June 4, 1831.

65. SPMD, Jan. 25, 1833.

66. SPMD, Dec. 24, 1832; Sept. 1, 1833.

67. SPMD, Jan. 5, 1833; May 8, 1833.

68. "An Act more effectually to provide for the government and protection of the Cherokee Indians, residing within the limits of Georgia, and to prescribe the bounds

of their occupant claims," Dec. 20, 1833, in Prince, *Digest of the Laws of the State of Georgia*, 281–82.

69. Battey, *History of Rome and Floyd County*, 85–87; Riley testimony quoted in Battey from the *Georgia Journal* (Milledgeville), Apr. 7, 1835. See also Payne Papers, 5:4.

70. *Census Roll, 1835, of the Cherokee Indians*; "Cherokee Valuations by Young & McMillan 1835," No. 158 Joseph Vann, Indian Office, Washington, DC, GC folder, GDAH. Wali Vann immigrated to Arkansas after 1828 and was evaluated as having possessed two attached dwelling houses near Mill Creek, a gristmill in good repair that had once belonged to James, a miller's house, twelve slave cabins, ten peach trees, and eight acres. See Valuations under the Treaty of 1828 Emigrations 1833 and 1834, no. 69, Polly Vann, University of Tennessee Digital Library Database, University of Tennessee, Knoxville; and "Vann Home Scene of Early History," Western History Collections, Cherokee Nation Papers, University of Oklahoma, Norman, OK.

Epilogue

1. Joseph Vann's Tennessee property was valued at $10,539. See Hoskins, "Cherokee Property Valuations in Tennessee." This record does not indicate when Joseph acquired the property; the property was appraised in 1836. See *Census Roll, 1835, of the Cherokee Indians*.

2. In 1832, Joseph Vann traveled to Washington with Chief John Ross and others to negotiate the removal threat. See Wilkins, *Cherokee Tragedy*, 249. In early December of 1835, Ross departed for Washington once again with Cherokee delegates; this group was still away during the negotiations and signing of the Treaty of New Echota. It stands to reason that Vann was also a member of this 1835 negotiating team that missed the treaty-making session. Gary Moulton (*John Ross*, 70, 72, 73) states that Schermerhorn purposefully planned the meeting during Ross's absence.

3. McFadden, "Saga of 'Rich Joe,'" 72–73. Vann transported a Cherokee family of seventeen and slaves numbering forty-eight to Indian Territory at a cost of $1,300. See United States to Vann for Commutation of Transportation, Jan. 29, 1839, Box 16, File 1116, Fourth Board of U.S. Commissioners Claim Papers, Record Group 75, National Archives and Records Administration, Washington, DC. According to the 1835 census, Vann owned 110 slaves before his departure. See *Census Roll, 1835, of the Cherokee Indians*, 3.

4. McFadden, "Saga of 'Rich Joe,'" 73.

5. "The Cherokee Vann Families," Oklahoma Writers' Project, Ex-Slaves, Oklahoma Historical Society; references given in Writers' Project document are Grant Foreman; "History of the Cherokees," by Emmett Starr; and Edward F. Vann, grandson of "old Rich Joe Vann."

6. McFadden, "Saga of 'Rich Joe,'" 73, 74.

7. Cotter, *Autobiography*, 39–40.

8. "Rich Joe Vann," Oklahoma Writers' Project, Oklahoma Historical Society, gives the cost of each colt as $5,000. McFadden ("Saga of 'Rich Joe,'" 75) records the cost of each colt at $500.

9. James Lloyd, "Explosion of the Lucy Walker"; "Cherokee Vann Families"; "Rich Joe Vann"; Cliff Robinson, "Steamboat Blew Up 114 Years Ago Near New Albany, Killing Over 50," *Louisville Courier-Journal*, Apr. 27, 1958, compiled by Herman McDaniel for Tim Howard, Whitfield-Murray Historical Society. Vann also transported cotton for Lewis Ross.

10. Elmer T. Peterson, "Derby Recalls Odd Disaster," May 15, 1960, Oklahoma Historical Society.

11. "Old Tragedy Is Detailed by Sooners," Oklahoma Writers' Project, Oklahoma Historical Society; the reference given in Writers' Project document is the *Alva Record*, Oct. 25, 1934.

12. Robinson, "Steamboat Blew Up"; "Cherokee Vann Families."

13. Peterson, "Derby Recalls"; "Wreck of the Lucy Walker," in Rev. D. Macdill, ed., *The Evangelical Guardian, by an Association of Ministers of the Associate Reformed Synod of the West*, vol. 2 (Rossville, OH: J. M. Christy, 1844), compiled by Herman McDaniel for Tim Howard, Whitfield-Murray Historical Society.

14. "Rich Joe Vann"; "Old Tragedy."

15. "Cherokee Vann Families"; "Rich Joe Vann"; "Old Tragedy"; Peterson, "Derby Recalls"; Zoe A. Tilghman, "The Voyage of Joe Vann," *Oklahoma's Orbit*, Jan. 29, 1961, Oklahoma Historical Society.

16. "Cherokee Vann Families."

17. Tiya Miles, VHOHP, Virginia Vann Perry; James Lloyd, "Explosion of the Lucy Walker."

18. Robinson, "Steamboat Blew Up."

19. Ibid.; James Lloyd, "Explosion of the Lucy Walker"; "Cherokee Vann Families"; "Rich Joe Vann." Only one source out of several says Vann's body was recovered: "Old Tragedy."

20. "Cherokee Vann Families."

21. Vann, "Reminiscences," 838. In addition to the unnamed former slave paraphrased by R. P. Vann and Lucinda Vann's narrative, two blacks formerly owned by members of the extended Vann family remembered the incident. Henry Henderson (owned by Martin Vann) said his father, A. Vann, "run a steamboat down the Arkansas River" (Baker and Baker, eds., *WPA Oklahoma Slave Narratives*, 194–97). Betty Robertson's father, Kalet (Caleb) Vann, was owned by "old Master Joseph Vann." After Caleb attempted an escape in the Cherokee Slave Revolt of 1842, Joseph Vann sent him to work on the *Lucy Walker*, effectively separating him from his family. Betty reported that Vann punished a number of the runaway slaves in this way. She said her father was "a kind of boss" of the steamboat, and that her father died in the 1844 explosion (Baker and Baker, eds., *WPA Oklahoma Slave Narratives*, 355–58). For a compilation of five WPA narratives focused on blacks owned by the

Vann family in Indian Territory, see McDaniel, *How Slaves Remembered "Rich Joe" Vann*.

22. Tiya Miles, VHOHP, Virginia Vann Perry. Celia Naylor (*African Cherokees*, 38) offers the intriguing supposition that Vann slaves may have sabotaged the boat as an act of resistance.

23. Lucinda Vann, in Baker and Baker, eds., *WPA Oklahoma Slave Narratives*, 435–41. Lucinda was owned by Jim and Jennie Doublehead Vann.

24. "Old Tragedy."

Conclusion

1. *The Georgia Communicator*, 6–7.
2. Legends, HOA, Inc., Legends of Settendown Creek.
3. Robert E. Chambers Interpretive Center Dedication Program, VHL; Robert E. Chambers, foreword to Lela Latch Lloyd, *If the Chief Vann House Could Speak*. Robert Chambers's grandson, Tom Greeson, and Greeson's wife, Jeannette Greeson, made the initial donation for the center. See "The Robert E. Chambers Interpretive Center Is Finally Finished," VHL.
4. In feedback on this book manuscript from Vann House employees, it became clear that despite the tenor of these specific speeches, the male-centered content of printed material and exhibit space biographies, and the unnamed mannequin of Joe Vann's wife in the Interpretive Center, stories about Cherokee women are often incorporated into the tours. Individual guides who have an interest in and knowledge of women's history at the site discuss Wali and Peggy Vann, as well as Nancy Ward and other War Women (a traditional title for women who engaged in war), in their presentations. This feedback also pointed out that the more recent exhibit on modern Cherokee life in the Interpretive Center includes profiles of several women. This is a fair rejoinder to my critique, but a positive next step for the site would be to formally include Cherokee women of the Vann family in both written and oral interpretations.
5. Tiya Miles, VHOHP, email interview with Jennifer Walford Vann, July 29, 2008.
6. Horton, "Slavery in American History," 45; Brundage, "Introduction," 16.
7. Unlike some other historic sites in the South, the Vann House is not a place that black tourists frequent or where black residents have taken an interest in interpretive aspects. This may be partly due to the largely white makeup of Murray County and the distance between the Vann House and Atlanta, the nearest city in the state with a sizeable black population. It might also be a result of little publicity about the Vann House being directed toward black communities and/or a lack of connection that blacks have felt with this particular site. The new attempt to incorporate black history at the Vann House, together with more targeted publicity, may draw a larger African American audience in the future.

8. Minter, *William Faulkner*, 200.

9. Walker, *Way Forward*, 42–59.

Appendix 1

1. As this book went to press in 2009, the Vann House had seen tremendous cuts to its staffing and budget at the hands of the state. Georgia's Department of Natural Resources cited budgetary concerns during an economic downturn as its reason for reducing full-time staff numbers by half and drastically decreasing hours of operation at the Vann House, as well as at a number of other state historic sites. The Friends of the Vann House community group, in partnership with Cherokee leaders in Oklahoma and North Carolina, were rallying once again to preserve the Vann home and its historical interpretation for the public.

2. Students in the class signed a release giving permission for their work to be used in this manner.

3. Eichstedt and Small, *Representations of Slavery*, 1, 2, 2–3. For a guide to southern plantation museums, see Gutek and Gutek, *Plantations and Outdoor Museums*.

4. Handler and Gable, *New History in an Old Museum*, 9.

5. Tiya Miles, tour with Nancy Carter Bland, Coosawattee, Murray County, GA, July 2004. Farish Carter bought the estate from Sarah Bosworth, who had acquired it through the Georgia land lottery in 1832. See Robert S. Davis Jr., "The Secrets Behind the Legends of Carter's Quarters," box 3, folder 2, no. 2549, Hargrett Rare Book and Manuscript Library, University of Georgia, Athens.

6. Respondents/interviewees for my Vann House Oral History Project were Cherokee researcher Jack Baker; Cherokee researcher David Cornsilk; Cherokee descended Moravian researcher Anna Smith; Cherokee/white Vann family descendants Virginia Vann Perry and Jennifer Walford Vann; black/freedpeople Vann descendant Lorraine Taylor; Cherokee freedpeople descendant Olive Anderson; Vann House rangers Julia Autry, William Chase Parker, Ethan Calhoun, and Curtis King; local Georgia historian Don Shadburn; and Cherokee history scholar Rowena McClinton. I also spoke informally with a number of people who had visited, worked at, or volunteered at the Vann House over the years, including former interpretive ranger Pat Hall and her husband, former superintendent James Edward Hall, who ran the site for thirty-five years after inheriting the position from Ed Hall's stepfather, the first site manager; Erskine Ellis and his wife Helen Ellis; former employee and Friends of the Vann House past president Tim Howard; and Cherokee Nation of Oklahoma supreme court justice Troy Wayne Poteete.

7. Justice, *Our Fire*, 31.

8. Farish Carter Papers, 1794, 1806–68, Baldwin and Murray Counties, Georgia, also Florida, Louisiana, and Tennessee, Reels 38–43, Southern Historical Collection, Manuscripts Department, Wilson Library, University of North Carolina, Chapel Hill.

9. Sensbach, *Separate Canaan*, 32, 37.

10. Payne Papers, 5:34.

11. Maelshagen's version often gives summaries rather than word-for-word translations. He also sometimes made mistakes on seemingly minor facts such as the racial identity/degree of Cherokee ancestry of particular people.

12. Gone, "Introduction."

13. Shoemaker, *Strange Likeness*, 9.

14. Baker and Baker, eds., *Oklahoma WPA Slave Narratives*; Minges, ed., *Black Indian Slave Narratives*.

15. Warrior, *People*, 184–85.

16. Ibid., 185.

17. Justice, *Our Fire*, 7, xvi.

18. Ibid., 16, 28.

19. Baptist and Camp, eds., *New Studies in the History of American Slavery*; David Brion Davis, *Inhuman Bondage*; Hall, *Slavery and African Ethnicities*; Jennifer L. Morgan, *Laboring Women*; Camp, *Closer to Freedom*; Harris, *In the Shadow of Slavery*; Singleton, ed., *"I, Too, Am American."*

20. Blassingame, *Slave Community*; Levine, *Black Culture*; Raboteau, *Slave Religion*; Stuckey, *Slave Culture*.

21. Brooks, DeCorse, and Walton, eds. *Small Worlds*, 3, 4.

22. The first close study of Cherokee slaveholding was published by J. B. Davis in 1933, the earliest period of African American and Native American historical writings in which the *Journal of Negro History* figured prominently. In an article in the *Chronicles of Oklahoma*, Davis argued that black slaveholding and the story of Cherokee civilization were connected and that Cherokees applied firm restrictions and employed harsh punishments. See Davis, "Slavery in the Cherokee Nation." In the 1970s and 1980s period referenced in this appendix, when slavery studies and black studies were flourishing in the aftermath of black civil rights and power movements, two full-length studies and a handful of articles appeared. Rudi Halliburton argued that Cherokees adopted black slavery as one of many "accoutrements of European civilization," that "[s]ome full-scale Southern-type Cherokee plantations existed in north Georgia," and that slavery in Indian nations was equivalent in harshness to slavery in white states. See Halliburton, "Origins of Black Slavery among the Cherokees," 489; and Halliburton, *Red over Black*, ix. Monroe Billington found through a statistical analysis of information in the WPA slave narratives that material treatment (such as amount of rations distributed, quality of clothing provided) seemed to be equivalent across these two spaces but that his results could not support larger claims in the comparison debate. See Billington, "Black Slavery in the Indian Territory." In her monograph that remains the most comprehensive overview of Cherokee slaveholding, Theda Perdue posited that Cherokees allowed their black slaves greater social mobility due to reduced need for slave labor, that cultural protocols made Cherokee slave codes less restrictive than white slave codes, and that

prior to Indian Removal, slaves did not run away. She noted: "Although Cherokee planters required hard work from their bondsmen, they probably treated their slaves much better on average than did their white counterparts" (Perdue, *Slavery and the Evolution of Cherokee Society*, 98). Most recently, in an effort to counter the leniency thesis, Celia Naylor has detailed and emphasized the frequency and cruelty of corporal punishment on Indian Territory plantations. See Naylor, *African Cherokees*, and Krauthamer, "Ar'n't I a Woman?" 158. For broader overviews of the historiography of black and Indian relations, see Krauthamer, "African Americans and Native Americans," and Miles and Krauthamer, "Africans and Native Americans."

23. Krauthamer, "African Americans and Native Americans," 8.

24. Naylor-Ojurongbe, "'Born and Raised'"; Naylor, *African Cherokees*; Krauthamer, "In Their 'Native Country'"; Zellar, *African Creeks*; Miles, *Ties That Bind*; Chang, "Where Will the Nation Be at Home?"

Appendix 3

1. Tiya Miles, conversation with Anna Smith, Mar. 1, 2007. The entire text of this memoir is taken from Abigail Mott, comp., *Biographical Sketches*, 44–46. This work is the property of the University of North Carolina at Chapel Hill. It may be used freely by individuals for research, teaching, and personal use as long as this statement of availability is included in the text. For more on the memoir form, see Faull, trans., *Moravian Women's Memoirs*.

Archival, Documentary, and Oral History Sources

Chief Vann House State Historic Site Library, Spring Place, Georgia
Dixie Bradley Bandy Scrapbook.
"Chieftain's Trail: Explore Native American History in Northwest Georgia."
Georgia Department of Natural Resources Brochure, n.d.
James McCartney v. Joseph Vann. Lawsuit filed in Roane County, Tennessee,
Sept. 1825 to Mar. 1829.
National Register of Historic Places Inventory. Vann House, entry number
69-10-10-0009, Oct. 28, 1969. United States Department of the Interior,
National Park Service.
Virginia Vann Perry Collection.
Robert E. Chambers Interpretive Center Dedication Program, July 27, 2002.
"The Robert E. Chambers Interpretive Center Is Finally Finished." Georgia
Department of Natural Resources. Vann House Staff Notes, Spring–
Summer 2001.
Serman, Nina. "Ground Penetrating Radar Survey of the Moravian Cemetery
(God's Acre) at Springplace." Report, Historic Preservation Division.
Georgia Department of Natural Resources, 2000.
Vann, William H., II, compiler. "Vann Generations with Cherokee Origins
from John Joseph Vann & James Clement Vann I of NC. SC. & GA.
ca 1750–1991."
Connecticut Historical Society, Hartford, Connecticut
Revd. John Gambold to Mrs. Lydia Huntly Sigourney, June 7, 1824. Hoadley
Box 6. Lydia Howard Huntley Sigourney Correspondence.
Georgia Department of Archives and History, Morrow, Georgia
T. Barnard to Edward Telfair, Esq., Governor, Aug. 22, 1786 (Flint River).
In Louise Frederick Hays, compiler. Unpublished Letters of Timothy
Barnard, 1784–1820. Department of Archives and History of the State
of Georgia, 1939.
Boudinot, Elias. "Address to the Whites." Record Group 4, Series Group
2, Series 46, Box 34, File 2: Subjects: Indians-Cherokees–Secondary
Material–New Echota.
"Cherokee Valuations by Young & McMillan 1835," No. 158 Joseph Vann.
Indian Office, Washington, DC. Record Group 61, Series Group 1,
Series 1, Box 4. Georgia Historical Commission Records. General
Correspondence Folder, 1951–54.
Description of horse, no date. File 2: Names, James Van [*sic*], Box 165.

Georgia Historical Commission Records. Record Group 61, Series Group 1, Series 1.
General Correspondence Folder, Box 4.
Data Summaries Folder, Box 6.
Vann House Folder, Box 1.
Benjamin Gold to Brother, Dec. 8, 1829. Record Group 4, Series Group 2, Series 46, Box 34, File 2: Subjects: Indians-Cherokees-Secondary Material-New Echota.
J. M. C. Montgomery to His Excellency Wilson Lumpkin, re. Cherokee Affairs, Feb. 10, 1833, 394. Cherokee Indian Letters, Talks and Treaties, 1786–1838.
Moravian Mission Diaries. Carl Maelshagen translation.
Gilcrease Museum, Tulsa, Oklahoma
John Ross Papers, 5126.474c. Council document regarding ownership of Vann slaves, May 5, 1811.
Hargrett Rare Book and Manuscript Library, University of Georgia, Athens, Georgia
Davis, Robert S., Jr. "The Secrets Behind the Legends of Carter's Quarters." Box 3, Folder 2, No. 2549.
Houghton Library, Harvard University, Cambridge, Massachusetts
Papers of the American Board of Commissioners for Foreign Missions
Ard Hoyt, Moody Hall, Wm. Chamberlin, and D. S. Butrick, Oostanahlee, to Samuel Worcester, June 30, 1818. 18.3.1. Cherokee Mission. Vol. 2, 1817–24. Unit 6, Reel 737.
Library of the American Philosophical Society, Philadelphia, Pennsylvania
Books in the Possession of John and Anna R. Gambold at Springplace Cherokee Country, Miscellaneous Manuscripts Collection (MLS-3).
Moravian Archives, Winston-Salem, North Carolina
Cherokee Mission Papers.
Springplace Mission Diary.
Springplace Mission Letters/Correspondence.
Church-Book for the People of Colour in and about Salem, N.C., Commencing the 24th Day of March, 1822.
Diary of the Small Negro Congregation in and around Salem, Mar. 4, 1822–Dec. 25, 1842, Book 4.
Oochgeelogy Mission Diary.
Protocol of the Helpers' Conference.
National Anthropological Archives, Smithsonian Institution, Washington, DC
Caldwell, Sheila, and Joseph R. Caldwell. "A Preliminary Report on the Vann House." River Basin Survey Records, Box 47, "Georgia 1947–1960." Vann House Photos and Report.
Newberry Library, Chicago, Illinois
Ayer Collection

Corners, M. A. H. Historical Traditions of Tennessee, Manuscript, captivity of Jane Brown and her family, 1851.

Hoskins, Shirley Coates. "Cherokee Property Valuations in Tennessee" (1984), No. 109.

John Howard Payne Papers.

Oklahoma Historical Society, Oklahoma City, Oklahoma
"The Chief Vann House." Georgia Historical Commission Brochure, circa 1967–71.

Oklahoma Writers' Project: Ex-Slaves.
"The Cherokee Vann Families."
"Rich Joe Vann."
"Old Tragedy Is Detailed By Sooners," Oct. 25, 1934.

Peterson, Elmer T. "Derby Recalls Odd Disaster," May 15, 1960.

South Carolina Department of Archives and History, Columbia, South Carolina
John Briant to John Vann, July 1751. Miscellaneous Records. Vol. 2, 28–29.

General Assembly Petition, Nov. 28, 1843. Series S165015, Box 111, Item 00084.

Robert Goudy v. John Vann (for debt), Oct. 23, 1758. South Carolina Court of Common Pleas. Judgment Rolls, Box 47A, No. 224A.

John Pope, State Plats 2 (Red Bank River), Mar. 21, 1805. Series S213192, Vol. 0040, Item 002, 386.

Betty, Peggy, and Sally Scott to Charles Goodwin (Power of Attorney), May 13, 1808. Secretary of State Miscellaneous Records (Columbia Series). Vol. B (1801–12), 575–77.

John Vann to Thomas Brown, Dec. 7, 1742. Miscellaneous Records, Volume EE, 344.

Southern Historical Collection, Manuscripts Department, Wilson Library, University of North Carolina, Chapel Hill, North Carolina
Farish Carter Papers, 1794, 1806–68. Baldwin and Murray Counties, Georgia; also Florida, Louisiana, and Tennessee, Reels 38–43.

Juliana Margaret Conner Papers (#174-z).
Diary of Juliana Margaret Conner from June 10th to Oct. 17th, 1827.

Tennessee State Library and Archives, Nashville, Tennessee
Cherokee Supreme Court Records, Cherokee Collection, Microfilm 815.

University of Oklahoma, Norman, Oklahoma
Western History Collections, Cherokee Nation Papers.
"Vann Home Scene of Early History." Unidentified periodical clipping, no date, Folder 7392. Furnished by W. B. Powell from Indian Springs, GA.

University of Tennessee Digital Library Database, University of Tennessee, Knoxville, Tennessee
Valuations under the Treaty of 1828 Emigrations, 1833 and 1834, No. 69, Polly Vann. Southeastern Native American Documents, 1730–1842,

⟨http://dlg.galileo.usg.edu/nativeamerican/jpg/pav045.jpg⟩,
Oct. 22, 2007.
Vann House Oral History Project. Conducted by Tiya Miles, Fall 2006–Fall 2008.
Yale Law School, New Haven, Conn.
    The Avalon Project at Yale Law School. Treaty with the Cherokee: 1785,
        ⟨www.yale.edu/lawweb/avalon/ntreaty/chr1785.htm⟩. Sept. 3, 2008.

Government Records

American State Papers. Documents. Legislative and Executive of the Congress of
    the United States, 1789–1815. Vol. 4, Indian Affairs.
Bureau of Indian Affairs. Records of the Cherokee Agency in Tennessee. Record
    Group 75. National Archives and Records Administration, Washington, DC
    (Newberry Library, Chicago, files as Microfilm 504).
Census Roll, 1835, of the Cherokee Indians East of the Mississippi and Index to the
    Roll. Microfilm T496: Roll 1. National Archives and Records Administration.
    Washington, DC, 1960.
Cherokee Boundary Papers. Record Group 75. Microfilm 234, Reel 73. National
    Archives and Records Administration, Southwest Branch. Fort Worth, Texas.
Fourth Board of U.S. Commissioners Claim Papers. Record Group 75. National
    Archives and Records Administration. Washington, DC.
Letters Received by the Secretary of War. Microfilm 221, Reel 70. National
    Archives and Records Administration, Southwest Branch. Fort Worth, Texas.
Special Files of the Office of Indian Affairs, 1807–1904. Microfilm M574. National
    Archives and Records Administration. Washington, DC.

Newspapers and Periodicals

Atlanta Constitution
Atlanta Journal
Chattanooga News-Free Press
Chattanooga Times
Chattanooga Times Free Press
Chatsworth Times
Cherokee Phoenix
The Dalton News
The Fayette County News
Friends of the Vann House Newsletter (Whitfield-Murray Historical Society,
    Friends of the Vann House)
The Georgia Communicator (The Georgia Association of Elementary School
    Principals, Sept. 6–7, 2005).
Louisville Courier-Journal
Missionary Herald

Oklahoma's Orbit (Sunday magazine of *The Oklahoman*)
Religious Intelligencer
Tulsa Daily World
Vann House Staff Notes (Chief Vann House State Historic Site)

Books, Journal Articles, and Unpublished Papers

Adair, James. *Adair's History of the American Indian*. Edited by Samuel Cole
    Williams. 1930. Reprint, New York: Promontory Press, 1974.
Adams, Jessica. *Wounds of Returning: Race, Memory, and Property on the Postslavery
    Plantation*. Chapel Hill: University of North Carolina Press, 2007.
Alden, John Richard. *John Stuart and the Southern Colonial Frontier*. Ann Arbor:
    University of Michigan Press, 1944.
Allen, Ivan. *The Cherokee Nation: Fort Mountain, Vann House, Chester Inns, New
    Echota*. Atlanta: I. Allen Co., 1959.
Bachelard, Gaston. *The Poetics of Space*. 1958. Reprint, Boston: Beacon Press, 1969.
Baker, T. Lindsay, and Julie P. Baker, eds. *The WPA Oklahoma Slave Narratives*.
    Norman: University of Oklahoma Press, 1996, 194–97.
Bandy, Dicksie Bradley. Foreword to *Early Georgia: Society for Georgia
    Archaeology* 2, Cherokee Issue, no. 2 (Spring 1957): 2.
Baptist, Edward E. "'Stol' and Fetched Here': Enslaved Migration, Ex-slave
    Narratives, and Vernacular History." In *New Studies in the History of American
    Slavery*, edited by Edward E. Baptist and Stephanie M. H. Camp, 243–74.
    Athens: University of Georgia Press, 2006.
Baptist, Edward E., and Stephanie M. H. Camp, eds. *New Studies in the History of
    American Slavery*. Athens: University of Georgia Press, 2006.
Bartram, William. "Observations on the Creek and Cherokee Indians." In
    Transactions of the American Ethnological Society. Vol. 3, pt. 1. New York:
    George P. Putnam, 1953.
———. *Travels Through North & South Carolina, Georgia, East & West Florida*,
    *the Cherokee Country, the Extensive Territories of the Muscogulges, or Creek
    Confederacy, and the Country of the Chactaws; Containing an Account of the
    Soil and Natural Productions of Those Regions, Together with Observations on the
    Manners of the Indians*. Philadelphia, PA: James & Johnson, 1791. Electronic
    ed., Documenting the American South, North Carolina Collection, University
    of North Carolina at Chapel Hill, ⟨http://docsouth.unc.edu/nc/bartram/
    bartram.html⟩. Sept. 8, Oct. 17, 2008.
Battey, George Magruder, Jr. *A History of Rome and Floyd County, 1540–1922*.
    Atlanta: Cherokee Publishing Company, 1969.
Beeson, Leola Selman. "Homes of Distinguished Cherokee Indians." *Chronicles
    of Oklahoma* 11, no. 3 (Sept. 1933): 927–41.
Bell, James W. *Chief James Vann: Cherokee Patriot*. Hodges, SC: Lindy
    Publications, 1999.

Beltran, G. Aguirre. "Tribal Origins of Slaves in New Mexico." *Association for the Study of African-American Life and History* 31, no. 3 (July 1946): 269–89.

Berlin, Ira. *Generations of Captivity: A History of African American Slaves.* Cambridge, MA: Harvard University Press, 2003.

Bibb, Henry. "Narrative of the Life and Adventures of Henry Bibb, an American Slave." In *I Was Born a Slave*, edited by Yuval Taylor, 1–102. Chicago: Lawrence Hill Books, 1999.

Billington, Monroe. "Black Slavery in the Indian Territory: The Ex-Slave Narratives." *Chronicles of Oklahoma* 61 (1982): 56–65.

Blackhawk, Ned. *Violence Over the Land: Indians and Empires in the Early American West.* Cambridge, MA: Harvard University Press, 2006.

Blair, William. *Cities of the Dead: Contesting the Memory of the Civil War in the South, 1865–1914.* Chapel Hill: University of North Carolina Press, 2004.

Blassingame, John W. *The Slave Community: Plantation Life in the Antebellum South.* 1972. Reprint, New York: Oxford University Press, 1979.

Blight, David W. "Epilogue: Southerners Don't Lie; They Just Remember Big." In *Where These Memories Grow: History, Memory, and Southern Identity*, edited by W. Fitzhugh Brundage, 347–54. Chapel Hill: University of North Carolina Press, 2000.

———. *Race and Reunion: The Civil War in American Memory.* Cambridge, MA: Harvard University Press, 2001.

Block, Sharon. *Rape and Sexual Power in Early America.* Chapel Hill: University of North Carolina Press, 2006.

Bodnar, John. *Remaking America: Public Memory, Commemoration, and Patriotism in the Twentieth Century.* Princeton, NJ: Princeton University Press, 1992.

Branham, Levi. *My Life and Travels.* 1929. Reprint, Dalton, GA: Whitfield-Murray Historical Society, 2000.

Braund, Kathryn E. Holland. *Deerskins and Duffels: Creek Indian Trade with Anglo-America, 1685–1815.* Lincoln: University of Nebraska Press, 1993.

Brooks, James F., Christopher R. N. DeCorse, and John Walton, eds. *Small Worlds: Method, Meaning, and Narrative in Microhistory.* Santa Fe, NM: School for Advanced Research Press, 2008.

Brown, John P. *Old Frontiers: The Story of the Cherokee Indians from Earliest Times to the Date of Their Removal to the West, 1838.* Kingsport, TN: Southern Publishers, Inc., 1938.

Brown, Kathleen M. "The Anglo-Algonquian Gender Frontier." In *Negotiators of Change: Historical Perspectives on Native American Women*, edited by Nancy Shoemaker, 26–48. New York: Routledge, 1995.

Brundage, W. Fitzhugh. "Introduction: No Deed But Memory." In *Where These Memories Grow: History, Memory, and Southern Identity*, edited by W. Fitzhugh Brundage, 1–28. Chapel Hill: University of North Carolina Press, 2000.

———. *The Southern Past: A Clash of Race and Memory.* Cambridge, MA: Harvard University Press, 2005.

Bunyan, John. *The Pilgrim's Progress from this World to That Which Is to Come*. 1678. Reprint, New York: Charles Scribner's Sons and Company, 1918.

Bynum, Victoria E. *Unruly Women: The Politics of Social and Sexual Control in the Old South*. Chapel Hill: University of North Carolina Press, 1992.

Calloway, Colin G. *The American Revolution in Indian Country: Crisis and Diversity in Native American Communities*. New York: Cambridge University Press, 1995.

Camp, Stephanie M. H. *Closer to Freedom: Enslaved Women & Everyday Resistance in the Plantation South*. Chapel Hill: University of North Carolina Press, 2004.

———. "The Pleasures of Resistance: Enslaved Women and Body Politics in the Plantation South, 1830–1861." In *New Studies in the History of American Slavery*, edited by Edward E. Baptist and Stephanie M. H. Camp, 87–126. Athens: University of Georgia Press, 2006.

Camp, Stephanie M. H., and Edward E. Baptist. "Introduction: A History of the History of Slavery in the Americas." In *New Studies in the History of American Slavery*, edited by Edward E. Baptist and Stephanie M. H. Camp, 1–18. Athens: University of Georgia Press, 2006.

Candler, Allen D., ed. *The Colonial Records of the State of Georgia*. Vol. 9, *January 1763 to December 1766*. Atlanta: The Franklin-Turner Company, 1907.

Chang, David A. Y. O. "Where Will the Nation Be at Home? Race, Nationalisms, and Emigration Movements in the Creek Nation." In *Crossing Waters, Crossing Worlds: The African Diaspora in Indian Country*, edited by Tiya Miles and Sharon P. Holland, 80–99. Durham, NC: Duke University Press, 2006.

"Cherokee Mission." *Periodical Accounts Relating to the Missions of the Church of the United Brethren, Established Among the Heathen*. Vol. 8. London: Brethren's Society for the Furtherance of the Gospel, 1821.

Chireau, Yvonne P. *Black Magic: Religion and the African American Conjuring Tradition*. Berkeley: University of California Press, 2003.

Clinton, Catherine. *The Plantation Mistress: Woman's World in the Old South*. New York: Pantheon Books, 1982, 80–81.

Cobb, James C. *Away Down South: A History of Southern Identity*. New York: Oxford University Press, 2005.

Cotter, William Jasper. *My Autobiography*. Nashville, TN: Publishing House Methodist Episcopal Church, 1917. Newberry Library, Chicago, IL.

Cox, John D. *Traveling South: Travel Narratives and the Construction of American Identity*. Athens: University of Georgia Press, 2005.

Creel, Margaret. *"A Peculiar People": Slave Religion and Community-Culture Among the Gullahs*. New York: New York University Press, 1988.

Crews, C. Daniel. *Faith and Tears: The Moravian Mission among the Cherokee*. Winston-Salem, NC: Moravian Archives, 2000.

———. *Neither Slave nor Free: Moravians, Slavery, and a Church That Endures*. Winston-Salem, NC: Moravian Archives, 1998.

———. *This We Most Certainly Believe: Thoughts on Moravian Theology*. Winston-Salem, NC: Moravian Archives, 2005.

Cumfer, Cynthia. *Separate Peoples, One Land: The Minds of Cherokees, Blacks, and Whites on the Tennessee Frontier*. Chapel Hill: University of North Carolina Press, 2007.

Davis, David Brion. *Inhuman Bondage: The Rise and Fall of Slavery in the New World*. New York: Oxford University Press, 2006.

Davis, J. B. "Slavery in the Cherokee Nation." *Chronicles of Oklahoma* 11, no. 4 (December 1933): 1056–72.

Davis, Ronald L. F. *The Black Experience in Natchez, 1720–1880, Special History Study*. Natchez National Historical Park, MS: National Park Service, 1993.

de Baillou, Clemens. "The Chief Vann House at Spring Place, Georgia." *Early Georgia* 2, no. 2 (Spring 1957): 3–11.

Deloria, Philip J. *Indians in Unexpected Places*. Lawrence: University Press of Kansas, 2004.

———. *Playing Indian*. New Haven, CT: Yale University Press, 1998.

Denson, Andrew. "Our Ancestors' Avarice: Remembering Cherokee Removal in Civil Rights Era Georgia." Paper version, accepted to *Southern Cultures* 14 (Winter 2008).

Easterby, J. H., ed., *The Colonial Records of South Carolina, The Journal of the Commons House of Assembly, September 10, 1745–June 17, 1746*. Columbia: South Carolina Archives Department, 1956.

———. *The Colonial Records of South Carolina, The Journal of the Commons House of Assembly, September 10, 1746–June 13, 1747*. Columbia: South Carolina Archives Department, 1958.

Eaton, Clement. *The Waning of the Old South Civilization, 1860's–1880's*. Mercer University Lamer Memorial Lectures, No. 10. Athens: University of Georgia Press, 1968.

Ehle, John. *Trail of Tears: The Rise and Fall of the Cherokee Nation*. New York: Anchor Books, 1988.

Eichstedt, Jennifer L., and Stephen Small. *Representations of Slavery: Race and Ideology in Southern Plantation Museums*. Washington, DC: Smithsonian Institution Press, 2002.

Elrod, Frary. *Historical Notes on Jackson County, Georgia*. Jefferson, GA: n.p., 1967.

Ethridge, Robbie. *Creek Country: The Creek Indians and Their World*. Chapel Hill: University of North Carolina Press, 2003.

"Extract of a Latter [*sic*] from Anna Rosina Gambold, Springplace, Cherokee Country, and from the Cherokee Youth Buck." May 6, 1818. *Periodical Accounts Relating to the Missions of the Church of the United Brethren, Established Among the Heathen*, No. 83, 55–60. London: Brethren's Society for the Furtherance of the Gospel, 1818.

Faull, Katherine M., trans. *Moravian Women's Memoirs: Their Related Lives, 1750–1820*. Syracuse, NY: Syracuse University Press, 1997.

Ferguson, Leland. "'The Cross Is a Magic Sign': Marks on Eighteenth-Century Bowls from South Carolina." In *"I, Too, Am American": Archaeological Studies of African-American Life*, edited by Theresa A. Singleton, 116–31. Charlottesville: University Press of Virginia, 1999.

Fisher, George, Accountant. *The American Instructor; or, Young Man's Best Companion*. Philadelphia: Printed and sold by Joseph Crukshank, 1787.

Fogelson, Raymond D. "An Analysis of Cherokee Sorcery and Witchcraft." In *Four Centuries of Southern Indians*, edited by Charles Hudson, 113–31. Athens: University of Georgia Press, 1975.

———. "On the 'Petticoat Government' of the Eighteenth-Century Cherokee." In *Personality and the Cultural Construction of Society*, edited by David Jordan and Marc Swartz, 161–81. Tuscaloosa: University of Alabama Press, 1990.

Forman, Henry Chandlee. *Virginia Architecture in the Seventeenth Century*. Williamsburg, VA: Virginia 350th Anniversary Celebration Corporation, 1957.

Fox-Genovese, Elizabeth. *Within the Plantation Household: Black and White Women of the Old South*. Chapel Hill: University of North Carolina Press, 1988.

Fries, Adelaide L., ed. *Records of the Moravians in North Carolina*. Vol. 6, *1793–1808*. Raleigh, NC: The North Carolina Historical Commission, 1943.

Gambold, Anna Rosina. "A List of Plants Found in the Neighbourhood of the Connasarga [*sic*] River, (Cherokee Country) Where Springplace Is Situated, Made by Mrs. Gambold, at the Request of the Rev. Elias Cornelius." Plants of the Cherokee Country, Art. 6. *The American Journal of Science* 1 (1818/1819).

———. "Margaret Ann Crutchfield: A Cherokee Convert." In *Biographical Sketches and Interesting Anecdotes of Persons of Color. To Which Is Added, a Selection of Pieces in Poetry*, compiled by Abigail Mott, 94–98. 1826. Reprint, New York: Mahlon Day, 1839.

George, David P., Jr., "Ninety Six Decoded: Origins of a Community's Name." *South Carolina Historical Magazine* 92 (Apr. 1991): 69–84.

Georgia 1800–1900: A Series of Selections from the Georgiana Library of a Private Collector: Public Exhibition. Series 10, "The Cherokee Indians of Georgia with Some Notice of The Timucuas and The Creeks." Atlanta: Atlanta Public Library, 1954–55.

"Georgia Gazette Riddle for July 21–25, 2008." *Georgia Gazette Blog*, ⟨http://georgia gazetteblogspot.com/2008/07/georgia-gazette-riddle-for-july-21-25.html⟩. Aug. 6, 2008.

Gilbert, William Harlen. *Smithsonian Institution Bureau of Ethnology Bulletin 133: Anthropological Papers Numbers 19–26*. "No. 23: The Eastern Cherokees." Washington, DC: Government Printing Office, 1943.

Gilmore, Jann Haynes. "Georgia's Historic Preservation Beginning: The Georgia Historical Commission (1951–1973)." *Georgia Historical Quarterly* 63 (Spring 1979): 9–21.

Glymph, Thavolia. *Out of the House of Bondage: The Transformation of the Plantation Household*. Cambridge: Cambridge University Press, 2008.

Gomez, Michael A. *Exchanging Our Country Marks: The Transformation of African Identities in the Colonial and Antebellum South*. Chapel Hill: University of North Carolina Press, 1998.

Gone, Joseph P. "Introduction: Mental Health Discourse as Western Cultural Proselytization." *Ethos* 36, no. 3 (2008): 310–15.

Goulding, F. R. *Sapelo; or, Child-Life on the Tidewater*. In *The Woodruff Stories*. Philadelphia: Claxton, Remsen & Haffelfinger, 1880.

Green, Rayna. "The Tribe Called Wannabee: Playing Indian in America and Europe." *Folklore* 99 (1988): 30–55.

Gutek, Gerald, and Patricia Gutek. *Plantations and Outdoor Museums in America's Historic South*. Columbia: University of South Carolina Press, 1996.

Hagy, James William, and Stanley J. Folmsbee, eds. "The Lost Archives of the Cherokee Nation." Part 2, 1772–1775. *East Tennessee Historical Society's Publications*, no. 44 (1972): 114–25.

Hall, Gwendolyn Mido. *Slavery and African Ethnicities in the Americas: Restoring the Links*. Chapel Hill: University of North Carolina Press, 2005.

Halliburton, R., Jr. "Origins of Black Slavery among the Cherokees." *Chronicles of Oklahoma* 52 (Winter 1974): 483–96.

———. *Red over Black: Black Slavery among the Cherokee Indians*. Westport, CT: Greenwood, 1977.

Hamilton, Kenneth G., trans. and ed. "Minutes of the Mission Conference Held in Springplace" (1802). *Atlanta Historical Bulletin* 15 (Winter 1970): 9–87.

———. "Minutes of the Mission Conference Held in Springplace" (1819). *Atlanta Historical Bulletin* 16 (Spring 1971): 31–59.

Handler, Richard, and Eric Gable. *The New History in an Old Museum: Creating the Past at Colonial Williamsburg*. Durham, NC: Duke University Press, 1997.

Harmon, Alexandra. "American Indians and Land Monopolies in the Gilded Age." *Journal of American History* 90, no. 1 (2003), ⟨http://www.historycooperative.org.proxy.lib.umich.edu/journals/jah/90.1.harmon.html⟩. Nov. 17, 2008.

Harris, Leslie M. *In the Shadow of Slavery: African Americans in New York City, 1626–1863*. Chicago: University of Chicago Press, 2003.

Hatley, Tom. *The Dividing Paths: Cherokees and South Carolinians Through the Era of Revolution*. New York: Oxford University Press, 1993.

Hawkins, Benjamin. "Benjamin Hawkins' Trip Across Georgia in 1796." Edited by Marion R. Hemperley. *The Georgia Historical Quarterly* (Spring 1971): 114–37.

———. *The Collected Works of Benjamin Hawkins, 1796–1810*. Edited by Thomas Foster. Tuscaloosa: University of Alabama Press, 2003.

Herskovits, Melville J. *The Myth of the Negro Past*. New York: Harper and Brothers, 1941.

Hicks, James R. "Jennie Conrad Taylor Aniwaya." Unpublished genealogical paper in author's possession.

———. "Vann Family." Unpublished genealogical paper. Also available as "Genealogy Report: Descendants of John Vann I" in "Cherokee Lineages," updated Dec. 4, 2005, ⟨http://familytreemaker.genealogy.com/users/h/i/c/James-R-Hicks-VA/⟩. Apr. 22, 2009.

Hill, Sarah H. "Weaving History: Cherokee Baskets from the Springplace Mission." *William and Mary Quarterly* 53, no. 1 (Jan. 1996): 115–36.

———. *Weaving New Worlds: Southeastern Cherokee Women and Their Basketry.* Chapel Hill: University of North Carolina Press, 1997.

hooks, bell. "Revolutionary 'Renegades': Native Americans, African Americans and Black Indians." Chap. 12 in *Black Looks: Race and Representation.* London: Turnaround, 1992.

Hopkins, Dwight N. *Down, Up, and Over: Slave Religion and Black Theology.* Minneapolis, MN: Fortress Press, 2000.

Horton, James Oliver. "Slavery in American History: An Uncomfortable National Dialogue." In *Slavery and Public History: The Tough Stuff of American Memory*, edited by James Oliver Horton and Lois E. Horton, 35–55. New York: New Press, 2006.

Horwitz, Tony. *Confederates in the Attic.* New York: Pantheon Books, 1998.

Howard, Tim, and Lela Latch Loyd. *The Vann House Speaks Again: Letters of Ermina Vann Campbell.* Roswell, GA: W. H. Wolfe Associates, 1989.

Jackson County, Georgia, Early Court Records, 1796–1831. "Wills and Estate Records 1796–1813." Transcribed by Faye Stone Poss. Alpharetta, GA: W. H. Wolfe Associates Historical Publications, 1994.

Jacobs, Harriet. *Incidents in the Life of a Slave Girl, Written by Herself.* 1861. Reprint, Cambridge, MA: Harvard University Press, 1987.

James, Stanlie. "Mothering: A Possible Black Feminist Link to Social Transformation?" In *Theorizing Black Feminisms: The Visionary Pragmatism of Black Women*, edited by Stanlie James and Abena Busia, 44–54. New York: Routledge, 1993.

Johnson, Caryl. "A West African Reflection in the Danish West Indies." *African Diaspora Studies*, no. 59 (June 2003): 79–84.

Johnston, Carolyn Ross. *Cherokee Women in Crisis: Trail of Tears, Civil War, And Allotment, 1838–1907.* Tuscaloosa: University of Alabama Press, 2003.

Joseph, J. W. "African-American Life in Georgia Through the Archaeological Looking Glass." Material Reflections of Georgia's African-American Past. *Early Georgia* 35, no. 2 (Fall 2007): 101–9.

Joyner, Charles. *Down by the Riverside: A South Carolina Slave Community.* Urbana: University of Illinois Press, 1985.

Justice, Daniel Heath. *Our Fire Survives the Storm: A Cherokee Literary History.* Minneapolis: University of Minnesota Press, 2006.

Kidwell, Clara Sue. *The Choctaws in Oklahoma: From Tribe to Nation, 1855–1970.* Norman: University of Oklahoma Press, 2007.

Kilpatrick, Alan. *The Night Has a Naked Soul: Witchcraft and Sorcery Among the Western Cherokee*. Syracuse, NY: Syracuse University Press, 1997.

Kilpatrick, Jack. "A Cherokee Conjuration to Cure a Horse." *Southern Folklore Quarterly* 28, no. 3 (1964): 216–19.

Kolchin, Peter. *American Slavery, 1619–1877*. 1993. Reprint, New York: Hill and Wang, 2003.

Krauthamer, Barbara. "African Americans and Native Americans." In *Origins*, edited by Colin Palmer and Howard Dodson, 91–136. Schomburg Studies on the Black Experience (SSBE), vol. 3. East Lansing: Michigan State University Press, 2008.

———. "Ar'n't I a Woman? Native Americans, Gender, and Slavery." *Journal of Women's History* 19, no. 2 (2007): 156–60.

———. "In Their 'Native Country': Freedpeople's Understandings of Culture and Citizenship in the Choctaw and Chickasaw Nations." In *Crossing Waters, Crossing Worlds: The African Diaspora in Indian Country*, edited by Tiya Miles and Sharon P. Holland, 100–120. Durham, NC: Duke University Press, 2006.

Kropp, Phoebe S. *California Vieja: Culture and Memory in a Modern American Place*. Berkeley: University of California Press, 2006.

Laws of the Cherokee Nation: Adopted by the Council at Various Periods. Tahlequah, C.N.: Cherokee Advocate Office, 1852.

Legends HOA, Inc. The Legends of Settendown Creek, ⟨http://www.legendson line.org/index.php?option=content&pcontent=1&task=vie w&id=29&Itemid =58&PHPSESSID=17fddf29612b88f99f995c2c9fe32b6e⟩. Aug. 11, 2008.

Levine, Lawrence W. *Black Culture and Black Consciousness*. 1977. Reprint, New York: Oxford University Press, 2007, xxv.

Linley, John. *The Georgia Catalog: Historic American Buildings Survey*. Athens: University of Georgia Press, 1983.

Longe, Alexander. "A Small Postcript of the Ways and Manners of the Indians Called Charikees." *Southern Indian Studies* 21 (1969): 3–49.

Lorde, Audre. *Zami: A New Spelling of My Name*. Freedom, CA: The Crossing Press, 1982.

Loskiel, George Henry. *Episcopus Fratrum, Extempore on a Wagon; A Metrical Narrative of a Journey from Bethlehem, P.A., to the Indian Town of Goshen, Ohio, in the Autumn of 1803*. Translated by J. Max Hark. Lancaster, PA: Samuel H. Zahm & Co., 1887.

Lloyd, James T. "Explosion of the Lucy Walker, Oct. 15, 1844." *Lloyd's Steamboat Directory and Disasters on the Western Waters*. Cincinnati, OH: P. J. T. Lloyd & Co., 1856.

Lloyd, Lela Latch. *If the Chief Vann House Could Speak*. Abilene, TX: Quality Printing Company, 1980.

Macdill, Rev. D., ed. *The Evangelical Guardian, By an Association of Ministers of the Associate Reformed Synod of the West*. Vol. 2. Rossville, OH: J. M. Christy, 1844.

Malone, Henry Thompson. "The Cherokees Become a Civilized Tribe." Cherokee Issue, *Early Georgia* 2, no. 2 (Spring 1957): 12–15.

———. *Cherokees of the Old South: A People in Transition.* Athens: University of Georgia Press, 1956.

Martin, C. Brenden. "To Keep the Spirit of Mountain Culture Alive: Tourism and Historical Memory in the Southern Highlands." In *Where These Memories Grow: History, Memory, and Southern Identity*, edited by W. Fitzhugh Brundage, 249–70. Chapel Hill: University of North Carolina Press, 2000.

Martin, Joel W. *Sacred Revolt: The Muskogees' Struggle for a New World.* Boston: Beacon Press, 1991.

May, Katja. *African Americans and Native Americans in the Creek and Cherokee Nations, 1830s to 1920s: Collision and Collusion.* New York: Garland Publishing, 1996.

McClinton, Rowena, ed. *The Moravian Springplace Mission to the Cherokees.* 2 vols. Lincoln: University of Nebraska Press, 2007.

McDaniel, Herman. *How Slaves Remembered "Rich Joe" Vann.* Self-published booklet, 2003. Available at the Vann House State Historic Site.

McDowell, William L., Jr., ed. *Documents Relating to Indian Affairs.* Vol. 1. Columbia: South Carolina Archives Department, 1958.

McFadden, Marguerite. "The Saga of 'Rich Joe' Vann." *Chronicles of Oklahoma* 61, no. 1 (1983): 68–79.

McKinley, Daniel. "Anna Rosina (Kliest) Gambold (1762–1821), Moravian Missionary to the Cherokees, with Special Reference to Her Botanical Interest." *Transactions of the Moravian Historical Society* 28 (1994): 67–70.

McLoughlin, William G. *Cherokee Renascence in the New Republic.* Princeton: Princeton University Press, 1986.

———. *Cherokees and Missionaries, 1789–1839.* 1984. Reprint, Norman: University of Oklahoma Press, 1995.

———. "James Vann: Intemperate Patriot." In *The Cherokee Ghost Dance: Essays on the Southeastern Indians, 1789–1861.* Macon, GA: Mercer University Press, 1984. ⟨www.measuringworth.com⟩. Apr. 14, 29, 2008.

Meriwether, Robert L. *The Expansion of South Carolina, 1729–1765.* Kingsport, TN: Southern Publishers Inc., 1940.

Miles, Tiya. "'Circular Reasoning': Recentering Cherokee Women in the Antiremoval Campaigns." *American Quarterly* 61, no. 2 (June 2009): 221–43.

———. "The Narrative of Nancy, A Cherokee Woman." Special Issue: Intermarriage and North American Indians, *Frontiers: A Journal of Women Studies* 29, no. 2 and 3 (2008): 59–80.

———. *Ties That Bind: The Story of an Afro-Cherokee Family in Slavery and Freedom.* Berkeley: University of California Press, 2005.

Miles, Tiya, and Barbara Krauthamer. "Africans and Native Americans." In *The Blackwell Companion to African American History*, edited by Alton Hornsby. Oxford: Blackwell, 2004.

Minges, Patrick, ed. *Black Indian Slave Narratives*. Winston-Salem, NC: John F. Blair, Publisher, 2004.

Minter, David. *William Faulkner, His Life and Work*. Baltimore, MD: Johns Hopkins University Press, 1980, 200.

"Mission Among the Cherokee Indians in North America." Sept. 1, 1820. *Periodical Accounts Relating to the Missions of the Church of the United Brethren, Established Among the Heathen*. Vol. 7. London: Brethren's Society for the Furtherance of the Gospel, 1820.

"The Mississippi Valley — Whole Lotta Shakin' Goin' On." United States Geological Survey, ⟨http://quake.usgs.gov/prepare/factsheets/NewMadrid/⟩. Apr. 25, 2008.

Mooney, James. *Historical Sketch of the Cherokee*. 1900. Reprint, Smithsonian Institution Press, 1975.

———. *Myths of the Cherokee*. 1900. Reprint, New York: Dover, 1995.

Morgan, Jennifer L. *Laboring Women: Reproduction and Gender in New World Slavery*. Philadelphia: University of Pennsylvania Press, 2004.

———. "'Some Could Suckle over Their Shoulder': Male Travelers, Female Bodies, and the Gendering of Racial Ideology." In *New Studies in the History of American Slavery*, edited by Edward E. Baptist and Stephanie M. H. Camp, 21–64. Athens: University of Georgia Press, 2006.

Morgan, Philip D. *Slave Counterpoint: Black Culture in the Eighteenth-Century Chesapeake and Lowcountry*. Chapel Hill: University of North Carolina Press, 1998.

Mott, Abigail, compiler. *Biographical Sketches and Interesting Anecdotes of Persons of Colour. To Which Is Added, a Selection of Pieces in Poetry*. New York: Mahlon Day, 1826. 1st ed., 2001. Electronic Edition: Academic Affairs Library, University of North Carolina at Chapel Hill, ⟨http://www.docsouth.unc.edu/neh/mott26/⟩. Dec. 10, 2005.

Moulton, Gary. E. *John Ross, Cherokee Chief*. Athens: University of Georgia Press, 1977.

Naylor, Celia E. *African Cherokees in Indian Territory: From Chattel to Citizens*. Chapel Hill: University of North Carolina Press, 2008.

Naylor-Ojurongbe, Celia E. "'Born and Raised among These People, I Don't Want to Know Any Other': Slave Acculturation in Nineteenth-Century Indian Territory." In *Confounding the Color Line: The Indian-Black Experience in North America*, edited by James F. Brooks, 161–91. Lincoln: University of Nebraska Press, 2002.

Nisbett, Richard E., and Dov Cohen. *Culture of Honor: The Psychology of Violence in the South*. Boulder, CO: Westview Press, 1996.

Norton, John. *The Journal of Major John Norton*. Edited by Carl F. Klinck and James J. Talman. 1816. Reprint, Toronto: Champlain Society, 1970.

Oakes, James. *The Ruling Race: A History of American Slaveholders*. 1982. Reprint, New York: W. W. Norton, 1998.

O'Donnell, James H., III. *Southern Indians in the American Revolution*. Knoxville: University of Tennessee Press, 1973.

———. "The Southern Indians in the War for American Independence." In *Four Centuries of Southern Indians*, edited by Charles Hudson, 46–64. Athens: University of Georgia Press, 1975.

Olmsted, Frederick Law. *The Cotton Kingdom: A Traveller's Observations on Cotton and Slavery in the American Slave States*. Edited by Arthur M. Schlesinger. New York: Knopf, 1953.

Owen, Narcissa. *A Cherokee Woman's America: Memoirs of Narcissa Owen, 1831–1907*. Edited by Karen L. Kilcup. Gainsville: University Press of Florida, 2005.

Palmer, Colin, and Howard Dodson, eds. *Origins*. Schomburg Studies on the Black Experience (SSBE), vol. 3. East Lansing: Michigan State University Press, 2008.

Parish, Peter J. *Slavery: History and Historians*. New York: Westview Press, 1989.

Penningroth, Dylan C. "My People, My People: The Dynamics of Community in Southern Slavery." In *New Studies in the History of American Slavery*, edited by Edward E. Baptist and Stephanie M. H. Camp, 166–76. Athens: University of Georgia Press, 2006.

Perdue, Theda. "Catharine Brown: Cherokee Convert to Christianity." In *Sifters: Native American Women's Lives*, edited by Theda Perdue, 77–91. New York: Oxford University Press, 2001.

———. *The Cherokee*. Edited by Frank W. Porter III. New York: Chelsea House Publishers, 1989.

———. "Cherokee Planters, Black Slaves, and African Colonization." *Chronicles of Oklahoma* 60, no. 3 (1982): 322–31.

———. *Cherokee Women: Gender and Culture Change, 1700–1835*. Lincoln: University of Nebraska Press, 1998.

———. *"Mixed-Blood" Indians: Racial Construction in the Early South*. Athens: University of Georgia Press, 2003.

———. *Slavery and the Evolution of Cherokee Society, 1540–1866*. Knoxville: University of Tennessee Press, 1979.

Perdue, Theda, and Michael D. Green. *The Columbia Guide to American Indians of the Southeast*. New York: Columbia University Press, 2001.

———, eds. *The Cherokee Removal: A Brief History with Documents*. 2nd ed. Boston: Bedford Books of St. Martin's Press, 2005.

Perkerson, Medora Field. *White Columns in Georgia*. New York: Rinehart & Co., 1952.

Philippe, Louis. *Diary of My Travels in America*. Translated by Stephen Becker. New York: Delacorte Press, 1977.

Phillips, Joyce Y., and Paul Gary Phillips, eds. *The Brainerd Journal: A Mission to the Cherokees, 1817–1823*. Lincoln: University of Nebraska Press, 1998.

Pommer, Barbara Vann. *The Curse of the House of Vann*. Old Hickory, TN: Vanns Trading Post, n.d. Georgia Department of Archives and History, Atlanta, GA.

Potter, Dorothy Williams, ed. *Passports of Southeastern Pioneers 1770–1823*. Baltimore, MD: Genealogical Publishing Co., Inc., 1994.

Pratt, Dorothy, and Richard Pratt. *A Guide to Early American Homes South*. New York: McGraw Hill, 1956.

Prince, Oliver H. *A Digest of the Laws of the State of Georgia*. Athens: Published by the author, 1837.

Raboteau, Albert J. *Slave Religion: The "Invisible Institution" in the Antebellum South*. 1978. Reprint, Oxford University Press, 2004.

Ramsey, J. G. M. *The Annals of Tennessee to the End of the Eighteenth Century*. 1853. Reprint, Johnson, TN: Overmountain Press, 1999.

Range, Willard. *A Century of Georgia Agriculture, 1850–1950*. Athens: University of Georgia Press, 1954.

"Reports of Christian Ludwig Benzien to the Unity Elders Conference, 1806, A Few Extracts Translated." In Adelaide Fries, ed., *Records of the Moravians in North Carolina*. Vol. 6, 2868. Raleigh, NC: The North Carolina Historical Commission, 1943.

Ridge, John. Letter to Albert Gallatin, Feb. 27, 1826. In *The Cherokee Removal: A Brief History with Documents*. 2nd ed., edited by Theda Perdue and Michael D. Green, 35–47. Boston: Bedford Books of St. Martin's Press, 2005.

Rising, Marsha Hoffman. "Pioneer Sketch [Joseph Crutchfield]." In *Opening the Ozarks: First Families in Southwest Missouri, 1835–1839*. Vol. 1. Derry, NH: American Society of Genealogists, 2005.

Rodning, Christopher B. "Reconstructing the Coalescence of Cherokee Communities in Southern Appalachia." In *The Transformation of the Southeastern Indians, 1540–1760*, edited by Robbie Ethridge and Charles Hudson, 155–75. Jackson: University Press of Mississippi, 2002.

Saunt, Claudio. *A New Order of Things: Property, Power, and the Transformation of the Creek Indians, 1733–1816*. Cambridge: Cambridge University Press, 1999, 155.

Schwarze, Rev. Edmund. *History of the Moravian Missions Among Southern Indian Tribes of the United States*. Transactions of the Moravian Historical Society, Special Series, vol. 1. Bethlehem, PA: Times Publishing Company, 1923.

Seebohm, Caroline, and Peter Woloszynski. *Under Live Oaks: The Last Great Houses of the Old South*. New York: Clarkson Potter, 2002.

Sensbach, Jon F. *African-Americans in Salem*. Booklet produced by Old Salem Incorporated, n.d.

———. *A Separate Canaan: The Making of an Afro-Moravian World in North Carolina, 1763–1840*. Chapel Hill: University of North Carolina Press, 1998.

Shadburn, Don L. *Unhallowed Intrusion: A History of Cherokee Families in Forsyth County, Georgia*. Cumming, GA: The Cottonpatch Press, 1993.

Shaw, Helen Louise. *British Administration of the Southern Indians, 1756–1783*. New York: AMS Press, 1931.

Shoemaker, Nancy. Introduction to *Negotiators of Change: Historical Perspectives* on *Native American Women*, edited by Nancy Shoemaker, 1–25. New York: Routledge, 1995.

———. *A Strange Likeness: Becoming Red and White in Eighteenth-Century North America*. New York: Oxford University Press, 2004.

Sigourney, Lydia Howard Huntley. *Myrtis, with Other Etchings and Sketches*. New York: Harper and Brothers, 1846.

———. *Traits of the Aborigines of America. A Poem*. Cambridge: The University Press Hillard and Metcalf Printers, 1822.

Simon, Rose. "Saved: The Gambold Collection of Moravian Devotional Books." *North Carolina Libraries*, Spring 1998, 4–10.

Singleton, Theresa A., ed. *"I, Too, Am American": Archaeological Studies of African-American Life*. Charlottesville: University Press of Virginia, 1999.

Slave Voyages Database, ⟨http://www.slavevoyages.org/tast/database/search.faces⟩. Sept. 4, 2008.

Smith, Andrea. *Conquest: Sexual Violence and American Indian Genocide*. Cambridge, MA: Southend Press, 2005.

Smith, Justine. "Resistance Disguised as Fundamentalism: Challenging the Myth of Cherokee Assimilation." Paper delivered at the American Academy of Religion Conference, Orlando, FL, Nov. 22, 1998.

Starkey, Marion L. *The Cherokee Nation*. 1973. Reprint, North Dighton, MA: JG Press, 1995.

Starr, Emmet. *History of the Cherokee Indians and Their Legends and Folklore*. Tulsa: Oklahoma Yesteryear Publications, 1993.

Stuckey, Sterling. *Slave Culture: Nationalist Theory and the Foundations of Black America*. New York: Oxford University Press, 1987.

Taylor, Alan. *The Divided Ground: Indians, Settlers, and the Northern Borderland of the American Revolution*. New York: Knopf, 2006.

Timberlake, Lieut. Henry. *Lieut. Henry Timberlake's Memoirs, 1756–1765*. Edited by Samuel Cole Williams. 1765. Reprint, Marietta, GA: Continental Book Company, 1948.

Vann, R. P. "Reminiscences of Mr. R. P. Vann, East of Webbers Falls, Oklahoma, September 28, 1932, as Told to Grant Foreman." *Chronicles of Oklahoma* 11, no. 2 (June 1933): 838–44.

Vlach, John Michael. *Back of the Big House: The Architecture of Plantation Slavery*. Chapel Hill: University of North Carolina Press, 1993.

Waldram, James B. *Revenge of the Windigo: The Construction of the Mind of North American Aboriginal Peoples*. Toronto: University of Toronto Press, 2004.

Walker, Alice. "Beyond the Peacock: The Reconstruction of Flannery O'Connor." In *In Search of Our Mothers' Gardens: Womanist Prose*. New York: Harcourt Books, 1983.

———. *The Way Forward Is with a Broken Heart*. New York: Random House, 2000.

Warrior, Robert. *The People and the Word: Reading Native Nonfiction*. Minneapolis: University of Minnesota Press, 2005, 184–85.

Whitfield-Murray Historical Society. *Murray County's Indian Heritage*. Fernandina Beach, FL: Wolfe Publishing, 1987.

Whitmire, Mildred E., ed. *Noland's Cherokee Diary: A U.S. Soldier's Story from Inside the Cherokee Nation*. Spartanburg, SC: The Reprint Company, Publishers, 1990.

Wilkins, Thurman. *Cherokee Tragedy: The Ridge Family and the Decimation of a People*. 2nd ed. Norman: University of Oklahoma Press, 1986.

Woodward, Grace Steele. *The Cherokees*. Norman: University of Oklahoma Press, 1963.

Wyatt-Brown, Bertram. *Southern Honor: Ethics and Behavior in the Old South*. 1982. Reprint, New York: Oxford University Press, 2007.

Yarbrough, Fay A. *Race and the Cherokee Nation: Sovereignty in the Nineteenth Century*. Philadelphia: University of Pennsylvania Press, 2008.

Yuhl, Stephanie E. "Rich and Tender Remembering: Elite White Women and an Aesthetic Sense of Place in Charleston, 1920s and 1930s." In *Where These Memories Grow: History, Memory, and Southern Identity*, edited by W. Fitzhugh Brundage, 227–48. Chapel Hill: University of North Carolina Press, 2000.

Zellar, Gary. *African Creeks: Estelvste and the Creek Nation*. Norman: University of Oklahoma Press, 2007, 257.

Chattanooga (Tenn.), 8

Cherokee, North Carolina (tourist attraction), 6

Cherokee Constitution, 113, 169, 175, 176; black slave restrictions in, 165

Cherokee Council, 5, 127–28, 167; anti-removal petition to, 160; Creek War and, 150; Georgia code against, 176; James Vann and, 63, 70, 124–25; James Vann's will revision by, 143, 144, 164; land losses of, 44, 70; Moravian mission school and, 145; Peggy Vann's slave inheritance and, 154–55; white removal edict of, 146–47, 148

Cherokee Eastern Band of North Carolina, 190

Cherokee language, 89; written form of, 169

Cherokee-Moravian Historical Society, 194, 195

Cherokee Nation: African acculturation to, 24–25, 89, 98–99; African cultural parallels with, 103–4; alcohol abuse and, 67, 113, 114, 128, 129; American Revolution and, 35, 41, 44–47, 48, 52, 111, 128; black slave culture and, 103–7, 217; black slave economic activity and, 92–93; black slaveholding by, 3–4, 5, 15, 21–25, 52, 56–59, 79–81, 87–90, 111, 165, 216–17, 254 (n. 18); black slave numbers of, 87, 254 (n. 18); black slave personal interactions with, 104–7; catastrophes and, 146, 148–50; ceremonial life of, 68; "chief" terminology and, 251 (n. 44); Chief Vann House as shrine to, 1, 3, 12, 14, 187–97; Christian conversions and, 2, 19, 20, 21, 22, 139–40, 160–61, 170–71, 233; Christian evangelism and, 151, 211–12; "civilized" practices of, 1, 12–13, 20–23, 41–42, 43, 49,

51, 52–53, 55, 65, 69–71, 111, 124, 128, 130, 143, 168–69, 175–76; clan retaliation code of, 33–34, 47, 123–24, 128–29; colonial-era vulnerability of, 33–34; common landownership by, 56–57, 62; consumer goods and, 43, 52, 58; creation story of, 130; cultural communality of, 62, 68; cultural shifts in, 128–30, 143, 146; domestic violence and, 15, 19, 113–14, 129; ethnopersonality of, 37–38; European white intermarriages with, 4, 5, 20, 32, 41–42; famine and, 146, 148; federal government dealings with, 5, 15, 20, 47, 111, 120–21, 126–27, 160; federal road and, 60–62; first recorded Christian convert in, 19, 139–40, 233; forced removal of, 5, 6, 8, 15, 19, 176–79, 181–84; gender role changes and, 109, 110–12, 129; gender-specific tasks and, 52, 124; Georgia gold discovery and, 176, 177; Georgia historic sites and, 7–10; Georgia land lottery and, 5, 19, 177, 206, 209; Georgia territory of, 8–9, 31, 38; ghost dance and, 150; ideals of, 37; insecurities of 1811 and 1812 and, 146–50; land holdings of, 4, 56–57, 168; land losses of, 1, 5, 16–17, 44–45, 47, 48, 70–71, 126–27, 128; map of settlements of, 27; as matrilineal society, 42, 51, 54, 89, 109, 112, 143; mixed-race children's identification with, 42, 51; Moravian mission school for, 5, 64–65, 68–69, 104–5, 134, 145, 149–50; Moravian mission to, 64–69, 190, 211; mourning customs of, 133, 134; national police force of, 19, 128, 131; New Echota capital of, 7, 16, 167, 169, 176; polygamy practiced by, 53–54, 103; resistance raids by, 35–36, 38, 47–48; scholarship on, 20–26, 201–18;

smallpox epidemic and, 40; spiritual beliefs of, 22, 25, 31–32, 68, 103, 130; spiritual revival (1811–12) of, 19, 146–50; survival philosophies of, 49; traditional housing of, 71; U.S. Supreme Court ruling and, 177; vanished heritage of, 14; war-captive slavery and, 59; white frontier harassment of, 29; white-removal edict of, 146–48; written language of, 169; written legal code adopted by, 143. *See also* Diamond Hill; Vann *headings*

Cherokee National Committee, 92, 169, 177, 181

Cherokee Nation of Oklahoma, 190, 193, 194, 195

Cherokee Phoenix (newspaper), 169, 177

Cherokee Rebellion (1806–10), 127

Cherokee Removal, 5, 6, 15, 19, 176–79, 181–84; Peggy's letter-writing campaign and, 160; Trail of Tears and, 8

Cherokee Slave Revolt (1842), 275 (n. 21)

Cherokee Supreme Court, 194

Cherokee War, 40–41, 43

Cherokee women. *See* Women, Cherokee

Chickamauga (Cherokee town), 47, 55

Chickamauga mission, 158

Chickamauga resistance (1782), 48, 49, 126

Chickasaws, 38, 39, 59

Chieftains Trail, 7–10, 17

Chief Vann House, 1–10, 166–69, 187–97; actual building date of, 21, 167, 168, 206–7; African American life at, xv, 190–97; annual events at, xi–xv, 187, 192, 193; architectural details of, 1, 2, 7, 167; architectural drawings of, 188; bold interior colors of, 7, 168, 182; brick facade of, 5, 12, 166; brick manufacture for, 166–67, 207; brochure for, 2,

7; Cherokee builder of (*see* Vann, Joseph); Cherokee expulsion from, 179; Christmas by Candlelight at, xi–xv, 187; description of, 167, 168; documentary record of, 208–13; floating staircase of, 7, 167, 169, 179; Georgian advocacy groups for, 7–8, 17, 187; Georgian private owners of, 5–6, 179, 194, 206; grounds of, 167, 169; illustrations of, x, xii, xiii, 152, 180; interpretive approaches to, 213–18; Interpretive Center of, 189, 190, 194; nineteenth-century visitors to, 165–66, 207–8; Oklahoma replica of, 182–83, 194–95; as racial house, 196–97; research process for, 201–18; restoration complex of, 7–10, 187–97; restoration in 1950s of, 1, 3–4, 6–7, 13, 187; restoration's fiftieth anniversary and, 192–97, 203; restoration's slave life exhibit at, 18, 191–95; significance of, xiv–xv, 14, 15–17, 19–20, 196–97; situation of, 7; souvenir images of, 3; as state historic site, 3, 6, 15; symbolism of, 3, 12, 14, 15–16, 196–97; visitor numbers to, xiv, 9–10; volunteers at, xiv

Chief Vann House Days, 192, 193

Chief Vann House State Historic Site, xi–xv, 3, 6, 166, 187–97

Children: black slave–Cherokee interactions of, 104–5, 161–62

Chireau, Yvonne, 99, 100

Choctaws, 38, 39

Chota: Cherokee loss of, 47 (*see also* New Echota)

Christianity: black slaves and, 83, 84, 88, 91, 99, 103, 136, 139, 156, 158, 159, 174–75, 254 (n. 26), 268 (n. 10); Cherokee converts to, 2, 19, 20, 21, 22, 139–40, 160–61, 170–71; James Vann's rejection of, 22, 29, 31–32, 68, 168; Peggy Scott's conversion/

Renee (slave), 95, 117, 137

Representations of Slavery (Eichstedt and Small), 204

Revolutionary War. *See* American Revolution

Rhodes, Marjorie, 7

Ridge, John (Cherokee chief), 20, 181

Ridge, Major (Cherokee chief), 7, 90, 150, 172

Ridge, Susanna (Peggy's aunt), 90, 171, 172

Ridge, The (slaveholder), 127

Riley, Spencer, 179

"Ring shout" ceremony, 98, 101

Robertson, Betty, 275 (n. 21)

Robinson, Ken, 238 (n. 7)

Rocky Mountain, 146

Rosana (slave child), 174

Rose (slave child), 155, 157

Ross, John (Cherokee chief), 74, 169, 181, 238 (n. 9)

Rowe, Richard, 46–47, 145

Runaway slaves, 95–96, 117–18, 137, 162

Running Water (Cherokee town), 47

Ruskin, Gertrude, 6

St. Philips Afro-Moravian Church, 175

Salem (Moravian community), 64, 66, 68, 69, 175, 254–55 (n. 27)

Salomo Michael (slave child), 174, 175

Sam (slave), 95–96, 119

Sanders family. *See* Saunders family

Sarah (slave), 89–90

Saunders, Alexander, 133

Saunders family, 91, 256–57 (n. 43)

Savannah River, 41, 54

Schermerhorn, John, 181

Schizophrenia, 31

Schmidt, Renatus, 159–60, 165, 173

Schneider, Martin, 72

Schweinitz, Frederic de, 63, 65

Scotland: Vann family origins in, 4, 39, 245 (n. 56)

Scott, Elizabeth (Betsy) (Peggy's sister). *See* Vann, Elizabeth (Betsy) Scott

Scott, Mary Polly (Peggy's sister). *See* Vann, Mary Polly Scott

Scott, Peggy. *See* Vann, Peggy Scott

Scott, Walter (Peggy's father), 51–52, 54

Second Middle Passage, 59, 137

Selu (Corn Mother), 130, 146

Senegambia, 88

Sequoyah (George Guess), 169

Settendown Creek, 189

Sevier, John, 48

Sexual assault, 46, 90

Shadburn, Don, 30–31, 207

Shawnees, 35, 44, 45, 146

Shoe Boots (Cherokee), 148–49, 150

Shoemaker, Nancy, 14, 212–13

Sigourney, Lydia Howard Huntley: *Traits of the Aborigines*, 173, 266 (n. 24)

Skia-gunsta, Chief, 43

Slave resistance, 93–97, 175; Vann robbery and, 117–20

Slavery. *See* Black slaves

Slavery and Public History (Horton, co-ed.), 191

Slave trade, African, 59

Slave trade, domestic: horrors of, 59, 136–37; James Vann and, 4, 58–59, 79–80, 83, 95

Small, Stephen, 204–5; *Representations of Slavery*, 204

Smith, Andrea, 32

Smith, Anna, 195, 233

Smith, Francis, 7

Smith, J. Frazer, 51

Smith, Justine, 21

Sorcery, 31

Sour Mush, Chief, 33, 45–46, 120

South Carolina, 87, 88; backcountry of, 38–39, 43, 45; Cherokee land losses to, 48; Cherokee War and, 40; Vann family origins in, 38–39, 245 (n. 56)

67, 110, 112, 115, 122; assessment of, 36–37, 215; biographical mythologies of, 34–36; biography of, 18; birth date of, 41, 245 (n. 56); birthplace of, 245 (n. 56); black slave property wealth of, 4, 5, 7, 8, 18, 48, 55, 56–57, 59–60, 63, 79, 88–89; black slave socialization with, 21–22, 24, 29, 67, 81, 102; black slave sources and, 79–80, 82, 88, 98; brutality of, 29, 37, 82, 116, 119–20; business ventures of, 4, 7, 22, 43, 48, 57–71, 79; Cherokee identity of, 32, 57–63, 71, 168; Cherokee land dealings and, 126–27; Cherokee name for, 245 (n. 56); Cherokee political prominence of, 5, 29, 36, 62–63, 70–71, 125; Cherokee resistance and, 35–36; Chief Vann House misattributed to, 168; childhood trauma of, 34–35, 36, 38, 46–47; children of, 14, 91, 104, 143 (see also Vann, Joseph); contradictory actions of, 29, 31, 38, 69, 71, 73–74; cultural identity questions about, 168; death of, 5, 19, 29–30, 131, 133, 134–35, 141–42, 145, 245 (n. 56); domestic slave trade and, 4, 58–59, 79–80, 83, 95; duel with brother-in-law of, 19, 122–26, 128, 129, 138, 144; emotional abuse by, 115; enemies of, 29, 30; English-language library of, 60, 122; entrepreneurial scale of, 62, 79; estate redistribution of, 19, 143, 144, 164; Euro-American practices and, 11, 49, 74, 114–15, 121, 122, 124; family background of, 4, 32, 39–41; family of, 5, 32; father's estate and, 48–49; federal officials and, 4, 28, 60, 62–63, 69–70, 73, 120–21, 127, 209, 214; frame plantation house of, 71–74, 207, 214; land holdings of, 4, 55–56; mental illness and, 31–32; modern psychological explanations for, 30–32; Moravian mission and, 18, 28, 29, 30, 31, 49, 64–71; multiple wives of, 5, 53–54 (see also Vann, Peggy Scott); murder of (see subhead death of); organized violence and, 126–30; personal appearance of, 6, 74; personal traits of, 28, 29, 30, 31, 32, 34, 48, 74, 116; plantation home of, 71–74, 79 (see also Diamond Hill); power of, 126; robbery/murder plot against, 117–21, 125, 126; self-defense precautions of, 124; as southern planter, 79; violence of, 19, 22, 23, 28, 30, 31, 33, 34–35, 36, 37, 80, 110–11, 112, 114–16, 119–21, 122, 126–30; violence toward slaves of, 111, 116, 128; wealth of, 4, 55, 56, 58, 60, 62, 63, 73, 79, 190; wife's property and, 55; will and estate of, 5, 16, 19, 48–49, 143–44; youthful influences on, 33–36, 47–48

Vann, Jennie (James's sister), 41, 48
Vann, Jennie Doublehead Foster (James's wife), 53, 164 (n. 58)
Vann, Jennie Foster (Joseph's wife), 183
Vann, Jennie Sprinston (Joseph's wife), 164–65
Vann, Jennifer Walford (descendant), 191
Vann, Jesse (James's son), 144
Vann, Jim (slave steamboat engineer), 186
Vann, Jimmy (James's son), 144
Vann, John (James's grandfather), 39–40, 43
Vann, John (James's great-grandfather), 244 (n. 52)
Vann, John (James's uncle), 40, 47–48, 89
Vann, Joseph (James's father), 4, 40, 41, 44, 245 (n. 56); estate of, 48–49; slaves owned by, 43; trade ventures of, 43, 48

Vann, Joseph (James's son), 5, 164–79; black slave property of, 22, 81, 164, 165, 182, 183, 186, 194–95; Cherokee removal and, 15, 19, 177, 178–79, 181, 182, 206–7; Chief Vann House built by, xiii, 5, 166–67, 169, 196; Chief Vann House replica built by, 182–83, 194–95; childhood mischief-making by, 104; cultural identification of, 168–69; Diamond Hill return of, 164–67; education of, 164; father's murder scene and, 29–30, 131, 133; as father's primary heir, 19, 143, 144, 145, 164; formal portrait of, 169; horse racing and, 183, 184; losses to Georgia of, 179; multiple wives of, 164–65, 183; Oklahoma prosperity of, 182–84, 194–95; personal traits of, 164; physical appearance of, 164, 170; President Monroe's overnight visit to, 165–66; steamboat accident death of, 5, 19, 183–86; Tennessee farmstead of, 181; wealth of, 164, 166, 183, 190

Vann, Lucinda (former slave), 186

Vann, Mary (James's daughter). See Stedman, Mary Vann

Vann, Mary Polly Scott (James's wife), 53, 54

Vann, Nancy (James's sister), 23, 41, 48, 66, 72, 83, 109, 116, 145, 206; beating of slave by, 117; husband's death in duel and, 122, 124, 138; Peggy's Christian conversion and, 140–41, 171; robbery plot and, 119, 120, 125; slave escapes from, 95–96

Vann, Nancy Brown (James's wife and Joseph's mother), 53, 164

Vann, Peggy Scott (James's wife) (later Margaret Ann Crutchfield), 5, 22, 53–57, 104, 114, 116, 123, 130, 137–45, 148, 149; attachment to slave Caty by, 82, 110, 115, 139, 268 (n. 10); bap-tismal name of, 139, 151; biography of, 18; birth of, 51; black slave relations with, 106, 136, 154–58, 163–64; black slave school of, 158–59; black slaves owned by, 54–55, 117, 142, 145, 154–58, 173–74; Cherokee identification of, 51; Christian conversion of, 19, 52, 137, 138–40, 145, 151, 152, 160; consumption of, 172; Crutchfield's courtship of, 153–54; cultural forces and, 22, 51–53, 109, 111–12; death and grave of, 5, 172–73, 174; Diamond Hill and, 5, 55–56, 73, 109–11, 145, 151, 190; Diamond Hill robbery and, 118, 119, 120; as domestic violence victim, 23–24, 109, 110, 112, 115, 121–22, 128; historical recognition of, 196; house of, 142, 154; independence as widow of, 140–42, 144–45, 151–52; influence of, 160–61; in-law relations with, 124, 140–41; isolation from kin of, 109–10, 111; James Vann's bequest to, 5, 143; letters of, 160, 209, 211; literacy of, 140, 152, 158, 160; maiden name reversion by, 142; marriage to Crutchfield of, 153–54, 160; marriage to James Vann of, 53–54, 109; memoir of, 233–35; Moravian missionaries and, 54, 67, 68, 138–39, 140, 142, 145, 147, 151–54, 156, 160, 170–73; Oothcaloga move by, 170–74; personal appearance of, 54, 55; personal traits of, 54, 56, 138; personal wealth of, 54–55, 154; reaction to James Vann's duel by, 124, 138; reaction to James Vann's murder by, 133–34

Vann, Polly Black (Joseph's wife), 164–65, 183

Vann, R. P. (Joseph's grandson), 185–86

Vann, Robert (James's son), 144

Vann, Sally (James's daughter), 144

Vann, Sarah Saunders, 90–91

Vann, Sister of Raven, 40
Vann, Wali (James's mother), 5, 22, 40, 41, 66, 109, 148, 149, 244 (n. 52); Arkansas move by, 274 (n. 70); beating of slave by, 116–17; Christian conversion of, 161, 171; Diamond Hill house of, 57, 71, 190; inheritance of, 49; missionary services and, 138; Peggy Vann's Christian conversion and, 140–41; reaction to son's death by, 134; robbery plot and, 125; slaves owned by, 43, 145, 261 (n. 5); socialization with black slaves by, 21, 22, 105–6; son's duel and, 122–23, 124, 138; son's estate and, 144, 154; son's murder and, 133; son's violence toward, 111, 115–16
Vann family, 15, 39–41; black slaveholding by, 21–22, 23, 29, 43, 48, 87, 125–26, 145, 186; chart of blacks associated with, 219–31; Chief Vann House Interpretive Center and, 190; descendants of, 16, 31, 185, 186, 191, 207; dispute over slaves by, 145; Euro-Cherokee background of, 41–43; generational cultural changes of, 21–23; loss of plantation of, 15; move to Georgia of, 48–49; origins of, 38, 39–40, 51, 244 (n. 52), 245 (n. 56); reaction to James Vann's murder by, 133–34; violent acts by women members of, 117, 128; wealth and success of, 43–44; WPA history project and, 213. *See also individual members*
Vann House. *See* Chief Vann House
Vann plantation. *See* Diamond Hill
Vann's party, 127
"Vann's Trail of Tears" (play), 187
Vannsville, 4–5, 57, 63
Virginia (slave child), 154, 158
Virginia (state), 45, 83; plantation layout of, 76–77

Vlach, John Michael, 75, 97
Vogt, Mr. (builder), 72–73

Wachovia (Moravian community), 64, 84
Wafford family, 70–71
Walker, Alice, 26, 197
Warrior, Robert, 213–14, 215; *The People and the Word: Reading Native Nonfiction*, 213–14
Warrior's Nephew. *See* Koychezetel, Chief
Washington, George, 53
Waters, Major (Vann relative), 33
Waters, Sally, 52–53
Watie, Buck. *See* Boudinot, Elias
Watie, David, 163, 174
Watts, John (Cherokee chief), 35, 48
Webbers Falls, 182
Well, Mary, 7
Westos, 59
"White Indians," 40
Whitfield-Murray Historical Society, xii, 6, 192, 194
Wilkins, Thurman, 30
Will (slave), 142, 154, 155, 156, 157–58
Witchcraft, 31–32, 99, 100, 103
Wohlfahrt, Johann Jacob, 66, 72–73, 110
Wolf Clan, 51
Women, black slave, 81–86, 93; abuse of, 116–17, 128; chores of, 77; community role of, 102; missionaries and, 105–6, 156–58
Women, Cherokee: antiremoval petition of, 160; Chief Vann House restoration and, 19, 190, 191, 196; cultural changes and, 23–24, 51–53, 109–14, 112, 117, 122–23, 128, 129; domestic violence threats against, 129; gender-specific tasks and, 52, 124; Moravian missionaries and, 66,

67; Peggy's spiritual guidance to, 160–61, 170–71; plantation household and, 19, 22; property rights of, 54, 55; slaveholding by, 125; traditional power of, 42, 54, 112, 113; treatment of black slaves by, 115, 116–17, 128; white intermarriages by, 4, 5, 41–42. *See also* Gender relations; Matrilineal society

Woodruff Stories, The (Goulding), 58
Woodward, Grace Steele, 20
Worcester v. Georgia, 177
Works Progress Administration, 182, 213

Zellar, Gary, 217
Zinzendorf, Nikolaus Ludwig von, 63–64